PROCLAMATION

PROCLAMATION OF SON AHMAN, EVEN JESUS CHRIST,
TO ALL PEOPLES OF THE EARTH, EVEN MY HOLY WILL
TO WARN ALL OF MY JUDGMENT UPON ALL PEOPLES

ISBN-13: 978-1-937271-03-9

PREFACE

Revelation of the Lord Jesus Christ
Given to President Warren S. Jeffs
Palestine, Texas
Sunday, October 2, 2011

1. Come ye, all ye people of the whole earth, unto me, and be ye ready for the coming of your Lord.

2. I send my own word to you to know I soon shall appear, making myself known to all people.

3. Let all now read of my coming in New Testament record.

4. Read Doctrine and Covenants of my holy word given through my holy Prophet and messenger of salvation, Joseph Smith; to know I have warned the people of the earth these many years to be ready.

5. Read Matthew chapter 24, to know I revealed of my return to earth in glory and power, to save mine elect who obey my Gospel of holy power.

6. I, your Lord Jesus Christ, now, in my loving power of my holy way being known on earth, send this, my Proclamation of my own revealing, to know my Holy Priesthood and my holy way of eternal marriage of my holy power of Celestial Plural Marriage has continued on earth, by my grace, attending my Holy Priesthood.

7. Let this Proclamation be known to all people of the earth.

8. I have caused my own word to go forth as a testimony I speak from the heavens, in plain language, to your understanding, to all people of every nation, having sent my own word to you; to be within reach to all people in your library book places; to be of a reading to any who will seek truth.

9. My Spirit shall witness to all honest and praying hearts and minds my word is only pure, true, peaceful, and of authority.

10. I shall fulfill my will in full as you, the people of every nation, prove your lives, whether you choose my ways or choose the way of evil; for my way is only pure, holy, noble, exalting, righteous, and is from Celestial eternal realm of my abiding.

11. Let this holy Proclamation be as a final message of a call to prepare, before I, your Lord Jesus Christ, your Redeemer and Savior over all appear in power.

12. Let all people hear and obey my will to survive my time of judgments upon all nations; to be ready for my coming, is my revelation to all; for I have named in my Proclamation the way to know my plan of salvation that continues on earth.

13. I, your Lord, have spoken, and shall fulfill all my will. Amen.

HOLY WORD OF JESUS CHRIST
TO ALL GOVERNING POWER OF CIVIL
GOVERNING POWER OF THE LAND OF THE
UNITED STATES OF AMERICA

INTRODUCTION

Thus Saith Jesus Christ, Even the Ruler Over All, Who Hath Now Sent You His Word of Judging and Cleansing Power, Who Now Declareth Judgment Upon Present Judge and Law Officials of Present Persecution Against My Fundamentalist Church of Jesus Christ of Latter-day Saints; to Know I Am Soon to Judge All in Government Positions of Unrighteous Prosecution Against My People, to Show My Will Concerning Present Court Persecuting Power; Which Judge Is Now to Be of My Holy Judging Upon Her and Others Who Have Mocked My Holy Religious and Pure Holy Law of Celestial Plural Marriage in Open Court: Let All Such Proceedings Cease Now!

Revelation of the Lord Jesus Christ
Given to President Warren S. Jeffs
San Angelo, Texas
Thursday, July 28, 2011

1. I send this, my own word of defending authority, to be as a full understanding of my holy power of holy authority, and of principles of eternal life; and to show how governing power of both local and national power in the days of my Church coming forth until now has been named; to know of my people always being the object of attack, with many tasks of government interference against my holy revealed religion, saith Jesus Christ, the God over all peoples.

2. Let my writing be examined by all government authorities in the nation, as from my own mouth, even my judging of peoples and lawmaking and court authority.

3. Let all now hear your Lord's will, to now release my servant Warren Jeffs and his brethren from imprisonment.

4. Read my will herein, and obey, saith your Lord, lest judgments, acute and keen, come upon Texas and the nation of the United States of America.

5. No longer be of a way of attacking my true Priesthood authority I have ordained, though he be in bondage.

6. I shall deliver my people, and leave their enemies who sought their destruction with neither root nor branch of posterity, which time is soon at hand; for I shall not allow my Celestial Law to be destroyed by ungodly power of governing power, unto the governing power that thus persecute my elect shall be brought low unto dissolution if they heed me not.

7. Be ye ready for my word to be fulfilled, and be of a pure holy way of living in your own families, communities, and this nation.

8. Let my people be no longer persecuted nor prosecuted.

9. Now read my own will to the people of present court prosecution of religious way of my holy will and revealing, and history of governmental attacks; and also naming Keyholders of my Holy Priesthood until now. Amen.

Thus Saith Jesus Christ to All of the People of the Nation, to Government Authorities of Every Place and Calling in Civil Power of Man's Governing, by the Grace of God Who Speaketh:

Revelation of the Lord Jesus Christ Given to President Warren S. Jeffs Eldorado, Texas Thursday, July 21, 2011

1. I am to be now recognized as the power of eternal authority on earth, to be honored as the Ruler over my world of my creating; to have my servant known to be my spokesman to all nations of all lands on the earth.

2. Hear my message of warning, to be of a full understanding of my eternal purpose of creating; to be known as soon to come in my glory unto my chosen people, to live the law of holy pure intent, principle, and practice; even to be of a holy way of Celestial revealing of pure and sacred keeping of laws of Eternal Power, unto the salvation of my Church.

3. Let all be of an awake and pure doing, to now receive my holy will; to know of the intent of thy Eternal Father, the Creator of all, in preparing a people for my coming.

4. Let all now be ready to learn my holy purpose of creation, as unto a labor of pure holy living in my holy Church.

5. Let my Celestial Law of Eternal Union of Eternal Plural Marriage now be protected by government power.

6. Let all now be of a delivering of my holy way, to be protected by the power of governing authority, according to the principle of religious and holy and sacred law of Celestial Union, guided by my own voice through my servant, revealing who is worthy of Eternal Marriage in my Church.

7. Let no one think those outside my Church can receive this, my holy law of pure sacred motive; to only be lived by he who is pure in moral doing and feeling, and she who is virtuous and of a motive of pure holy religion; to attain a salvation unto my Kingdom of Eternal Authority of a Celestial power of eternal and holy pure living.

8. Let all now see I have spoken my will, and shall soon call to accounting they who persecute through governing power of legal action, or by violent effort, or combination of those who oppose my revealed faith and Priesthood authority, Church of Jesus Christ of Latter-day Saints, known among men as the name of Fundamentalist Church of Jesus Christ of Latter-day Saints.

9. Let my people be of freedom of religious and pure living.

10. My Celestial Law of Union in Marriage is of holy way; to be a principle not of any evil nor false nor of a work of men only, but of thy Lord who is over all people; who is to be soon appearing to all nations in the power of my might; to be known as Ruler over all; who shall be as a flaming fire unto all people in my glory.

11. Now let my people be of free exercise of my holy law of Eternal Power; soon to be my elect who dwell in my eternal place of Celestial power on the land of America, a Zion to be of my creating, even new and holy power of Celestial Eternal Authority.

12. Let my people be as free to be my holy laboring agents for the salvation of all nations; for I am God, who is the Framer of the earth, and who is the full power of holy and Celestial governing power.

13. Let all now be my whole and full warning of awake and preparing children; to know I am to be a holy revealing of all secrets of all peoples of all generations, as my holy revealing is sent forth from the city New and Holy Jerusalem, a power of full governing power over all peoples.

14. Let my people have all their free religious rights protected.

15. Let the present attack against my people through government interfering be stopped.

16. I am the God over all.

17. Let my word be conveyed to governing power on the land of my coming, even to dwell among men on earth for a Millennial Reign of Peace.

18. Let all now be of a preparing, to be of a surviving the judgments of my power on all wicked, corrupt, and violent peoples in every nation; to be preserving the more righteous unto my holy way of salvation of eternal life.

19. Let my will now be fulfilled, unto you who do my holy will being blessed, unto my giving preserving of your people and nation, each one.

20. Let no one be of violent way, to bring harm on other nations or people, even in thy own nation.

21. Let leaders be of a fatherly kind way, to lift up the needy, to be just and equitous unto all in the governing power you hold, by my grace.

22. I have sent you my own will.

23. Let all be of full preparing for my holy will to be manifest.

24. Receive my previous will revealing my holy way.

25. Let my Church be pure in all holy conduct, in all my law of sacred giving.

26. Let the court release my servant.

27. Let his brethren also be set free.

28. They only abide my Celestial Law of a more pure holy conduct and religious love for God and my purpose of preparing for my holy power of Zion to come forth on the land of Zion, even America.

29. Let my whole way be learned.

30. Judge my people no more as of evil way.

31. Let them be of free exercise of religion.

32. I, your Lord, have preserved this land for my Zion to rise.

33. Do not obstruct Zion.

34. Let all be peace.

35. Now hear my will: Learn of my law and of the labor of my servants, the Prophets, in establishing my Kingdom of pure holy way.

36. Let my truths be honored.

37. Let my holy walk be your way.

38. Let no aggressive way be exerting to destroy my people, who have been called by my revealing Celestial eternal laws that do not alter.

39. My law of Eternal Union is an holy pure law, only to be my Church preparing for my own will in their lives.

40. Let my people be free to have their lands and houses, to be of a work of pure living; no hindering of my Church by powers of governing power; to be of free labor, as is guaranteed by the law of original power of full religious freedom.

41. Let my people now have all their pure holy way be protected, to have my law their way. Amen.

TABLE OF CONTENTS
Chapter 1
Administration of President Joseph Smith, Jun.

Thus Saith Son Ahman, Jesus Christ, to the Power of Governing in the Court of Prosecuting Labor, and to the Leaders of National Power -- Let My Word Be Heard in Your Several Placings of Your Influencing and Governing Power, Even This, My Warning to Not Abuse My Innocent People, But Maintain Their Rights of Governing Protecting of Religious Way of My Holy Order of Union Celestial in My Holy Church on Earth. Let There Cease to Be the Continued Way and Idea You Can Be of a Prosecuting Labor Against My Holy Way of Eternal Lives of Celestial Union Power Above All Peoples and Their Claims of Power to Rule Over All the People in Their Lands of Man Organizing Power. Thus Am I Now Giving My Will to Be Known Among All Surviving People on Earth. Hear Thou My Way of Truth by This, My Revealing to All:

**Son Ahman Gives Truth of
Eternal Power to Joseph Smith,
a God of Power**

**President Rulon Jeffs' Testimony of

**Testimony of President Brigham

Chapter 2
Administration of President Brigham Young

Chapter 3
Administration of President John Taylor

Chapter 4
Administration of President John W. Woolley

Chapter 5
Administration of President Lorin C. Woolley

Chapter 6
Administration of President John Y. Barlow

Chapter 7
Administration of President Leroy S. Johnson

Chapter 8
Administration of President Rulon Jeffs

Chapter 9
Administration of President Warren S. Jeffs

Appendix A

Warnings of Previous Sending
to Leaders of the Nation

Appendix B

Appendix of My New Word of Pure Power Printed in This My Proclamation to All Peoples on All Lands Referencing Pages to Find My Word in This Publishing

Appendix C

Documents Showing the Legal and Religious Establishing and Continuing of the Fundamentalist Church of Jesus Christ of Latter-day Saints Among Men on Earth, Thy Lord Establishing His Church April 6, 1830, Through Joseph Smith, Continued on Earth Through My Priesthood; Now a Legal Organization According to Law of Land Among Men, Saith Jesus Christ, Your Lord

Chapter 1
Administration of President Joseph Smith, Jun.

Joseph Smith, "Revelator of My Holy Will to All Nations"

Revelation of the Lord Jesus Christ Given to President Warren S. Jeffs
San Angelo, Texas
Tuesday, July 26, 2011

1. Thus saith the Lord, who is Jesus Christ, to all people of holy way of living my holy way:

2. Now be of rejoicing.

3. My Holy Priesthood shall be with you, for nothing can stay my holy will from being fulfilled.

4. I shall have my holy will manifest, to have full way of Joseph Smith, my holy Revelator of pure giving to the generation in which my holy will has to be fulfilled.

5. Now be of an open mind, and no longer be of a slow preparing, for all I have revealed shall be fulfilled, given through my servant Joseph.

6. He shall yet be among you, the people of my holy way, and he shall be the One Mighty and Strong sent to set in order my house; even my Priesthood, Church, and Kingdom on earth.

7. Let all give heed to my holy way being fulfilled, to Zion being established in full.

8. Let my believing pure vessels be purified by the Holy Spirit.

9. Receive ye my holy will in full purpose of heart, that all may be done according to my revealing power. Amen.

Joseph Smith's First Visitation

President Joseph Smith, Jun.
Pearl of Great Price, Joseph Smith 2

5. Some time in the second year after our removal to Manchester, there was in the place where we lived an unusual excitement on the subject of religion. It commenced with the Methodists, but soon became general among all the sects in that region of country. Indeed, the whole district of country seemed affected by it, and great multitudes united themselves to the different religious parties, which created no small stir and division amongst the people, some crying, "Lo, here!" and others, "Lo, there!" Some were contending for the Methodist faith, some for the Presbyterian, and some for the Baptist.

6. For, notwithstanding the great love which the converts to these different faiths expressed at the time of their conversion, and the great zeal manifested by the respective clergy, who were active in getting up and promoting this extraordinary scene of religious feeling, in order to have everybody converted, as they were pleased to call it, let them join what sect they pleased; yet when the converts began to file off, some to one party and some to another, it was seen that the seemingly good feelings of both the priests and the converts were more pretended than real; for a scene of great confusion and bad feeling ensued -- priest contending against priest, and convert against convert; so that all their good feelings one for another, if they ever had any, were entirely lost in a strife of words and a contest about opinions.

7. I was at this time in my fifteenth year. My father's family was proselyted to the Presbyterian faith, and four of them joined that church, namely, my mother, Lucy; my brothers Hyrum and Samuel Harrison; and my sister Sophronia.

8. During this time of great excitement my mind was called up to serious reflection and great uneasiness; but though my feelings were deep and often poignant, still I kept myself aloof from all these parties, though I attended their

several meetings as often as occasion would permit. In process of time my mind became somewhat partial to the Methodist sect, and I felt some desire to be united with them; but so great were the confusion and strife among the different denominations, that it was impossible for a person young as I was, and so unacquainted with men and things, to come to any certain conclusion who was right and who was wrong.

9. My mind at times was greatly excited, the cry and tumult were so great and incessant. The Presbyterians were most decided against the Baptists and Methodists, and used all the powers of both reason and sophistry to prove their errors, or, at least, to make the people think they were in error. On the other hand, the Baptists and Methodists in their turn were equally zealous in endeavoring to establish their own tenets and disprove all others.

10. In the midst of this war of words and tumult of opinions, I often said to myself: What is to be done? Who of all these parties are right; or, are they all wrong together? If any one of them be right, which is it, and how shall I know it?

11. While I was laboring under the extreme difficulties caused by the contests of these parties of religionists, I was one day reading the Epistle of James, first chapter and fifth verse, which reads: *If any of you lack wisdom, let him ask of God, that giveth to all men liberally, and upbraideth not; and it shall be given him.*

12. Never did any passage of scripture come with more power to the heart of man than this did at this time to mine. It seemed to enter with great force into every feeling of my heart. I reflected on it again and again, knowing that if any person needed wisdom from God, I did; for how to act I did not know, and unless I could get more wisdom than I then had, I would never know; for the teachers of religion of the different sects understood the same passages of scripture so differently as to destroy all confidence in settling the question by an appeal to the Bible.

13. At length I came to the conclusion that I must either remain in darkness and confusion, or else I must do as James directs, that is, ask of God. I at length came to the determination to "ask of God," concluding that if he gave wisdom to them that lacked wisdom, and would give liberally, and not upbraid, I might venture.

14. So, in accordance with this, my determination to ask of God, I retired to the woods to make the attempt. It was on the morning of a beautiful, clear day, early in the spring of eighteen hundred and twenty. It was the first time in my life that I had made such an attempt, for amidst all my anxieties I had never as yet made the attempt to pray vocally.

15. After I had retired to the place where I had previously designed to go, having looked around me, and finding myself alone, I kneeled down and began to offer up the desire of my heart to God. I had scarcely done so, when immediately I was seized upon by some power which entirely overcame me, and had such an astonishing influence over me as to bind my tongue so that I could not speak. Thick darkness gathered around me, and it seemed to me for a time as if I were doomed to sudden destruction.

16. But, exerting all my powers to call upon God to deliver me out of the power of this enemy which had seized upon me, and at the very moment when I was ready to sink into despair and abandon myself to destruction -- not to an imaginary ruin, but to the power of some actual being from the unseen world, who had such marvelous power as I had never before felt in any being -- just at this moment of great alarm, I saw a pillar of light exactly over my head, above the brightness of the sun, which descended gradually until it fell upon me.

17. It no sooner appeared than I found myself delivered from the enemy which held me bound. When the light rested upon me I saw two Personages, whose brightness and glory defy all description, standing above me in the air. One of them spake unto me, calling me by name and said, pointing to the other -- *This is My Beloved Son. Hear Him!*

18. My object in going to inquire of the Lord was to know which of all the sects was right, that I might know which to join. No sooner, therefore, did I get possession of myself, so as to be able to speak, than I asked the Personages who stood above me in the light, which of all the sects was right -- and which I should join.

19. I was answered that I must join none of them, for they were all wrong; and the Personage who addressed me said that all their creeds were an abomination in his sight; that those professors

were all corrupt; that: "they draw near to me with their lips, but their hearts are far from me, they teach for doctrines the commandments of men, having a form of godliness, but they deny the power thereof."

20. He again forbade me to join with any of them; and many other things did he say unto me, which I cannot write at this time. When I came to myself again, I found myself lying on my back, looking up into heaven. When the light had departed, I had no strength; but soon recovering in some degree, I went home. And as I leaned up to the fireplace, mother inquired what the matter was. I replied, "Never mind, all is well -- I am well enough off." I then said to my mother, "I have learned for myself that Presbyterianism is not true." It seems as though the adversary was aware, at a very early period of my life, that I was destined to prove a disturber and an annoyer of his kingdom; else why should the powers of darkness combine against me? Why the opposition and persecution that arose against me, almost in my infancy?

21. Some few days after I had this vision, I happened to be in company with one of the Methodist preachers, who was very active in the before mentioned religious excitement; and, conversing with him on the subject of religion, I took occasion to give him an account of the vision which I had had. I was greatly surprised at his behavior; he treated my communication not only lightly, but with great contempt, saying it was all of the devil, that there were no such things as visions or revelations in these days; that all such things had ceased with the apostles, and that there would never be any more of them.

22. I soon found, however, that my telling the story had excited a great deal of prejudice against me among professors of religion, and was the cause of great persecution, which continued to increase; and though I was an obscure boy, only between fourteen and fifteen years of age, and my circumstances in life such as to make a boy of no consequence in the world, yet men of high standing would take notice sufficient to excite the public mind against me, and create a bitter persecution; and this was common among all the sects -- all united to persecute me.

23. It caused me serious reflection then, and often has since, how very strange it was that an obscure boy, of a little over fourteen years of age, and one, too, who was doomed to the necessity of obtaining a scanty maintenance by his daily labor, should be thought a character of sufficient importance to attract the attention of the great ones of the most popular sects of the day, and in a manner to create in them a spirit of the most bitter persecution and reviling. But strange or not, so it was, and it was often the cause of great sorrow to myself.

24. However, it was nevertheless a fact that I had beheld a vision. I have thought since, that I felt much like Paul, when he made his defense before King Agrippa, and related the account of the vision he had when he saw a light, and heard a voice; but still there were but few who believed him; some said he was dishonest, others said he was mad; and he was ridiculed and reviled. But all this did not destroy the reality of his vision. He had seen a vision, he knew he had, and all the persecution under heaven could not make it otherwise; and though they should persecute him unto death, yet he knew, and would know to his latest breath, that he had both seen a light and heard a voice speaking unto him, and all the world could not make him think or believe otherwise.

25. So it was with me. I had actually seen a light, and in the midst of that light I saw two Personages, and they did in reality speak to me; and though I was hated and persecuted for saying that I had seen a vision, yet it was true; and while they were persecuting me, reviling me, and speaking all manner of evil against me falsely for so saying, I was led to say in my heart: Why persecute me for telling the truth? I have actually seen a vision; and who am I that I can withstand God, or why does the world think to make me deny what I have actually seen? For I had seen a vision; I knew it, and I knew that God knew it, and I could not deny it, neither dared I do it; at least I knew that by so doing I would offend God, and come under condemnation.

26. I had now got my mind satisfied so far as the sectarian world was concerned -- that it was not my duty to join with any of them, but to continue as I was until further directed. I had found the testimony of James to be true -- that a man who lacked wisdom might ask of God, and obtain, and not be upbraided.

27. I continued to pursue my common

vocations in life until the twenty-first of September, one thousand eight hundred and twenty-three, all the time suffering severe persecution at the hands of all classes of men, both religious and irreligious, because I continued to affirm that I had seen a vision.

Visitation of Angel Moroni to Joseph Smith; The Book of Mormon a Revealed Work

President Joseph Smith, Jun.
Pearl of Great Price, Joseph Smith 2

28. During the space of time which intervened between the time I had the vision and the year eighteen hundred and twenty-three -- having been forbidden to join any of the religious sects of the day, and being of very tender years, and persecuted by those who ought to have been my friends and to have treated me kindly, and if they supposed me to be deluded to have endeavored in a proper and affectionate manner to have reclaimed me -- I was left to all kinds of temptations; and, mingling with all kinds of society, I frequently fell into many foolish errors, and displayed the weakness of youth, and the foibles of human nature; which, I am sorry to say, led me into divers temptations, offensive in the sight of God. In making this confession, no one need suppose me guilty of any great or malignant sins. A disposition to commit such was never in my nature. But I was guilty of levity, and sometimes associated with jovial company, etc., not consistent with that character which ought to be maintained by one who was called of God as I had been. But this will not seem very strange to any one who recollects my youth, and is acquainted with my native cheery temperament.

29. In consequence of these things, I often felt condemned for my weakness and imperfections; when, on the evening of the above-mentioned twenty-first of September, after I had retired to my bed for the night, I betook myself to prayer and supplication to Almighty God for forgiveness of all my sins and follies, and also for a manifestation to me, that I might know of my state and standing before him; for I had full confidence in obtaining a divine manifestation, as I previously had one.

30. While I was thus in the act of calling upon God, I discovered a light appearing in my room, which continued to increase until the room was lighter than at noonday, when immediately a personage appeared at my bedside, standing in the air, for his feet did not touch the floor.

31. He had on a loose robe of most exquisite whiteness. It was a whiteness beyond anything earthly I had ever seen; nor do I believe that any earthly thing could be made to appear so exceedingly white and brilliant. His hands were naked, and his arms also, a little above the wrist; so, also, were his feet naked, as were his legs, a little above the ankles. His head and neck were also bare. I could discover that he had no other clothing on but this robe, as it was open, so that I could see into his bosom.

32. Not only was his robe exceedingly white, but his whole person was glorious beyond description, and his countenance truly like lightning. The room was exceedingly light, but not so very bright as immediately around his person. When I first looked upon him, I was afraid; but the fear soon left me.

33. He called me by name, and said unto me that he was a messenger sent from the presence of God to me, and that his name was Moroni; that God had a work for me to do; and that my name should be had for good and evil among all nations, kindreds, and tongues, or that it should be both good and evil spoken of among all people.

34. He said there was a book deposited, written upon gold plates, giving an account of the former inhabitants of this continent, and the source from whence they sprang. He also said that the fulness of the everlasting Gospel was contained in it, as delivered by the Savior to the ancient inhabitants;

35. Also, that there were two stones in silver bows -- and these stones, fastened to a breastplate, constituted what is called the Urim and Thummim -- deposited with the plates; and the possession and use of these stones were what constituted "seers" in ancient or former times; and that God had prepared them for the purpose of translating the book.***

42. Again, he told me, that when I got those plates of which he had spoken -- for the time that they should be obtained was not yet fulfilled -- I should not show them to any person; neither the

breastplate with the Urim and Thummim; only to those to whom I should be commanded to show them; if I did I should be destroyed. While he was conversing with me about the plates, the vision was opened to my mind that I could see the place where the plates were deposited, and that so clearly and distinctly that I knew the place again when I visited it.

43. After this communication, I saw the light in the room begin to gather immediately around the person of him who had been speaking to me, and it continued to do so until the room was again left dark, except just around him; when, instantly I saw, as it were, a conduit open right up into heaven, and he ascended till he entirely disappeared, and the room was left as it had been before this heavenly light had made its appearance.

44. I lay musing on the singularity of the scene, and marveling greatly at what had been told to me by this extraordinary messenger; when, in the midst of my meditation, I suddenly discovered that my room was again beginning to get lighted, and in an instant, as it were, the same heavenly messenger was again by my bedside.

45. He commenced, and again related the very same things which he had done at his first visit, without the least variation; which having done, he informed me of great judgments which were coming upon the earth, with great desolations by famine, sword, and pestilence; and that these grievous judgments would come on the earth in this generation. Having related these things, he again ascended as he had done before.

46. By this time, so deep were the impressions made on my mind, that sleep had fled from my eyes, and I lay overwhelmed in astonishment at what I had both seen and heard. But what was my surprise when again I beheld the same messenger at my bedside, and heard him rehearse or repeat over again to me the same things as before; and added a caution to me, telling me that Satan would try to tempt me (in consequence of the indigent circumstances of my father's family), to get the plates for the purpose of getting rich. This he forbade me, saying that I must have no other object in view in getting the plates but to glorify God, and must not be influenced by any other motive than that of building his kingdom; otherwise I could not get them.

47. After this third visit, he again ascended into heaven as before, and I was again left to ponder on the strangeness of what I had just experienced; when almost immediately after the heavenly messenger had ascended from me for the third time, the cock crowed, and I found that day was approaching, so that our interviews must have occupied the whole of that night.

48. I shortly after arose from my bed, and, as usual, went to the necessary labors of the day; but, in attempting to work as at other times, I found my strength so exhausted as to render me entirely unable. My father, who was laboring along with me, discovered something to be wrong with me, and told me to go home. I started with the intention of going to the house; but, in attempting to cross the fence out of the field where we were, my strength entirely failed me, and I fell helpless on the ground, and for a time was quite unconscious of anything.

49. The first thing that I can recollect was a voice speaking unto me, calling me by name. I looked up, and beheld the same messenger standing over my head, surrounded by light as before. He then again related unto me all that he had related to me the previous night, and commanded me to go to my father and tell him of the vision and commandments which I had received.

50. I obeyed; I returned to my father in the field, and rehearsed the whole matter to him. He replied to me that it was of God, and told me to go and do as commanded by the messenger. I left the field, and went to the place where the messenger had told me the plates were deposited; and owing to the distinctness of the vision which I had had concerning it, I knew the place the instant that I arrived there.

51. Convenient to the village of Manchester, Ontario county, New York, stands a hill of considerable size, and the most elevated of any in the neighborhood. On the west side of this hill, not far from the top, under a stone of considerable size, lay the plates, deposited in a stone box. This stone was thick and rounding in the middle on the upper side, and thinner towards the edges, so that the middle part of it was visible above the ground, but the edge all around was covered with earth.

52. Having removed the earth, I obtained

a lever, which I got fixed under the edge of the stone, and with a little exertion raised it up. I looked in, and there indeed did I behold the plates, the Urim and Thummim, and the breastplate, as stated by the messenger. The box in which they lay was formed by laying stones together in some kind of cement. In the bottom of the box were laid two stones crossways of the box, and on these stones lay the plates and the other things with them.

53. I made an attempt to take them out, but was forbidden by the messenger, and was again informed that the time for bringing them forth had not yet arrived, neither would it, until four years from that time; but he told me that I should come to that place precisely in one year from that time, and that he would there meet with me, and that I should continue to do so until the time should come for obtaining the plates.

54. Accordingly, as I had been commanded, I went at the end of each year, and at each time I found the same messenger there, and received instruction and intelligence from him at each of our interviews, respecting what the Lord was going to do, and how and in what manner his kingdom was to be conducted in the last days.***

59. At length the time arrived for obtaining the plates, the Urim and Thummim, and the breastplate. On the twenty-second day of September, one thousand eight hundred and twenty-seven, having gone as usual at the end of another year to the place where they were deposited, the same heavenly messenger delivered them up to me with this charge: that I should be responsible for them; that if I should let them go carelessly, or through any neglect of mine, I should be cut off; but that if I would use all my endeavors to preserve them, until he, the messenger, should call for them, they should be protected.

Priesthood Authority Restored to the Earth

President Joseph Smith, Jun.
Pearl of Great Price, Joseph Smith 2

66. On the 5th day of April, 1829, Oliver Cowdery came to my house, until which time I had never seen him. He stated to me that having been teaching school in the neighborhood where my father resided, and my father being one of those who sent to the school, he went to board for a season at his house, and while there the family related to him the circumstances of my having received the plates, and accordingly he had come to make inquiries of me.

67. Two days after the arrival of Mr. Cowdery (being the 7th of April) I commenced to translate the Book of Mormon, and he began to write for me.

68. We still continued the work of translation, when, in the ensuing month (May, 1829), we on a certain day went into the woods to pray and inquire of the Lord respecting baptism for the remission of sins, that we found mentioned in the translation of the plates. While we were thus employed, praying and calling upon the Lord, a messenger from heaven descended in a cloud of light, and having laid his hands upon us, he ordained us, saying:

69. *Upon you my fellow servants, in the name of Messiah, I confer the Priesthood of Aaron, which holds the keys of the ministering of angels, and of the gospel of repentance, and of baptism by immersion for the remission of sins; and this shall never be taken again from the earth until the sons of Levi do offer again an offering unto the Lord in righteousness.*

70. He said this Aaronic Priesthood had not the power of laying on hands for the gift of the Holy Ghost, but that this should be conferred on us hereafter; and he commanded us to go and be baptized, and gave us directions that I should baptize Oliver Cowdery, and that afterwards he should baptize me.

71. Accordingly we went and were baptized. I baptized him first, and afterwards he baptized me -- after which I laid my hands upon his head and ordained him to the Aaronic Priesthood, and afterwards he laid his hands on me and ordained me to the same Priesthood -- for so we were commanded.

72. The messenger who visited us on this occasion and conferred this Priesthood upon us, said that his name was John, the same that is called John the Baptist in the New Testament, and that he acted under the direction of Peter, James and John, who held the keys of the Priesthood of Melchizedek, which Priesthood, he said, would in due time be conferred on us,

and that I should be called the first Elder of the Church, and he (Oliver Cowdery) the second. It was on the fifteenth day of May, 1829, that we were ordained under the hand of this messenger, and baptized.

73. Immediately on our coming up out of the water after we had been baptized, we experienced great and glorious blessings from our Heavenly Father. No sooner had I baptized Oliver Cowdery, than the Holy Ghost fell upon him, and he stood up and prophesied many things which should shortly come to pass. And again, so soon as I had been baptized by him, I also had the spirit of prophecy, when, standing up, I prophesied concerning the rise of this Church, and many other things connected with the Church, and this generation of the children of men. We were filled with the Holy Ghost, and rejoiced in the God of our salvation.

74. Our minds being now enlightened, we began to have the scriptures laid open to our understandings, and the true meaning and intention of their more mysterious passages revealed unto us in a manner which we never could attain to previously, nor ever before had thought of. In the meantime we were forced to keep secret the circumstances of having received the Priesthood and our having been baptized, owing to a spirit of persecution which had already manifested itself in the neighborhood.

75. We had been threatened with being mobbed, from time to time, and this, too, by professors of religion. And their intentions of mobbing us were only counteracted by the influence of my wife's father's family (under Divine providence), who had become very friendly to me, and who were opposed to mobs, and were willing that I should be allowed to continue the work of translation without interruption; and therefore offered and promised us protection from all unlawful proceedings, as far as in them lay.

Restoring Melchizedek Priesthood on Earth

President Rulon Jeffs
Rulon Jeffs' Sermons 1:249 December 16, 1962 SLC
Now brethren and sisters, we read in Section 110 that all of the heads of previous dispensations came and gave their keys to Joseph Smith; Elias delivering the gospel of Abraham to him, Moses the keys of the gathering, and Elijah the keys of the sealing powers of the holy Priesthood. Peter, James, and John had previously come and given him their keys of the meridian dispensation of the Kingdom of God -- Peter, James, and John, not just John alone. We read in many places in the Doctrine and Covenants where Joseph has these keys, the fullness of the keys of the holy Priesthood, and of the last Dispensation of the Fullness of Times, never to be taken from him in heaven or in earth. And he holds them today.

We testify that Joseph Smith is the third member of the Godhead, and in this last and great dispensation, he holds all of the keys, and is still directing the affairs of this dispensation under the direction of Jesus and Father Adam. He stood by directing the proceedings when this special dispensation of the Priesthood was given under John Taylor in 1886; and he is still directing this work in the same way.

President Brigham Young
JD 1:134 April 6, 1853 SLC
Joseph was ordained an Apostle -- that you can read and understand. After he was ordained to this office, then he had the right to organize and build up the kingdom of God, for he had committed unto him the *keys* of the *Priesthood*, which is after the order of Melchizedec -- the *High Priesthood*, which is after the order of the Son of God. And this, remember, *by being ordained an Apostle.****

I know that Joseph received his Apostleship from Peter, James, and John, before a revelation on the subject was printed, and he never had a right to organize a Church before he was an Apostle.

Revelation of the Lord Jesus Christ Given to President Joseph Smith, Jun. August 1830 Doctrine and Covenants, Section 27
12. And also with Peter, and James, and John, whom I have sent unto you, by whom I have ordained you and confirmed you to be apostles, and especial witnesses of my name, and bear the keys of your ministry and of the same things which I revealed unto them;

Revelation of the Lord Jesus Christ
Given to President Joseph Smith, Jun.
September 6, 1842
Doctrine and Covenants Section 128

20. And again, what do we hear? Glad tidings from Cumorah! Moroni, an angel from heaven, declaring the fulfilment of the prophets -- the book to be revealed. A voice of the Lord in the wilderness of Fayette, Seneca county, declaring the three witnesses to bear record of the book! The voice of Michael on the banks of the Susquehanna, detecting the devil when he appeared as an angel of light! The voice of Peter, James, and John in the wilderness between Harmony, Susquehanna county, and Colesville, Broome county, on the Susquehanna river, declaring themselves as possessing the keys of the kingdom, and of the dispensation of the fulness of times!

President John Taylor
Mediation and Atonement, Page 159

We read that Moses and Elias came to administer to Jesus, on the Mount, while Peter, James and John were with him. Who were this Moses and this Elias? Moses was a great Prophet, appointed by the Lord to deliver Israel from Egyptian bondage, and lead them to the promised land; and he held the keys of the gathering dispensation, which keys he afterwards conferred upon Joseph Smith in the Kirtland Temple. Who was Elias? Elijah; which name in the old Scriptures is made synonymous with Elias; and who held, according to the testimony of Joseph Smith as elsewhere stated, the keys of the Priesthood. These men, who held those keys and officiated upon the earth, having left the earth, now come, associated with Jesus, to administer to Peter, James and John, and confer upon them the Priesthood which they hold; and these three ancient Apostles conferred the Priesthood upon Joseph Smith and Oliver Cowdery in this dispensation.

President Joseph Smith, Jun.
Teachings of the Prophet Joseph Smith, Page 346

Here, then, is eternal life -- to know the only wise and true God; and you have got to learn how to be Gods yourselves, and to be kings and priests to God, the same as all Gods have done before you, namely, by going from one small degree to another, and from a small capacity to a great one; from grace to grace, from exaltation to exaltation, until you attain to the resurrection of the dead, and are able to dwell in everlasting burnings, and to sit in glory, as do those who sit enthroned in everlasting power.

Revelation of the Lord Jesus Christ
Given to President Joseph Smith, Jun.
November 1, 1831
Doctrine and Covenants, Section 1

1. Hearken, O ye people of my church, saith the voice of him who dwells on high, and whose eyes are upon all men; yea, verily I say: Hearken ye people from afar; and ye that are upon the islands of the sea, listen together.

2. For verily the voice of the Lord is unto all men, and there is none to escape; and there is no eye that shall not see, neither ear that shall not hear, neither heart that shall not be penetrated.

3. And the rebellious shall be pierced with much sorrow; for their iniquities shall be spoken upon the housetops, and their secret acts shall be revealed.

4. And the voice of warning shall be unto all people, by the mouths of my disciples, whom I have chosen in these last days.

5. And they shall go forth and none shall stay them, for I the Lord have commanded them.

6. Behold, this is mine authority, and the authority of my servants, and my preface unto the book of my commandments, which I have given them to publish unto you, O inhabitants of the earth.

7. Wherefore, fear and tremble, O ye people, for what I the Lord have decreed in them shall be fulfilled.

8. And verily I say unto you, that they who go forth, bearing these tidings unto the inhabitants of the earth, to them is power given to seal both on earth and in heaven, the unbelieving and rebellious;

9. Yea, verily, to seal them up unto the day when the wrath of God shall be poured out upon the wicked without measure --

10. Unto the day when the Lord shall come to recompense unto every man according to his work, and measure to every man according to the measure which he has measured to his fellow man.

11. Wherefore the voice of the Lord is unto the ends of the earth, that all that will hear may hear:

12. Prepare ye, prepare ye for that which is to come, for the Lord is nigh;

13. And the anger of the Lord is kindled, and his sword is bathed in heaven, and it shall fall upon the inhabitants of the earth.

14. And the arm of the Lord shall be revealed; and the day cometh that they who will not hear the voice of the Lord, neither the voice of his servants, neither give heed to the words of the prophets and apostles, shall be cut off from among the people;

15. For they have strayed from mine ordinances, and have broken mine everlasting covenant;

16. They seek not the Lord to establish his righteousness, but every man walketh in his own way, and after the image of his own God, whose image is in the likeness of the world, and whose substance is that of an idol, which waxeth old and shall perish in Babylon, even Babylon the great, which shall fall.

17. Wherefore, I the Lord, knowing the calamity which should come upon the inhabitants of the earth, called upon my servant Joseph Smith, Jun., and spake unto him from heaven, and gave him commandments;

18. And also gave commandments to others, that they should proclaim these things unto the world; and all this that it might be fulfilled, which was written by the prophets --

19. The weak things of the world shall come forth and break down the mighty and strong ones, that man should not counsel his fellow man, neither trust in the arm of flesh --

20. But that every man might speak in the name of God the Lord, even the Savior of the world;

21. That faith also might increase in the earth;

22. That mine everlasting covenant might be established;

23. That the fulness of my gospel might be proclaimed by the weak and the simple unto the ends of the world, and before kings and rulers.

24. Behold, I am God and have spoken it;

these commandments are of me, and were given unto my servants in their weakness, after the manner of their language, that they might come to understanding.

25. And inasmuch as they erred it might be made known;

26. And inasmuch as they sought wisdom they might be instructed;

27. And inasmuch as they sinned they might be chastened, that they might repent;

28. And inasmuch as they were humble they might be made strong, and blessed from on high, and receive knowledge from time to time.

29. And after having received the record of the Nephites, yea, even my servant Joseph Smith, Jun., might have power to translate through the mercy of God, by the power of God, the Book of Mormon.

30. And also those to whom these commandments were given, might have power to lay the foundation of this church, and to bring it forth out of obscurity and out of darkness, the only true and living church upon the face of the whole earth, with which I, the Lord, am well pleased, speaking unto the church collectively and not individually --

31. For I the Lord cannot look upon sin with the least degree of allowance;

32. Nevertheless, he that repents and does the commandments of the Lord shall be forgiven;

33. And he that repents not, from him shall be taken even the light which he has received; for my Spirit shall not always strive with man, saith the Lord of Hosts.

34. And again, verily I say unto you, O inhabitants of the earth: I the Lord am willing to make these things known unto all flesh;

35. For I am no respecter of persons, and will that all men shall know that the day speedily cometh; the hour is not yet, but is nigh at hand, when peace shall be taken from the earth, and the devil shall have power over his own dominion.

36. And also the Lord shall have power over his saints, and shall reign in their midst, and shall come down in judgment upon Idumea, or the world.

37. Search these commandments, for they

are true and faithful, and the prophecies and promises which are in them shall all be fulfilled.

38. What I the Lord have spoken, I have spoken, and I excuse not myself; and though the heavens and the earth pass away, my word shall not pass away, but shall all be fulfilled, whether by mine own voice or by the voice of my servants, it is the same.

39. For behold, and lo, the Lord is God, and the Spirit beareth record, and the record is true, and the truth abideth forever and ever. Amen.

The Articles of Faith of the Church of Jesus Christ of Latter-day Saints

President Joseph Smith, Jun.
Pearl of Great Price, Page 60

1. We believe in God, the Eternal Father, and in His son, Jesus Christ, and in the Holy Ghost.

2. We believe that men will be punished for their own sins, and not for Adam's transgression.

3. We believe that through the Atonement of Christ, all mankind may be saved, by obedience to the laws and ordinances of the Gospel.

4. We believe that the first principles and ordinances of the Gospel are: first, Faith in the Lord Jesus Christ; second, Repentance; third, Baptism by immersion for the remission of sins; fourth, Laying on of hands for the gift of the Holy Ghost.

5. We believe that a man must be called of God, by prophecy, and by the laying on of hands, by those who are in authority, to preach the Gospel and administer in the ordinances thereof.

6. We believe in the same organization that existed in the Primitive Church, namely, apostles, prophets, pastors, teachers, evangelists, etc.

7. We believe in the gift of tongues, prophecy, revelation, visions, healing, interpretation of tongues, etc.

8. We believe the Bible to be the word of God as far as it is translated correctly; we also believe the Book of Mormon to be the word of God.

9. We believe all that God has revealed, all that He does now reveal, and we believe that He will yet reveal many great and important things pertaining to the Kingdom of God.

10. We believe in the literal gathering of Israel and in the restoration of the Ten Tribes; that Zion (the New Jerusalem) will be built upon the American continent; that Christ will reign personally upon the earth; and, that the earth will be renewed and receive its paradisiacal glory.

11. We claim the privilege of worshiping Almighty God according to the dictates of our own conscience, and allow all men the same privilege, let them worship how, where, or what they may.

12. We believe in being subject to kings, presidents, rulers, and magistrates, in obeying, honoring, and sustaining the law.

13. We believe in being honest, true, chaste, benevolent, virtuous, and in doing good to all men; indeed, we may say that we follow the admonition of Paul -- We believe all things, we hope all things, we have endured many things, and hope to be able to endure all things. If there is anything virtuous, lovely, or of good report or praiseworthy, we seek after these things.

JOSEPH SMITH.

One Man on the Earth at a Time Holds the Sealing Power to Seal Blessings Unto Eternal Life

Revelation of the Lord Jesus Christ Given to President Warren S. Jeffs San Angelo, Texas Tuesday, July 26, 2011

1. The revelations on my Holy Right to Rule, in my holy will manifested through my Seer and Prophet, Joseph Smith, are in Doctrine and Covenants as my guide to all people, to know that my authority has been restored among men to govern my holy law of plural marriage in my stead, as I reveal through my representative I have named, to be known now as Warren Jeffs, my Prophet, who is now of the full authority to administer all blessings of my holy Church on earth.

2. Let all now know that my holy authority to seal eternal blessings upon men of my Church, and also women of

my Church, is Warren Jeffs, the One Man I place the full power of sealing keys of my Melchizedek Priesthood, to administer lives of pure abiding to receive endless lives through Priesthood sealing keys.

3. The sealing keys are of my guiding, empowering; presenting my will as Mouthpiece of God on earth; being the power of eternal power, of Celestial eternal power now upon earth.

4. Let all know I have set upon my Prophet the gift to know me by the revelations of my will in a flow of holy revealing, to know my will, to give to my people the way of truth of holy and eternal way unto life eternal.

5. Let all be of a full way of receiving my will as I reveal my authority to be on earth; to honor thy God, to be of my holy power, to have life given through authorizing power now on earth, to guide all people of faith unto saving principles of eternal truths.

6. Let my Church now be of a full believing to be of my holy way; to be of the new era of peace; to have full way of coming to my holy place of receiving eternal gifts of love, light, peace, knowledge, justice, truth, power eternal; to be of my holy Order of Union Power.

7. Let all people know I have given my will, to be of a full power of pure light, knowledge, and truth; to be of a full way of pure holy guiding to all people who desire truth, unto them having all things being my Kingdom, all to be made holy and of eternal way of life everlasting.

8. Such does my eternal power of holy authority perform, by my holy power attending the administering power of Priesthood.

9. Receive ye my servant to receive me, saith your Lord, even Jesus Christ, who reigneth over all, justified by my holy sacrifice; redeeming all people of every time of the world from the grave, to stand before my holy presence to be judged according to the deeds done in the flesh.

10. Now receive ye my will, even Son Ahman, who is Jesus Christ: I am He who ruleth, who has all power, who sees and has knowing of all things in each person's life.

11. I am the rightful and true King over all.

12. Hear my holy word, will, and purposes in bringing all peoples of the earth on this globe of probationary testing.

13. I give my holy will and must be obeyed.

14. Now learn my holy will, to be obedient to my law of righteous dominion on earth and in Celestial worlds, even being my holy will to all peoples of the earth:

15. Let my servant go free to do my will.

16. He is in bondage because corrupt men have joined with a combination of several branches of earthly governing power in several places on the land of Zion, even known now as America, both North and South.

17. I have the right to rule.

18. No one has any authority to dictate God who made them.

19. Now be of good cheer, as I cause my dominion of Zion to soon take the reign of governing power over all peoples of the earth.

         Chapter 1 -- Administration of Joseph Smith, Jun.

20. Let all now acknowledge my having the right to rule over all nations, kindreds, tongues, and governing powers.

21. And if present nations of the earth seek to overthrow my Church and Kingdom, even Zion, they shall be brought low, to no longer be a nation, nor a people; who will now be of a full accounting, having knowledge now of my revealed power and divine authority on earth.

22. You "come unto me" through obedience to my law and Gospel. Amen.

Revelation of the Lord Jesus Christ Given to President Joseph Smith, Jun. July 12, 1843 Doctrine and Covenants, Section 132

7. And verily I say unto you, that the conditions of this law are these: All covenants, contracts, bonds, obligations, oaths, vows, performances, connections, associations, or expectations, that are not made and entered into and sealed by the Holy Spirit of promise, of him who is anointed, both as well for time and for all eternity, and that too most holy, by revelation and commandment through the medium of mine anointed, whom I have appointed on the earth to hold this power (and I have appointed unto my servant Joseph to hold this power in the last days, and there is never but one on the earth at a time on whom this power and the keys of this priesthood are conferred), are of no efficacy, virtue, or force in and after the resurrection from the dead; for all contracts that are not made unto this end have an end when men are dead.

Revelation of the Lord Jesus Christ Given to President Joseph Smith, Jun. September 1830 Doctrine and Covenants, Section 28

1. Behold, I say unto thee, Oliver, that it shall be given unto thee that thou shalt be heard by the church in all things whatsoever thou shalt teach them by the Comforter, concerning the revelations and commandments which I have given.

2. But, behold, verily, verily, I say unto thee, no one shall be appointed to receive commandments and revelations in this church excepting my servant Joseph Smith, Jun., for he receiveth them even as Moses.

3. And thou shalt be obedient unto the things which I shall give unto him, even as Aaron, to declare faithfully the commandments and the revelations, with power and authority unto the church.

4. And if thou art led at any time by the Comforter to speak or teach, or at all times by the way of commandment unto the church, thou mayest do it.

5. But thou shalt not write by way of commandment, but by wisdom;

6. And thou shalt not command him who is at thy head, and at the head of the church;

7. For I have given him the keys of the mysteries, and the revelations which are sealed, until I shall appoint unto them another in his stead.

Revelation of the Lord Jesus Christ Given to President Warren S. Jeffs San Angelo, Texas Tuesday, July 26, 2011

1. I, your Lord, have only One Man at a time on earth to be my holy Revelator of my new word.

Revelation of the Lord Jesus Christ Given to President Joseph Smith, Jun. February 1831 Doctrine and Covenants, Section 43

1. O hearken, ye elders of my church, and give ear to the words which I shall speak unto you.

2. For behold, verily, verily, I say unto you, that ye have received a commandment for a law unto my church, through him whom I have appointed unto you to receive commandments and revelations from my hand.

3. And this ye shall know assuredly -- that there is none other appointed unto you to receive commandments and revelations until he be taken, if he abide in me.

4. But verily, verily, I say unto you, that none else shall be appointed unto this gift except it be through him; for if it be taken from him he shall

not have power except to appoint another in his stead.

5. And this shall be a law unto you, that ye receive not the teachings of any that shall come before you as revelations or commandments;

6. And this I give unto you that you may not be deceived, that you may know they are not of me.

7. For verily I say unto you, that he that is ordained of me shall come in at the gate and be ordained as I have told you before, to teach those revelations which you have received and shall receive through him whom I have appointed.***

12. And if ye desire the glories of the kingdom, appoint ye my servant Joseph Smith, Jun., and uphold him before me by the prayer of faith.

13. And again, I say unto you, that if ye desire the mysteries of the kingdom, provide for him food and raiment, and whatsoever thing he needeth to accomplish the work wherewith I have commanded him;

14. And if ye do it not he shall remain unto them that have received him, that I may reserve unto myself a pure people before me.

Revelation of the Lord Jesus Christ Given to President Warren S. Jeffs
San Angelo, Texas
Tuesday, July 26, 2011

1. It is my holy will concerning Celestial Law of Plural Eternal Union:

2. My power is described as the only way to receive plural marriage.

3. Let all know the true power of governing power over my Church on earth is the Holy Melchizedek Priesthood, of the full order of Prophet, Seer, and Revelator.

4. Be of the way of knowing, by prayerful walk, and by my grace attending you, who is my Prophet, Seer, and Revelator to give my will to all people.

5. I have given to my Keyholder in the Melchizedek Priesthood the full key and knowledge of God to bring a people into the presence of your Lord.

6. Such is the call of our Lord, to now cease present proceedings of unjust attack in a court, not having power to be judge over my Celestial authority; even to be subservient to my Holy Priesthood authorized servant on my land of the full Kingdom of God ruling over all nations; which is the holy Order of Union Power of the dominion of my coming eternal power of Zion on earth.

7. Now hear my will: Be ye my holy will fulfilling --

8. Let my servant be free to do my will on earth; to let freedom of religion be your justification.

9. Let all now learn my holy will concerning the power of eternal authority of keys of holy power of my holy Order of Eternal Priesthood, that I have given my power of full and eternal authority to my servant on earth, to be of full power of my holy eternal authority.

10. Let all be of my eternal Kingdom, as you are my son or daughter on earth sent to do thy Lord's will.

Revelation of the Lord Jesus Christ Given to President Joseph Smith, Jun.
July 12, 1843
Doctrine and Covenants, Section 132

7. And verily I say unto you, that the conditions of this law are these: All covenants, contracts, bonds, obligations, oaths, vows, performances, connections, associations, or expectations, that are not made and entered into and sealed by the Holy Spirit of promise, of him who is anointed, both as well for time and for all eternity, and that too most holy, by revelation and commandment through the medium of mine anointed, whom I have appointed on the earth to hold this power (and I have appointed unto my servant Joseph to hold this power in the last days, and there is never but one on the earth at

a time on whom this power and the keys of this priesthood are conferred), are of no efficacy, virtue, or force in and after the resurrection from the dead; for all contracts that are not made unto this end have an end when men are dead.***

45. For I have conferred upon you the keys and power of the priesthood, wherein I restore all things, and make known unto you all things in due time.

46. And verily, verily, I say unto you, that whatsoever you seal on earth shall be sealed in heaven; and whatsoever you bind on earth, in my name and by my word, saith the Lord, it shall be eternally bound in the heavens; and whosesoever sins you remit on earth shall be remitted eternally in the heavens; and whosesoever sins you retain on earth shall be retained in heaven.

47. And again, verily I say, whomsoever you bless I will bless, and whomsoever you curse I will curse, saith the Lord; for I, the Lord, am thy God.

48. And again, verily I say unto you, my servant Joseph, that whatsoever you give on earth, and to whomsoever you give any one on earth, by my word and according to my law, it shall be visited with blessings and not cursings, and with my power, saith the Lord, and shall be without condemnation on earth and in heaven.

49. For I am the Lord thy God, and will be with thee even unto the end of the world, and through all eternity; for verily I seal upon you your exaltation, and prepare a throne for you in the kingdom of my Father, with Abraham your father.***

58. Now, as touching the law of the priesthood, there are many things pertaining thereunto.

59. Verily, if a man be called of my Father, as was Aaron, by mine own voice, and by the voice of him that sent me, and I have endowed him with the keys of the power of this priesthood, if he do anything in my name, and according to my law and by my word, he will not commit sin, and I will justify him.

60. Let no one, therefore, set on my servant Joseph; for I will justify him; for he shall do the sacrifice which I require at his hands for his transgressions, saith the Lord your God.

Obedience to Priesthood Is Obedience to God

President Rulon Jeffs
Rulon Jeffs' Sermons 3:504 April 4, 1976 CCA

The first law of heaven goes through my mind, which I feel to speak upon with the help of the Lord here today. The first law of heaven is obedience. Jesus said, "The first and greatest commandment, or law, is that we love our Father in heaven with all our heart, might, mind, and strength." These two are the same, brothers and sisters. Jesus said, "If you love Me, obey My commandments." That Being whom we love, we list to obey, and so it is indeed part and parcel of the first and great commandment and law of God, both in heaven and in earth.

If we love God, we love His Priesthood, because He is Priesthood. In fact, the holy Priesthood is God with us, if we understand Priesthood. It has been said, and truthfully, that -- and I am sure if you will trace the history, you will find it is true -- that man who apostatizes from this work, the work of the Priesthood, the work of God, has done so because he did not understand Priesthood. So we have, by the mercy and blessing of God, delegated to His chosen servants, and particularly I mention the keyholder, the keys of the holy Priesthood, from which we obtain the blessings of salvation. Therefore, it is necessary, if we take it to its correct and ultimate conclusion, that we obey Priesthood, which is the same as obeying God.

Some men who do not understand seem to feel that obedience is giving up our free agency. On the contrary; to enjoy our free agency, we must obey God. Disobedience to the law will bring about an abridgement of our agency, ***

So, brethren and sisters, President Johnson and those of the same order of Priesthood which holds that same Priesthood with him, are called of God. They belong to God, and as I have said many times in rather strong terms, hands off! It is for us to obey the principles of truth which is given us by that Priesthood and the keys thereof. If we will obey His servants, we will be obeying God. God cannot be here personally, and He has delegated His power and authority in the very highest that is given to man to President Johnson in this day and time. Brothers and sisters, if we do not draw near to him and be subject to his direction, when the time of visitation and of judgments come, we may not be in the right place, standing in holy places.

You brethren holding the holy Melchizedek Priesthood, heads of families, should have your families rallying around you in such a way that they would move as by a hair, that they might stand in holy places, and make your homes a temple. Those are the holy places that we must stand in, unless our head calls for us to go some place while the overflowing scourge passes over, for it is coming in soon.

I try to liken our condition, brothers and sisters, to that of the Zion's camp. God called upon Joseph to gather five hundred men to go up and redeem Zion. The least He would be satisfied with would be one hundred, but he gathered two hundred. Now, I am sure that God knew by His foreknowledge that this would not be accomplished, the redemption of Zion, though the set time had been given, September of 1836.

The conditions of this great work and mission that was given these men was that they should go and follow their head as by a hair, and go without murmuring, walking in perfect obedience, being one with him, walking as one man; so perfect in their unity and their oneness that they would have put to flight all of the mobs and the armies and the aliens and could have redeemed Zion. Had they complied with all of the conditions of that great commandment that was given them, they could have done it, because there was a set time, had they complied.

We have heard many, many times in recent years and times that the Gospel of preparation is upon us. We will not become prepared, brothers and sisters, short of this thing that I am speaking of here today; and that is obedience to Priesthood, obedience to President Johnson, our head, and the medium through which the word of God comes, and thus we will be obeying God. He is giving us these instructions and commandments by reason of the revelations of God with him, therefore this law of obedience is upon us; which, if we do, we will obey the law of sacrifice and come to know that our course is pleasing to God. And by the power of faith, the power of the Holy Ghost, through the Priesthood, we will accomplish this great work

of preparation and be raised up as a people, out of the heart's core of this people. Not everyone under the sound of my voice will be called up, I can promise you that, or else God never spoke by the mouth of His Prophets.

So, where do we stand, brothers and sisters? Are we walking in perfect obedience, in perfect love? Love and obedience are the same thing. Whom we love, we list to obey, as Jesus said. Now let us, therefore, love God, love His Priesthood, love the truth, the true and correct principles that are expounded and given to us by that Priesthood, and become one, that we may have power with God through faith. Faith is power with God, in the application of these principles of obedience and love.

Erastus Snow
JD 24:159 June 24, 1883 Parowan

Brother Cannon speaks of President Young and President Taylor, and other good men, our leaders, being led, as it were, by a hair in obedience to the Priesthood, which implies simply obedience to truth and to correct doctrine, and to righteousness. This is the explanation the Prophet Joseph Smith gave to a certain lawyer in his time who came to see him and his people and expressed astonishment and surprise at the ease with which he controlled the people, and said it was something that was not to be found among the learned men of the world. Said he: "We cannot do it. What is the secret of your success?" "Why," said the Prophet, "I do not govern the people. I teach them correct principles and they govern themselves."

Power of Priesthood

Revelation of the Lord Jesus Christ
Given to President Joseph Smith, Jun.
May 6, 1833
Doctrine and Covenants, Section 84

17. Which priesthood continueth in the church of God in all generations, and is without beginning of days or end of years.

18. And the Lord confirmed a priesthood also upon Aaron and his seed, throughout all their generations, which priesthood also continueth and abideth forever with the priesthood which is after the holiest order of God.

19. And this greater priesthood administereth the gospel and holdeth the key of the mysteries

of the kingdom, even the key of the knowledge of God.

20. Therefore, in the ordinances thereof, the power of godliness is manifest.

21. And without the ordinances thereof, and the authority of the priesthood, the power of godliness is not manifest unto men in the flesh;

22. For without this no man can see the face of God, even the Father, and live.***

35. And also all they who receive this priesthood receive me, saith the Lord;

36. For he that receiveth my servants receiveth me;

37. And he that receiveth me receiveth my Father;

38. And he that receiveth my Father receiveth my Father's kingdom; therefore all that my Father hath shall be given unto him.

39. And this is according to the oath and covenant which belongeth to the priesthood.

40. Therefore, all those who receive the priesthood, receive this oath and covenant of my Father, which he cannot break, neither can it be moved.

41. But whoso breaketh this covenant after he hath received it, and altogether turneth therefrom, shall not have forgiveness of sins in this world nor in the world to come.

42. And wo unto all those who come not unto this priesthood which ye have received, which I now confirm upon you who are present this day, by mine own voice out of the heavens; and even I have given the heavenly hosts and mine angels charge concerning you.

43. And I now give unto you a commandment to beware concerning yourselves, to give diligent heed to the words of eternal life.

44. For you shall live by every word that proceedeth forth from the mouth of God.

45. For the word of the Lord is truth, and whatsoever is truth is light, and whatsoever is light is Spirit, even the Spirit of Jesus Christ.

46. And the Spirit giveth light to every man that cometh into the world; and the Spirit enlighteneth every man through the world, that hearkeneth to the voice of the Spirit.

47. And every one that hearkeneth to the voice of the Spirit cometh unto God, even the Father.

48. And the Father teacheth him of the covenant which he has renewed and confirmed upon you, which is confirmed upon you for your sakes, and not for your sakes only, but for the sake of the whole world.

49. And the whole world lieth in sin, and groaneth under darkness and under the bondage of sin.

50. And by this you may know they are under the bondage of sin, because they come not unto me.

51. For whoso cometh not unto me is under the bondage of sin.

52. And whoso receiveth not my voice is not acquainted with my voice, and is not of me.

53. And by this you may know the righteous from the wicked, and that the whole world groaneth under sin and darkness even now.***

63. And as I said unto mine apostles, even so I say unto you, for you are mine apostles, even God's high priests; ye are they whom my Father hath given me; ye are my friends;

Priesthood to Be of Pure Love

Revelation of the Lord Jesus Christ
Given to President Joseph Smith, Jun.
March 20, 1839
Doctrine and Covenants, Section 121

41. No power or influence can or ought to be maintained by virtue of the priesthood, only by persuasion, by long-suffering, by gentleness and meekness, and by love unfeigned;

42. By kindness, and pure knowledge, which shall greatly enlarge the soul without hypocrisy, and without guile --

43. Reproving betimes with sharpness, when moved upon by the Holy Ghost; and then showing forth afterwards an increase of love toward him whom thou hast reproved, lest he esteem thee to be his enemy;

44. That he may know that thy faithfulness is stronger than the cords of death.

45. Let thy bowels also be full of charity towards all men, and to the household of faith, and let virtue garnish thy thoughts unceasingly; then shall thy confidence wax strong in the presence of God; and the doctrine of the priesthood shall distil upon thy soul as the dews from heaven.

46. The Holy Ghost shall be thy constant companion, and thy scepter an unchanging scepter of righteousness and truth; and thy dominion shall be an everlasting dominion, and without compulsory means it shall flow unto thee forever and ever.

Sealing Powers Restored
(My Will of Holy Celestial Power)

Revelation of the Lord Jesus Christ Given to President Warren S. Jeffs San Angelo, Texas Tuesday, July 26, 2011

1. I, your Lord, appearing to Joseph Smith in my holy temple, declared eternal power to rest upon my people.

2. I sent the Keyholders of keys and power to deliver to my One Man holding full Priesthood authority, to also hold keys of Priesthood in full, which is the keys of Elijah, to seal Celestial unions of marriage, even plural marriage upon faithful sons and daughters of my holy Church on earth.

Revelation of the Lord Jesus Christ Given to President Joseph Smith, Jun. April 3, 1836 Doctrine and Covenants, Section 110

1. The veil was taken from our minds, and the eyes of our understanding were opened.

2. We saw the Lord standing upon the breastwork of the pulpit, before us; and under his feet was a paved work of pure gold, in color like amber.

3. His eyes were as a flame of fire; the hair of his head was white like the pure snow; his countenance shone above the brightness of the sun; and his voice was as the sound of the rushing of great waters, even the voice of Jehovah, saying:

4. I am the first and the last; I am he who liveth, I am he who was slain; I am your advocate with the Father.

5. Behold, your sins are forgiven you; you are clean before me; therefore, lift up your heads and rejoice.

6. Let the hearts of your brethren rejoice, and let the hearts of all my people rejoice, who have, with their might, built this house to my name.

7. For behold, I have accepted this house, and my name shall be here; and I will manifest myself to my people in mercy in this house.

8. Yea, I will appear unto my servants, and speak unto them with mine own voice, if my people will keep my commandments, and do not pollute this holy house.

9. Yea the hearts of thousands and tens of thousands shall greatly rejoice in consequence of the blessings which shall be poured out, and the endowment with which my servants have been endowed in this house.

10. And the fame of this house shall spread to foreign lands; and this is the beginning of the blessing which shall be poured out upon the heads of my people. Even so. Amen.

11. After this vision closed, the heavens were again opened unto us; and Moses appeared before us, and committed unto us the keys of the gathering of Israel from the four parts of the earth, and the leading of the ten tribes from the land of the north.

12. After this, Elias appeared, and committed the dispensation of the gospel of Abraham, saying that in us and our seed all generations after us should be blessed.

13. After this vision had closed, another great and glorious vision burst upon us; for Elijah the prophet, who was taken to heaven without tasting death, stood before us, and said:

14. Behold, the time has fully come, which was spoken of by the mouth of Malachi -- testifying that he [Elijah] should be sent, before the great and dreadful day of the Lord come --

15. To turn the hearts of the fathers to the children, and the children to the fathers, lest the whole earth be smitten with a curse --

16. Therefore, the keys of this dispensation

are committed into your hands; and by this ye may know that the great and dreadful day of the Lord is near, even at the doors.

The Government of God

President Joseph Smith, Jun.
Teachings of the Prophet Joseph Smith, Page 248

An Editorial by the Prophet On the Failure of Man-made Governments and the Right of God to Rule

The government of the Almighty has always been very dissimilar to the governments of men, whether we refer to His religious government, or to the government of nations. The government of God has always tended to promote peace, unity, harmony, strength, and happiness; while that of man has been productive of confusion, disorder, weakness, and misery.

Man's Government Brings Misery and Destruction

The greatest acts of the mighty men have been to depopulate nations and to overthrow kingdoms; and whilst they have exalted themselves and become glorious, it has been at the expense of the lives of the innocent, the blood of the oppressed, the moans of the widow, and the tears of the orphan.

Egypt, Babylon, Greece, Persia, Carthage, Rome -- each was raised to dignity amidst the clash of arms and the din of war; and whilst their triumphant leaders led forth their victorious armies to glory and victory, their ears were saluted with the groans of the dying and the misery and distress of the human family; before them the earth was a paradise, and behind them a desolate wilderness; their kingdoms were founded in carnage and bloodshed, and sustained by oppression, tyranny, and despotism. The designs of God, on the other hand, have been to promote the universal good of the universal world; to establish peace and good will among men; to promote the principles of eternal truth; to bring about a state of things that shall unite man to his fellow man; cause the world to "beat their swords into plowshares, and their spears into pruning hooks," make the nations of the earth dwell in peace, and to bring about the millennial glory, when "the earth shall yield its increase, resume its paradisean glory, and become as the garden of the Lord."

Failure of the Governments of Men

The great and wise of ancient days have failed in all their attempts to promote eternal power, peace and happiness. Their nations have crumbled to pieces; their thrones have been cast down in their turn, and their cities, and their mightiest works of art have been annihilated; or their dilapidated towers, or time-worn monuments have left us but feeble traces of their former magnificence and ancient grandeur. They proclaim as with a voice of thunder, those imperishable truths -- that man's strength is weakness, his wisdom is folly, his glory is his shame.

Monarchial, aristocratical, and republican governments of their various kinds and grades, have, in their turn, been raised to dignity, and prostrated in the dust. The plans of the greatest politicians, the wisest senators, and most profound statesmen have been exploded; and the proceedings of the greatest chieftains, the bravest generals, and the wisest kings have fallen to the ground. Nation has succeeded nation, and we have inherited nothing but their folly. History records their puerile plans, their short-lived glory, their feeble intellect and their ignoble deeds.

Has Man Increased in Intelligence?

Have we increased in knowledge or intelligence? Where is there a man that can step forth and alter the destiny of nations and promote the happiness of the world? Or where is there a kingdom or nation that can promote the universal happiness of its own subjects, or even their general well-being? Our nation, which possesses greater resources than any other, is rent, from center to circumference, with party strife, political intrigues, and sectional interest; our counselors are panic stricken, our legislators are astonished, and our senators are confounded, our merchants are paralyzed, our tradesmen are disheartened, our mechanics out of employ, our farmers distressed, and our poor crying for bread, our banks are broken, our credit ruined, and our states overwhelmed in debt, yet we are, and have been in peace.

Man Not Able to Govern Himself

What is the matter? Are we alone in this thing? Verily no. With all our evils we are better situated than any other nation. Let

Egypt, Turkey, Spain, France, Italy, Portugal, Germany, England, China, or any other nation, speak, and tell the tale of their trouble, their perplexity, and distress, and we should find that their cup was full, and that they were preparing to drink the dregs of sorrow. England, that boasts of her literature, her science, commerce, &c., has her hands reeking with the blood of the innocent abroad, and she is saluted with the cries of the oppressed at home. Chartism, O'Connelism, and radicalism are gnawing her vitals at home; and Ireland, Scotland, Canada, and the east are threatening her destruction abroad. France is rent to the core, intrigue, treachery, and treason lurk in the dark, and murder, and assassination stalk forth at noonday. Turkey, once the dread of European nations, has been shorn of her strength, has dwindled into her dotage, and has been obliged to ask her allies to propose to her tributary terms of peace; and Russia and Egypt are each of them opening their jaws to devour her. Spain has been the theater of bloodshed, of misery and woe for years past. Syria is now convulsed with war and bloodshed. The great and powerful empire of China, which has for centuries resisted the attacks of barbarians, has become tributary to a foreign foe, her batteries thrown down, many of her cities destroyed, and her villages deserted. We might mention the Easter Rajahs, the miseries and oppressions of the Irish; the convulsed state of Central America; the situation of Texas and Mexico; the state of Greece, Switzerland and Poland; nay, the world itself presents one great theater of misery, woe, and "distress of nations with perplexity." All, all, speak with a voice of thunder, that man is not able to govern himself, to legislate for himself, to protect himself, to promote his own good, nor the good of the world.

The Design of Jehovah

It has been the design of Jehovah, from the commencement of the world, and is His purpose now, to regulate the affairs of the world in His own time, to stand as a head of the universe, and take the reins of government in His own hand. When that is done, judgment will be administered in righteousness; anarchy and confusion will be destroyed, and "nations will learn war no more." It is for want of this great governing principle,

that all this confusion has existed; "for it is not in man that walketh, to direct his steps;" this we have fully shown.

If there was anything great or good in the world, it came from God. The construction of the first vessel was given to Noah, by revelation. The design of the ark was given by God, "a pattern of heavenly things." The learning of the Egyptians, and their knowledge of astronomy was no doubt taught them by Abraham and Joseph, as their records testify, who received it from the Lord. The art of working in brass, silver, gold, and precious stones, was taught by revelation, in the wilderness. The architectural designs of the Temple at Jerusalem, together with its ornaments and beauty, were given of God. Wisdom to govern the house of Israel was given to Solomon, and the Judges of Israel; and if he had always been their king, and they subject to his mandate, and obedient to his laws, they would still have been a great and mighty people -- the rulers of the universe, and the wonder of the world.

Government Established by God

If Nebuchadnezzar, or Darius, or Cyrus, or any other king possessed knowledge or power, it was from the same source, as the Scriptures abundantly testify. If, then, God puts up one, and sets down another at His pleasure, and made instruments of kings, unknown to themselves, to fulfill His prophecies, how much more was he able, if man would have been subject to His mandate, to regulate the affairs of this world, and promote peace and happiness among the human family!

The Lord has at various times commenced this kind of government, and tendered His services to the human family. He selected Enoch, whom He directed, and gave His law unto, and to the people who were with him; and when the world in general would not obey the commands of God, after walking with God, he translated Enoch and his church, and the Priesthood or government of heaven was taken away.

Abraham was guided in all his family affairs by the Lord; was conversed with by angels, and by the Lord; was told where to go, and when to stop; and prospered exceedingly in all that he put his hand unto; it was because he and his family obeyed the counsel of the Lord.

 Chapter 1 -- Administration of Joseph Smith, Jun.

When Egypt was under the superintendence of Joseph it prospered, because he was taught of God; when they oppressed the Israelites, destruction came upon them. When the children of Israel were chosen with Moses at their head, they were to be a peculiar people, among whom God should place His name; their motto was: "The Lord is our lawgiver; the Lord is our Judge; the Lord is our King; and He shall reign over us." While in this state they might truly say, "Happy is that people, whose God is the Lord." Their government was a theocracy; they had God to make their laws, and men chosen by Him to administer them; He was their God, and they were His people. Moses received the word of the Lord from God Himself; he was the mouth of God to Aaron, and Aaron taught the people, in both civil and ecclesiastical affairs; they were both one, there was no distinction; so will it be when the purposes of God shall be accomplished: when "the Lord shall be King over the whole earth" and "Jerusalem His throne." "The law shall go forth from Zion, and the word of the Lord from Jerusalem."

Universal Peace to Come from God

This is the only thing that can bring about the "restitution of all things spoken of by all the holy Prophets since the world was" -- "the dispensation of the fullness of times, when God shall gather together all things in one." Other attempts to promote universal peace and happiness in the human family have proved abortive; every effort has failed; every plan and design has fallen to the ground; it needs the wisdom of God, the intelligence of God, and the power of God to accomplish this. The world has had a fair trial for six thousand years; the Lord will try the seventh thousand Himself; "He whose right it is, will possess the kingdom, and reign until He has put all things under His feet;" iniquity will hide its hoary head, Satan will be bound, and the works of darkness destroyed; righteousness will be put to the line, and judgment to the plummet, and "he that fears the Lord will alone be exalted in that day." To bring about this state of things, there must of necessity be great confusion among the nations of the earth; "distress of nations with perplexity." Am I asked what is the cause of the present distress? I would answer, "Shall there be evil in a city and the Lord hath not done it?"

Earth Now Groaning Under Corruption

The earth is groaning under corruption, oppression, tyranny and bloodshed; and God is coming out of His hiding place, as He said He would do, to vex the nations of the earth. Daniel, in his vision, saw convulsion upon convulsion; he "beheld till the thrones were cast down, and the Ancient of Days did sit;" and one was brought before him like unto the Son of Man; and all nations, kindred, tongues, and peoples, did serve and obey Him. It is for us to be righteous, that we may be wise and understand; for none of the wicked shall understand; but the wise shall understand, and they that turn many to righteousness shall shine as the stars for ever and ever.

It Behooves Us to Be Wise

As a Church and a people it behooves us to be wise, and to seek to know the will of God, and then be willing to do it; for "blessed is he that heareth the word of the Lord, and keepeth it," say the Scriptures. "Watch and pray always," says our Savior, "that ye may be accounted worthy to escape the things that are to come on the earth, and to stand before the Son of Man." If Enoch, Abraham, Moses, and the children of Israel, and all God's people were saved by keeping the commandments of God, we, if saved at all, shall be saved upon the same principle. As God governed Abraham, Isaac and Jacob as families, and the children of Israel as a nation; so we, as a Church, must be under His guidance if we are prospered, preserved and sustained. Our only confidence can be in God; our only wisdom obtained from Him; and He alone must be our protector and safeguard, spiritually and temporally, or we fall.

We have been chastened by the hand of God heretofore for not obeying His commands, although we never violated any human law, or transgressed any human precept; yet we have treated lightly His commands, and departed from His ordinances, and the Lord has chastened us sore, and we have felt His arm and kissed the rod; let us be wise in time to come and ever remember that "to obey is better than sacrifice, and to hearken than the fat of rams." The Lord has told us to build the Temple and the Nauvoo House; and that command is as binding upon us as any other; and that man who engages not in these things is as much a transgressor as though he broke any other commandment; he is not a doer of God's will, not a fulfiller of His laws.

The Saints Subject to Divine Counsel

In regard to the building up of Zion, it has to be done by the counsel of Jehovah, by the revelations of heaven; and we should feel to say, "If the Lord go not with us, carry us not up hence." We would say to the Saints that come here, we have laid the foundation for the gathering of God's people to this place, and they expect that when the Saints do come, they will be under the counsel that God has appointed. The Twelve are set apart to counsel the Saints pertaining to this matter; and we expect that those who come here will send before them their wise men according to revelation; or if not practicable, be subject to the counsel that God has given, or they cannot receive an inheritance among the Saints, or be considered as God's people, and they will be dealt with as transgressors of the laws of God. We are trying here to gird up our loins, and purge from our midst the workers of iniquity; and we hope that when our brethren arrive from abroad, they will assist us to roll forth this good work, and to accomplish this great design, that "Zion may be built up in righteousness; and all nations flock to her standard;" that as God's people, under His direction, and obedient to His law, we may grow up in righteousness and truth; that when His purposes shall be accomplished, we may receive an inheritance among those that are sanctified. (July 15, 1842.) D.H.C. 5:61-66.

Plural Marriage Established; Reward of Those Who Abide Their Covenants Unto the End

Revelation of the Lord Jesus Christ Given to President Warren S. Jeffs San Angelo, Texas Tuesday, July 26, 2011

Celestial Plural Marriage Established by Revelation of God

1. Thus saith the Lord, even your Savior over all flesh, to all peoples of every nation on earth; and to governing authority on my land of Zion where I am to soon come to dwell among men a thousand years; to govern all peoples as your God and King, all to my right to rule:

2. I have been your Lord all your eternal existence as a son or daughter of God.

3. I am a God of eternal power.

4. I have all knowledge, light, truth eternal, Priesthood power and authority from my Father, the God of Holy Priesthood power over all.

5. I am Son Ahman, even Jesus Christ, whose holy will and atoning and perfect way hath caused you to have hope eternal, to be of such a way to learn of eternal way of life everlasting.

6. I have instituted eternal laws of progression of pure holy conduct and of faith, to bring children on earth to be of my holy order of eternal lives.

7. Celestial Marriage is a law and principle of eternal life of my holy power of Priesthood, to exalt pure sons to Godhood; daughters to a Celestial, eternal, happy life of mothers of children in eternal union of my guiding, perfecting, and exalting; unto a mother of creating sons and daughters of spirit power on an eternal earth of high Celestial power; to be eternal parents, to be of pure begetters of children eternally.

8. Let all know this law is of me and is eternal, unchangeable, and is a holy, pure, exalting law of salvation, and must be lived by my revealing; and by my holy revealing, appointing unions eternal as I reveal all truth, of pure truth, who is of worthy condition to be a God of Creation.

9. Such is this law of pure religious and holy intent, practice, and eternal result of my power guiding all in this law by my Holy Priesthood.

10. Thus, I reveal to all people of the earth that I shall uphold my Priesthood power I cause to reveal my will; and I shall be the holy power to perfect my people who abide faithfully my law.

11. Let my holy will now be of a way to understand I revealed my law of Celestial Union of Plural Marriage to my servant on earth, even my servant who held all the powers of Priesthood authority in the beginning of this time of preparing for my holy power coming to earth from Celestial realms of my eternal domain, which rules over all people and shall be of my whole and holy power.

12. Let all now be receiving my word as given through Joseph Smith, my holy Seer of the time of final preparing for my coming, to be my law under my revealing, not to be given to any outside my Holy Priesthood.

13. All must be of my true faith and Kingdom to be receiving my holy law.

14. No one can enter into this law who is not of my Church and Kingdom.

15. Therefore, this law is of religion of heaven revealed by your God to His Prophet of full Priesthood authority and power eternal, to be my law, not of any government power among men to be of a way of justice power over my Church, for it is mine, not of man.

16. Therefore, thy Lord revealeth all needed truth, that my law will be preserved on earth, to prepare my Church for my coming; which law is Celestial and is not to be of earth only.

17. I am God. I have my eternal law to reveal, guide, and preserve.

18. Let my truth be upheld by my Priesthood.

19. Let all government powers of man not interfere in the religious free living of my holy way; to no longer be of a prosecuting power against my holy religion.

20. Receive ye my will on the truths revealed through my servant Joseph Smith, and as I caused others of my servants of Priesthood power to continue on earth; to have a pure people raised unto your God for His coming.

Revelation of the Lord Jesus Christ Given to President Joseph Smith, Jun. July 12, 1843 Doctrine and Covenants, Section 132

1. Verily, thus saith the Lord unto you my servant Joseph, that inasmuch as you have inquired of my hand to know and understand wherein I, the Lord, justified my servants Abraham, Isaac, and Jacob, as also Moses, David and Solomon, my servants, as touching the principle and doctrine of their having many wives and concubines --

2. Behold, and lo, I am the Lord thy God, and will answer thee as touching this matter.

3. Therefore, prepare thy heart to receive and obey the instructions which I am about to give unto you; for all those who have this law revealed unto them must obey the same.

4. For behold, I reveal unto you a new and an everlasting covenant; and if ye abide not that covenant, then are ye damned; for no one can reject this covenant and be permitted to enter into my glory.

5. For all who will have a blessing at my hands shall abide the law which was appointed for that blessing, and the conditions thereof, as were instituted from before the foundation of the world.

6. And as pertaining to the new and everlasting covenant, it was instituted for the fulness of my glory; and he that receiveth a fulness thereof must and shall abide the law, or he shall be damned, saith the Lord God.

7. And verily I say unto you, that the conditions of this law are these: All covenants, contracts, bonds, obligations, oaths, vows, performances, connections, associations, or

expectations, that are not made and entered into and sealed by the Holy Spirit of promise, of him who is anointed, both as well for time and for all eternity, and that too most holy, by revelation and commandment through the medium of mine anointed, whom I have appointed on the earth to hold this power (and I have appointed unto my servant Joseph to hold this power in the last days, and there is never but one on the earth at a time on whom this power and the keys of this priesthood are conferred), are of no efficacy, virtue, or force in and after the resurrection from the dead; for all contracts that are not made unto this end have an end when men are dead.

8. Behold, mine house is a house of order, saith the Lord God, and not a house of confusion.

9. Will I accept of an offering, saith the Lord, that is not made in my name?

10. Or will I receive at your hands that which I have not appointed?

11. And will I appoint unto you, saith the Lord, except it be by law, even as I and my Father ordained unto you, before the world was?

12. I am the Lord thy God; and I give unto you this commandment -- that no man shall come unto the Father but by me or by my word, which is my law, saith the Lord.

13. And everything that is in the world, whether it be ordained of men, by thrones, or principalities, or powers, or things of name, whatsoever they may be, that are not by me or by my word, saith the Lord, shall be thrown down, and shall not remain after men are dead, neither in nor after the resurrection, saith the Lord your God.

14. For whatsoever things remain are by me; and whatsoever things are not by me shall be shaken and destroyed.

15. Therefore, if a man marry him a wife in the world, and he marry her not by me nor by my word, and he covenant with her so long as he is in the world and she with him, their covenant and marriage are not of force when they are dead, and when they are out of the world; therefore, they are not bound by any law when they are out of the world.

16. Therefore, when they are out of the world

they neither marry nor are given in marriage; but are appointed angels in heaven, which angels are ministering servants, to minister for those who are worthy of a far more, and an exceeding, and an eternal weight of glory.

17. For these angels did not abide my law; therefore, they cannot be enlarged, but remain separately and singly, without exaltation, in their saved condition, to all eternity; and from henceforth are not gods, but are angels of God forever and ever.

18. And again, verily I say unto you, if a man marry a wife, and make a covenant with her for time and for all eternity, if that covenant is not by me or by my word, which is my law, and is not sealed by the Holy Spirit of promise, through him whom I have anointed and appointed unto this power, then it is not valid neither of force when they are out of the world, because they are not joined by me, saith the Lord, neither by my word; when they are out of the world it cannot be received there, because the angels and the gods are appointed there, by whom they cannot pass; they cannot, therefore, inherit my glory; for my house is a house of order, saith the Lord God.

19. And again, verily I say unto you, if a man marry a wife by my word, which is my law, and by the new and everlasting covenant, and it is sealed unto them by the Holy Spirit of promise, by him who is anointed, unto whom I have appointed this power and the keys of this priesthood; and it shall be said unto them -- Ye shall come forth in the first resurrection; and if it be after the first resurrection, in the next resurrection; and shall inherit thrones, kingdoms, principalities, and powers, dominions, all heights and depths -- then shall it be written in the Lamb's Book of Life, that he shall commit no murder whereby to shed innocent blood, and if ye abide in my covenant, and commit no murder whereby to shed innocent blood, it shall be done unto them in all things whatsoever my servant hath put upon them, in time, and through all eternity; and shall be of full force when they are out of the world; and they shall pass by the angels, and the gods, which are set there, to their exaltation and glory in all things, as hath been sealed upon their heads, which glory shall be a fulness and a continuation of the seeds forever and ever.

20. Then shall they be gods, because they

have no end; therefore shall they be from everlasting to everlasting, because they continue; then shall they be above all, because all things are subject unto them. Then shall they be gods, because they have all power, and the angels are subject unto them.

21. Verily, verily, I say unto you, except ye abide my law ye cannot attain to this glory.

22. For strait is the gate, and narrow the way that leadeth unto the exaltation and continuation of the lives, and few there be that find it, because ye receive me not in the world neither do ye know me.

23. But if ye receive me in the world, then shall ye know me, and shall receive your exaltation; that where I am ye shall be also.

24. This is eternal lives -- to know the only wise and true God, and Jesus Christ, whom he hath sent. I am he. Receive ye, therefore, my law.

25. Broad is the gate, and wide the way that leadeth to the deaths; and many there are that go in thereat, because they receive me not, neither do they abide in my law.

26. Verily, verily, I say unto you, if a man marry a wife according to my word, and they are sealed by the Holy Spirit of promise, according to mine appointment, and he or she shall commit any sin or transgression of the new and everlasting covenant whatever, and all manner of blasphemies, and if they commit no murder wherein they shed innocent blood, yet they shall come forth in the first resurrection, and enter into their exaltation; but they shall be destroyed in the flesh, and shall be delivered unto the buffetings of Satan unto the day of redemption, saith the Lord God.

27. The blasphemy against the Holy Ghost, which shall not be forgiven in the world nor out of the world, is in that ye commit murder wherein ye shed innocent blood, and assent unto my death, after ye have received my new and everlasting covenant, saith the Lord God; and he that abideth not this law can in nowise enter into my glory, but shall be damned, saith the Lord.

28. I am the Lord thy God, and will give unto thee the law of my Holy Priesthood, as was ordained by me and my Father before the world was.

29. Abraham received all things, whatsoever he received, by revelation and commandment, by my word, saith the Lord, and hath entered into his exaltation and sitteth upon his throne.

30. Abraham received promises concerning his seed, and of the fruit of his loins -- from whose loins ye are, namely, my servant Joseph -- which were to continue so long as they were in the world; and as touching Abraham and his seed, out of the world they should continue; both in the world and out of the world should they continue as innumerable as the stars; or, if ye were to count the sand upon the seashore ye could not number them.

31. This promise is yours also, because ye are of Abraham, and the promise was made unto Abraham; and by this law is the continuation of the works of my Father, wherein he glorifieth himself.

32. Go ye, therefore, and do the works of Abraham; enter ye into my law and ye shall be saved.

33. But if ye enter not into my law ye cannot receive the promise of my Father, which he made unto Abraham.

34. God commanded Abraham, and Sarah gave Hagar to Abraham to wife. And why did she do it? Because this was the law; and from Hagar sprang many people. This, therefore, was fulfilling, among other things, the promises.

35. Was Abraham, therefore, under condemnation? Verily I say unto you, Nay; for I, the Lord, commanded it.

36. Abraham was commanded to offer his son Isaac; nevertheless, it was written: Thou shalt not kill. Abraham, however, did not refuse, and it was accounted unto him for righteousness.

37. Abraham received concubines, and they bore him children; and it was accounted unto him for righteousness, because they were given unto him, and he abode in my law; as Isaac also and Jacob did none other things than that which they were commanded; and because they did none other things than that which they were commanded, they have entered into their exaltation, according to the promises, and sit upon thrones, and are not angels but are gods.

38. David also received many wives and

concubines, and also Solomon and Moses my servants, as also many others of my servants, from the beginning of creation until this time; and in nothing did they sin save in those things which they received not of me.

39. David's wives and concubines were given unto him of me, by the hand of Nathan, my servant, and others of the prophets who had the keys of this power; and in none of these things did he sin against me save in the case of Uriah and his wife; and, therefore he hath fallen from his exaltation, and received his portion; and he shall not inherit them out of the world, for I gave them unto another, saith the Lord.

40. I am the Lord thy God, and I gave unto thee, my servant Joseph, an appointment, and restore all things. Ask what ye will, and it shall be given unto you according to my word.

41. And as ye have asked concerning adultery, verily, verily, I say unto you, if a man receiveth a wife in the new and everlasting covenant, and if she be with another man, and I have not appointed unto her by the holy anointing, she hath committed adultery and shall be destroyed.

42. If she be not in the new and everlasting covenant, and she be with another man, she has committed adultery.

43. And if her husband be with another woman, and he was under a vow, he hath broken his vow and hath committed adultery.

44. And if she hath not committed adultery, but is innocent and hath not broken her vow, and she knoweth it, and I reveal it unto you, my servant Joseph, then shall you have power, by the power of my Holy Priesthood, to take her and give her unto him that hath not committed adultery but hath been faithful; for he shall be made ruler over many.

45. For I have conferred upon you the keys and power of the priesthood, wherein I restore all things, and make known unto you all things in due time.

46. And verily, verily, I say unto you, that whatsoever you seal on earth shall be sealed in heaven; and whatsoever you bind on earth, in my name and by my word, saith the Lord, it shall be eternally bound in the heavens; and whosoever sins you remit on earth shall be remitted eternally in the heavens; and whosoever sins you retain on earth shall be retained in heaven.

47. And again, verily I say, whomsoever you bless I will bless, and whomsoever you curse I will curse, saith the Lord; for I, the Lord, am thy God.

48. And again, verily I say unto you, my servant Joseph, that whatsoever you give on earth, and to whomsoever you give any one on earth, by my word and according to my law, it shall be visited with blessings and not cursings, and with my power, saith the Lord, and shall be without condemnation on earth and in heaven.

49. For I am the Lord thy God, and will be with thee even unto the end of the world, and through all eternity; for verily I seal upon you your exaltation, and prepare a throne for you in the kingdom of my Father, with Abraham your father.

50. Behold, I have seen your sacrifices, and will forgive all your sins; I have seen your sacrifices in obedience to that which I have told you. Go, therefore, and I make a way for your escape, as I accepted the offering of Abraham of his son Isaac.

51. Verily, I say unto you: A commandment I give unto mine handmaid, Emma Smith, your wife, whom I have given unto you, that she stay herself and partake not of that which I commanded you to offer unto her; for I did it, saith the Lord, to prove you all, as I did Abraham, and that I might require an offering at your hand, by covenant and sacrifice.

52. And let mine handmaid, Emma Smith, receive all those that have been given unto my servant Joseph, and who are virtuous and pure before me; and those who are not pure, and have said they were pure, shall be destroyed, saith the Lord God.

53. For I am the Lord thy God, and ye shall obey my voice; and I give unto my servant Joseph that he shall be made ruler over many things; for he hath been faithful over a few things, and from henceforth I will strengthen him.

54. And I command mine handmaid, Emma Smith, to abide and cleave unto my servant Joseph, and to none else. But if she will not

abide this commandment she shall be destroyed, saith the Lord; for I am the Lord thy God, and will destroy her if she abide not in my law.

55. But if she will not abide this commandment, then shall my servant Joseph do all things for her, even as he hath said; and I will bless him and multiply him and give unto him an hundredfold in this world, of fathers and mothers, brothers and sisters, houses and lands, wives and children, and crowns of eternal lives in the eternal worlds.

56. And again, verily I say, let mine handmaid forgive my servant Joseph his trespasses; and then shall she be forgiven her trespasses, wherein she has trespassed against me; and I, the Lord thy God, will bless her, and multiply her, and make her heart to rejoice.

57. And again, I say, let not my servant Joseph put his property out of his hands, lest an enemy come and destroy him; for Satan seeketh to destroy; for I am the Lord thy God, and he is my servant; and behold, and lo, I am with him, as I was with Abraham, thy father, even unto his exaltation and glory.

58. Now, as touching the law of the priesthood, there are many things pertaining thereunto.

59. Verily, if a man be called of my Father, as was Aaron, by mine own voice, and by the voice of him that sent me, and I have endowed him with the keys of the power of this priesthood, if he do anything in my name, and according to my law and by my word, he will not commit sin, and I will justify him.

60. Let no one, therefore, set on my servant Joseph; for I will justify him; for he shall do the sacrifice which I require at his hands for his transgressions, saith the Lord your God.

61. And again, as pertaining to the law of the priesthood -- if any man espouse a virgin, and desire to espouse another, and the first give her consent, and if he espouse the second, and they are virgins, and have vowed to no other man, then is he justified; he cannot commit adultery for they are given unto him; for he cannot commit adultery with that that belongeth unto him and to no one else.

62. And if he have ten virgins given unto him by this law, he cannot commit adultery, for

they belong to him, and they are given unto him; therefore is he justified.

63. But if one or either of the ten virgins, after she is espoused, shall be with another man, she has committed adultery, and shall be destroyed; for they are given unto him to multiply and replenish the earth, according to my commandment, and to fulfil the promise which was given by my Father before the foundation of the world, and for their exaltation in the eternal worlds, that they may bear the souls of men; for herein is the work of my Father continued, that he may be glorified.

64. And again, verily, verily, I say unto you, if any man have a wife, who holds the keys of this power, and he teaches unto her the law of my priesthood, as pertaining to these things, then shall she believe and administer unto him, or she shall be destroyed, saith the Lord your God; for I will destroy her; for I will magnify my name upon all those who receive and abide in my law.

65. Therefore, it shall be lawful in me, if she receive not this law, for him to receive all things whatsoever I, the Lord his God, will give unto him, because she did not believe and administer unto him according to my word; and she then becomes the transgressor; and he is exempt from the law of Sarah, who administered unto Abraham according to the law when I commanded Abraham to take Hagar to wife.

66. And now, as pertaining to this law, verily, verily, I say unto you, I will reveal more unto you, hereafter; therefore, let this suffice for the present. Behold, I am Alpha and Omega. Amen.

On My Way of Revealing Necessity of Revelation Being Needed to Be My True Religion of Heaven --

Revelation of the Lord Jesus Christ Given to President Warren S. Jeffs San Angelo, Texas Wednesday, July 27, 2011

1. Let all now be of a holy way.

2. Let my way be of a pure holy way of revealing marriage unions, to be my law

of holy eternal revealing; not of man, but of me, your Lord Jesus Christ; He who is over all and who dictates and guides His servant to administer my holy way, not to others not in my Church and Priesthood law.

3. Let my people quietly abide the sacred covenants they have received to be as an example to guide souls to see as God sees in all things.

4. No longer live in prejudicing the people of the world who do not understand eternal law.

5. Let no one set on my servant and Keyholder on earth, as he is my vessel of holy power to bless pure holy vessels on the way of my giving increase in salvation power eternal.

6. Let my servant Warren Jeffs be free to conduct my affairs in my Church as I shall name, without government interference or persecution, for I shall preserve the faithful in the way unto eternal life. Amen.

President Joseph Smith, Jun.
Teachings of the Prophet Joseph Smith, Page 257

Our heavenly Father is more liberal in His views, and boundless in His mercies and blessings, than we are ready to believe or receive; and, at the same time, is more terrible to the workers of iniquity, more awful in the executions of His punishments, and more ready to detect every false way, than we are apt to suppose Him to be. He will be inquired of by His children. He says, "Ask and ye shall receive, seek and ye shall find;" but, if you will take that which is not your own, or which I have not given you, you shall be rewarded according to your deeds; but no good thing will I withhold from them who walk uprightly before me, and do my will in all things -- who will listen to my voice and to the voice of my servant whom I have sent; for I delight in those who seek diligently to know my precepts, and abide by the law of my kingdom; for all things shall be made known unto them in mine own due time, and in the end they shall have joy.

Celestial Plural Marriage Established by the Revelations of God

Testimony of President Brigham Young

President Brigham Young
JD 16:166 August 31, 1873 Paris, Idaho

After this doctrine was received, Joseph received a revelation on celestial marriage. You will recollect, brethren and sisters, that it was in July, 1843, that he received this revelation concerning celestial marriage. This doctrine was explained and many received it as far as they could understand it. Some apostatized on account of it; but others did not, and received it in their faith. This, also, is a great and noble doctrine. I have not time to give you many items upon the subject, but there are a few hints that I can throw in here that perhaps may be interesting.***...the people of God, therefore, have been commanded to take more wives. The women are entitled to salvation if they live according to the word that is given to them; and if their husbands are good men, and they are obedient to them, they are entitled to certain blessings, and they will have the privilege of receiving certain blessings that they cannot receive unless they are sealed to men who will be exalted.

President Brigham Young
JD 11:239 June 3, 1866 SLC

We are told that if we would give up polygamy -- which we know to be a doctrine revealed from heaven, and it is God and the world for it -- but suppose this Church should give up this holy order of marriage, then would the devil, and all who are in league with him against the cause of God, rejoice that they had prevailed upon the Saints to refuse to obey one of the revelations and commandments of God to them. Would they be satisfied with this? No; but they would next want us to renounce Joseph Smith as a true prophet of God, then the Book of Mormon, then baptism for the remission of sins and the laying on of hands for the reception of the Holy Ghost. Then they would wish us to disclaim the gift of prophecy, and the other gifts and graces of the Holy Spirit, on the ground that they are done away and no longer needed in our day, also prophets and apostles, etc.

President Brigham Young
JD 13:239 February 20, 1870 SLC

Well, I need not talk about this; but I will

say that the principle of patriarchal marriage is one of the highest and purest ever revealed to the children of men. I do not say that it will not injure a great many. I heard brother Joseph Smith say a number of times, "There is no question but it will be the means of damning many of the Elders of Israel; it is nevertheless true and must be revealed; and the Lord designs that it shall be revealed and go forth, and that this people must receive the oracles of truth, and they must receive this holy ordinance, and that that pertains to the celestial world; and they will retrograde if they do not embrace more of the celestial law than they have yet."

I say, with regard to this principle, if it was good in the days of Abraham and of the Patriarchs and Prophets, or at any other period of the world's history, and the fact that the Lord commanded His servants anciently to observe it, is conclusive proof that it was so considered by Him, why is it not good now?

Testimony of Heber C. Kimball

Heber C. Kimball
JD 5:203 October 12, 1856 SLC

Let the Presidency of this Church, and the Twelve Apostles, and all the authorities unite and say with one voice that they will oppose that doctrine, and the whole of them would be damned. What are you opposing it for? It is a principle that God has revealed for the salvation of the human family. He revealed it to Joseph the Prophet in this our dispensation; and that which he revealed he designs to have carried out by his people.

Heber C. Kimball
JD 4:224 February 8, 1857 SLC

Do you suppose that Joseph and Hyrum and all those good men would associate with those ancient worthies, if they had not been engaged in the same practices? They had to do the works of Abraham, Isaac, and Jacob, in order to be admitted where they are; -- they had to be polygamists in order to be received into their society. God knows that I am not ashamed of those good men now, and how much more I shall prize my associate polygamists, when I am further advanced in knowledge, I do not know. I am talking in earnest, and from the experience I have had.

Testimony of President John Taylor

President John Taylor
JD 24:230 (Unknown Date) Trip to Bear Lake

This you will see is strictly in accordance with what I have told you Joseph Smith told the Twelve -- that if this law was not practiced, if they would not enter into this covenant, then the kingdom of God could not go one step further. Now, we did not feel like preventing the kingdom of God from going forward. We professed to be the Apostles of the Lord, and did not feel like putting ourselves in a position to retard the progress of the kingdom of God. The revelation, as you have heard, says that, "all those who have this law revealed unto them must obey the same." Now, that is not my word. I did not make it. It was the Prophet of God who revealed that to us in Nauvoo, and I bear witness of this solemn fact before God, that He did reveal this sacred principle to me and others of the Twelve, and in this revelation it is stated that it is the will and law of God that "all those who have this law revealed unto them must obey the same."***

Now, as I have already said, the reason was very obvious why a law of this kind should be had. As a people we professed to be Latter-day Saints. We professed to be governed by the word, and will, and law of God. We had a religion that might do to live by, but we had none to die by. But this was a principle that God had revealed unto us, and it must be obeyed. I had always entertained strict ideas of virtue, and I felt as a married man that this was to me, outside of this principle, an appalling thing to do. The idea of my going and asking a young lady to be married to me, when I had already a wife! It was a thing calculated to stir up feelings from the innermost depth of the human soul. I had always entertained the strictest regard for chastity. I had never in my life seen the time when I have known of a man deceiving a woman -- and it is often done in the world, where notwithstanding the crime, the man is received into society, and the poor woman is looked upon as a pariah and an outcast -- I have always looked upon such a thing as infamous, and upon such a man as a villain, and I hold to-day the same ideas. Hence, with the feelings I had entertained, nothing but a knowledge of God, and the revelations of God, and the truth of them, could have induced me to embrace such a principle as this. We seemed to put off, as far as we could, what might be termed the evil day. Some time after these things were made known to us, I was riding out of Nauvoo on horseback, and met Joseph Smith coming in, he, too, being on horseback. Some of you who were acquainted with Nauvoo, know where the graveyard was. We met upon the road going on to the hill there. I bowed to Brother Joseph, and having done the same to me he said; "Stop;" and he looked at me very intently. "Look here," said he, "those things that have been spoken of must be fulfilled, and if they are not entered into right away, the keys will be turned." Well, what did I do? Did I feel to stand in the way of this great, eternal principle, and treat lightly the things of God? No. I replied: "Brother Joseph, I will try and carry these things out," and I afterwards did, and I have done it more times than once; but then I have never broken a law of the United States in doing so, and I am at their defiance to prove to the contrary.

Testimony of William Clayton

William Clayton
The Historical Record Volume 6, Page 224

The following statement was sworn to before John T. Caine, a notary public, in Salt Lake City, Feb. 16, 1874:

"Inasmuch as it may be interesting to future generations of the members of the Church of Jesus Christ of Latter-day Saints to learn something of the first teachings of the principle of plural marriage by President Joseph Smith, the Prophet, Seer, Revelator and Translator of said Church, I will give a short relation of facts which occurred within my personal knowledge, and also matters related to me by President Joseph Smith.

"I was employed as a clerk in President Joseph Smith's office, under Elder Willard Richards, and commenced to labor in the office on the 10th day of February, 1842. I continued to labor with Elder Richards until he went east to fetch his wife to Nauvoo.

"After Elder Richards started east I was necessarily thrown constantly into the company of President Smith, having to attend to his public and private business, receiving and recording tithings and donations, attending to land and other matters of business. During this period I necessarily became well acquainted with Emma Smith, the wife of the Prophet Joseph, and also with the children -- Julia M. (an adopted daughter), Joseph, Frederick and Alexander, very much of the business being transacted at the residence of the Prophet.

"On the 7th of October, 1842, in the presence of Bishop Newel K. Whitney and his wife Elizabeth Ann, President Joseph Smith appointed me Temple Recorder, and also his private clerk, placing all records, books, papers, etc., in my care, and requiring me to take charge of and preserve them, his closing words being, 'When I have any revelations to write, you are the one to write them.'

"During this period the Prophet Joseph frequently visited my house in my company, and became well acquainted with my wife Ruth, to whom I had been married five years. One day in the month of February, 1843, date not remembered, the Prophet invited me to walk with him. During our walk, he said he had learned that there was a sister back in England, to whom I was very much attached. I replied there was, but nothing further than an attachment such as a brother and sister in the Church might rightfully entertain for each other. He then said, 'Why don't you send for her?' I replied, 'In the first place, I have no authority to send for her, and if I had, I have not the means to pay expenses.' To this he answered, 'I give you authority to send for her, and I will furnish you with means,' which he did. This was the first time the Prophet Joseph talked with me on the subject of plural marriage. He informed me that the doctrine and principle was right in the sight of our Heavenly Father, and that it was a doctrine which pertained to celestial order and glory. After giving me lengthy instructions and informations concerning the doctrine of celestial or plural marriage, he concluded his remarks by the words, 'It is your privilege to have all the wives you want.' After this introduction, our conversations on the subject of plural marriage were very frequent, and he appeared to take particular pains to inform and instruct me in respect to the principle. He also informed me that he had other wives *living* besides his first wife Emma, and in particular gave me to understand that Eliza R. Snow,

Louisa Beman, Desdemona W. Fullmer and others were his lawful wives in the sight of Heaven.

"On the 27th of April, 1843, the Prophet Joseph Smith married to me Margaret Moon, for time and eternity, at the residence of Elder Heber C. Kimball; and on the 22nd of July, 1843, he married to me, according to the order of the Church, my first wife Ruth.

"On the 1st day of May, 1843, I officiated in the office of an Elder by marrying Lucy Walker to the Prophet Joseph Smith, at his own residence.

"During this period the Prophet Joseph took several other wives. Amongst the number I well remember Eliza Partridge, Emily Partridge, Sarah Ann Whitney, Helen Kimball and Flora Woodworth. These all, he acknowledged to me, were his lawful, wedded wives, according to the celestial order. His wife Emma was cognizant of the fact of some, if not all, of these being his wives, and she generally treated them very kindly.

"On the morning of the 12th of July, 1843, Joseph and Hyrum Smith came into the office in the upper story of the 'brick store,' on the bank of the Mississippi River. They were talking on the subject of plural marriage. Hyrum said to Joseph, 'If you will write the revelation on celestial marriage, I will take and read it to Emma, and I believe I can convince her of its truth, and you will hereafter have peace.' Joseph smiled and remarked, 'You do not know Emma as well as I do.' Hyrum repeated his opinion and further remarked, 'The doctrine is so plain, I can convince any reasonable man or woman of its truth, purity or heavenly origin,' or words to their effect. Joseph then said, 'Well, I will write the revelation and we will see.' He then requested me to get paper and prepare to write. Hyrum very urgently requested Joseph to write the revelation by means of the Urim and Thummim, but Joseph, in reply, said he did not need to, for he knew the revelation perfectly from beginning to end.

"Joseph and Hyrum then sat down and Joseph commenced to dictate the revelation on celestial marriage, and I wrote it, sentence by sentence, as he dictated. After the whole was written, Joseph asked me to read it through, slowly and carefully, which I did, and he pronounced it correct. He then remarked that there was much more that he could write, on the same subject, but what was written was sufficient for the present.

"Hyrum then took the revelation to read to Emma. Joseph remained with me in the office until Hyrum returned. When he came back, Joseph asked him how he had succeeded. Hyrum replied that he had never received a more severe talking to in his life, that Emma was very bitter and full of resentment and anger.

"Joseph quietly remarked, 'I told you you did not know Emma as well as I did.' Joseph then put the revelation in his pocket, and they both left the office.

"The revelation was read to several of the authorities during the day. Towards evening Bishop Newel K. Whitney asked Joseph if he had any objections to his taking a copy of the revelation; Joseph replied that he had not, and handed it to him. It was carefully copied the following day by Joseph C. Kingsbury. Two or three days after the revelation was written Joseph related to me and several others that Emma had so teased, and urgently entreated him for the privilege of destroying it, that he became so weary of her teasing, and to get rid of her annoyance, he told her she might destroy it and she had done so, but he had consented to her wish in this matter to pacify her, realizing that he knew the revelation perfectly, and could rewrite it at any time if necessary.

"The copy made by Joseph C. Kingsbury is a true and correct copy of the original in every respect. The copy was carefully preserved by Bishop Whitney, and but few knew of its existence until the temporary location of the Camps of Israel at Winter Quarters, on the Missouri River, in 1846.

"After the revelation on celestial marriage was written Joseph continued his instructions, privately, on the doctrine, to myself and others, and during the last year of his life we were scarcely ever together, alone, but he was talking on the subject, and explaining that doctrine and principles connected with it. He appeared to enjoy great liberty and freedom in his teachings, and also to find great relief in having a few to whom he could unbosom his feelings on that great and glorious subject.

"From him I learned that the doctrine of plural and celestial marriage is the most holy and important doctrine ever revealed to man on the earth, and that without obedience to that principle no man can ever attain to the fulness of exaltation in celestial glory.

(Signed)   WILLIAM CLAYTON
"Salt Lake City, February 16th, 1874."

Testimony of Eliza R. Snow

Eliza R. Snow
The Historical Record Volume 6, Page 224

The following was also published in the *Deseret News* (weekly) of Oct. 22, 1879:

"Recently, to my great astonishment, I read an article headed 'Last Testimony of Sister Emma,' published in the *Saints' Advocate*, a pamphlet issued in Plano, Ill.

"In the article referred to, her son Joseph reports himself as interviewing his mother on the subject of polygamy, asking questions concerning his father. Did his father teach the principle? Did he practice or approve of it? Did his father have other wives than herself? To all of these and similar inquiries, Sister Emma is represented as answering in the negative, positively affirming that Joseph, the Prophet, had no other wife or wives than her; that he neither taught the principle of plurality of wives, publicly or privately.

"I once dearly loved 'Sister Emma,' and now, for me to believe that she, a once highly honored woman, should have sunk so low, even in her own estimation, as to deny what she *knew* to be true, seems a palpable absurdity. If what purports to be her 'last testimony' was really her testimony, she died with a libel on her lips -- a libel against her husband -- against his wives -- against the truth, and a libel against God; and in publishing that libel, her son has fastened a stigma on the character of his mother, that can never be erased. It is a *fact* that Sister Emma, of her own free will and choice, gave her husband four wives, two of whom are now living, and ready to testify that she, not only gave them to her husband, but that she taught them the doctrine of plural marriage and urged them to accept it. And, if her son wished to degrade

his mother in the estimation of her former associates, those familiar with the incidents of the period referred to, he could not do it more effectually than by proving her denial of any knowledge of polygamy (celestial marriage), and its practice by her husband. Even if her son ignored his mother's reputation for veracity, he better had waited until his father's wives were silent in death, for now they are here living witnesses of the divinity of plural marriage, as revealed by the Almighty, through Joseph Smith, who was commanded to introduce it by taking other wives.

"So far as Sister Emma personally is concerned, I would gladly have been silent and let her memory rest in peace, had not her misguided son, through a sinister policy, branded her name with gross wickedness -- charging her with the denial of a sacred principle which she had heretofore not only acknowledged but had acted upon -- a principle than which there is none more important comprised in the Gospel of the Son of God.

"It may be asked, Why defend plurality of wives, since the United States government forbids its practice? The action of the executors of this government can neither change nor annihilate a fundamental truth; and this nation, in preventing the practice of plural marriage, shoulders a heavier responsibility than any nation has ever assumed, with one exception -- that of the ancient Jews. If the government can afford it, we can. The controversy is with God -- not us.

ELIZA R. SNOW
A wife of Joseph Smith, the Prophet.

Testimony of Eliza Partridge

The Historical Record Volume 6, Page 223
"Eliza M. Partridge's Affidavit.

"Territory of Utah,   }
County of Millard. } ss.

"Be it remembered that on the first day of July, A.D. 1869, personally appeared before me, Edward Partridge, probate judge in and for said county, Eliza M. (Partridge) Lyman, who was by me sworn in due form of law, and upon her oath saith, that on the 11th day of May, 1843, at the City of Nauvoo, County of Hancock, State of Illinois, she was married or sealed to Joseph

Smith, President of the Church of Jesus Christ of Latter-day Saints, by James Adams, a High Priest in said Church, *** in the presence of Emma (Hale) Smith and Emily D. Partridge.

(Signed)   ELIZA. M. (P.) LYMAN.

"Subscribed and sworn to by the said Eliza Maria Lyman, the day and year first above written.

[SEAL.]   EDWARD PARTRIDGE,
Probate Judge.

Testimony of Lucy W. Kimball

Lucy W. Kimball
The Historical Record Volume 6, Page 229

"When the Prophet Joseph Smith first mentioned the principle of plural marriage to me I became very indignant, and told him emphatically that I did not wish him ever to mention it to me again, as my feelings and education revolted against any thing of such a nature. He counseled me, however, to pray to the Lord for light and understanding in relation thereto, and promised me if I would do so sincerely, I should receive a testimony of the correctness of the principle. At length I concluded to follow this advice, and the consequence was that the Prophet's promise unto me was fulfilled to the very letter. Before praying I felt gloomy and downcast; in fact, I was so entirely given up to despair that I felt tired of life; but after I had poured out my heart's contents before God, I at once became calm and composed; a feeling of happiness took possession of me, and at the same time I received a powerful and irresistible testimony of the truth of plural marriage, which testimony has abided with me ever since. Shortly afterwards I consented to become the Prophet's wife, and was married to him May 1, 1843, Elder William Clayton officiating. I am also able to testify that Emma Smith, the Prophet's first wife, gave her consent to the marriage of at least four other girls to her husband, and that she was well aware that he associated with them as wives within the meaning of all that word implies. This is proven by the fact that she herself, on several occasions, kept guard at the door to prevent disinterested persons from intruding, when these ladies were in the house.

LUCY W. KIMBALL."

Testimony of Lydia Knight

Lydia Knight
Lydia Knight's History, Page 95

"I had always believed in the principle of celestial marriage, since I received a testimony of its truth in an early day from the Prophet Joseph's teachings. I have heard him teach it in public as well as in private; have heard him relate the incident of the angel coming to him with a drawn sword, commanding him to obey the law, or he should lose his priesthood as well as his life if he did not go forward in this principle; and I had received a strong testimony of its truth when under the Prophet's teachings."***

"It may be some will enquire of me, 'how do you like plurality after living in it and getting the experience you desired? What are your feelings now?' I will say I like it first-rate; my belief is strengthened; I do believe it is a principle that if not abused, will purify and exalt those that enter into it with purity of purpose, and so abide therein."

Persecutions of the Priesthood, Church, and Kingdom of God by the People of the Nation of the United States of America

Persecutions in the State of New York

Joseph Smith Receives the Plates; Persecution Becomes Severe by Enemies Seeking to Destroy the Prophet Joseph Smith

President Joseph Smith, Jun.
Pearl of Great Price, Joseph Smith 2

59. At length the time arrived for obtaining the plates, the Urim and Thummim, and the breastplate. On the twenty-second day of September, one thousand eight hundred and twenty-seven, having gone as usual at the end of another year to the place where they were deposited, the same heavenly messenger delivered them up to me with this charge: that I should be responsible for them; that if I should let them go carelessly, or through any neglect of mine, I should be cut off; but that if I would use all my endeavors to preserve them, until he, the messenger, should call for them, they should be protected.

60. I soon found out the reason why I had received such strict charges to keep them safe,

and why it was that the messenger had said that when I had done what was required at my hand, he would call for them. For no sooner was it known that I had them, than the most strenuous exertions were used to get them from me. Every stratagem that could be invented was resorted to for that purpose. The persecution became more bitter and severe than before, and multitudes were on the alert continually to get them from me if possible. But by the wisdom of God, they remained safe in my hands, until I had accomplished by them what was required at my hand. When, according to arrangements, the messenger called for them, I delivered them up to him; and he has them in his charge until this day, being the second day of May, one thousand eight hundred and thirty-eight.

61. The excitement, however, still continued, and rumor with her thousand tongues was all the time employed in circulating falsehoods about my father's family, and about myself. If I were to relate a thousandth part of them, it would fill up volumes. The persecution, however, became so intolerable that I was under the necessity of leaving Manchester, and going with my wife to Susquehanna county, in the State of Pennsylvania.

The Prophet Joseph Arrested and Tried Twice -- 1830

President Joseph Smith, Jun.
Documentary History of the Church 1:88

We had appointed a meeting for this evening, for the purpose of attending to the confirmation of those who had been the same morning baptized. The time appointed had arrived and our friends had nearly all collected together, when to my surprise, I was visited by a constable, and arrested by him on a warrant, on the charge of being a disorderly person, of setting the country in an uproar by preaching the Book of Mormon, etc. The constable informed me, soon after I had been arrested, that the plan of those who had got out the warrant was to get me into the hands of the mob, who were now lying in ambush for me; but that he was determined to save me from them, as he had found me to be a different sort of person from what I had been represented to him. I soon found that he had told me the truth in this matter, for not far from Mr. Knight's house, the wagon in which we had set out was surrounded by a mob, who seemed only to await

some signal from the constable; but to their great disappointment, he gave the horse the whip, and drove me out of their reach.

Whilst driving in great haste one of the wagon wheels came off, which left us once more very nearly surrounded by them, as they had come on in close pursuit. However, we managed to replace the wheel and again left them behind us. He drove on to the town of South Bainbridge, Chenango county, where he lodged me for the time being in an upper room of a tavern; and in order that all might be right with himself and with me also, he slept during the night with his feet against the door, and a loaded musket by his side, whilst I occupied a bed which was in the room; he having declared that if we were interrupted unlawfully, he would fight for me, and defend me as far as it was in his power.

On the day following, a court was convened for the purpose of investigating those charges which had been preferred against me. A great excitement prevailed on account of the scandalous falsehoods which had been circulated, the nature of which will appear in the sequel.***

At length the trial commenced amidst a multitude of spectators, who in general evinced a belief that I was guilty of all that had been reported concerning me, and of course were very zealous that I should be punished according to my crimes.***

Several other attempts were made to prove something against me, and even circumstances which were alleged to have taken place in Broome county, were brought forward, but these my lawyers would not admit of as testimony against me; in consequence of which my persecutors managed to detain the court until they had succeeded in obtaining a warrant from Broome county, which warrant they served upon me at the very moment that I was acquitted by this court.

The constable who served this second warrant upon me had no sooner arrested me than he began to abuse and insult me; and so unfeeling was he with me, that although I had been kept all the day in court without anything to eat since the morning, yet he hurried me off to Broome county, a distance of about fifteen miles, before he allowed me any kind of food whatever. He took me to a tavern, and gathered in a number of men, who used every means to abuse, ridicule and insult me. They spit upon me, pointed their fingers at me, saying, "Prophesy, prophesy!" and thus did they imitate those who crucified the Savior of mankind, not knowing what they did.

We were at this time not far distant from my own house. I wished to be allowed the privilege of spending the night with my wife at home, offering any wished for security for my appearance; but this was denied me. I applied for something to eat. The constable ordered me some crusts of bread and water, which was the only food I that night received. At length we retired to bed. The constable made me lie next the wall. He then laid himself down by me and put his arm around me, and upon my moving in the least, would clench me fast, fearing that I intended to escape from him; and in this very disagreeable manner did we pass the night.

Next day I was brought before the magistrate's court at Colesville, Broome county, and put upon my trial. My former faithful friends and lawyers were again at my side; my former persecutors were arrayed against me. Many witnesses were again called forward and examined, some of whom swore to the most palpable falsehoods, and like the false witnesses which had appeared against me the day previous, they contradicted themselves so plainly that the court would not admit their testimony. Others were called, who showed by their zeal that they were willing enough to prove something against me, but all they could do was to tell something which somebody else had told them.***

Mr. Seymour now addressed the court, and in a long and violent harangue endeavored to blacken my character and bring me in guilty of the charges which had been brought against me.***

Mr. Davidson and Mr. Reid followed on my behalf. They held forth in true colors the nature of the prosecution, the malignancy of intention, and the apparent disposition to persecute their client, rather than to afford him justice.*** In fact, these men, although not regular lawyers, were upon this occasion able to put to silence their opponents, and convince the court that I was innocent. They spoke like men inspired of God, whilst those who were arrayed against me trembled under the sound of their voices, and quailed before them like criminals before a bar of justice.

The majority of the assembled multitude had now begun to find that nothing could be sustained against me. Even the constable who arrested me, and treated me so badly, now came and apologized to me, and asked my forgiveness for his behavior towards me; and so far was he changed, that he informed me that the mob were determined, if the court acquitted me, that they would have me, and rail-ride me, and tar and feather me; and further, that he was willing to favor me and lead me out in safety by a private way.

The court found the charges against me not sustained; I was accordingly acquitted, to the great satisfaction of my friends and vexation of my enemies, who were still determined upon molesting me. But through the instrumentality of my new friend the constable, I was enabled to escape them and make my way in safety to my wife's sister's house, where I found my wife awaiting with much anxiety the issue of those ungodly proceedings, and in company with her I arrived next day in safety at my own house.

President Joseph Smith, Jun.
Documentary History of the Church 1:97

Thus were we persecuted on account of our religious faith -- in a country the Constitution of which guarantees to every man the indefeasible right to worship God according to the dictates of his own conscience -- and by men, too, who were professors of religion, and who were not backward to maintain the right of religious liberty for themselves, though they could thus wantonly deny it to us. For instance, Cyrus McMaster, a Presbyterian of high standing in his church, was one of the chief instigators of these persecutions; and he at one time told me personally that he considered me guilty without judge or jury. The celebrated Dr. Boyington, also a Presbyterian, was another instigator of these deeds of outrage; whilst a young man named Benton, of the same religious faith, swore out the first warrant against me. I could mention many others also, but for brevity's sake, will make these suffice for the present.

Persecutions in the State of Ohio

Mob Violence at Hiram, Ohio -- 1832

President Joseph Smith, Jun.
Documentary History of the Church 1:261

On the 24th of March, the twins before mentioned, which had been sick of the measles for some time, caused us to be broken of our rest in taking care of them, especially my wife. In the evening I told her she had better retire to rest with one of the children, and I would watch with the sicker child. In the night she told me I had better lie down on the trundle bed, and I did so, and was soon after awakened by her screaming murder, when I found myself going out of the door, in the hands of about a dozen men; some of whose hands were in my hair, and some had hold of my shirt, drawers and limbs. The foot of the trundle bed was towards the door, leaving only room enough for the door to swing open. My wife heard a gentle tapping on the windows which she then took no particular notice of (but which was unquestionably designed for ascertaining whether or not we were all asleep), and soon after the mob burst open the door and surrounded the bed in an instant, and, as I said, the first I knew I was going out of the door in the hands of an infuriated mob. I made a desperate struggle, as I was forced out, to extricate myself, but only cleared one leg, with which I made a pass at one man, and he fell on the door steps. I was immediately overpowered again; and they swore by G—, they would kill me if I did not be still, which quieted me. As they passed around the house with me, the fellow that I kicked came to me and thrust his hand, all covered with blood, into my face and with an exulting hoarse laugh, muttered *"Ge, gee, G— d— ye, I'll fix ye."*

They then seized me by the throat and held on till I lost my breath. After I came to, as they passed along with me, about thirty rods from the house, I saw Elder Rigdon stretched out on the ground, whither they had dragged him by his heels. I supposed he was dead. I began to plead with them, saying, "You will have mercy and spare my life, I hope." To which they replied, "G— d— ye, call on yer God for help, we'll show ye no mercy;" and the people began to show themselves in every direction; one coming from the orchard had a plank; and I expected they would kill me, and carry me off on the plank. They then turned to the right, and went on

about thirty rods further; about sixty rods from the house, and thirty from where I saw Elder Rigdon, into the meadow, where they stopped, and one said, "Simonds, Simonds," (meaning, I supposed, Simonds Ryder,) "pull up his drawers, pull up his drawers, he will take cold." Another replied: *"Ain't ye going to kill 'im? ain't ye going to kill 'im?"* when a group of mobbers collected a little way off, and said: "Simonds, Simonds, come here;" and "Simonds" charged those who had hold of me to keep me from touching the ground (as they had done all the time), lest I should get a spring upon them. They held a council, and as I could occasionally overhear a word, I supposed it was to know whether or not it was best to kill me. They returned after a while, when I learned that they had concluded not to kill me, but to beat and scratch me well, tear off my shirt and drawers, and leave me naked. One cried, "Simonds, Simonds, *where's the tar bucket?"* "I don't know," answered one, *"where 'tis, Eli's left it."* They ran back and fetched the bucket of tar, when one exclaimed, with an oath, *"Let us tar up his mouth;"* and they tried to force the tar-paddle into my mouth; I twisted my head around, so that they could not; and they cried out, *"G— d— ye, hold up yer head and let us give ye some tar."* They then tried to force a vial into my mouth, and broke it in my teeth. All my clothes were torn off me except my shirt collar; and one man fell on me and scratched my body with his nails like a mad cat, and then muttered out: *"G— d— ye, that's the way the Holy Ghost falls on folks!"*

They then left me, and I attempted to rise, but fell again; I pulled the tar away from my lips, so that I could breathe more freely, and after a while I began to recover, and raised myself up, whereupon I saw two lights. I made my way towards one of them, and found it was Father Johnson's. When I came to the door I was naked, and the tar made me look as if I were covered with blood, and when my wife saw me she thought I was all crushed to pieces, and fainted. During the affray abroad, the sisters of the neighborhood had collected at my room. I called for a blanket, they threw me one and shut the door; I wrapped it around me and went in.***

My friends spent the night in scraping and removing the tar, and washing and cleansing my body; so that by morning I was ready to be clothed again. This being the Sabbath morning, the people assembled for meeting at the usual hour of worship, and among them came also the mobbers;...

Persecutions in the State of Missouri

Mob Violence Against the Saints in Jackson County, Missouri -- 1833

President Joseph Smith, Jun.
Documentary History of the Church 1:390

ON the 20th of July, the mob collected, and demanded the discontinuance of the Church printing establishment in Jackson county, the closing of the store, and the cessation of all mechanical labors. The brethren refused compliance, and the consequence was that the house of W. W. Phelps, which contained the printing establishment, was thrown down, the materials taken possession of by the mob, many papers destroyed, and the family and furniture thrown out of doors.

The mob then proceeded to violence towards Edward Partridge, the Bishop of the Church, as he relates in his autobiography:

I was taken from my house by the mob, George Simpson being their leader, who escorted me about half a mile, to the court house, on the public square in Independence; and then and there, a few rods from said court house, surrounded by hundreds of the mob, I was stripped of my hat, coat and vest and daubed with tar from head to foot, and then had a quantity of feathers put upon me; and all this because I would not agree to leave the county, and my home where I had lived two years.

Before tarring and feathering me I was permitted to speak. I told them that the Saints had suffered persecution in all ages of the world; that I had done nothing which ought to offend anyone; that if they abused me, they would abuse an innocent person; that I was willing to suffer for the sake of Christ; but, to leave the country, I was not then willing to consent to it. By this time the multitude made so much noise that I could not be heard: some were cursing and swearing, saying, "call upon your Jesus," etc.; others were equally noisy in trying to still the rest, that they might be enabled to hear what I was saying.

Until after I had spoken, I knew not what they intended to do with me, whether to kill me, to whip me, or what else I knew not. I bore my abuse with so much resignation and meekness, that it appeared to astound the multitude, who permitted me to retire in silence, many looking very solemn, their sympathies having been touched as I thought;

and as to myself, I was so filled with the Spirit and love of God, that I had no hatred towards my persecutors or anyone else.

Charles Allen was next stripped and tarred and feathered, because he would not agree to leave the county, or deny the Book of Mormon. Others were brought up to be served likewise or whipped.***

In the course of this day's wicked, outrageous, and unlawful proceedings, many solemn realities of human degradation, as well as thrilling incidents were presented to the Saints. An armed and well organized mob, in a government professing to be governed by law, with the Lieutenant Governor (Lilburn W. Boggs), the second officer in the state, calmly looking on, and secretly aiding every movement, saying to the Saints, "You now know what our Jackson boys can do, and you must leave the county;" and all the justices, judges, constables, sheriffs, and military officers, headed by such western missionaries and clergymen as the Reverends McCoy, Kavanaugh, Hunter, Fitzhugh, Pixley, Likens, and Lovelady, consisting of Methodists, Baptists, Presbyterians, and all the different sects of religionists that inhabited that country, with that great moral reformer, and register of the land office at Lexington, forty miles east, known as the head and father of the Cumberland Presbyterians, even the Reverend Finis Ewing, publicly publishing that "Mormons were the common enemies of mankind, and ought to be destroyed" -- all these solemn realities were enough to melt the heart of a savage; while there was not a *solitary offense* on record, or proof, that a Saint had broken the law of the land.

Expulsion of the Saints from Jackson County, Missouri -- 1833

President Joseph Smith, Jun.
Documentary History of the Church 1:426

THURSDAY night, the 31st of October, gave the Saints in Zion abundant proof that no pledge on the part of their enemies, written or verbal, was longer to be regarded; for on that night, between forty and fifty persons in number, many of whom were armed with guns, proceeded against a branch of the Church, west of the Big Blue, and unroofed and partly demolished ten dwelling houses; and amid the shrieks and screams of the women and children, whipped and beat in a savage and brutal manner, several of the men: while their horrid threats frightened women and children into the wilderness. Such of the men as could escape fled for their lives; for very few of them had arms, neither were they organized; and they were threatened with death if they made any resistance; such therefore as could not escape by flight, received a pelting with stones and a beating with guns and whips. On Friday, the first of November, women and children sallied forth from their gloomy retreats, to contemplate with heartrending anguish the ravages of a ruthless mob, in the lacerated and bruised bodies of their husbands, and in the destruction of their houses, and their furniture. Houseless and unprotected by the arm of the civil law in Jackson county, the dreary month of November staring them in the face and loudly proclaiming an inclement season at hand; the continual threats of the mob that they would drive every "Mormon" from the county; and the inability of many to move, because of their poverty, caused an anguish of heart indescribable.

On Friday night, the 1st of November, a party of the mob proceeded to attack a branch of the Church settled on the prairie, about twelve or fourteen miles from the town of Independence. Two of their number were sent in advance, as spies, viz., Robert Johnson, and —— Harris, armed with two guns and three pistols. They were discovered by some of the Saints, and without the least injury being done to them, said mobber Robert Johnson struck Parley P. Pratt over the head with the breech of his gun, after which they were taken and detained till morning; which action, it was believed, prevented a general attack of the mob that night. In the morning the two prisoners, notwithstanding their attack upon Parley P. Pratt the evening previous, were liberated without receiving the least injury.

The same night, (Friday), another party in Independence commenced stoning houses, breaking down doors and windows and destroying furniture. This night the brick part attached to the dwelling house of A. S. Gilbert, was partly pulled down, and the windows of his dwelling broken in with brickbats and rocks, while a gentleman, a stranger, lay sick with fever in his house. The same night three doors of the store of Messrs. Gilbert & Whitney were split open, and after midnight the goods, such as calicos, handkerchiefs, shawls, cambrics, lay scattered in the streets. An express came from Independence after midnight to a party of the brethren who had organized about half a mile from the town for the safety of their lives, and brought the information that the mob were tearing down houses, and scattering goods of the store in the streets. Upon receiving this information the company of brethren referred to marched into Independence, but the main body of the mob fled at their approach. One Richard McCarty, however, was caught in the act of throwing rocks and brickbats into the doors, while the goods lay scattered around him in the streets. He was immediately taken before Samuel Weston, Esq., justice of the peace, and complaint was then made to said Weston, and a warrant requested, that McCarty might be secured; but Weston refused to do anything in the case at that time, and McCarty was liberated.

The same night some of the houses of the Saints in Independence had long poles thrust through the shutters and sash into the rooms of defenseless women and children, from whence their husbands and fathers had been driven by the dastardly attacks of the mob, which were made by ten, fifteen, or twenty men upon a house at a time. Saturday, the 2nd of November, all the families of the Saints in Independence moved with their goods about half a mile out of town and organized to the number of thirty, for the preservation of life and personal effects. The same night a party from Independence met a party from west of the Blue, and made an attack upon a branch of the Church located at the Blue, about six miles from the village of Independence. Here they tore the roof from one dwelling and broke open another house; they found the owner, David Bennett, sick in bed, and beat him most inhumanly, swearing they would blow out his brains. They discharged a pistol at him, and the ball cut a deep gash across the top of his head. In this skirmish a young man of the mob, was shot in the thigh; but by which party the shot was fired is not known.

The next day, Sunday, November 3rd, four of the brethren, viz., Joshua Lewis, Hiram Page, and two others, were dispatched for Lexington to see the circuit judge, and obtain a peace warrant. Two other brethren called on Esquire Silvers, in Independence, and asked him for a peace warrant, but he refused to issue one on account, as he afterwards declared, of his fears of the mob. This day many of the citizens, professing friendship, advised the Saints to leave the county as speedily as possible; for the Saturday night affray had enraged the whole county, and the people were determined to come out on Monday and massacre indiscriminately; and, in short, it was commonly declared among the mob, that *"Monday would be a bloody day."*

Monday came, and a large party of the mob gathered at the Blue, took the Ferry boat belonging to the Church, threatened lives, etc. But they soon abandoned the ferry, and went to Wilson's store, about one mile west of the Blue. Word had been previously sent to a branch of the Church, several miles west of the Blue, that the mob were destroying property on the east side of the river, and the sufferers there wanted help to preserve lives and property. Nineteen men volunteered, and started to their assistance; but discovering that fifty or sixty of the mob had gathered at said Wilson's they turned back. At this time two small boys passed on their way to Wilson's who gave information to the mob, that the "Mormons" were on the road west of them. Between forty and fifty of the mob armed with guns, immediately started on horseback and on foot in pursuit; after riding about two or two and a half miles, they discovered them, when the said company of nineteen brethren immediately dispersed, and fled in different directions. The mob hunted them, turning their horses meantime into a corn field belonging to the Saints. Corn fields and houses were searched, the mob at the same time threatening women and children that they would pull down their houses and kill them if they did not tell where the men had fled. Thus they were employed in hunting the men and threatening the women, when a company of thirty of the brethren from the prairie, armed with seventeen guns, made their appearance.

The former company of nineteen had dispersed, and fled, and but one or two of them returned in time to take part in the subsequent battle. On the approach of the latter company of thirty men, some of the mob cried, "Fire, G— d— ye, fire." Two or three guns were then fired by the mob, which fire was returned by the other party without loss of time. This company is the same that is represented by the mob as having gone forth in the evening of the above incident bearing the olive branch of peace. The mob retreated immediately after the first fire, leaving some of their horses in Whitmer's corn field, and two of their number, Hugh L. Brazeale and Thomas Linvill dead on the ground. Thus fell Hugh L. Brazeale, who had been heard to say, "With ten fellows, I will wade to my knees in blood, but that I will drive the 'Mormons' from Jackson county." The next morning the corpse of Brazeale was discovered on the battle ground with a gun by his side. Several were wounded on both sides, but none mortally among the brethren except Andrew Barber, who expired the next day. This attack of the mob was made about sunset, Monday, November the 4th; and the same night, runners were dispatched in every direction under pretense of calling out the militia; spreading every rumor calculated to alarm and excite the uninformed as they went; such as that the "Mormons" had taken Independence, and that the Indians had surrounded it, the "Mormons" and Indians being colleagued together.***

On the morning of the 5th of November, Independence began to be crowded with individuals from different parts of the county armed with guns and other weapons; and report said the militia had been called out under the sanction or at the instigation of Lieutenant Governor Boggs; and that one Colonel Pitcher had the command. Among this militia (so-called) were included the most conspicuous characters of the mob; and it may truly be said that the appearance of the ranks of this body was well calculated to excite suspicion of their horrible designs.

Very early on the same morning, several branches of the Church received intelligence that a number of their brethren were in prison, and the determination of the mob was to kill them; and that the branch of the Church near the town of Independence was in imminent danger, as the main body of the mob was gathered at that place. In this critical situation, about one hundred of the Saints, from different branches, volunteered for the protection of their brethren near Independence, and proceeded on the road towards Independence, and halted about one mile west of the town, where they awaited further information concerning the movements of the mob. They soon learned that the prisoners were not massacred, and that the mob had not fallen upon the branch of the Church near Independence, as had been reported. They were also informed, that the militia had been called out for their protection; but in this they placed little confidence, for the body congregated had every appearance of a mob; and subsequent events fully verified their suspicions.

On application to Colonel Pitcher, it was found that there was no alternative, but for the Church to leave the county forthwith, and deliver into his hands certain men to be tried for murder, said to have been committed by them in the battle, as he called it, of the previous evening. The arms of the Saints were also demanded by Colonel Pitcher. Among the committee appointed to receive the arms of the brethren were several of the most unrelenting of the old July mob committee, who had directed in the demolishing of the printing office, and the personal injuries inflicted on brethren that day, viz., Henry Chiles, Abner Staples, and Lewis Franklin, who had not ceased to pursue the Saints, from the first to the last, with feelings the most hostile.

These unexpected requisitions of the Colonel, made him appear like one standing at the head of both civil and military law, stretching his authority beyond the constitutional limits that regulate both civil and military power in our Republic. Rather than to have submitted to these unreasonable requirements, the Saints would have cheerfully shed their blood in defense of their rights, the liberties of their country and of their wives and children; but the fear of violating law, in resisting this pretended militia, and the flattering assurance of protection and honorable usage promised by Lieutenant Governor Boggs, in whom, up to this time, they had reposed confidence, induced the Saints to submit, believing that he did not tolerate so gross a violation of all law, as had been practiced in Jackson county. But as so glaringly exposed in the sequel, it was the design and craft of this man to rob an innocent people of their arms by stratagem, and leave more than one thousand defenseless men, women and children to be driven from their homes among strangers in a strange land to seek shelter from the stormy blast of winter. All earth and hell cannot deny that a baser knave, a greater traitor, and a more wholesale butcher, or murderer of

mankind ever went untried, unpunished, and unhung -- since hanging is the popular method of execution among the Gentiles in all countries professing Christianity, instead of blood for blood, according to the law of heaven. The conduct of Colonels Lucas and Pitcher, had long proven them to be open and avowed enemies of the Saints. Both of these men had their names attached to the mob circular, as early as the July previous, the object of which was to drive the Saints from Jackson county. But with assurances from the Lieutenant Governor and others that the object was to disarm the combatants on both sides, and that peace would be the result, the brethren surrendered their arms to the number of fifty or upwards.

The men present, who were accused of being in the battle the evening before, also gave themselves up for trial; but after detaining them one day and a night on a pretended trial for murder, in which time they were threatened and brick-batted, Colonel Pitcher, after receiving a watch of one of the prisoners to satisfy "costs of court," took them into a corn field, and said to them, *"Clear!"* [Meaning, of course, clear out, leave.]

After the Saints had surrendered their arms, which had been used only in self-defense, the tribes of Indians in time of war let loose upon women and children, could not have appeared more hideous and terrific, than did the companies of ruffians who went in various directions, well armed, on foot and on horseback, bursting into houses without fear, knowing the arms were secured; frightening distracted women with what they would do to their husbands if they could catch them; warning women and children to flee immediately, or they would tear their houses down over their heads, and massacre them before night. At the head of these companies appeared the *Reverend Isaac McCoy*, with a gun upon his shoulder, ordering the Saints to leave the county forthwith, and surrender what arms they had. Other pretended preachers of the Gospel took a conspicuous part in the persecution, calling the "Mormons" the "common enemy of mankind," and exulting in their afflictions.

On Tuesday and Wednesday nights, the 5th and 6th of November, women and children fled in every direction before the merciless mob.

One party of about one hundred and fifty women and children fled to the prairie, where they wandered for several days with only about six men to protect them. Other parties fled to the Missouri river, and took lodging for the night where they could find it. One Mr. Barnet opened his house for a night's shelter to a wandering company of distressed women and children, who were fleeing to the river. During this dispersion of the women and children, parties of the mob were hunting the men, firing upon some, tying up and whipping others, and pursuing others with horses for several miles.

Thursday, November 7th, the shores of the Missouri river began to be lined on both sides of the ferry, with men, women and children; goods, wagons, boxes, chests, and provisions; while the ferrymen were busily employed in crossing them over. When night again closed upon the Saints, the wilderness had much the appearance of a camp meeting. Hundreds of people were seen in every direction; some in tents, and some in the open air, around their fires, while the rain descended in torrents. Husbands were inquiring for their wives, and women for their husbands; parents for children, and children for parents. Some had the good fortune to escape with their families, household goods, and some provisions; while others knew not the fate of their friends, and had lost all their effects. The scene was indescribable, and would have melted the hearts of any people upon earth, except the blind oppressor, and the prejudiced and ignorant bigot. Next day the company increased, and they were chiefly engaged in felling small cottonwood trees, and erecting them into temporary cabins, so that when night came on, they had the appearance of a village of wigwams, and the night being clear, the occupants began to enjoy some degree of comfort.

Lieutenant Governor Boggs has been represented as merely a curious and disinterested observer of these events; yet he was evidently the head and front of the mob; for as may easily be seen by what follows, no important move was made without his sanction. He certainly was the secret mover in the affairs of the 20th and 23rd of July; and, as will appear in the sequel, by his authority the mob was converted into militia, to effect by stratagem what he knew, as well as his hellish host, could not be done by legal force.

As Lieutenant Governor, he had only to wink, and the mob went from maltreatment to murder. The horrible calculations of this second Nero were often developed in a way that could not be mistaken. Early on the morning of the 5th, say at 1 o'clock a.m., he came to Phelps, Gilbert, and Partridge, and told them to flee for their lives. Now, unless he had given the order to murder no one would have attempted it, after the Church had agreed to go away. His conscience, however, seemed to vacillate at its moorings, and led him to give the secret alarm to these men.

The Saints who fled from Jackson county, took refuge in the neighboring counties, chiefly in Clay county, the inhabitants of which received them with some degree of kindness. Those who fled to the county of Van Buren were again driven, and compelled to flee, and these who fled to Lafayette county, were soon expelled, or the most of them, and had to move wherever they could find protection.

The Prophet's Description of the Renewed Missouri Persecutions -- 1838

President Joseph Smith, Jun.
Documentary History of the Church 3:67

There is great excitement at present among the Missourians, who are seeking if possible an occasion against us. They are continually chafing us, and provoking us to anger if possible, one sign of threatening after another, but we do not fear them, for the Lord God, the Eternal Father is our God, and Jesus the Mediator is our Savior, and in the great I Am is our strength and confidence.

We have been driven time after time, and that without cause; and smitten again and again, and that without provocation; until we have proved the world with kindness, and the world has proved us, that we have no designs against any man or set of men, that we injure no man, that we are peaceable with all men, minding our own business, and our business only. We have suffered our rights and our liberties to be taken from us; we have not avenged ourselves of those wrongs; we have appealed to magistrates, to sheriffs, to judges, to government and to the President of the United States, all in vain; yet we have yielded peaceably to all these things. We have not complained at the Great God, we murmured not, but peaceably left all; and retired into the back country, in the broad and wild prairies, in the barren and desolate plains, and there commenced anew; we made the desolate places to bud and blossom as the rose; and now the fiend-like race is disposed to give us no rest.

Government Militia Comes Against Far West -- 1838

President Joseph Smith, Jun.
Documentary History of the Church 3:76

This day [September 12, 1832] also a communication was sent to Governor Boggs, dated Daviess county, containing all the falsehoods and lies that the evil genius of mobocrats, villains, and murderers could invent, charging the "Mormons" with every crime they themselves had been guilty of, and calling the "Mormons" impostors, rebels, Canadian refugees, emissaries of the prince of darkness, and signed, "The Citizens of Daviess and Livingston Counties."

Under this date, General Atchison informed the Governor, by letter from headquarters at Richmond, that on the solicitation of the citizens and the advice of the judge of the circuit, he had ordered out four companies of fifty men each from the militia of Clay county, and a like number from Ray; also four hundred men to hold themselves in readiness if required, all mounted riflemen, except one company of infantry. The troops were to proceed immediately to the scene of excitement and insurrection.

Expulsion of the Saints From De Witt, Missouri

President Joseph Smith, Jun.
Documentary History of the Church 3:156

Under the same date, [October 6th] from the mob camp near De Witt, eleven blood-thirsty fellows, viz., Congrave Jackson, Larkin H. Woods, Thomas Jackson, Rolla M. Daviess, James Jackson, Jun., Johnson Jackson, John L. Tomlin, Sidney S. Woods, Geo. Crigler, William L. Banks, and Whitfield Dicken, wrote a most inflammatory, lying and murderous communication to the citizens of Howard county, calling upon them as friends and fellow citizens, to come to their immediate rescue, as the "Mormons" were then firing upon them and they would have to act on the defensive until they could procure more assistance.

A. C. Woods, a citizen of Howard county,

made a certificate to the same lies, which he gathered in the mob camp; he did not go into De Witt, or take any trouble to learn the truth of what he certified. While the people will lie and the authorities will uphold them, what justice can honest men expect?***

The messenger, Mr. Caldwell, who had been dispatched to the governor for assistance, returned, but instead of receiving any aid or even sympathy from his Excellency, we were told that "the quarrel was between the Mormons and the mob," and that "we might fight it out."

About this time a mob, commanded by Hyrum Standly, took Smith Humphrey's goods out of his house, and said Standly set fire to Humphrey's house and burned it before his eyes, and ordered him to leave the place forthwith, which he did by fleeing from De Witt to Caldwell county. The mob had sent to Jackson county and got a cannon, powder and balls, and bodies of armed men had gathered in, to aid them, from Ray, Saline, Howard, Livingston, Clinton, Clay, Platte counties and other parts of the state, and a man by the name of Jackson, from Howard county, was appointed their leader.

The Saints were forbidden to go out of the town under pain of death, and were shot at when they attempted to go out to get food, of which they were destitute. As fast as their cattle or horses got where the mob could get hold of them, they were taken as spoil, as also other kinds of property. By these outrages the brethren were obliged, most of them, to live in wagons or tents.

Application had been made to the judge of the Circuit Court for protection, and he ordered out two companies of militia, one commanded by Captain Samuel Bogart, a Methodist minister, and one of the worst of the mobocrats. The whole force was placed under the command of General Parks, another mobber, if his letter speaks his feelings, and his actions do not belie him, for he never made the first attempt to disperse the mob, and when asked the reason of his conduct, he always replied that Bogart and his company were mutinous and mobocratic, that he dare not attempt a dispersion of the mob. Two other principal men of the mob were Major Ashly, member of the Legislature, and Sashiel Woods, a Presbyterian clergyman.

General Parks informed us that a greater part of his men under Captain Bogart had mutinied, and that he would be obliged to draw them off from the place, for fear they would join the mob; consequently he could offer us no assistance.

We had now no hopes whatever of successfully resisting the mob, who kept constantly increasing; our provisions were entirely exhausted, and we were worn out by continually standing on guard, and watching the movements of our enemies, who, during the time I was there, fired at us a great many times. Some of the brethren perished from starvation; and for once in my life, I had the pain of beholding some of my fellow creatures fall victims to the spirit of persecution, which did then, and has since, prevailed to such an extent in Upper Missouri. They were men, too, who were virtuous and against whom no legal process could for one moment be sustained, but who, in consequence of their love of God, attachment to His cause, and their determination to keep the faith, were thus brought to an untimely grave.

In the meantime Henry Root and David Thomas, who had been the soul cause of the settlement of our people in De Witt, solicited the Saints to leave the place. Thomas said he had assurances from the mob, that if they would leave the place they would not be hurt, and that they would be paid for all losses which they had sustained, and that they had come as mediators to accomplish this object, and that persons should be appointed to set a value on the property which they had to leave, and that they should be paid for it. The Saints finally, through necessity, had to comply, and leave the place. Accordingly the committee was appointed -- Judge Erickson was one of the committee, and Major Florey, of Rutsville, another, the names of others are not remembered. They appraised the real estate, that was all.

When the people came to start, many of their horses, oxen and cows were gone, and could not be found. It was known at the time, and the mob boasted of it, that they had killed the oxen and lived on them. Many houses belonging to my brethren were burned, their cattle driven away, and a great quantity of their property was destroyed by the mob. The people of De Witt utterly failed to fulfill their pledge to pay the Saints for the losses they sustained. The governor having turned a deaf ear to our entreaties, the militia having mutinied, the greater part of them being ready to join the mob, the brethren, seeing no prospect of relief, came to the conclusion to leave that place, and seek a shelter elsewhere. Gathering up as many wagons as could be got ready, which was about seventy, with a remnant of the property they had been able to save from their ruthless foes, they left De Witt and started for Caldwell county on the afternoon of Thursday, October 11, 1838. They traveled that day about twelve miles, and encamped in a grove of timber near the road.

That evening a woman, of the name of Jensen, who had some short time before given birth to a child, died in consequence of the exposure occasioned by the operations of the mob, and having to move before her strength would properly admit of it. She was buried in the grove, without a coffin.

During our journey we were continually harassed and threatened by the mob, who shot at us several times, whilst several of our brethren died from the fatigue and privation which they had to endure, and we had to inter them by the wayside, without a coffin, and under circumstances the most distressing. We arrived in Caldwell on the twelfth of October.

Governor Boggs' Exterminating Order
Documentary History of the Church 3:175

HEADQUARTERS MILTIA, CITY OF JEFFERSON,
October 27, 1838.

SIR: -- Since the order of the morning to you, directing you to cause four hundred mounted men to be raised within your division, I have received by Amos Rees, Esq., and Wiley C. Williams, Esq., one of my aids, information of the most appalling character, which changes the whole face of things, and places the Mormons in the attitude of open and avowed defiance of the laws, and of having made open war upon the people of this state. Your orders are, therefore, to hasten your operations and endeavor to reach Richmond, in Ray county, with all possible speed. the Mormons must be treated as enemies and *must be exterminated* or driven from the state, if necessary for the public good. Their outrages are beyond all description. If you can increase your force, you are authorized to do so, to any extent you may think necessary. I have just issued orders to Major-General Wallock, of Marion county, to raise five hundred men, and to march them to the northern part of Daviess and there to unite with General Doniphan, of Clay, who has been ordered with five hundred men to proceed to the same point for the purpose of intercepting the retreat of the Mormons to the north. They have been directed to communicate with you by express; and you can also communicate with them if you find it necessary. Instead, therefore, of proceeding as at first directed, to reinstate the citizens of Daviess in their homes, you will proceed immediately to Richmond, and there operate against the Mormons. Brigadier-General Parks, of Ray, has been ordered to have four hundred men of his brigade in readiness to join you at Richmond. The whole force will be placed under your command.

L. W. Boggs,
Governor and Commander-in-Chief.

To General Clark.

Great excitement now prevailed, and mobs were heard of in every direction, who seemed determined on our destruction. They burned the houses in the country, and took off all the cattle they could find. They destroyed corn fields, took many prisoners, and threatened death to all the Mormons.

President Joseph Smith, Jun.
Documentary History of the Church 3:178

LILBURN W. BOGGS had become so hardened by mobbing the Saints in Jackson county, and his conscience so "seared as with a hot iron," that he was considered a fit subject for the gubernatorial chair; and it was probably his hatred to truth and the "Mormons," and his blood-thirsty, murderous disposition, that raised him to the station he occupied. His exterminating order of the twenty-seventh aroused every spirit in the state, of the like stamp of his own; and the Missouri mobocrats were flocking to the standard of General Clark from almost every quarter.

Clark, although not the ranking officer, was selected by Governor Boggs as the most fit instrument to carry out his murderous designs; for bad as they were in Missouri, very few commanding officers were yet sufficiently hardened to go all lengths with Boggs in this contemplated inhuman butchery, and expulsion from one of the should-be free and independent states of the Republic of North America, where the Constitution declares, that *every man shall have the privilege of worshiping God according to the dictates of his own conscience;* and this was all the offense the Saints had been guilty of.

President Joseph Smith, Jun.
Documentary History of the Church 3:182

The mob began to encamp at Richmond on the twenty-sixth, and by this time amounted to about two thousand men, all ready to fulfill the exterminating order, and join the standard of the governor. They took up a line of march for Far West, traveling but part way, where they encamped for the night.

Tuesday, October 30. -- The advance guard of the mob were patrolling the country and taking many prisoners, among whom were Brother Stephen Winchester, and Brother Carey, whose skull they laid open by a blow from a rifle barrel. In this mangled condition, the mob laid him in their wagon and went on their way, denying him every comfort, and thus he remained that afternoon and night.

General Clark was in camp at Chariton under a forced march to Richmond, with about a thousand men, and the governor's exterminating order.

For the history of this day at Haun's Mills, on Shoal creek, I quote the following affidavit of Elder Joseph Young, First President of the Seventies:

Haun's Mill Massacre

Joseph Young's Narrative of the Massacre at Haun's Mill

On Sunday, twenty-eighth October, we arrived about twelve o'clock, at Haun's Mills, where we found a number of our friends collected together, who were holding a council, and deliberating on the best course for them to pursue, to defend themselves against the mob, who were collecting in the neighborhood under the command of Colonel Jennings, of Livingston county, and threatening them with house burning and killing. The decision of the council was, that our friends there should place themselves in an attitude of self defense. Accordingly about twenty-eight of our men armed themselves, and were in constant readiness for an attack of any small body of men that might come down upon them.

The same evening, for some reason best known to themselves, the mob sent one of their number to enter into a treaty with our friends, which was accepted, on the condition of mutual forbearance on both sides, and that each party, as far as their influence extended, should exert themselves to prevent any further hostilities upon either party.

At this time, however, there was another mob collecting on Grand river, at William Mann's, who were threatening us, consequently we remained under arms.

Monday passed away without molestation from any quarter.

On Tuesday, the 30th, that bloody tragedy was acted, the scene of which I shall never forget. More than three-fourths of the day had passed in tranquility, as smiling as the preceding one. I think there was no individual of our company that was apprised of the sudden and awful fate that hung over our heads like an overwhelming torrent, which was to change the prospects, the feelings and the circumstances of about thirty families. The banks of Shoal creek on either side teemed with children sporting and playing, while their mothers were engaged in domestic employments, and their fathers employed in guarding the mills and other property, while others were engaged in gathering in their crops for their winter consumption. The weather was very pleasant, the sun shone clear, all was tranquil, and no one expressed any apprehension of the awful crisis that was near us -- even at our doors.

It was about four o'clock, while sitting in my cabin with my babe in my arms, and my wife standing by my side, the door being open, I cast my eyes on the opposite bank of Shoal creek and saw a large company of armed men, on horses, directing their course towards the mills with all possible speed. As they advanced through the scattering trees that stood on the edge of the prairie they seemed to form themselves into a three square position, forming a vanguard in front.

At this moment, David Evans, seeing the superiority of their numbers, (there being two hundred and forty of them, according to their own account), swung his hat, and cried for peace. This not being heeded, they continued to advance, and their leader, Mr. Nehemiah Comstock, fired a gun, which was followed by a solemn pause of ten or twelve seconds, when, all at once, they discharged about one hundred rifles, aiming at a blacksmith shop into which our friends had fled for safety; and charged up to the shop, the cracks of which between the logs were sufficiently large to enable them to aim directly at the bodies of those who had there fled for refuge from the fire of their murderers. There were several families tented in the rear of the shop, whose lives were exposed, and amidst a shower of bullets fled to the woods in different directions.

After standing and gazing on this bloody scene for a few minutes, and finding myself in the uttermost danger, the bullets having reached the house where I was living, I committed my family to the protection of heaven, and leaving the house on the opposite side, I took a path which led up the hill, following in the trail of three of my brethren that had fled from the shop. While ascending the hill we were discovered by the mob, who immediately fired at

us, and continued so to do till we reached the summit. In descending the hill, I secreted myself in a thicket of bushes, where I lay till eight o'clock in the evening, at which time I heard a female voice calling my name in an under tone, telling me that the mob had gone and there was no danger. I immediately left the thicket, and went to the house of Benjamin Lewis, where I found my family (who had fled there) in safety, and two of my friends mortally wounded, one of whom died before morning. Here we passed the painful night in deep and awful reflections on the scenes of the preceding evening.

After daylight appeared, some four or five men, who with myself, had escaped with our lives from the horrid massacre, and who repaired as soon as possible to the mills, to learn the condition of our friends, whose fate we had but too truly anticipated. When we arrived at the house of Mr. Haun, we found Mr. Merrick's body lying in the rear of the house, Mr. McBride's in front, literally mangled from head to foot. We were informed by Miss Rebecca Judd, who was an eye witness, that he was shot with his own gun, after he had given it up, and then cut to pieces with a corn cutter by a Mr. Rogers of Daviess county, who keeps a ferry on Grand river, and who has since repeatedly boasted of this act of savage barbarity. Mr. York's body we found in the house, and after viewing these corpses, we immediately went to the blacksmith's shop, where we found nine of our friends, eight of whom were already dead; the other, Mr. Cox, of Indiana, struggling in the agonies of death and soon expired. We immediately prepared and carried them to the place of interment. The last office of kindness due to the remains of departed friends, was not attended with the customary ceremonies or decency, for we were in jeopardy, every moment expecting to be fired upon by the mob, who, we supposed, were lying in ambush, waiting for the first opportunity to despatch the remaining few who were providentially preserved from the slaughter of the preceding day. However, we accomplished without molestation this painful task. The place of burying was a vault in the ground, formerly intended for a well, into which we threw the bodies of our friends promiscuously. Among those slain I will mention Sardius Smith, son of Warren Smith, about nine years old, who, through fear, had crawled under the bellows in the shop, where he remained till the massacre was over, when he was discovered by a Mr. Glaze, of Carroll county, who presented his rifle near the boy's head, and literally blowed off the upper part of it. Mr. Stanley, of Carroll, told me afterwards that Glaze boasted of this fiend-like murder and heroic deed all over the country.

The number killed and mortally wounded in this wanton slaughter was eighteen or nineteen, whose names as far as I recollect were as follows: Thomas McBride, Levi N. Merrick, Elias Benner, Josiah Fuller, Benjamin Lewis, Alexander Campbell, Warren Smith, Sardius Smith, George S. Richards, Mr. William Napier, Augustine Harmer, Simon Cox, Mr. [Hiram] Abbott, John York, Charles Merrick, (a boy eight or nine years old), [John Lee, John Byers], and three or four others, whose names I do not recollect, as they were strangers, to me. Among the wounded who recovered were Isaac Laney, Nathan K. Knight, Mr. [William] Yokum, two brothers by the name of [Jacob and George] Myers, Tarlton Lewis, Mr. [Jacob] Haun, and several others, [Jacob Foutz, Jacob Potts, Charles Jimison, John Walker, Alma Smith, aged about nine years]. Miss Mary Stedwell, while fleeing, was shot through the hand, and, fainting, fell over a log, into which they shot upwards of twenty balls.

To finish their work of destruction, this band of murderers, composed of men from Daviess, Livingston, Ray, Carroll, and Chariton counties, led by some of the principal men of that section of the upper country, (among whom I am informed were Mr. Ashby, of Chariton, member of the state legislature; Colonel Jennings, of Livingston county, Thomas O. Bryon, clerk of Livingston county; Mr. Whitney, Dr. Randall, and many others), proceeded to rob the houses, wagons, and tents, of bedding and clothing; drove off horses and wagons, leaving widows and orphans destitute of the necessaries of life; and even stripped the clothing from the bodies of the slain. According to their own account, they *fired seven* rounds in this awful butchery, making upwards of sixteen hundred shots at a little company of men, about thirty in number. I hereby certify the above to be a true statement of facts, according to the best of my knowledge.

JOSEPH YOUNG.***

A younger brother of the boy here killed, aged eight, was shot through the hip. The little fellow himself states that seeing his father and brother both killed, he thought they would shoot him again if he stirred, and so feigned himself dead, and lay perfectly still, till he heard his mother call him after dark.

Nathan K. Knight saw a Missourian cut down Father McBride with a corn-cutter, and also saw them stripping the dying, and heard the boys crying for mercy. Brother Knight made his escape across the mill-dam, after receiving wounds through his lungs and finger. After the massacre was over, he was led to a house by a woman, and whilst lying there wounded he heard Mr. Jesse Maupin say that he blew one of the boys' brains out. Some time later whilst walking the streets of Far West Brother Knight was met by three Missourians who threatened to butcher him, and one of them by the name of Rogers drew a butcher knife, and said that he had not got his corn-cutter with him, that he cut down McBride with, "but by —— I have got something that will do as well;" but by a great chance Brother Knight made his escape from the ruffian.

General Atchison withdrew from the army at Richmond as soon as the governor's extermination order was received. Up to this time we were ignorant at Far West of the movements of the mob at Richmond, and the governor's order of extermination.

On the 30th of October a large company of armed soldiers were seen approaching Far West. They came up near to the town, and then drew back about a mile, and encamped for the night. We were informed that they were militia, ordered out by the governor for the purpose of stopping our proceedings, it having been represented to his excellency, by wicked and designing men from Daviess that we were the aggressors, and had committed outrages in Daviess county. They had not yet got the governor's order of extermination, which I believe did not arrive till the next day.

Joseph Smith and Other Leading Men Are Taken Prisoner

Wednesday, October 31. -- The militia of Far West guarded the city the past night, and arranged a temporary fortification of wagons, timber, etc., on the south. The sisters, many of them, were engaged in gathering up their most valuable effects, fearing a terrible battle in the morning, and that the houses might be fired and they obliged to flee. The enemy was five to one against us.

About eight o'clock a flag of truce was sent from the enemy, which was met by several of our people, and it was hoped that matters would be satisfactorily arranged after the officers had heard a true statement of all the circumstances. Colonel Hinkle went to meet the flag, and secretly made the following engagement: First, to give up their [the Church's] leaders to be tried and punished; second, to make an appropriation of the property of all who had taken up arms, for the payment of their debts, and indemnify for the damage done by them; third, that the remainder of the Saints should leave the state, and be protected while doing so by the militia; but they were to be permitted to remain under protection until further orders were received from the commander-in-chief; fourth, to give up their arms of every description, which would be receipted for.

The enemy was reinforced by about one thousand five hundred men today, and news of the destruction of property by the mob reached us from every quarter.

Towards evening I was waited upon by Colonel Hinkle, who stated that the officers of the militia desired to have an interview with me and some others, hoping that the difficulties might be settled without having occasion to carry into effect the exterminating orders which they had received from the governor. I immediately complied with the request, and in company with Elders Sidney Rigdon and Parley P. Pratt, Colonel Wight and George W. Robinson, went into the camp of the militia. But judge of my surprise, when, instead of being treated with that respect which is due from one citizen to another, we were taken as prisoners of war, and treated with the utmost contempt. The officers would not converse with us, and the soldiers, almost to a man, insulted us as much as they felt disposed, breathing out threats against me and my companions. I cannot begin to tell the scene which I there witnessed. The loud cries and yells of more than one thousand voices, which rent the air and could be heard for miles, and the horrid and blasphemous threats and curses which were poured upon us in torrents, were enough to appall the stoutest heart. In the evening we had to lie down on the cold ground, surrounded by a strong guard, who were only kept back by the power of God from depriving us of life. We petitioned the officers to know why we were thus treated, but they utterly refused to give us any answer, or to converse with us. After we arrived in the camp, Brother Stephen Winchester and eleven other brethren who were prisoners, volunteered, with permission of the officers, to carry Brother Carey into the city to his family, he having lain exposed to the weather for a show to the

inhuman wretches, without having his wound dressed or being nourished in any manner. He died soon after he reached home.

The Prophet and Others Condemned to Be Shot

Thursday, November 1. -- Brothers Hyrum Smith and Amasa Lyman were brought prisoners into camp. The officers of the militia held a court martial, and sentenced us to be shot, on Friday morning, on the public square of Far West as a warning to the "Mormons." However, notwithstanding their sentence and determination, they were not permitted to carry their murderous sentence into execution. Having an opportunity of speaking to General Wilson, I inquired of him why I was thus treated. I told him I was not aware of having done anything worthy of such treatment; that I had always been a supporter of the Constitution and of democracy. His answer was, "<u>I know it, and that is the reason why I want to kill you, or have you killed</u>."

The City of Far West Plundered

<u>The militia went into the town, and without any restraint whatever, plundered the houses, and abused the innocent and unoffending inhabitants and left many destitute</u>. They went to my house, drove my family out of doors, carried away most of my property. General Doniphan declared he would have nothing to do with such cold-blooded murder, and that he would withdraw his brigade in the morning.

Governor Boggs wrote General Clark from Jefferson City, that he considered full and ample powers were vested in him [Clark] to carry into effect the former orders; says Boggs:

Excerpt from Governor Boggs' Communication to General Lucas -- 1838

The case is now a very plain one -- the "Mormons" must be subdued; and peace restored to the community; you will therefore proceed without delay to execute the former orders. Full confidence is reposed in your ability to do so; your force will be amply sufficient to accomplish the object. Should you need the aid of artillery, I would suggest that an application be made to the commanding officer of Fort Leavenworth, for such as you may need. You are authorized to request the loan of it in the name of the state of Missouri. The ringleaders of this rebellion should be made an example of; and if it should become necessary for the public peace, the "Mormons" should be exterminated, or expelled from the state.

This morning General Lucas ordered the Caldwell militia to give up their arms. Hinkle, having made a treaty with the mob on his own responsibility, to carry out his treachery, marched the troops out of the city, and the brethren gave up their arms, their own property, which no government on earth had a right to require.

The mob (called Governor's troops) then marched into town, and under pretense of searching for arms, tore up floors, upset haystacks, plundered the most valuable effects they could lay their hands on, wantonly wasted and destroyed a great amount of property, compelled the brethren at the point of the bayonet to sign deeds of trust to pay the expenses of the mob, even while the place was desecrated by the chastity of women being violated. About eighty men were taken prisoners, the remainder were ordered to leave the state, and were forbidden, under threat of being shot by the mob to assemble more than three in a place.***

Joseph Bids Farewell to His Family

Myself and fellow prisoners were taken to the town, into the public square, and before our departure we, after much entreaty, were suffered to see our families, being attended all the while by a strong guard. I found my wife and children in tears, who feared we had been shot by those who had sworn to take our lives, and that they would see me no more. When I entered my house, they clung to my garments, their eyes streaming with tears, while mingled emotions of joy and sorrow were manifested in their countenances. I requested to have a private interview with them a few minutes, but this privilege was denied me by the guard. I was then obliged to take my departure. Who can realize the feelings which I experienced at that time, to be thus torn from my companion, and leave her surrounded with monsters in the shape of men, and my children, too, not knowing how their wants would be supplied; while I was to be taken far from them in order that my enemies might destroy me when they thought proper to do so. My partner wept, my children clung to me, until they were thrust from me by the swords of the guards. I felt overwhelmed while I witnessed the scene, and could only recommend them to the care of

that God whose kindness had followed me to the present time, and who alone could protect them, and deliver me from the hands of my enemies, and restore me to my family.

Defense Witnesses Threatened and Imprisoned; Judge Austin A. King Is an Unjust Judge

President Joseph Smith, Jun.
Documentary History of the Church 3:210

We were called upon for our witnesses, and we gave the names of some forty or fifty. Captain Bogart was despatched with a company of militia to procure them. He arrested all he could find, thrust them into prison, and we were not allowed to see them.

During the week we were again called upon most tauntingly for witnesses; we gave the names of some others, and they were thrust into prison, so many as were to be found.

In the meantime*** [six] volunteered, and were sworn, on the defense, but were prevented as much as possible by threats from telling the truth. We saw a man at the window by the name of Allen, and beckoned him to come in, and had him sworn, but when he did not testify to please the court, several rushed upon him with their bayonets, and he fled the place; three men took after him with loaded guns, and he barely escaped with his life. It was of no use to get any more witnesses, even if we could have done so.

Thus this mock investigation continued from day to day, till Saturday, when several of the brethren were discharged by Judge King,***

Our Church organization was converted, by the testimony of the apostates, into a temporal kingdom, which was to fill the whole earth, and subdue all other kingdoms.

The judge, who by the by was a Methodist, asked much concerning our views of the prophecy of Daniel: "In the days of these kings shall the God of heaven set up a kingdom which shall break in pieces all other kingdoms, and stand forever," * * * * "and the kingdom and the greatness of the kingdom, under the whole heaven, shall be given to the Saints of the Most High." As if it were treason to believe the Bible.***

The remaining prisoners were all released or admitted to bail, except Lyman Wight, Caleb

Baldwin, Hyrum Smith, Alexander McRae, Sidney Rigdon, and myself, who were sent to Liberty, Clay county, to jail, to stand our trial for treason and murder. Our treason consisted of having whipped the mob out of Daviess county, and taking their cannon from them; the murder, of killing the man in the Bogart battle; also Parley P. Pratt, Morris Phelps, Luman Gibbs, Darwin Chase, and Norman Shearer, who were put into Richmond jail to stand their trial for the same "crimes."

During the investigation we were confined in chains and received much abuse. The matter of driving away witnesses or casting them into prison, or chasing them out of the county, was carried to such length that our lawyers, General Doniphan and Amos Rees, told us not to bring our witnesses there at all; for if we did, there would not be one of them left for final trial; for no sooner would Bogart and his men know who they were, than they would put them out of the country.

As to making any impression on King, Doniphan said, if a cohort of angels were to come down, and declare we were innocent, it would all be the same; for he (King) had determined from the beginning to cast us into prison. We never got the privilege of introducing our witnesses at all; if we had, we could have disproved all the evidence of our enemies.

President Joseph Smith, Jun.
Documentary History of the Church 3:242

After we were cast into prison, we heard nothing but threatenings, that, if any judge or jury, or court of any kind, should clear any of us, we should never get out of the state alive.

President Joseph Smith, Jun.
Documentary History of the Church 3:306

Thursday, April 4. -- Brothers Kimball and Turley called on Judge King, who was angry at their having reported the case to the governor, and, said he, "I could have done all the business for you properly, if you had come to me; and I would have signed the petition for all except Joe, and he is not fit to live."

President Joseph Smith, Jun.
Documentary History of the Church 3:308

Saturday, April 6. -- Judge King evidently fearing a change of venue, or some movement on our part to escape his unhallowed persecution

(and most probably expecting that we would be murdered on the way) hurried myself and fellow prisoners off to Daviess county, under a guard of about ten men, commanded by Samuel Tillery, deputy jailer of Clay county. We were promised that we should go through Far West, which was directly on our route, which our friends at that place knew, and expected us; but instead of fulfilling their promise, they took us around the city, and out of the direct course some eighteen miles; far from habitations, where every opportunity presented for a general massacre.***

[In Daviess County] *Tuesday, April 9.* -- Our trial commenced before a drunken grand jury, Austin A. King, presiding judge, as drunk as the jury; for they were all drunk together. Elder Stephen Markham had been dispatched by the committee to visit us.*** Brother Markham brought us a written copy of a statute which had passed the legislature, giving us the privilege of a change of venue on our own affidavit.

Judge Morin arrived from Mill Port, and was favorable to our escape from the persecution we were enduring, and spent the evening with us in prison.

The State of Missouri Rewards the Mobbers
President Joseph Smith, Jun.
Documentary History of the Church 3:243

The state appropriated two thousand dollars to be distributed among the people of Daviess and Caldwell counties, the "Mormons" of Caldwell not excepted. The people of Daviess thought they could live on "Mormon" property, and did not want their thousand, consequently it was pretended to be given to those of Caldwell. Judge Cameron, Mr. McHenry, and others attended to the distribution. Judge Cameron would drive in the brethren's hogs (many of which were identified) and shoot them down in the streets; and without further bleeding, and half dressing, they were cut up and distributed by McHenry to the poor, at a charge of four and five cents per pound; which, together with a few pieces of refuse goods, such as calicoes at double and treble prices soon consumed the two thousand dollars; doing the brethren very little good, or in reality none, as the property destroyed by them, [i.e. the distributing commission] was equal to what they gave the Saints.

The proceedings of the legislature were

warmly opposed by a minority of the house -- among whom were David R. Atchison of Clay county and all the members from St. Louis and Messrs. Rollins and Gordon, from Boone county, and by various other members from other counties; but the mob majority carried the day, for the guilty wretches feared an investigation -- knowing that it would endanger their lives and liberties. Some time during this session the legislature appropriated two hundred thousand dollars to pay the troops for driving the Saints out of the state.

The Prophet Escapes From Imprisonment in Missouri

President Joseph Smith, Jun.
Documentary History of the Church 3:319

Monday, April 15. -- Having procured a change of venue we started for Boone county, and were conducted to that place by a strong guard.***

This evening our guard got intoxicated. We thought it a favorable opportunity to make our escape; knowing that the only object of our enemies was our destruction; and likewise knowing that a number of our brethren had been massacred by them on Shoal Creek, amongst whom were two children; and that they sought every opportunity to abuse others who were left in that state; and that they were never brought to an account for their barbarous proceedings, which were winked at and encouraged by those in authority. We thought that it was necessary for us, inasmuch as we loved our lives, and did not wish to die by the hand of murderers and assassins; and inasmuch as we loved our families and friends, to deliver ourselves from our enemies, and from that land of tyranny and oppression, and again take our stand among a people in whose bosoms dwell those feelings of republicanism and liberty which gave rise to our nation: feelings which the inhabitants of the State of Missouri were strangers to. Accordingly, we took advantage of the situation of our guard and departed, and that night we traveled a considerable distance.

Redress Denied by the President of the United States

George Q. Cannon
Life of Joseph Smith the Prophet, Page 328

Some time after the Saints had completed their exodus [from Missouri] Hyrum Smith epitomized the awful events in the following words:

Governor Boggs and Generals Clark, Lucas, Wilson and Gilliam, also Austin A. King, have committed treasonable acts against the citizens of Missouri, and did violate the Constitution of the United States and also the constitution and laws of the state of Missouri, and did exile and expel, at the point of the bayonet, some twelve or fourteen thousand inhabitants of the state, and did murder some three or four hundred of men, women and children in cold blood, in the most horrid and cruel manner possible. And the whole of it was caused by religious bigotry and persecution, and because the Mormons dared to worship Almighty God according to the dictates of their own conscience, and agreeably to His divine will, as revealed in the scriptures of eternal truth.

President Joseph Smith, Jun.
Documentary History of the Church 4:80

During my stay I had an interview with Martin Van Buren, the President, who treated me very insolently, and it was with great reluctance he listened to our message, which, when he had heard, he said: *"Gentlemen, your cause is just, but I can do nothing for you;"* and *"If I take up for you I shall lose the vote of Missouri."* His whole course went to show that he was an office-seeker, that self-aggrandizement was his ruling passion, and that justice and righteousness were no part of his composition. I found him such a man as I could not conscientiously support at the head of our noble Republic. I also had an interview with Mr. John C. Calhoun, whose conduct towards me very ill became his station. I became satisfied there was little use for me to tarry, to press the just claims of the Saints on the consideration of the President or Congress, and stayed but a few days, taking passage in company with Porter Rockwell and Dr. Foster on the railroad and stages back to Dayton, Ohio.

Persecutions in the State of Illinois

Joseph Smith Arrested on False Accusations; Attempt to Forcibly Take Him to Missouri; Abuses by the Officers upon Joseph

(Compiled By Church Historian)
Documentary History of the Church, Introduction 5:24

A second attempt of Missouri to drag the Prophet from the state of Illinois by extradition procedure, was even more infamous than the first. No sooner was Joseph released from arrest and departed from Springfield than John C. Bennett arrived there and wrote some of his friends in Nauvoo his intention to leave immediately for Missouri and obtain a new indictment by a grand jury on the old charge of "murder, treason, burglary, theft," etc., brought against the Prophet, Hyrum Smith, Lyman Wight, Parley P. Pratt *et al.,* in 1838, hoping that upon this charge he might succeed in getting out extradition papers on the ground that the Prophet was a fugitive from the justice of the state of Missouri. It will be remembered that a former attempt was made under this same charge, in June, 1841, when the Prophet was tried on writ of *habeas corpus* at Monmouth, Warren county, Illinois, before Judge Douglas and set at liberty. It was on this occasion that Esquire O. H. Browning declared that to ask Joseph Smith "to go to Missouri for a trial was adding insult to injury" (Vol. IV, chapter XX)

An indictment on these old charges was finally obtained, supposedly at the instance of Bennett and the Prophet's old Missouri enemies, at a special term of the Circuit Court of Daviess county, Missouri, on the 5th of June, 1843. Governor Reynolds, of Missouri issued a requisition on Governor Ford for Joseph Smith, and appointed J. H. Reynolds as agent of Missouri to receive the Prophet from the authorities of Illinois.

President Joseph Smith, Jun.
Documentary History of the Church 5:439-456

I sent William Clayton to Dixon at ten a.m., to try and find out what was going on there. He met Mr. Joseph H. Reynolds, the sheriff of Jackson county, Missouri, and Constable Harmon T. Wilson, of Carthage, Illinois, about half way, but they being disguised, they were not known by him; and when at Dixon they represented themselves as Mormon elders who wanted to see the prophet. They hired a man and team to carry them, for they had run their horses almost to death.

They arrived at Mr. Wasson's while the family were at dinner, about two p.m. They came to the door and said they were Mormon elders, and wanted to see Brother Joseph. I was in the yard going to the barn when Wilson stepped to the end of the house and saw me. He accosted me in a very uncouth, ungentlemanly manner, when Reynolds stepped up to me, collared me,

then both of them presented cocked pistols to my breast, without showing any writ or serving any process. Reynolds cried out, "G— d— you, if you stir I'll shoot; G— d— if you, stir one inch, I shoot you, be still, or I'll shoot you, by G—." I enquired "What is the meaning of all this?" "I'll show you the meaning, by G—; and if you stir one inch, I'll shoot you, G— d— you." I answered, "I am not afraid of your shooting; I am not afraid to die." I then bared my breast and told them to shoot away. "I have endured so much oppression, I am weary of life; and kill me, if you please. I am a strong man, however, and with my own natural weapons could soon level both of you; but if you have any legal process to serve, I am at all times subject to law, and shall not offer resistance." Reynold replied, "G— d— you, if you say another word I will shoot you, by G—." I answered, "Shoot away; I am not afraid of your pistols."

By this time Stephen Markham walked deliberately towards us. When they saw him coming, they turned their pistols from me to him, and threatened his life if he came any nearer; but he paid no attention to their threats, and continued to advance nearer. They then turned their pistols on me again, jamming them against my side, with their fingers on the triggers, and ordered Markham to stand still or they would shoot me through. As Markham was advancing rapidly towards me, I said, "You are not going to resist the officers, are you, Brother Markham?" He replied, "No, not if they are officers: I know the law too well for that."

They then hurried me off, put me in a wagon without serving any process, and were for hurrying me off without letting me see or bid farewell to my family or friends, or even allowing me time to get my hat or clothes, or even suffer my wife or children to bring them to me. I then said, "Gentlemen, if you have any legal process, I wish to obtain a writ of habeas corpus," and was answered,-- "G— d— you, you shan't have one." They still continued their punching me on both sides with their pistols.

Markham then sprung and seized the horses by the bits, and held them until my wife could bring my hat and coat. Reynolds and Wilson again threatening to shoot Markham, who said, "There is no law on earth that requires a sheriff to take a prisoner without his clothes." Fortunately at this moment I saw a man passing, and said to him, "These men are kidnapping me, and I wish a writ of habeas corpus to deliver myself out of their hands. But as he did not appear to go, I told Markham to go, and he immediately proceeded to Dixon on horseback, where the sheriff also proceeded with me at full speed, without even allowing me to speak to my family or bid them good bye. The officers held their pistols with the muzzles jamming into my side for more than eight miles, and they only desisted on being reproached by Markham for their cowardice in so brutally ill-treating an unarmed, defenseless prisoner. On arriving at the house of Mr. McKennie, the tavern-keeper, I was thrust into a room and guarded there, without being allowed to see anybody; and fresh horses were ordered to be ready in five minutes.

I again stated to Reynolds, "I wish to get counsel," when he answered. G— d— you, you shan't have counsel: one word more, G— d— you, and I'll shoot you."

"What is the use of this so often?" said I. "I have repeatedly told you to shoot; and I now tell you again to shoot away!" I saw a person passing and shouted to him through the window, "I am falsely imprisoned here, and I want a lawyer. Lawyer Edward Southwick came, and had the door banged in his face, with the old threat of shooting him if he came any nearer.

Another lawyer (Mr. Shepherd G. Patrick) afterwards came and received the same treatment, which began to cause considerable excitement in Dixon.

A Mr. Lucien P. Sanger asked Markham what was the matter, when he told him all, and stated that the sheriff intended to drag me away immediately to Missouri, and prevent my taking out a writ of habeas corpus.

Sanger soon made this known to Mr. Dixon, the owner of the house, and his friends, who gathered around the hotel door, and gave Reynolds to understand that if that was their mode of doing business in Missouri, they had another way of doing it in Dixon. They were a law-abiding people and Republicans, and gave Reynolds to understand that he should not take me away without giving me the opportunity of a fair trial, and that I should have justice done

me; but that if he persisted in his course, they had a very summary way of dealing with such people.

Mr. Reynolds finding further resistance to be useless, allowed Mr. Patrick and Mr. Southwick to come into the room to me, (but Wilson was inside guarding the door, and Reynolds guarded the outside of the door,) when I told them I had been taken prisoner by these men without process; I had been insulted and abused by them. I showed them my flesh, which was black for about eighteen inches in circumference on each side, from their punching me with their pistols; and I wanted them to sue out a writ of habeas corpus, whereupon Reynolds swore he should only wait half-an-hour to give me a chance. A messenger was immediately sent by Mr. Dixon to Mr. Chamberlain, the Master-in-Chancery, who lived six miles distant, and, another message to Cyrus H. Walker, who happened to be near, to have them come down and get out the writ of habeas corpus.

A writ was sued out by Markham before a justice of the peace against Reynolds and Wilson for threatening his life. They were taken into custody by the constable. He sued out another writ for assault and threatening my life, whereupon they were again arrested.

At this time Markham rushed into the room and put a pistol (unobserved) into my pocket, although Reynolds and Wilson had their pistols cocked at the same time and were threatening to shoot him.

About midnight he sued out a writ for a violation of the law in relation to writs of habeas corpus, Wilson having transferred me to the custody of Reynolds, for the purpose of dragging me to Missouri, and thereby avoiding the effect and operation of said writ, contrary to law, which was put over to be heard at ten o'clock tomorrow morning; and I was conducted back to the room and guarded through the night.***

About eight, the master-in-chancery arrived and issued a writ of habeas corpus returnable before the Hon. John D. Caton, Judge of the 9th Judicial Circuit at Ottawa, which was duly served on Reynolds and Wilson.

Mr. Cyrus Walker, who was out electioneering to become the representative for Congress, told me that he could not find time to be my lawyer unless I could promise him my vote. He being considered the greatest criminal lawyer in that part of Illinois, I determined to secure his aid, and promised him my vote. He afterwards went to Markham and joyfully said, "I am now sure of my election, as Joseph Smith has promised me his vote, and I am going to defend him."

President Joseph Smith, Jun.
Documentary History of the Church 5:466

If our enemies are determined to oppress us and deprive us of our constitutional rights and privileges as they have done and if the authorities that are on the earth will not sustain us in our rights, nor give us that protection which the laws and constitution of the United States, and of this State guarantee unto us, then we will claim them from a higher power -- from heaven -- yea, from God Almighty.

George Q. Cannon
Life of Joseph Smith the Prophet, Page 497

Under advice of the lawyers, Joseph with his captors was brought before the municipal court at Nauvoo, and all the writs and other papers were filed there. The case was heard upon its merits, and the Prophet was discharged. The lawyers concurred that in all the transactions since the day of his arrest Joseph had held himself amendable to the law and its officers; and that the decision of the municipal court of Nauvoo was not only legal and just but was within the power of this tribunal under the city charter.

Thus Saith Son Ahman, Jesus Christ, to the Power of Governing in the Court of Prosecuting Labor, and to the Leaders of National Power -- Let My Word Be Heard in Your Several Placings of Your Influencing and Governing Power, Even This, My Warning to Not Abuse My Innocent People, But Maintain Their Rights of Governing Protecting of Religious Way of My Holy Order of Union Celestial in My Holy Church on Earth. Let There Cease to Be the Continued Way and Idea You Can Be of a Prosecuting Labor Against My Holy Way of Eternal Lives of

Celestial Union Power Above All Peoples and Their Claims of Power to Rule Over All the People in Their Lands of Man Organizing Power. Thus Am I Now Giving My Will to Be Known Among All Surviving People on Earth. Hear Thou My Way of Truth by This, My Revealing to All:

Revelation of the Lord Jesus Christ Given to President Warren S. Jeffs San Angelo, Texas Saturday, July 30, 2011

1. I who is over all peoples, your Lord Jesus Christ, declare to my present nation on the land of Zion, even the power of governing over the people of the nation of United States of America: I, your Lord, have caused history truth to be as a full seeing into abuse of governing power against my servant Joseph Smith, because he testified of my holy appearing and guiding to the people of my land of Zion, even to the nation.

2. Let my people now find true peace and preserving of religious freedom, as I, your Lord, ordained, in raising up nation free of religious exercise of the founding of my Constitution of inspiring power I caused to guide founding authorities.

3. Let all now be of a giving an accounting soon at hand, where I shall be the God over all my holy Zion, and over all remaining nations on earth.

4. You shall see my holy Zion is of a preserving, not of government prosecution, where you are defiling innocence and sacred trust in present court.

5. Let all now be of a stop! of the prosecuting power.

6. I shall send my will to you of my holy way to establish peace on my land as you uphold my will.

7. Let my servant go, to do my will with my people of the Fundamentalist Church of Jesus Christ of Latter-day Saints; to establish my holy way upon which Zion must be built; even laws of my holy revealing, and abiding by my power.

8. It is now time to be of a ceasing of thy prosecuting power against members of my Church now under attack for religious practice, which is of a freedom guaranteed by constitutional and governing law of pure principle of rights and freedoms, of national power, over state power now afflicting my servant and my holy law of Celestial Marriage, requiring my own guiding.

9. You are now in a way of opposing God.

10. I am He who bore the sins of all who will repent and turn to a way of pure holy way of living.

11. Let all now know I shall send a judging on all of the people who combine against my holy way of pure power of Eternal Union of my revealing.

12. Let all people now be knowing of my coming to give reward to all people.

13. Let the court dismiss all counts against my servant.

14. Let my people be of free living my law of pure holy way.

15. Let it now be a new way of governing, to be as caring and protecting power over innocent peoples, who only live for God and His holy way to build up my holy place of my coming, even New Jerusalem, soon to be of full power over all people.

16. Let my will be sounded to this nation.

17. Let all now be forewarned.

18. Let all now have my will known, to be of full exercise of their choosing to do right toward my people who abide higher religious revealing law of family way; yea, as more holy, as is the heavens holy more than the earth and false ways of governing and living on earth.

19. Let all be holy among my holy way.

20. Let all be a full preparing; to be of the Zion of my making soon at hand, even endow my pure holy way being known to all people.

21. Let this, my will, be of a presenting.

22. Let it now be my will above your way of governing, saith God over all, to uphold my right to rule, lest my cleansing power Celestial is as a whirlwind upon the nation of my coming, to cleanse the gross evils off my land; to be a pure and holy way remaining on the land of holiness, even Zion, my Chosen.

23. Let all now be of a full repenting; for I am God; and now am causing my will to be known to all people on earth; warnings justifying me to send forth judgment upon all who are of wicked; intent against life, innocence, purity, holy way of my revealing; even to purge every peoples of the more wicked; preserving my people of purity of living if they abide their covenant of Celestial purity with me, their Lord, who is Jesus Christ, even the God of the Resurrection; bringing life, salvation, happiness on earth, and happiness eternal in the heavens, unto souls well preparing for Eternal Union power of eternal life, through my Holy Priesthood of my sending all needful way of holy and revealed truth, blessings of Priesthood revealing power, which is my authority in heaven, now bestowed on my servant on earth by my own way;

to be a holy vessel of administering my holy will to all nations, peoples, and tongues; to be as a voice to the people of this generation; yet not acknowledged as being my Holy Priesthood power among men on earth; being all my power sent from heaven to earth; that my obedient children are blessed by their Lord with eternal power to be exalting in my holy power of Godhood.

24. Let my people be above reproach.

25. Let all be to me as a son or daughter of obedient way.

26. I am Jehovah Christ, even Son Ahman, Jesus Christ; the Holy Power over all creation.

27. Let all people in the nation of government power of constitutional guarantee of freedom of religion, now be of a voice to please God in preserving my obedient, peaceful people in religious rights of free living pure holy way of abiding in family and Church governing; private and sacred to me and to my people of a Celestial way of heavenly power on earth in their individual lives, by my revealing who is worthy of Celestial Union Eternal.

28. Let it be of law in the land by constitutional preserving power, to allow my Celestial Law of Plural Marriage be of a new way of pure justice, freedom; preserving religious rights of a peaceful and holy way of life on earth of thy God's sending Priesthood power on earth; to be my authority of law above the changing law of many, to preserve to my people my way to earn salvation eternal.

29. This is the will of God to the leader of the nation and to all government powers on this land of United States of America.

30. Let my people be free now, is my call to all governing powers on the land of Zion, where I shall appear in my power of pure holy power over all things.

31. I am He who created all things, is above all things, the Life and Light of all peoples, tongues, kindreds, nations on earth.

32. I am God over all, saith your Lord, who is Jesus Christ, even I who send this holy will to court, and to leaders of governing power, as my own will revealing truth, that shall be as a foundation of pure holy way of my Kingdom soon to rise and be the governing power over all nations; New Jerusalem being the city of power, governing all peoples by my holy power.

33. I am to soon cleanse all peoples of evil practices of murder of unborn children, as well as secret combinations in nations and between national leaders of murder and combinations of evil to get gain by evil, immoral, licentious way of corrupting innocence and virtue.

34. Let all beware.

35. I come suddenly.

36. Be ye ready.

37. I am above all, and have the right to rule over all flesh, saith Son Ahman, your Lord and Holy Redeemer. Amen.

Martyrdom of Joseph Smith and Hyrum Smith in Carthage Jail -- June 27, 1844

(Compiled by Church Historian)
Documentary History of the Church 6:602

5:30 a. m. -- Arose. Joseph requested Dan Jones to descend and inquire of the guard the cause of the disturbance in the night. Frank Worrell, the officer of the guard, who was one of the Carthage Greys, in a very bitter spirit said, "We have had too much trouble to bring Old Joe here to let him ever escape alive, and unless you want to die with him you had better leave before sundown; and you are not a damned bit better than him for taking his part, and you'll see that I can prophesy better than Old Joe, for neither he nor his brother, nor anyone who will remain with them will see the sun set today."

Joseph directed Jones to go to Governor Ford and inform him what he had been told by the officer of the guard. While Jones was going to Governor Ford's quarters, he saw an assemblage of men, and heard one of them, who was apparently a leader, making a speech, saying that, "Our troops will be discharged this morning in obedience to orders, and for a sham we will leave the town; but when the Governor and the McDonough troops have left for Nauvoo this afternoon, we will return and kill those men, if we have to tear the jail down." This sentiment was applauded by three cheers from the crowd.

Captain Jones went to the Governor, told him what had occurred in the night, what the officer of the guard had said, and what he had heard while coming to see him, and earnestly solicited him to avert the danger.

His Excellency replied, "You are unnecessarily alarmed for the safety of your friends, sir, the people are not that cruel."

Irritated by such a remark, Jones urged the necessity of placing better men to guard them than professed assassins, and said, "The Messrs. Smith are American citizens, and have surrendered themselves to your Excellency upon your pledging your honor for their safety; they are also Master Masons, and as such I demand of you protection of their lives."

Governor Ford's face turned pale, and Jones remarked, "If you do not do this, I have but one more desire, and that is if you leave their lives in the hands of those men to be sacrificed --

"What is that, sir?" he asked in a hurried tone.

"It is," said Jones, "that the Almighty will preserve my life to a proper time and place, that I may testify that you have been timely warned of their danger."

Jones then returned to the prison, but the guard would not let him enter. He again returned to the hotel, and found Governor Ford standing in front of the McDonough troops, who were in line ready to escort him to Nauvoo.

The disbanded mob retired to the rear, shouting loudly that they were only going a short distance out of town, when they would return and kill old Joe and Hyrum as soon as the Governor was far enough out of town.

Jones called the attention of the Governor to the threats then made, but the Governor took no notice of them, although it was impossible for him to avoid hearing them.

Jones then requested the Governor to give him passports for himself and friends to pass in and out of the prison, according to his promise made to the prisoners. He refused to give them, but he told General Deming to give one to Dr. Willard Richards, Joseph Smith's private secretary.

The Prophet's Life Is Threatened

While obtaining this, Jones' life was threatened, and Chauncey L. Higbee said to him in the street, "We are determined to kill Joe and Hyrum, and you had better go away to save yourself."

At 7 a. m., Joseph, Hyrum, Dr. Richards, Stephen Markham and John S. Fullmer ate breakfast together. Mr. Crane ate with them, and wanted to know if the report was true that Joseph fainted three times on Tuesday, while being exhibited to the troops. He was told it was a false report.***

Dr. Southwick was in the meeting, seeing what was going on. He afterward told Stephen Markham that the purport of the meeting was to take into consideration the best way to stop Joseph Smith's career, as his views on government were widely circulated and took like wildfire. They said if he did not get into the Presidential chair this election, he would be sure to the next time; and if Illinois and Missouri would join together and kill him, they would not be brought to justice for it. There were delegates in said meeting from every state in the Union except three. Governor Ford and Captain Smith were also in the meeting.

Captain Dunn and his company were ordered to accompany the Governor to Nauvoo. The Carthage Greys, who had but two days before been under arrest for insulting the commanding general, and whose conduct had been more hostile to the prisoners than that of any other company, were selected by Governor Ford to guard the prisoners at the jail; and other troops composed of the mob whom the Governor had found at Carthage, and had mustered into the service of the State and who had been promised "full satisfaction" and that they should be marched to Nauvoo, were disbanded and discharged in Carthage; yet Governor Ford suffered two or three hundred armed men to remain encamped about eight miles off on the Warsaw road, apparently under the control of Col. Levi Williams, a notoriously sworn enemy to Joseph, and who had on many occasions threatened the destruction of Nauvoo and the death of Joseph. Moreover it was the duty of the Governor to dismiss the troops into the hands of their several officers in order to be marched home and there disbanded, and not to have disbanded them at a distance from home, and at a time and place when they were predisposed to acts of lawless violence, rapine and murder.

Cyrus H. Wheelock, states that previous to leaving Carthage he said to the Governor, "Sir, you must be aware by this time that the prisoners have no fears in relation to any lawful demands made against them, but you have heard sufficient to justify you in the belief that their enemies would destroy them if they had them in their power; and now, sir, I am about to leave for Nauvoo, and I fear for those men; they are safe as regards the law, but they are not safe from the hands of traitors, and midnight assassins who thirst for their blood and have determined to spill it; and under these circumstances I leave with a heavy heart."

Ford replied: "I was never in such a dilemma in my life; but your friends shall be protected, and have a fair trial by the law; in this *pledge* I am not alone; I have obtained the *pledge* of the whole of the army to sustain me."

The Martyrdom

(Compiled By Church Historian)
Documentary History of the Church 6:617

Immediately there was a little rustling at the outer door of the jail, and a cry of surrender, and also a discharge of three or four firearms followed instantly. The doctor glanced an eye by the curtain of the window, and saw about a hundred armed men around the door.

It is said that the guard elevated their firelocks, and boisterously threatening the mob discharged their firearms over their heads. The mob encircled the building, and some of them rushed by the guard up the flight of stairs, burst open the door, and began the work of death, while others fired in through the open windows.

In the meantime Joseph, Hyrum, and Elder Taylor had their coats off. Joseph sprang to his coat for his six-shooter, Hyrum for his single barrel, Taylor for Markham's large hickory cane, and Dr. Richards for Taylor's cane. All sprang against the door, the balls whistled up the stairway, and in an instant one came through the door.

Joseph Smith, John Taylor and Dr. Richards sprang to the left of the door, and tried to knock aside the guns of the ruffians.

Hyrum was retreating back in front of the door and snapped his pistol, when a ball struck him in the left side of his nose, and he fell on his back on the floor saying, "I am a dead man!" As he fell on the floor another ball from the outside entered his left side, and passed through his body with such force that it completely broke to pieces the watch he wore in his vest pocket, and at the same instant another ball from the door grazed his breast, and entered his head by the throat; subsequently a fourth ball entered his left leg.

A shower of balls was pouring through all parts of the room, many of which lodged in the ceiling just above the head of Hyrum.

Joseph reached round the door casing, and discharged his six shooter into the passage, some barrels missing fire. Continual discharges of musketry came into the room. Elder Taylor continued parrying the guns until they had got them about half their length into the room, when he found that resistance was vain, and he attempted to jump out of the window, where a ball fired from within struck him on his left thigh, hitting the bone, and passing through to within half an inch of the other side. He fell on the window sill, when a ball fired from the outside struck his watch in his vest pocket, and threw him back into the room.

After he fell into the room he was hit by two more balls, one of them injuring his left wrist considerably, and the other entering at the side of the bone just below the left knee. He rolled under the bed, which was at the right of the window in the south-east corner of the room.

While he lay under the bed he was fired at several times from the stairway; one ball struck him on the left hip, which tore the flesh in a shocking manner, and large quantities of blood were scattered upon the wall and floor.

When Hyrum fell, Joseph exclaimed, "Oh dear, brother Hyrum!" and opening the door a few inches he discharged his six shooter in the stairway (as stated before), two or three barrels of which missed fire.

Joseph, seeing there was no safety in the room, and no doubt thinking that it would save the lives of his brethren in the room if he could get out, turned calmly from the door, dropped his pistol on the floor, and sprang into the window when two balls pierced him from the door, and one entered his right breast from without, and he fell outward into the hands of his murderers, exclaiming, "O Lord, my God!"

Announcement of the Death of Joseph and Hyrum Smith

President John Taylor
Doctrine and Covenants, Section 135

1. To seal the testimony of this book and the Book of Mormon, we announce the martyrdom of Joseph Smith the Prophet, and Hyrum Smith the Patriarch. They were shot in Carthage jail, on the 27th of June, 1844, about five o'clock p.m., by an armed mob -- painted black -- of from 150 to 200 persons. Hyrum was shot first and fell calmly, exclaiming: *I am a dead man!* Joseph leaped from the window, and was shot dead in the attempt, exclaiming: *O Lord my God!* They were both shot after they were dead, in a brutal manner, and both received four balls.

2. John Taylor and Willard Richards, two of the Twelve, were the only persons in the room at the time; the former was wounded in a savage manner with four balls, but has since recovered; the latter, through the providence of God, escaped, without even a hole in his robe.

3. Joseph Smith, the Prophet and Seer of the Lord, has done more, save Jesus only, for the salvation of men in this world, than any other man that ever lived in it. In the short space of twenty years, he has brought forth the Book of Mormon, which he translated by the gift and power of God, and has been the means of publishing it on two continents; has sent the fulness of the everlasting gospel, which it contained, to the four quarters of the earth; has brought forth the revelations and commandments which compose this book of Doctrine and Covenants, and many other wise documents and instructions for the benefit of the children of men; gathered many thousands of the Latter-day Saints, founded a great city, and left a fame and name that cannot be slain. He lived great, and he died great in the eyes of God and his people; and like most of the Lord's anointed in ancient times, has sealed his mission and his works with his own blood; and so has his brother Hyrum. In life they were not divided, and in death they were not separated!

4. When Joseph went to Carthage to deliver himself up to the pretended requirements of the law, two or three days previous to his assassination, he said: "I am going like a lamb to the slaughter; but I am calm as a summer's morning; I have a conscience void of offense towards God, and towards all men. I SHALL DIE INNOCENT, AND IT SHALL YET BE SAID OF ME -- HE WAS MURDERED IN COLD BLOOD." -- The same morning, after Hyrum had made ready to go -- shall it be said to the slaughter? yes, for so it was -- he read the following paragraph, near the close of the twelfth chapter of Ether, in the Book of Mormon, and turned down the leaf upon it:

5. *And it came to pass that I prayed unto the Lord that he would give unto the Gentiles grace, that they might have charity. And it came to pass that the Lord said unto me: If they have not charity it mattereth not unto thee, thou hast been faithful; wherefore thy garments are clean. And because thou hast seen thy weakness, thou shalt be made strong, even unto the sitting down in the place which I have prepared in the mansions of my Father. And now I....bid farewell unto the Gentiles; yea, and also unto my brethren whom I love, until we shall meet before the judgment-seat of Christ, where all men shall know that my garments are not spotted with your blood.* The testators are now dead, and their testament is in force.

6. Hyrum Smith was forty-four years old in February, 1844, and Joseph Smith was thirty-eight in December, 1843; and henceforward their names will be classed among the martyrs of religion; and the reader in every nation will be reminded that the Book of Mormon, and this book of Doctrine and Covenants of the church, cost the best blood of the nineteenth century to bring them forth for the salvation of a ruined world; and that if the fire can scathe a green tree for the glory of God, how easy it will burn up the dry trees to purify the vineyard of corruption. They lived for glory; they died for glory; and glory is their eternal reward. From age to age shall their names go down to posterity as gems for the sanctified.

7. They were innocent of any crime, as they had often been proved before, and were only confined in jail by the conspiracy of traitors and wicked men; and their *innocent blood* on the floor of Carthage jail is a broad seal affixed to "Mormonism" that cannot be rejected by any court on earth, and their *innocent blood* on the escutcheon of the State of Illinois, with the broken faith of the State as pledged by the governor, is a witness to the truth of the everlasting gospel that all the world cannot impeach; and their *innocent blood* on the banner of liberty, and on the *magna charta* of the United States, is an ambassador for the religion of Jesus Christ, that will touch the hearts of honest men among all nations; and their *innocent blood*, with the innocent blood of all the martyrs under the altar that John saw, will cry unto the Lord of Hosts till he avenges that blood on the earth. Amen.

Son Ahman Gives Truth of Eternal Power to Joseph Smith, A God of Power

Revelation of the Lord Jesus Christ Given to President Warren S. Jeffs San Angelo, Texas Friday, July 29, 2011

1. I who am Endless, even your Lord Jesus Christ, declare that my servant Joseph Smith, my holy Prophet, Seer, and Revelator, performed a work that is now to soon burst forth in my holy power still on him as the third member of the Ruling Power over this world; to be my holy Son of God who is to be of the full and ordained Gods in Celestial and eternal Priesthood authority in heaven; to come to earth to rule on my land and place of power, of Celestial governing power over all peoples, under Christ; to be a holy power of governing authority; to subdue all powers to be of my Kingdom on earth.

2. Let all people revere the holy name and perfect mission of Joseph Smith; restoring my Gospel, Priesthood, and Kingdom of God, Church and holy order of power Celestial to earth.

3. Such is his mission to yet be done on earth; all peoples learning of his grandeur and eternal power of my giving him dominion over all peoples; to be the power of eternal authority over all peoples; as I have ordained upon him to be an holy Celestial God over all peoples on earth, as a God of pure governing power.

4. Not one law was of a leaving out.

5. All was restored through this great Prophet of God, unto my full Kingdom being restored on earth; he being my Messenger of the power of life and holy way, unto being a full God of Eternal Union Power.

6. Let all rejoice in the God of all for Joseph Smith, and the grand mission performing now, to be of a fulfilling of the promise of my coming, even Jesus Christ, to all nations knowing of my power.

7. Let all now be my Zion on earth to receive more eternal truths.

8. Let all be my pure holy way of Eternal Union, in my holy way of my New Jerusalem soon to come forth in fulness. Amen.

President Rulon Jeffs' Testimony of the Prophet Joseph Smith

Joseph Smith Is the Third Member of the Godhead and the Witness and Testator

President Rulon Jeffs
Rulon Jeffs' Sermons 2:8 August 7, 1966 SLC

I testify to you that Joseph Smith, the Prophet, the Witness and Testator, is the One Mighty and Strong who shall come and set in order His House. And we should be so ordering our lives, brothers and sisters, that we will be found worthy to meet him and be instructed of him; for he will come, under the direction of the Holy One of Israel, and he will speak to His servants first, and then to those who are worthy.

President Rulon Jeffs
Rulon Jeffs' Sermons 2:42 February 5, 1967 SLC

TPJS Page 190
The Three Personages

Everlasting covenant was made between three personages before the organization of this earth, and relates to their dispensation of things to men on the earth; these personages, according to Abraham's record, are called God the first, the Creator; God the second, the Redeemer; and God the third, the witness or Testator.

It is a wonderful thing to contemplate who this Witness and Testator is, and that it is not beneath the place and the dignity of Joseph Smith to class him among the grand Presidency of this earth, the Godhead: the Father, the Son, and the Holy Ghost. This great man who witnessed the Father and the Son together as a fourteen-year-old boy, and undoubtedly subsequent to this, stood in Their presence, and was indeed Their Witness and Testator, standing in the office of the Holy Ghost. Heber C. Kimball made the statement on one occasion: "Let me tell you, the Holy Ghost is a man." Now who is that man? Joseph Smith. The Holy Ghost is also that great spiritual power and essence, the foundation of all things, that emanates from the Father and issues forth from Himself throughout all His creations, and is the instrument of God in creating this earth and all of His dominions, and is the power and gift by which we are able to come back to Him. There is another very important thing that I think might be called to our attention, and that is something that the Prophet Joseph said himself, of himself, although he did not give it in so many words.

TPJS Page 364

The last time I spoke on this stand it was on the resurrection of the dead, when I promised to continue my remarks upon that subject. I still feel a desire to say something on this subject. Let us this very day begin anew, and now say, with all our hearts, we will forsake our sins and be righteous. I shall read the 24th chapter of Matthew, and give it a literal rendering and reading; and when it is rightly understood, it will be edifying.

I thought the very oddity of its rendering would be edifying anyhow -- "And it will be preached, the Gospel of the kingdom, in the whole world, to a witness over all people: and then will the end come." I will now read it in German [which he did, and many Germans who were present said he translated it correctly].

The Savior said when these tribulations should take place, it should be committed to a man who should be a witness over the whole world: the keys of knowledge, power and revelations should be revealed to a witness who should hold the testimony to the world. It has always been my province to dig up hidden mysteries -- new things -- for my hearers. Just at the time when some men think that I have no right to the keys of the Priesthood -- just at that time I have the greatest right. The Germans are an exalted people. The old German translators are the most nearly correct -- most honest of any of the translators; and therefore I get testimony to bear me out in the revelations that I have preached for the last fourteen years. The old German, Latin, Greek and Hebrew translations all say it is true: they cannot be impeached, and therefore I am in good company.

All the testimony is that the Lord in the last days would commit the keys of the Priesthood to a witness over all people. Has the Gospel of the kingdom commenced in the last days? And will God take it from the man until He takes him Himself? I have read it precisely as the words flowed from the lips of Jesus Christ. John the Revelator saw an angel flying through the midst of heaven, having the everlasting Gospel to preach unto them that dwell on the earth.

The scripture is ready to be fulfilled when great wars, famines, pestilence, great distress, judgments, &c., are ready to be poured out on the inhabitants of the earth. John saw the angel having the holy Priesthood, who should preach the everlasting Gospel to all nations. God had an angel -- a special messenger -- ordained and prepared for that purpose in the last days. Woe, woe be to that man or set of men who lift up their hands against God and His witness in these last days: for they shall deceive almost the very chosen ones!

Joseph Smith is that Witness. It is my testimony to you that everyone who has stood in his place since he was taken, has been able to speak with the same authority. They are not that Witness as he is; no one can take his place, or his kingdom, or his Priesthood. But this is the authority that we are dealing with, brothers and sisters. Joseph Smith stands next to Jesus Christ, Himself, as John Taylor wrote, as we have recorded in Section 135; and I thought it might even be well to read that if it be edifying to us today. Sometimes we have some of these scriptures before us that we never think to read, and we need to have them read to us from this stand occasionally, I think; learn to appreciate what we have and who these men are that God has raised up.

President Rulon Jeffs
Rulon Jeffs' Sermons 2:138 May 19, 1968 SLC
Joseph later corrected this to say, "Again, this Gospel of the kingdom shall be preached in all the world, to a witness over all nations." That witness is Joseph the Prophet, that great Witness and Testator who filled the office of the Holy Ghost and stands in that office as to the Godhead -- the Father, the Son, and the Holy Ghost, the Godhead of this earth. How blessed we are to have the message and the testimony and the witness of this great man in our day and time.

President Rulon Jeffs
Rulon Jeffs' Sermons 2:173 November 17, 1968 SLC
I appreciate my brethren, President Johnson who presides over us, his great faith and love for this work and this people. It reminds me, as I contemplate Brother Johnson, the great love of the Prophet Joseph Smith for all men and especially the saints, desiring nothing but their salvation and exaltation. He was sent at the head of the last dispensation to do the great work of the gathering, the bringing together of Israel, and to bring together all the former dispensations under the Lord Jesus Christ, preparatory to the coming

of the Lord in glory, so that the great Millennium might be ushered in after the redemption of Zion. I desire, brothers and sisters, to read some of the words of Joseph, which I think might help us to appreciate him more as the One Mighty and Strong and the great Witness and Testator.

Testimony of President Brigham Young Concerning the Calling and Mission of the Prophet Joseph Smith

President Brigham Young
JD 5:332 October 7, 1857 SLC
What is the nature and beauty of Joseph's mission? You know that I am one of his Apostles. When I first heard him preach, he brought heaven and earth together; and all the priests of the day could not tell me anything correct about heaven, hell, God, angels, or devils: they were as blind as Egyptian darkness. When I saw Joseph Smith, he took heaven, figuratively speaking, and brought it down to earth; and he took the earth, brought it up, and opened up, in plainness and simplicity, the things of God; and that is the beauty of his mission. I had a testimony, long before that, that he was a Prophet of the Lord, and that was consoling. Did not Joseph do the same to your understandings? Would he not take the Scriptures and make them so plain and simple that everybody could understand? Every person says, "Yes, it is admirable; it unites the heavens and the earth together;" and as for time, it is nothing, only to learn us how to live in eternity.

President Brigham Young
JD 7:289 October 9, 1859 SLC
Joseph Smith holds the keys of this last dispensation, and is now engaged behind the vail in the great work of the last days. I can tell our beloved brother Christians who have slain the Prophets and butchered and otherwise caused the death of thousands of Latter-day Saints, the priests who have thanked God in their prayers and thanksgiving from the pulpit that we have been plundered, driven, and slain, and the deacons under the pulpit, and their brethren and sisters in their closets, who have thanked God, thinking that the Latter-day Saints were wasted away, something that no doubt will mortify them -- something that, to say the least, is a matter of deep regret to them -- namely, that no man or woman in this dispensation will ever

enter into the celestial kingdom of God without the consent of Joseph Smith. From the day that the Priesthood was taken from the earth to the winding-up scene of all things, every man and woman must have the certificate of Joseph Smith, junior, as a passport to their entrance into the mansion where God and Christ are -- I with you and you with me. I cannot go there without his consent. He holds the keys of that kingdom for the last dispensation -- the keys to rule in the spirit-world; and he rules there triumphantly, for he gained full power and a glorious victory over the power of Satan while he was yet in the flesh, and was a martyr to his religion and to the name of Christ, which gives him a most perfect victory in the spirit-world. He reigns there as supreme a being in his sphere, capacity, and calling, as God does in heaven. Many will exclaim -- "Oh, that is very disagreeable! It is preposterous! We cannot bear the thought!" But it is true.

I will now tell you something that ought to comfort every man and woman on the face of the earth. Joseph Smith, junior, will again be on this earth dictating plans and calling forth his brethren to be baptized for the very characters who wish this was not so, in order to bring them into a kingdom to enjoy, perhaps, the presence of angels or the spirits of good men, if they cannot endure the presence of the Father and the Son; and he will never cease his operations, under the directions of the Son of God, until the last ones of the children of men are saved that can be, from Adam till now.

Should not this thought comfort all people? They will, by-and-by, be a thousand times more thankful for such a man as Joseph Smith, junior, than it is possible for them to be for any earthly good whatever. It is his mission to see that all the children of men in this last dispensation are saved, that can be, through the redemption. You will be thankful, every one of you, that Joseph Smith, junior, was ordained to this great calling before the worlds were. I told you that the doctrine of election and reprobation is a true doctrine. It was decreed in the counsels of eternity, long before the foundations of the earth were laid, that he should be the man, in the last dispensation of this world, to bring forth the word of God to the people, and receive the fulness of the keys and power of the Priesthood

of the Son of God. The Lord had his eye upon him, and upon his father and upon his father's father, and upon their progenitors clear back to Abraham, and from Abraham to the flood, from the flood to Enoch, and from Enoch to Adam. He has watched that family and that blood as it has circulated from its fountain to the birth of that man. He was foreordained in eternity to preside over this last dispensation, as much so as Pharaoh was fore-ordained to be a wicked man, or as was Jesus to be the Saviour of the world because he was the oldest son in the family.***

Joseph Smith, junior, was foreordained to come through the loins of Abraham, Isaac, Jacob, Joseph, and so on down through the Prophets and Apostles; and thus he came forth in the last days to be a minister of salvation, and to hold the keys of the last dispensation of the fulness of times.

President Brigham Young
JD 15:138 August 24, 1872 Farmington

I am going to stop my talking by saying that, in the millennium, when the kingdom of God is established on the earth in power, glory and perfection, and the reign of wickedness that has so long prevailed is subdued, the Saints of God will have the privilege of building their temples, and of entering into them, becoming, as it were, pillars in the temples of God, and they will officiate for their dead. Then we will see our friends come up, and perhaps some that we have been acquainted with here. If we ask who will stand at the head of the resurrection in this last dispensation, the answer is -- Joseph Smith, Junior, the Prophet of God. He is the man who will be resurrected and receive the keys of the resurrection, and he will seal this authority upon others, and they will hunt up their friends and resurrect them when they shall have been officiated for, and bring them up. And we will have revelations to know our forefathers clear back to Father Adam and Mother Eve, and we will enter into the temples of God and officiate for them. Then man will be sealed to man until the chain is made perfect back to Adam, so that there will be a perfect chain of priesthood from Adam to the winding-up scene.

This will be the work of the Latter-day Saints in the millennium.

Joseph Suffered Because He Is the Messenger to the People of the Entire Earth

President Brigham Young
JD 9:366 August 31, 1862 SLC

This whole people were cast out for believing that <u>God spake to Joseph Smith and chose him to be his messenger -- his Apostle -- to this generation</u>. I testify to you that we were not cast out for teaching and practising the Patriarchal doctrine, as our enemies now declare, for at that time it [had] not been published to the world, but it was for believing, preaching and practising the doctrines of the New Testament; for believing in the events to take place in the latter days, as foretold by the ancient Prophets; and, for believing the declarations of Joseph Smith, that Jesus was indeed the Christ and the Saviour of all men, but especially of them that believe, and that he had set to his hand the second time to gather his people, to establish his kingdom, to build up Zion, redeem Jerusalem, empty the earth of wickedness and bring in everlasting righteousness.

Revelation of the Lord Jesus Christ Given to President Warren S. Jeffs San Angelo, Texas Saturday, July 30, 2011

1. Thus saith the Lord Jesus Christ to all nations, kindreds, tongues, peoples of all the earth:

2. I have sent Joseph Smith as my great Prophet, Seer, and Revelator, to restore my revealings of the Gospel of preparation in my holy order of restoring to earth all Priesthood authorities, powers, retributions, powers eternal; to now be among men with thy Lord as he who is under Christ, to be Governor over all.

3. Let my will be known, that Joseph Smith is the third member of the Godhead that now rules over this earth.

4. Let all now know that every nation in this now present earth, that you mock God when you deride against His labor through Joseph Smith.

5. He who opposes any labor I called upon Joseph to perform, you are then deriding against me, saith your Lord Jesus Christ, to this generation, knowing I, your God, that I speak as to be understood, saith:

6. Let my people go who have received my Celestial Law of Eternal Union of Celestial Power of Marriage Eternal.

7. Let all beware to not treat lightly my holy way of Priesthood power, authority, and dominion; for my holy way is to only be of eternal power Celestial.

8. Thus, you who are not acquainted with my Church and Kingdom, come learn of me eternal truths that exalt the mind to be of a full-hearted way of obeying my will of Eternal Union law of Celestial authority, power, and dominion; not to be slow in final preparing, but to now be ready to receive Joseph Smith again among you, now soon at hand.

9. Let all now be of resounding rejoicing, that you know Joseph Smith shall be on earth, among my Priesthood; to direct my will to the people of the earth in all lands, languages, isles of the sea, as well as parts of earth returning.

10. Great is the day of my coming in glory.

11. No evil again can remain on my land of Zion.

12. Let only pure way of doing be of my whole labor of preparing, among all people of the earth; for my holy coming in eternal power is nigh and must be met in a pure way of living.

13. Repent ye, Repent ye, all ye peoples of every nation, lest you fall short of any blessing needful for eternal progression,

in the eternal realm of Ahman, even God over all creation.

14. I am Son Ahman, Jesus Christ, over all the earth, as my Father hath appointed.

15. I am the Holy One of Israel who speaketh, who shall gather mine Israel unto Zion to live Eternal Power of truth Celestial.

16. Let all now realize without Joseph Smith's mission being fulfilled, all peoples would be lost unto never-ending sadness and despair, for his work is my will and way done in full organizing of Eternal Union power over all people.

17. Let my will now be known, to realize I am now speaking from my own eternal home through my Mouthpiece of pure receiving and revealing holy truth, eternal truth; that exalts the soul unto Godhood or Goddesshood in Celestial realms of everlasting burnings of heavenly power.

18. Let all now heed my will, and now be ready for more of my word, even concerning the other Israel soon to return to this globe.

19. I am the Creator of the earth, and all flesh on the earth.

20. I am a God of Creation power eternal.

21. You cannot escape from a God who sees and knows all things, who has all power to accomplish every good thing of my Father's naming; to bring immortality and eternal lives to a few who will listen and obey my every word I send through my servant on earth, even my holy servant now in bondage by the land of governing power, which power is over all the earth; I being your God and King, even Jesus Christ, by my holy Priesthood authority given me of my Father.

22. Let all be holy, pure, righteous, in spirit and in truth, to be of a full preparing against the time of my glorious appearing, prophesied of by my holy Prophets.

23. Let United States governing power of just and holy preserving of religious freedom, now deliver my holy servant Warren Jeffs from bondage, to now dwell freely among my Church; to have all needed things be of a full ready way, to allow my elect to be gathering unto my appointed gathering place, New Jerusalem; to have all things fully ready for my glory to be their deliverance for mine Israel, my chosen; to be of Celestial eternal power in my Kingdom.

24. Let all now be aware of coming power of cleansing the earth.

25. Let all have only my will to be done; then do my will, and not be hearers only, being as hypocrites, professing to know my name, yet you do not know me, because you have a form of godliness, but you deny the power thereof; even my Priesthood authority I have ordained to dwell among you, even my Keyholder and Mouthpiece, holding the sealing power of Elijah in full Priesthood power and all people; to deliver Israel unto the Zion of pure governing power; to bless all peoples of every nation, to have all being of a revealing of my truths Celestial unto holy, pure, noble, exalting, inspiring ways, being upheld by every power on earth, because they heed my will.

26. I will own anyone, whether they be national power or individual personal devotion, who come unto me, your Lord Jesus Christ, through my authority on earth; to be an administering authorized agent, to perform labor of holy and pure way of my revealing.

27. Let all people now rejoice in thy

God who created you, and for Him now making Himself known to all people, to be preparing for my coming unto all people, to them knowing, in fear of transgressing my right to rule; unto all who remain shall know your Lord.

28. Be ye clean and pure.

29. Cease the attack against my Holy Priesthood and people.

30. Now be truly just, and honored as governing power that preserves purity and pure religious and constitutional power of preserving freedoms; who will cleanse people of your ruling of murder, and Sodom, of immoral ways, which afflicts your very inward workings as a people, corrupting all you do by the corrupt way allowed by governing power over this present people now dwelling on my Zion, a land of future cleansing in full, even soon at hand; is the will of thy God who now revealeth truth without interfering of governing powers; who seek to prosecute an innocent religion of pure revealing from my own will being manifest.

31. My love shines over all peoples, holding them in their place.

32. Come unto me, your Savior, O ye people of the world, and come out of Babylon; which evil power shall soon be subdued by my holy arms stretched out all the day long for salvation to be your eternal power as you abide in me.

33. Let Judge recuse herself for honor's sake, for truth is she is of a way of pride, defending her rulings of unrighteous way, afflicting my Church; to be of an affliction that sought to destroy my Celestial and Eternal Law by seeking to be as God over my Church to declare policy of way of doing in my holy way of pure Celestial Law of Priesthood governing power yesterday; when I caused my servant to voice my will, to call on you to not be of a Judge over religion, when it was in your ability to stop the attack of government against a religious and holy way constitutionally guaranteed in religious practice freedom; a freedom for all peoples to enjoy in pure way of a revealed Priesthood and religious authority God, that rules over all, hath ordained, and shall yet be the Eternal Head of my Church, in heaven and on earth.

34. O ye who afflict my Church, sorrowful shall you be in days to come if you repent not of your wicked, perverse ways of ignoble corrupt way; to allow evil of immoral practice in every way of living in this nation, in politics, in governing power, in social evils, and in allowing murder of innocence, yea, the most helpless of creations, the unborn children; a sin that corrupts your very way of life, before a just God, who shall now no longer uphold your nation as a power over other nations, lest you corrupt the way of all the earth.

35. Thus, my promises concerning your overthrow as a nation of corruption shall be fulfilled by the Almighty power of Eternal Power.

36. Let these evils cease, saith God, lest you go to a judging of thy God, unto you not having place on earth anymore, is the warning voice of God over all. Amen.

Chapter 2

Administration of President Brigham Young

Let Brigham Young Be Upheld as a Prophet of Power, Who Also Sought Celestial Power of Holy Way of Union Celestial

Revelation of the Lord Jesus Christ Given to President Warren S. Jeffs San Angelo, Texas Saturday, July 30, 2011

1. I, your Lord Jesus Christ, reveal truth of my servant Brigham Young as a holy son of my sending, to continue my Priesthood on earth; having received my holy Order of Eternal Power by the hand of my servant Joseph Smith; and having proved pure as a man of holy way, to be of full Priesthood power of Keyholder and Mouthpiece of my sending; even as Moses.

2. Let all rejoice in your God for the mission of Brigham Young; as he continues to labor in my holy Order of Holy Union, a holy angel sent to do my bidding among my holy way of governing all my pure way of Priesthood in every department of my domain, to be of my order of Priesthood power to sons of God who are worthy to be receiving angelic visiting.

3. Let my holy way be known, that Priesthood is eternal; and faithful sons of Celestial Power in my Priesthood are ministering power of Celestial Priesthood power, in eternal labor of advancing my Kingdom.

4. Let my Priesthood be pure, to increase unto the gift of becoming like me in full power of Eternal Priesthood; to be as God in the inherited dominion they earn, by faith and obeying my every will and way of pure and holy increase, worlds without end.

5. Let all know he is with me in all power of Priesthood power, by my holy way abiding in him.

6. Let my Priesthood be of great power in mortal life, so as to be of greater power in Celestial realm of pure holy power of Priesthood; as my son, Brigham Young, now is; as an holy pure son of God, able to disseminate truth eternal to worthy men in my holy Order of Eternal Union; Gods of Creation in everlasting lives.

7. Let all know Brigham Young was faithful unto the end, and is with me in Celestial power of my Godhood-giving power in lives of my pure in heart, who are constant unto me.

8. Let all, every one, be of full power of pure obeying, to magnify Priesthood, like unto this faithful son of Priesthood, holding the keys of Elijah, and having proved humble and holy, worthy to be with his Lord in all-consuming power of fire of heaven as a power of continual heavenly authority; to administer to chosen vessels in the world of departed spirits, and also to those on earth who love God with an undivided heart, with all their soul and might, in increasing power Celestial; to be Gods of holy Order of Union Power; to govern domain of my appointing.

9. Let all my people rejoice in His continuing the keys of sealing power on earth through chosen sons of Priesthood and holy power, who abide in me, through the gift of revealing my will; which is the way of my holy way of governing authority; always abiding in my holy

will, unto full confidence bestowed as a God in Celestial realms of eternal gift, of my Celestial holy way of my holy power extended to men, to give full glory of pure exalting; to be holy men of pure eternal Priesthood authority of Holy Priesthood revealing my truths unto the way of union eternal.

10. Let all now be of holy way. Amen.

Saints of God Were Driven West

Battle of Nauvoo -- 1845

President Brigham Young
Documentary History of the Church 7:439

Thursday, [September] 11, -- I received a letter from Sheriff J. B. Backenstos announcing the death of General Miner R. Deming, who died at half past ten o'clock yesterday of congestive fever; during his illness his life was repeatedly threatened by the mob, he was prevented from sleeping at night by their yells and hideous screams, as they kept up a continual row in the streets of Carthage near the general's residence which greatly aggravated his fever, and doubtless caused his death.

I answered Sheriff Backenstos' letter assuring him of our regret at the loss the cause of liberty, law, and order had sustained in the unexpected death of General Deming, and informed him of the burning of the houses of the citizens of Morley Settlement by the mob yesterday, and requested him to take immediate steps to suppress the mob, advised him to inform the governor that he may take the necessary measures to protect the lives and property of the people in this country.

A messenger from Lima reports eight houses burned.***

SOLOMON HANCOCK'S ANSWER TO BRIGHAM YOUNG

By letter from Solomon Hancock, Yelrome, we learn that the mob have burned all the houses on the south side of the branch [brook] , and left last evening for Lima, said they would return this morning as soon as light, and swear they will sweep through and burn everything to Nauvoo. Colonel Levi Williams is at the head of the mob.

President Brigham Young
Documentary History of the Church 7:443

Sunday, 14. -- *** I said, in relation to the mob burning houses, I was willing they should do so, until the surrounding counties should be convinced that we were not the aggressors, peradventure they may conclude to maintain the supremacy of the law by putting down mob violence and bringing offenders to justice.

I counseled the brethren to bring their families and grain here, and called for volunteers with wagons and teams to aid in removing the saints to this place; one hundred and thirty-four teams were procured and started forthwith. The brethren agreed to continue until they had brought in all their families, effects and grain of the saints in the settlements attacked by the mob.***

Monday, 15. -- Seven a. m., the police met at my house and put me up a stable.

Sheriff Backenstos went to Warsaw and tried his best to summon a posse to stop the burning but could not raise one.

Forty-four buildings have been burned by the mob. Several houses have been burned in the Prairie branch, Green Plain precinct.

Michael Barnes a constable from Carthage, and his brother came into Nauvoo with writs for H. C. Kimball, Willard Richards, John E. Page, Daniel Garn, Wm. and George A. Smith, and myself, issued by Captain Smith of the Carthage Greys, on the complaint of _____ Backman. The charges were for aiding and abetting Joseph Smith in treasonable designs against the state, for being officers in the Nauvoo Legion, for building an arsenal, for keeping cannon in times of peace, for holding a private council in Nauvoo, and for holding correspondence with the Indians.***

I received a letter from J. B. Backenstos, dated, Carthage, September 15th, in which he stated his inability to raise law and order citizens to quell the mob and requested us to hold two thousand well armed men in readiness for immediate service at any hour that he may call for them and added: that if we will not defend our own lives and property that we cannot reasonably expect any considerable support from those citizens commonly called 'Jack-Mormons'. 'Colonel Levi Williams has ordered out his brigade of militia, I am certain the turnout will be slim, we must whip them.'

In reply I advised him to wait a few days and see if there are any law and order citizens in the county that are not Mormons, and if it proved there were none else to stand up for the Constitution and laws of the state, it would then be time enough for us, as the old citizens had heretofore advised us to 'hold still'! 'Keep cool'! 'Be quiet'! etc., etc., we were determined to do so.

The first regiment, second cohort of the Nauvoo Legion met and organized, choosing the old officers, to place themselves in readiness to act at the sheriff's call.***

Tuesday, 16. -- Sheriff Backenstos arrived in great haste and somewhat excited, said that the mob had driven him from his house in Carthage yesterday, and he went to Warsaw and stayed over night. He soon ascertained that the people were so enraged at him for trying to stop the house-burning that there was little probability of getting away alive, but finally prevailed on an influential mobocrat to escort him out of Warsaw this morning, who came with him about three and a half miles and on leaving cautioned him that if he saw two men together to avoid them for there were deep plans laid to kill him. Soon after he was pursued by a party of the mob on horseback, three of whom took the lead, one of the three had a swifter horse and gained a hundred yards in advance of his party in a short time when his horse stumbled and threw his rider. Backenstos maintained his speed, driving as fast as his horse could go.

The mob took the nearest road to cross his track and on his arrival at the old railroad crossing, the mob were within about 200 yards, they being on horseback and he in a buggy, they had gained on him considerably.

Orrin P. Rockwell and John Redding were refreshing themselves near the crossing as they had been out to bring in some of the burnt-out families who were sick, and on looking up saw Backenstos coming down the hill at full speed, and asked what was the matter. Backenstos replied the mob were after and determined to kill him and commanded them in the name of the people of the state to protect him, Rockwell

replied, fear not, we have 50 rounds (two fifteen-shooter rifles besides revolvers).

Sheriff Backenstos then turned to the mob and commanded them to stop, and as they continued to advance raising their guns, he ordered Rockwell to fire; he did so aiming at the clasp of the belt on one of the mob, which proved to be Frank Worrell, who fell from his horse and the rest turned back and soon brought up a wagon and put his body into it. ***

Tuesday, 30. -- *** I went with the Twelve to Elder Taylor's and saw Judge Douglas and Sheriff Backenstos.

They said it was hard to make the people, the other side of the Illinois river, believe that it was not the Mormons that were burning houses in Hancock county.

They wished us to go and see General Hardin. In company with H. C. Kimball, W. Richards, John Taylor, George A. Smith and Amasa M. Lyman, I went on to the hill and met General Hardin and staff surrounded by his troops, four hundred in number. He read us his orders from the governor to come here and keep the peace if he had to keep the county under martial law: said he wished to search for the bodies of two dead men who were last seen in Nauvoo and it was supposed they had been murdered.

I told him he was welcome to search for dead bodies or anything else he pleased. He inquired if I knew anything about them or of crimes having been committed in Nauvoo. I replied I knew nothing of the kind, but that I had reliable information that some hundred houses had been burned in the south part of the county and probably if he would go there, he would find the persons who had done it.

I tendered him the hospitality of the city and a home at my house, to which he replied drily, 'I always stay in camp.'

General Hardin marched his troops to, and searched the Temple, Masonic Hall, Nauvoo House, and the stables of the Mansion.***

President Brigham Young
Documentary History of the Church 7:481
General Hardin has pledged himself to the mob that he will come to Nauvoo with his troops and either arrest Orrin P. Rockwell and some others of the brethren or he 'will unroof every house in

Nauvoo'. Three hundred of our enemies have volunteered to come with him from Quincy and they expect to be joined by others on the way.

There seems to be no disposition abroad but to massacre the whole body of this people, and nothing but the power of God can save us from the cruel ravages of the bloodthirsty mob.***

Bishop Miller, Sheriff Backenstos, and those who went with them to Quincy, have all returned safely.

Backenstos is bound over to court in three thousand dollar bonds. General Hardin has gone to Springfield.

Tuesday, 14. -- Major Warren came into the city with a detachment of the troops.

President Brigham Young
Documentary History of the Church 7:486

Saturday, 25. -- 4 p.m., A. W. Babbitt arrived from Carthage and stated that when the brethren went in yesterday as witnesses of the house-burning the grand jury refused to hear their testimony, or to admit any of them into the jury room, which effectually shields the house-burners from justice and blockades the way for the sufferers to obtain redress.***

This morning Hosea Stout and John Scott stationed themselves at the mound, seven miles east of Nauvoo, and extended a few men for miles north and south to ascertain and express any hostile movements which might be made towards Nauvoo.

Major Warren, Judge Purple, J. B. Backenstos, Judge Ralston and Mr. Brannan with a detachment of troops came into town and Warren demanded an explanation in relation to seeing some fifteen or twenty of our express men on the prairie.

I went to the Mansion and in plain but mild language stated the reason why our men were there. Warren in a great rage declared he would issue his manifesto on Monday morning and put the county under martial law. After this Elder John Taylor made some very just and spirited remarks in relation to the foul treachery or criminal imbecility of the governor's protection, telling Mr. Warren that we had placed our express men in a position to communicate the earliest intelligence should any mob violence be attempted upon our brethren while at Carthage and further said: 'We lack confidence in the governor's troops under your command while hundreds of murderers, robbers and house-burners roam at large unwhipped of justice. We shall take measures to protect ourselves. I, Sir, have been shot all to pieces under the 'protection' of the governor's troops. Our leading men have been murdered in Carthage and we shall not trust ourselves unprotected again until the state gives some evidence more than it has done of its justice and humane intentions to enforce its laws.'

President Brigham Young
Documentary History of the Church 7:510

Saturday, November 1, 1845. -- *** The following editorial appeared in the Times and Seasons:

GREAT PERSECUTION OF THE CHURCH OF JESUS CHRIST OF LATTER-DAY SAINTS IN ILLINOIS

'After we had begun to realize the abundance of one of the most fruitful seasons known for a long time, and while many hundreds of saints were laboring with excessive, and unwearied diligence to finish the Temple and rear the Nauvoo House, suddenly in the forepart of September, the mob commenced burning the houses and grain of the saints in the south part of Hancock county. Though efforts were made by the sheriff to stay the torch of the incendiary and parry off the deluge of arson, still a 'fire and sword' party continued the work of destruction for about a week, laying in ashes nearly two hundred buildings and much grain.

Nor is this all: as it was in the sickly season, many feeble persons, thrown out into the scorching rays of the sun, or wet with the dampening dews of the evening, died, being persecuted to death in a Christian land of law and order; and while they are fleeing and dying, the mob, embracing doctors, lawyers, statesmen, Christians of various denominations, with the military from colonels down, were busily engaged in filching or plundering, taking furniture, cattle and grain. In the midst of this horrid revelry, having failed to procure aid among the 'old citizens', the sheriff summoned a sufficient posse to stay the 'fire shower of ruin', but not until some of the offenders had paid for the aggression with their lives.

This, however, was not the end of the matter. Satan sits in the hearts of the people to rule for evil, and the surrounding counties began to fear that law, religion, and equal rights, in the hands of the Latter-day Saints, would feel after iniquity or terrify their neighbors to larger acts of 'reserved rights', and so they began to open a larger field of woe. To cut this matter short they urged the necessity (to stop the effusion of blood), to expel the church, or as they call them, the Mormons, from the United States, 'peaceably if they could, and forcibly if they must', unless they would transport themselves by next spring. Taking into consideration the great value of life, and the blessings of peace, a proposition upon certain specified conditions was made to a committee of Quincy, and which it was supposed from the actions of conventions was accepted. But we are sorry to say, that the continued depredations of the mob and the acts of a few individuals, have greatly lessened the confidence of every friend of law, honor and humanity, in everything promised by the committees and conventions, though we have already made great advances towards outfitting for a move next spring.

A few troops stationed in the county, have not entirely kept the mob at bay: several buildings have been burned in the month of October.

We shall, however, make every exertion on our part, as we have always done, to preserve the law and our engagements sacred, and leave the event with God, for he is sure.

It may not be amiss to say, that the continued abuses, persecutions, murders, and robberies practiced upon us by a horde of land pirates with impunity in a Christian republic, and land of liberty, (while the institutions of justice, have either been too weak to afford us protection or redress, or else they too have been a little remiss) have brought us to the solemn conclusion that our exit from the United States is the only alternative by which we can enjoy our share of the elements which our heavenly Father created free for all.

We can then shake the dust from our garments, suffering wrong rather than do wrong, leaving this nation alone in her glory, while the residue of the world, points the finger of scorn, till the indignation and consumption decreed, make a full end.

In our patience we [will] possess our souls and work out a more exceeding and eternal weight of glory, preparing, by withdrawing the power and priesthood from the Gentiles, for the great consolation of Israel, when the wilderness shall blossom as the rose, and Babylon fall like a millstone cast into the sea. The just shall live by faith; but the folly of fools will perish with their bodies of corruption: then shall the righteous shine: Amen.'"

President Brigham Young
Documentary History of the Church 7:523

Saturday, 15. -- ***

DEATH OF EDMUND DURFEE -- SHOT BY A MOB OF HOUSE-BURNERS

A considerable party of the mob set fire to a stack of straw near Solomon Hancock's barn and concealed themselves. Hancock and others went out to put out the fire which was the only way to save the building, when they were fired upon by the burners, and Elder Edmund Durfee killed on the spot, many balls flew around the rest of the brethren, but none of the rest were hurt.***

Sunday, 16. -- *** I received the following:

BACKENSTOS' NOTE TO THE TWELVE

'To the Twelve: On last night Elder Edmund Durfee was basely murdered by the mob in the Green Plains precinct, what shall be done to avenge his blood? the troops afford us no protection.

Yours etc.,

November 16th, 1845.   J. B. BACKENSTOS.'

President Brigham Young
Documentary History of the Church 7:527

Tuesday, 18. -- The Twelve met in council at Dr. Richards'.

Mr. Brayman, attorney for the state, wrote a letter to the council desiring witnesses against the murderers of Durfee to be sent to Carthage, also affidavits; forwarded in relation to the burning of Rice's house, and advising us of the arrest of George Backman, Moss and Snyder, who were charged with the murder of Elder Edmund Durfee, Sen.

The council replied immediately and requested the witnesses to start in the morning for Carthage to perform their part in another judicial farce.***

NAUVOO NEIGHBOR -- EXTRA

Nauvoo, November 19th, 1845

MURDER AND ARSON
EDMUND DURFEE SHOT -- TWO HOUSES BURNED

'As may be seen by the affidavits below, it falls to our painful lot to chronicle two more outrages upon the lives and rights of the Latter-day Saints, since they have been using all diligence to secure their crops, build wagons, and leave next spring.

Mr. Durfee was one of the most industrious, inoffensive and good men that could be found, and having his house burnt in September last, moved to Nauvoo and went on Saturday last for a load of grain, was shot dead in cold blood, at midnight while striving with others to save property from the flames by an armed mob!

As to the destruction of the houses and

property, and the treatment on that occasion---let the affidavit speak for itself.

We have nearly two thousand five hundred wagons commenced for our Pacific journey next spring, but such outrages certainly are not calculated to aid us in getting ready. We have borne the Missouri persecution; we have mourned the loss of the Prophet and Patriarch, Joseph and Hyrum Smith; we feel the destruction of one or two hundred houses the present season, and our hearts are pained at the murder of Edmund Durfee, because he was a good man; but, we, as in all cases of the saints, leave the disposition of these matters in the care of a wise God, and the perpetrators, to the mercy of (as they say), a country of laws, and be those laws honored or disgraced we cannot be charged with revenge; and we do beseech the people and the authorities not to impute crime to us, to raise excitement, when we see our accusers wiping the blood of innocent men, women, and children, from their garments, as though this was the realm of Nero.

If thieves and robbers escape to Nauvoo, our rule is to deliver them up to the law of the land, and that is all that we can do.

We believe there is virtue and humanity among high-minded men, that know what honor is, and we appeal to them to lend a helping hand, while we are outfitting for our intended removal in the spring. Give us peace, for you that hold the balances of power can! And when we have settled on the other side of America you will know of a truth that we were friends and not enemies to life, law, and liberty! That we were good men, engaged in a good cause, and will receive the meed of praise we deserve for universal benevolence, and everlasting friendship to goodness.

The jealousy of the present generation is so great against the saints, that we have deemed it our duty to give this and the accompanying affidavits, that the world may know the continued ravages, and bloody outrages of a midnight mob; and for another important reason, that as Major Warren has pledged himself to use every exertion in his power to allay excitement, prevent the destruction of property, and stop the shedding of blood, we cannot feel anything better than that he will exhibit his honor and clemency in our

behalf, that we may prepare for our exodus in peace henceforth.'

President Brigham Young
Documentary History of the Church 7:541

ACQUITTAL OF SHERIFF BACKENSTOS FOR
THE KILLING OF FRANK A. WORRELL

News has arrived that Sheriff Backenstos, who went to Peoria in charge of Henry W. Miller, coroner of Hancock county, and was tried before Judge Purple on the charge of the 'murder' of Frank A. Worrell, was acquitted. The moral atmosphere around the judge was so different, than when at Carthage, that in all his charges and rulings, he appeared like another judge, and as though he had never been afflicted with mobocratic mania.

The jury said if there had been no witnesses only on the part of the state, it would not have required more than two minutes to have made up their verdict. There are two of the mob witnesses in jail for perjury and Backenstos is gone to Springfield to request the governor to withdraw his troops.

Story of Bogus Brigham

President Brigham Young
JD 14:218 July 23, 1871 Logan

While brother George A. Smith was referring to the circumstance of William Miller going to Carthage, it brought to my mind reflections of the past. Perhaps to relate the circumstance as it occurred would be interesting.

I do not profess to be much of a joker, but I do think this to be one of the best jokes ever perpetrated. By the time we were at work in the Nauvoo Temple, officiating in the ordinances, the mob had learned that "Mormonism" was not dead, as they had supposed. We had completed the walls of the Temple, and the attic story from about half way up of the first windows, in about fifteen months. It went up like magic, and we commenced officiating in the ordinances. Then the mob commenced to hunt for other victims; they had already killed the Prophets Joseph and Hyrum in Carthage jail, while under the pledge of the State for their safety, and now [they] wanted Brigham, the President of the Twelve Apostles, who were then acting as the Presidency of the Church.

I was in my room in the Temple; it was in the

south-east corner of the upper story. I learned that a posse was lurking around the Temple, and that the United States Marshal was waiting for me to come down, whereupon I knelt down and asked my Father in heaven, in the name of Jesus, to guide and protect me that I might live to prove advantageous to the Saints. Just as I arose from my knees and sat down in my chair, there came a rap at my door. I said, "Come in," and brother George D. Grant, who was then engaged driving my carriage and doing chores for me, entered the room. Said he, "Brother Young, do you know that a posse and the United States Marshal are here?" I told him I had heard so. On entering the room brother Grant left the door open. Nothing came into my mind what to do, until looking directly across the hall I saw brother William Miller leaning against the wall. As I stepped towards the door I beckoned to him; he came. Said I to him, "Brother William, the Marshal is here for me; will you go and do just as I tell you? If you will, I will serve them a trick." I knew that brother Miller was an excellent man, perfectly reliable and capable of carrying out my project. Said I, "Here, take my cloak;" but it happened to be brother Heber C. Kimball's; our cloaks were alike in color, fashion and size. I threw it around his shoulders, and told him to wear my hat and accompany brother George D. Grant. He did so. I said to brother Grant, "George, you step into the carriage and look towards brother Miller, and say to him, as though you were addressing me, 'Are you ready to ride?' You can do this, and they will suppose brother Miller to be me, and proceed accordingly," which they did.

Just as brother Miller was entering the carriage, the Marshal stepped up to him, and, placing his hand upon his shoulder, said, "You are my prisoner." Brother William entered the carriage and said to the Marshal, "I am going to the Mansion House, won't you ride with me?" They both went to the Mansion House. There were my sons Joseph A., Brigham, jun., and brother Heber C. Kimball's boys, and others who were looking on, and all seemed at once to understand and partake of the joke. They followed the carriage to the Mansion House and gathered around brother Miller, with tears in their eyes, saying, "Father, or President Young, where are you going?" Brother Miller looked at them kindly, but made no reply; and the Marshal really thought he had got "Brother Brigham."

Lawyer Edmonds, who was then staying at the Mansion House, appreciating the joke, volunteered to brother Miller to go to Carthage with him and see him safe through. When they arrived within two or three miles of Carthage, the Marshal with his posse stopped. They arose in their carriages, buggies and waggons, and, like a tribe of Indians going into battle, or as if they were a pack of demons, yelling and shouting, they exclaimed, "We've got him! we've got him! We've got him!" When they reached Carthage the Marshal took the supposed Brigham into an upper room of the hotel, and placed a guard over him, at the same time telling those around that he had got him. Brother Miller remained in the room until they bid him come to supper. While there, parties came in, one after the other, and asked for Brigham. Brother Miller was pointed out to them. So it continued, until an apostate Mormon, by the name of Thatcher, who had lived in Nauvoo, came in, sat down and asked the landlord where Brigham Young was. The landlord, pointing across the table to brother Miller, said, "That is Mr. Young." Thatcher replied, "Where? I can't see any one that looks like Brigham." The landlord told him it was that fat, fleshy man eating. "Oh, hell!" exclaimed Thatcher, "that's not Brigham; that is William Miller, one of my old neighbors." Upon hearing this the landlord went, and, tapping the Sheriff on the shoulder, took him a few steps to one side, and said, "You have made a mistake, that is not Brigham Young; it is William Miller, of Nauvoo." The Marshal, very much astonished, exclaimed, "Good heavens! and he passed for Brigham." He then took brother Miller into a room, and, turning to him, said, "What in hell is the reason you did not tell me your name?" Brother Miller replied, "You have not asked me my name." "Well," said the Sheriff, with another oath, "What is your name?" "My name," he replied, "is William Miller." Said the Marshal, "I thought your name was Brigham Young. Do you say this for a fact?" "Certainly I do," said brother Miller. "Then," said the Marshal, "why did you not tell me this before?" "I was under no obligations to tell you," replied brother Miller, "as you did not ask me." Then the Marshal, in a rage, walked out of the room, followed by brother

Miller, who walked off in company with Lawyer Edmonds, Sheriff Backenstos, and others, who took him across lots to a place of safety; and this is the real pith of the story of "Bogus" Brigham, as far as I can recollect.

The Saints Begin Their Exodus in Freezing Weather

President Brigham Young
Documentary History of the Church 7:552

Friday, 26.[1846] -- *** Sheriff Backenstos informed me that the United States deputy marshal was in town with writs for the Twelve and Brother George Miller.

President Brigham Young
Documentary History of the Church 7:567

Sunday, 11.[1846] -- The General Council met and arranged to make an early start west.***

The captains of fifties and tens made reports of the number in their respective companies, who were prepared to start west immediately, should the persecutions of our enemies compel us to do so: one hundred and forty horses and seventy wagons were reported ready for immediate service.

President Brigham Young
Documentary History of the Church 7:577

Sheriff Backenstos has returned from Springfield, and says, that Governor Ford has turned against us, and that Major Warren is making calculations to prevent our going away.

I received a letter from Josiah Lamborn, Esq., Springfield, stating that Governor Ford was decidedly in favor of General J. J. Hardin's policy, which is, that of suspending all civil offices, the collection of taxes, and placing the county under martial law.***

Thursday, 29. -- ***Quite a number of the governor's troops are prowling around our city; I am informed that they are seeking to arrest some of the leading men of the church.***

Monday, [February] 2. [1846] -- *** Ten a. m., the Twelve, Trustees and a few others met in council, to ascertain the feelings of the brethren that were expecting to start westward. We agreed that it was imperatively necessary to start as soon as possible. I counseled the brethren to procure boats and hold them in readiness to convey our wagons and teams over the river, and let everything for the journey be in readiness,

that when a family is called to go, everything necessary may be put into the wagon within four hours, at least, for if we are here many days, our way will be hedged up. Our enemies have resolved to intercept us whenever we start. I should like to push on as far as possible before they are aware of our movements. In order to have this counsel circulated, I sent messengers to notify the captains of hundreds and fifties to meet at 4 p. m. at Father Cutlers'.

At four o'clock, I met with the captains of hundreds and fifties, and laid my counsel before them, to which they all consented, and dispersed to carry it into execution.

President Brigham Young
Documentary History of the Church 7:585

Sunday, 15.[1846] -- I crossed the river with my family accompanied by W. Richards and family and George A. Smith. We traveled on four miles, when we came to the bluff. I would not go on until I saw all the teams up. I helped them up the hill with my own hands. At dusk started on, and reached Sugar Creek about 8 p. m., having traveled nine miles. The roads were very bad.

President Brigham Young
Documentary History of the Church 7:592

Thursday, 19. -- From Dr. Richards' *Camp Journal:*

'The wind blew steadily from the northwest accompanied by snow which fell to the depth of seven or eight inches, but much thawed as it fell, the storm was unceasing, and the evening was very cold, which caused much suffering in the camp, for there were many who had no tents or any comfortable place to lodge: many tents were blown down, some of them were unfinished and had no ends.'

President Brigham Young
Documentary History of the Church 7:596

Tuesday, 24. -- ***The cold has been severe the past night, a snowstorm this morning which continued during the forenoon, blowing from the northwest, which prevented Captain Bent's Company from moving; the cold was severe through the day and increased as night approached.***

Wednesday, 25. -- The morning was colder than any one since the encampment, but the sun rose clear, the whole camp appeared cheerful and happy.

Nine a. m., the blast of the bugle and the raising of the flag called the brethren together.

Persecution Against Leaders of Priesthood

President Brigham Young
JD 19:61 July 24, 1877 SLC

We lived in the State of Illinois a few years; and here, as elsewhere, persecution overtook us. It came from Missouri, centering itself upon Joseph, and fastened itself upon others. We lived in Illinois from 1839 to 1844, by which time they again succeeded in kindling the spirit of persecution against Joseph and the Latter-day Saints.*** They took Joseph and Hyrum, and as a guarantee for their safety, Governor Thomas Ford pledged the faith of the State of Illinois. They were imprisoned, on the pretense of safe keeping, because the mob was so enraged and violent. The Governor left them in the hands of the mob, who entered the prison and shot them dead.*** After the mob had committed these murders they came upon us and burned our houses and our grain. When the brethren would go out to put out the fire, the mob would lie concealed under fences, and in the darkness of the night, they would shoot them. At last they succeeded in driving us from the State of Illinois.

Orson F. Whitney
The Life of Heber C. Kimball, Page 359 ©1888

It soon became evident to the enemy that the death of the Prophet, so far from destroying, or even impeding Mormonism, had only given it fresh impetus, an energy which they feared, if allowed to increase, might prove irresistible. They therefore renewed the attack, Brigham, Heber and the Twelve now being the especial objects of their animus.***

The chief inciters of the opposition were the Laws, the Fosters, and the Higbees, apostates who had betrayed and sacrificed Joseph and Hyrum, with others who now joined them in their warfare against the Twelve. The most strenuous efforts were made, generally under cover of law, to get President Young into their power; and even his life, it is said, was attempted by the midnight assassin. Knowing their fell purpose, and remembering the fate of the martyrs, Joseph and Hyrum, who had tested the virtue of official pledges and the protecting majesty of the law in Illinois, Brigham and Heber wisely determined not to be taken.

President John Taylor
Life of John Taylor, Page 164

[Speaking to Major Warren] "I will touch upon the things of the present in a moment -- You may think this outrage was an outbreak -- a sudden ebullition of feeling that the governor could not control; but who was it that did this deed? The governor's troops, sir, were among the foremost of that bloody gang. And where, sir -- tell me where is our redress? You talk about the majesty of the law! What has become of those murderers? Have they been hung or shot, or in any way punished? No, sir, you know they have not. With their hands yet reeking in blood, having become hardened in their deeds of infamy, knowing that they will not be punished, they are now applying the torch to the houses of those they have already so deeply injured. What has been done to them under your administration? Have they been brought to justice, have they been punished for their infamous proceedings? No, sir; not one of them. They are still burning houses under your supervision; and you have either been unwilling or unable to stop them. Houses have been burned since your arrival here; men have been kidnapped, cattle stolen, our brethren abused and robbed when going after their corn. Are we to stand still and let marauders and house-burners come into our city under the real or assumed name of "governor's troops," and yet offer no resistance to their nefarious deeds? Are we to be held still by you, sir, while they thrust the hot iron into us? I tell you plainly for one I will not do it. I speak now on my own responsibility, and I tell you, sir, I will not stand it. I care nothing for your decrees, your martial law or any other law, I mean to protect myself; and if my brethren are to be insulted and abused in going after their own corn, and pursuing their lawful business -- if nobody else will go to protect them I will. They shall not be abused under pretext of law or anything else; and there is not a patriot in the world but what would bear me out in it.

"Where is the spirit of '76? Where is the fire that burned in the bosoms of those who fought and bled for liberty? Is there no one who will stand up in defense of the oppressed? If a man had the least spark of humanity burning in his bosom -- if he were not hardened and desperate, he would be ashamed to oppress a people already goaded by a yoke too intolerable to be borne, and that, too, in a boasted land of liberty. Talk about law! Sir, I stand before you as a victim of law. I feel warm on this subject -- who would not? I have seen my best friends shot down while under legal protection. What is our governor? These scenes have been enacted under his supervision. What are our generals and judges? They have aided in these matters. If an honorable jury is legally selected, a house-burner or perhaps a murderer makes affidavit that he has reason to believe they are partial and the judge will order a mobocratic sheriff and jury for the purpose of acquitting the guilty and condemning the innocent. What are all these legal men but a pack of scoundrels? And you will talk to us of law and order, and threaten us with punishment for disobeying your commands and protecting our rights! What are we? Are we beasts? I tell you for one, sir, I shall protect myself, law or no law, judge or no judge, governor or no governor. I will not stand such infernal rascality, and if I have to fight it out, I will sell my life as dearly as I can."

Government of the United States Rejects My People of Priesthood, Saith Jesus Christ

President Brigham Young
JD 19:62 July 24, 1877 SLC

Three congressmen came in the Fall of 1845, and had a Conference with the Twelve and others; they were desirous that we should leave the United States. We told them we would do so, we had staid long enough with them; we agreed to leave the State of Illinois in consequence of that religious prejudice against us that we could not stay in peace any longer. These men said the people were prejudiced against us. Stephen A. Douglass, one of the three had been acquainted with us. He said "I know you, I knew Joseph Smith; he was a good man," and this people was a good people; but the prejudices of the priests and the ungodly are such that, said he, "Gentlemen, you cannot stay here and live in peace." We agreed to leave.*** We left Nauvoo in February, 1846. There remained behind a few of the very poor, the sick and the aged, who suffered again from the violence of the mob: they were whipped and beaten, and had their houses burned.

Orson F. Whitney
The Life of Heber C. Kimball, Page 360

The anti-Mormons were clamoring for the removal of the entire community of Latter-day Saints from the state, and they, seeing no alternative but to comply with this outrageous demand, or experience a repetition of the murderous scenes of Missouri, had resolved to again sacrifice their homes and seek a land of peace and liberty in the wilds of the savage west.

Before coming to the conclusion to thus expatriate themselves, the Saints, through their leaders, had petitioned the President of the United States, James K. Polk, and the Governors of all the states excepting Missouri and Illinois, for aid and protection from the efforts of those who were plotting their destruction. But the appeal was in vain.

President Brigham Young
JD 11:17 December 11, 1864 SLC

The Lord has thrown his people on several occasions, into circumstances of destitution and dependence, to try the leaders of the nation, and has thus said unto them, what will you now do for my poor and afflicted people; and their reply has been, "We will destroy them, if we can." They think they will destroy us yet. In this, however, they are mistaken, "for God hath not appointed us to wrath, but to obtain salvation by our Lord Jesus Christ."***

When we were driven from Nauvoo, our Elders went to the East to lay our case before the judges, governors, and rulers of the different States to ask for an asylum; but none was offered us. We sent men through the Eastern country to try and raise some means for the destitute women and children, whose husbands, fathers and brothers had gone into the Mexican war at the call of the General Government, leaving their wives and children and aged fathers and mothers upon the open prairies without home or shelter, and the brethren who went East hardly got enough to bear their expenses. The great men of the nation were asked if they would do anything for the Lord's people. No; not a thing would they do, but hoped they would perish in the wilderness. "Therefore," saith the Lord, "behold, the destroyer I have sent forth to destroy and lay waste mine enemies: and not many years hence they shall not be left to pollute mine heritage, and to blaspheme my name upon the lands which I have consecrated for the gathering together of my saints." In the year 1845 I addressed letters to all the Governors of States and Territories in the Union, asking them for an asylum, within their borders, for the Latter-day Saints. We were refused such privilege, either by silent contempt or a flat denial in every instance. They all agreed that we could not come within the limits of their Territory or State. Three members of Congress came to negociate with us to leave the confines of the United States, and of the public domain. It was understood that we were going to Vancouver Island; but we had our eye on Mexico, and here we are located in the midst of what was then northern Mexico. Fears have been entertained that we shall again be meddled with; but you will find that the enemies of the cause of God will have plenty of business besides digging gold and silver and fighting the Saints, and I trust Utah will be left as unnoticed as it is in the President's message. I thank them for what they have done and for what they have not done. I thank the Lord that He has led this people, and suffered them to be driven from place to place. I thank the Lord that we have the words of eternal life; and if we live by them, our feet are as sure and as fast as these everlasting hills. I know where the Saints will dwell.

George A. Smith
JD 6:87 November 29, 1857 SLC

We petitioned the several States and also the United States for an asylum where we could enjoy ourselves; and all our petitions were answered with coldness and indifference, and there was not a place in the United States where a man that professed to be a Latter-day Saint could have peace. There was nothing but to be mobbed, driven, his houses burned, wherever he might be; and no governor, no legislature, no authority would extend any better prospect than the repetition of the murder, robberies, and persecution we had suffered in Missouri, and that we were then enduring in Illinois.

Holy Temple in Nauvoo Defiled

President Brigham Young
JD 2:32 April 6, 1853 SLC

While these things were transpiring with the Saints in the wilderness, the Temple at Nauvoo passed into the hands of the enemy, who polluted it to that extent the Lord not only ceased to occupy it, but He loathed to have it called by His name, and permitted the wrath of its possessors to purify it by fire, as a token of what will speedily fall on them and their habitations, unless they repent.

Government Demand for Troops on My Driven People of Priesthood, Saith the Lord

Orson F. Whitney
The Life of Heber C. Kimball, Page 369 ©1888

Word was brought to head-quarters on the Missouri, that a United States army officer with a squad of soldiers had arrived at Mt. Pisgah, with a requisition for five hundred men, to be furnished by the Mormons, to enter the army and march to California to take part in the war against Mexico.

Imagination can alone picture the surprise, almost dismay, with which this startling news was received. What! the nation whose people had thrust them from its borders, robbed them of their homes and driven them into the wilderness, where it was hoped they might perish, now calling upon them for aid? And this in full face of the fact that their own oft reiterated appeals for help had been denied?

It was even so. Five hundred able-bodied men, the flower of the camp, were wanted. And this in the heart of an Indian country, in the midst of an exodus unparalleled for its dangers and hardships, when every active man was needed as a bulwark of defense and a staff for the aged and feeble. For even delicate women, thus far, had in some instances been driving teams and tending stock, owing to the limited number of men available.

Government Conspiracy to Destroy the People of God

President Brigham Young
JD 8:335 February 17, 1861 SLC

Did Thomas H. Benton aid in gathering the Saints? Yes, he was the mainspring and action of governments in driving us into these mountains. He obtained orders from President Polk to summon the militia of Missouri, and destroy every "Mormon" man, woman, and child, unless they turned out five hundred men to fight the battles of the United States in Mexico. He said that we were aliens to the Government, and to prove it he said -- "Mr. President, make a requisition on that camp for five hundred men, and I will prove to you that they are traitors to our Government." We turned out the men, and many of them are before me to-day; among whom is father Pettigrew -- a man that ought to have been asked into the Cabinet to give the President counsel; but they asked him to travel on foot across the Plains to fight our country's battles against Mexico. We turned out the men, and Mr. Benton was disappointed.

President Brigham Young
JD 10:106 March 8, 1863 SLC

This is the outside pressure. It forced us from Ohio to Missouri, from Missouri to Illinois, and from Illinois into the wilderness. We were accused of disloyalty, alienation, and apostacy from the Constitution of our country. We were accused of being secessionists. I am, so help me God, and ever expect to be a secessionist from their wickedness, unrighteousness, dishonesty and unhallowed principles in a religious point of view; but am I or this people secessionists with regard to the glorious Constitution of our country? No. Were we secessionists when we so promptly responded to the call of the General Government, when we were houseless and friendless on the wild prairies of Pottowattamie? I think not. We there told the brethren to enlist, and they obeyed without a murmur.***

I knew then as well as I do now that the Government would call for a battalion of men out of that part of Israel, to test our loyalty to the Government. Thomas H. Benton, if I have been rightly informed, obtained the requisition to call for that battalion, and, in case of non-compliance with that requisition, to call on the militia of Missouri and Iowa, and other States, if necessary, and to call volunteers from Illinois, from which State we had been driven, to destroy the camp of Israel. This same Mr. Benton said to the President of the United States, in the presence of some other persons, "Sir, they are a pestilential race, and ought to become extinct."

I will again urge upon this people to so live that they will have the knowledge they desire, as we have knowledge not of all, but only of that which is necessary. Have we not shown to the world that we love the Constitution of our country and its institutions better than do those who have been and are now distracting the nation? You cannot find a community, placed under the circumstances that we were, that would have done as we did on the occasion of furnishing the Mormon Battalion, after our leading men had been slain and we had been compelled to leave our farms, gardens, homes and firesides, while, at the same time, the general Government was called upon in vain to put a stop to such a series of abuses against an innocent people.

Brigham Young Arrives in Salt Lake, Late, After Pioneers on July 24, 1847

Orson F. Whitney
History of Utah, Volume 1 Page 303

On April 16th, at about 2 p. m., the pioneers broke camp and traveled three miles.***

During the next few days the camp was thoroughly organized under the direction of President Young. In addition to the captains of tens, already named, there were captains of hundreds and fifties appointed.***

Thus organized, equipped and instructed, the pioneers proceeded on their way, slowly traveling up the north bank of the Platte.***

Orson F. Whitney
History of Utah, Volume 1 Page 323

The rear wagons, with the sick President, were at the same time approaching East Canyon. On the 22nd they encamped there, and on the 23rd crossed Big Mountain. The President, reclining in Apostle Woodruff's carriage, requested to have it turned upon the summit so that he might see those portions of the Valley that were now visible. Gazing long and earnestly at the prospect, he exclaimed: "Enough. This is the right place. Drive on."***

It was late in the forenoon of the day following -- the memorable 24th -- that the rear wagons rolled through the mouth of Emigration Canyon, and Brigham Young, the founder of Utah, looked his first upon the full glory of the Valley by the Lake.

After the death of Joseph Smith, when it seemed as if every trouble and calamity had come upon the Saints, Brigham Young, who was President of the Twelve,*** …sought the Lord to know what they should do, and where they should lead the people for safety, and while they were fasting and praying daily on this subject, President Young had a vision of Joseph Smith, who showed him the mountain that we now call Ensign Peak, immediately north of Salt Lake City, and there was an ensign fell upon that peak, and Joseph said, "Build under the point where the colors fall and you will prosper and have peace." The Pioneers had no pilot or guide, none among them had ever been in the country or knew anything about it. However, they travelled under the direction of President Young until they reached this valley. When they entered it President Young pointed to that peak, and said he, "I want to go there." He went up to the point and said, "This is Ensign Peak."

Missionaries Sent to the Nations of the Earth to Gather Israel to the Mountains

Son Ahman, Your Lord, Speaketh of the Pure Governing Power of All Nations of Millennial Time of Holy Pure and Authoritative Governing of Celestial Power; My Holy Power of Eternal Celestial Authority:

Revelation of the Lord Jesus Christ Given to President Warren S. Jeffs Galveston, Texas Thursday, September 8, 2011

1. Thus saith God, over all, to all nations: My holy way shall be the Millennium of holy pure noble righteous power.

2. Let all know the holy way shall be known by the holy word of my testimony of the holy Prophets being of a fulfilling; even to gather to my Zion.

3. Let all know my time is soon at hand, to cleanse all peoples of every nation; leaving the way of pure power of Zion to be of your holy power of my sending.

4. Let all know I am soon to be of a full power to be among all people of every nation.

5. Let all come to my New Jerusalem as I establish my governing power over the whole earth.

6. Let all be of a hearing my doctrine of civil governing authority.

7. Let my holy will be thy way of the power to govern. Amen.

Isaiah 2 (Inspired Version)

1. The word that Isaiah the son of Amoz saw concerning Judah and Jerusalem:

2. And it shall come to pass in the last days, when the mountain of the Lord's house shall be established in the top of the mountains, and shall be exalted above the hills, and all nations shall flow unto it.

3. And many people shall go and say, Come ye, and let us go up to the mountain of the Lord, to the house of the God of Jacob; and he will teach us of his ways, and we will walk in his paths; for out of Zion shall go forth the law, and the word of the Lord from Jerusalem;

4. And he shall judge among the nations, and shall rebuke many people; and they shall beat their swords into plowshares, and their spears into pruning hooks; nation shall not lift up sword against nation, neither shall they learn war any more.

President Joseph Smith, Jun.
Teachings of the Prophet Joseph Smith, Page 92

Much has been said and done of late by the general government in relation to the Indians (Lamanites) within the territorial limits of the United States. One of the most important points in the faith of the Church of the Latter-day Saints, through the fullness of the everlasting Gospel, is the gathering of Israel (of whom the Lamanites constitute a part) that happy time when Jacob shall go up to the house of the Lord, to worship Him in spirit and in truth, to live in holiness; when the Lord will restore His judges as at the first, and His counselors as at the beginning;

when every man may sit under his own vine and fig tree, and there will be none to molest or make afraid; when He will turn to them a pure language, and the earth will be filled with sacred knowledge, as the waters cover the great deep; when it shall no longer be said, the Lord lives that brought up the children of Israel out of the land of Egypt, but the Lord lives that brought up the children of Israel from the land of the north, and from all the lands whither He has driven them. That day is one, all important to all men.

In view of its importance, together with all that the prophets have said about it before us, we feel like dropping a few ideas in connection with the official statements from the government concerning the Indians. In speaking of the gathering, we mean to be understood as speaking of it according to scripture, the gathering of the elect of the Lord out of every nation on earth, and bringing them to the place of the Lord of Hosts, when the city of righteousness shall be built, and where the people shall be of one heart and one mind, when the Savior comes: yea, where the people shall walk with God like Enoch, and be free from sin. The word of the Lord is precious; and when we read that the veil spread over all nations will be destroyed, and the pure in heart see God, and reign with Him a thousand years on earth, we want all honest men to have a chance to gather and build up a city of righteousness, where even upon the bells of the horses shall be written *"Holiness to the Lord."*

The Book of Mormon has made known who Israel is, upon this continent. And while we behold the government of the United States gathering the Indians, and locating them upon lands to be their own, how sweet it is to think that they may one day be gathered by the Gospel!

President Joseph Smith, Jun.
Teachings of the Prophet Joseph Smith, Page 183

The greatest temporal and spiritual blessings which always come from faithfulness and concerted effort, never attended individual exertion or enterprise. The history of all past ages abundantly attests this fact. In addition to all temporal blessings, there is no other way for the Saints to be saved in these last days, [than by the gathering] as the concurrent testimony of all the holy prophets clearly proves, for it is written -- "They shall come from the east, and be gathered from the west; the north shall give

up, and the south shall keep not back." "The sons of God shall be gathered from afar, and his daughters from the ends of the earth."

It is also the concurrent testimony of all the prophets, that this gathering together of all the Saints, must take place before the Lord comes to "take vengeance upon the ungodly," and "to be glorified and admired by all those who obey the Gospel." The fiftieth Psalm, from the first to the fifth verse inclusive, describes the glory and majesty of that event. (Jan. 8, 1841.) DHC 4:272.

President Joseph Smith, Jun.
Teachings of the Prophet Joseph Smith, Page 254

In regard to the building up of Zion, it has to be done by the counsel of Jehovah, by the revelations of heaven; and we should feel to say, "If the Lord go not with us, carry us not up hence." We would say to the Saints that come here, we have laid the foundation for the gathering of God's people to this place, and they expect that when the Saints do come, they will be under the counsel that God has appointed. The Twelve are set apart to counsel the Saints pertaining to this matter; and we expect that those who come here will send before them their wise men according to revelation; or if not practicable, be subject to the counsel that God has given, or they cannot receive an inheritance among the Saints, or be considered as God's people, and they will be dealt with as transgressors of the laws of God. We are trying here to gird up our loins, and purge from our midst the workers of iniquity; and we hope that when our brethren arrive from abroad, they will assist us to roll forth this good work, and to accomplish this great design that "Zion may be built up in righteousness; and all nations flock to her standard;" that as God's people, under His direction, and obedient to His law, we may grow up in righteousness and truth; that when His purposes shall be accomplished, we may receive an inheritance among those that are sanctified. (July 15, 1842.) DHC 5:61-66.

President Joseph Smith, Jun.
Teachings of the Prophet Joseph Smith, Page 308

It was the design of the councils of heaven before the world was, that the principles and laws of the priesthood should be predicated upon the gathering of the people in every age of the world. Jesus did everything to gather the people, and they would not be gathered, and He therefore poured out curses upon them. Ordinances instituted in the heavens before the foundation of the world, in the priesthood, for the salvation of men, are not to be altered or changed. All must be saved on the same principles.

President Joseph Smith, Jun.
Teachings of the Prophet Joseph Smith, Page 310

The doctrine of baptism for the dead is clearly shown in the New Testament; and if the doctrine is not good, then throw the New Testament away; but if it is the word of God, then let the doctrine be acknowledged; and it was the reason why Jesus said unto the Jews, "How oft would I have gathered thy children together, even as a hen gathereth her chickens under her wings, and ye would not!" -- that they might attend to the ordinances of baptism for the dead as well as other ordinances of the priesthood, and receive revelations from heaven, and be perfected in the things of the kingdom of God -- but they would not. This was the case on the day of Pentecost: those blessings were poured out on the disciples on that occasion. God ordained that He would save the dead, and would do it by gathering His people together.

President Brigham Young
JD 11:125 June 18, 1865 SLC

It is through the proclamation of the gospel that this great people have been gathered from their homes in distant parts of the earth. It is not in the power of man to accomplish such a work of gathering thousands of men, women, and children from different nations to a distant inland country, and unite them together and make of them a powerful nation. They heard the sound of the gospel, they repented of their sins, and were baptized for the remission of them, and received the Holy Ghost by the laying on of hands; this Spirit caused them to gather themselves together for the truth's sake; they came here because the voice of the Lord called them together from the ends of the earth. They needed not to be persuaded to gather themselves together, for they knew it was the will of God by the power of the Spirit which they had received through the ordinances of the gospel. Here sits brother George D. Watt, our reporter, who was the first man to receive the gospel in a foreign land; there had not been a word spoken to him about gathering to America; but he prophesied that the land of America was the land of Zion, and that the Lord would gather His people to that land in the last days, and thus he prophesied by the Spirit of prophecy which he had received by embracing the gospel.

Law of Eternal Marriage Made Known to All People as a Holy Way of Pure Holy Law of Exaltation

Son Ahman Saith Thus to the People of the Earth, of Full Way of Knowing I Am Continuing My Law of Celestial Union on the Land of Zion. Amen.

Revelation of the Lord Jesus Christ Given to President Warren S. Jeffs Galveston, Texas Thursday, September 8, 2011

1. Thus saith the Lord unto the people who are of holy and noble cause; unto a full and pure living my holy law of Eternal Power: My holy way is holy, pure, of Celestial Power of Eternal Union in holy marriage.

2. Let all know I sent my servant Brigham Young to reveal to the people of all nations my holy law must be lived to gain eternal exaltation. Thus did I cause all people to learn my holy way.

3. I am the Author of this holy law.

4. Let my people be of a full way of religious and of a pure living of this, my holy law of Eternal Power.

5. I am the God over all.

6. I shall fulfill my way of eternal and holy laws of Priesthood, not to be controlled by man's governing.

7. Thus do I give my way to all, that you may let alone my Celestial way, to be of a pure power of my revealing, unto the holy law of the government of heaven being a law of progress eternal. Thus do I reveal my holy law as a pure way eternal.

8. Let governing power of civil law

not be of a way of being of a governing my holy law.

9. I am the Giver of all my holy way Celestial.

10. Let my people be of a way of Eternal Union of holy religious living of constitutional guarantee of freedom of worship. Amen.

The Celestial Law Is Summarized as Perfect Christlike Obedience

President John Taylor
JD 26:350 February 20, 1884 SLC

That is taking this nation as an example, all laws that are proper and correct, and all obligations entered into which are not violative of the constitution should be kept inviolate. But if they are violative of the constitution, then the compact between the rulers and the ruled is broken and the obligation ceases to be binding. Just as a person agreeing to purchase anything and to pay a certain amount for it, if he receives the article bargained for, and does not pay its price, he violates his contract; but if he does not receive the article he is not required to pay for it. Again we ask, what is this celestial law? The celestial law above referred to is absolute submission and obedience to the law of God. It is exemplified in the words of Jesus, who, when He came to introduce the Gospel said, "I came not to do my will but the will of the Father that sent me;" and His mission was to do the will of the Father who sent him, or to fulfill a celestial law.

The Celestial Law to Be Lived in a Pure and Holy Way

President John Taylor
JD 24:295 October 7, 1883 SLC

We have embraced the Gospel. We have placed ourselves in another position from that of the world. We have entered into sacred covenants with the Lord, and He expects us to fulfill our covenants, and those who do not fulfill them will be condemned. There are certain rules and regulations that exist in the heavens, as well as on the earth. We are told that before we can enter into the celestial kingdom of God, we shall have to pass by the angels, and the Gods, and if the Latter-day Saints aim at a celestial exaltation, they must live and abide by the celestial law, or they will not get it, any more than the Gentiles will. Hear it, ye Latter-day Saints! God expects you to be pure, virtuous, holy, upright, prayerful, honest, obedient to His law, and not to follow the devices and desires of your own hearts. God has revealed many things to you, and He will reveal many more. He expects you to abide His law, and those who do not want to abide it, had better quit to-day, the sooner the better, for God expects us to do His will in all things.

Joseph F. Smith
Gospel Doctrine, Page 272

I desire to emphasize this. I want the young men of Zion to realize that this institution of marriage is not a man-made institution. It is of God. It is honorable, and no man who is of marriageable age is living his religion who remains single. It is not simply devised for the convenience alone of man, to suit his own notions, and his own ideas; to marry and then divorce, to adopt and then to discard, just as he pleases. There are great consequences connected with it, consequences which reach beyond this present time, into all eternity, for thereby souls are begotten into the world, and men and women obtain their being in the world. Marriage is the preserver of the human race. Without it, the purposes of God would be frustrated; virtue would be destroyed to give place to vice and corruption, and the earth would be void and empty.

President Brigham Young
JD 13:272 July 24, 1870 SLC

Should we not obey the requirements of Heaven? Certainly we should. Would it be the least injurious to the human family to receive the Gospel of the Son of God, and to have the man Christ Jesus to rule over them? Not at all; but, on the contrary, it would fill them with peace, joy, love, kindness, and intelligence. Would the principles of the Gospel, if obeyed, teach us to control ourselves? They would. They will teach men and women to govern and control their own passions.

President Brigham Young
JD 13:239 February 20, 1870 SLC

...I will say that the principle of patriarchal marriage is one of the highest and purest ever revealed to the children of men.

In the summer of 1852 the tenet of celestial or plural marriage -- commonly called polygamy -- which was destined to become in after years the leading question of the so-called "Utah Problem," was for the first time publicly proclaimed by the Church of Jesus Christ of Latter-day Saints. It had been practiced, as seen, at Nauvoo, and subsequently at Winter Quarters and in Utah; but up to this time the Church had never enunciated it. The practice, however, had long been evident, even to strangers visiting Utah; little or no effort being made by the Saints to conceal it. It had also been much commented upon, not only by such critics as Judge Brocchus and his colleagues, and others equally inimical to the Mormons, but by friendly visitors as well.***

It was during a special conference of the Church, held at Salt Lake City on the 28th and 29th of August, that the public avowal of plural marriage was made. The conference convened in the building which afterwards became known as the "Old Tabernacle," though it was then quite new, having been completed for dedication on the 6th of the preceding April.***

There on the 29th of August, 1852, the revelation on Celestial Marriage, first recorded from the lips of the Prophet Joseph Smith on July 12th, 1843, was read to the assembled Saints and sustained by the uplifted hands of the large congregation as a doctrine of their faith and a revelation from the Almighty. The same day Apostle Orson Pratt preached to the conference the first authorized public discourse on the subject of plural marriage. Thousands of copies of the revelation were published and circulated throughout the Union and carried by missionaries to various parts of the world. One of these is preserved in the Deseret Museum. It is the proof revised by Editor Willard Richards, and authenticated by James McKnight, at that time foreman of the *Deseret News*.

Temples Built by Priesthood for the Work of Holy Ordinances of Salvation

President Brigham Young
JD 18:262 October 8, 1876 SLC

Now, I will make a proposition, and you may have five years to do the work I am about to assign you. To the people of the Sevier Valley, Millard County, Iron County, Piute County, Beaver County, with Juab, Kane, Washington, and Sanpete Counties, I will say, Go to work and build a Temple in Sanpete. As soon as you are ready to commence, I will provide the plan. The ground is already selected. We do not ask whether you are able to do this; but ask yourselves if you have faith sufficient to do it, for we know that you are perfectly able to do it if you are willing, and do it inside of three years from next April. Then to the people of Box Elder County, the Malad Valley, Cache Valley, Soda Springs, and Bear Lake Valley, Rich County, and the people on Bear River, I say, unite your labor and commence as soon as you can to build a Temple in Cache Valley. Again, to the people of Weber County, Davis County, Morgan and Summit Counties, Salt Lake County, Tooele and Utah Counties, with the people east and west, I will say, Go to work and finish the Temple in this city forthwith. Can you accomplish the work, you Latter-day Saints of these several counties? Yes, that is a question I can answer readily, you are perfectly able to do it, the question is, Have you the necessary faith? Have you sufficient of the Spirit of God in your hearts to enable you to say, Yes, by the help of God our Father, we will erect these buildings to his name. There will be little money comparatively needed, it is nearly all labor, such as you can perform. If the people had paid their Tithing, and paid the hands employed on the Temple in proportion as I have done, that building would have been finished before now. But I am not obliged to build Temples for the people; this is our common duty, in order that all may have the privilege to officiate for themselves and their dead. How long, Latter-day Saints, before you will believe the Gospel as it is? The Lord has declared it to be his will that his people enter into covenant, even as Enoch and his people did, which of necessity must be before we shall have the privilege of building the Centre Stake of Zion, for the power and glory of God will be there, and none but the pure in heart will be able to live and enjoy it. Go to now, with your might and with your means, and finish this Temple. Why, for what reason? The reasons are very obvious, and you understand them.

President Joseph Smith, Jun.
Teachings of the Prophet Joseph Smith, Page 182

The Temple of the Lord is in process of

erection here, where the Saints will come to worship the God of their fathers, according to the order of His house and the powers of the Holy Priesthood, and will be so constructed as to enable all the functions of the Priesthood to be duly exercised, and where instructions from the Most High will be received, and from this place go forth to distant lands.

President Joseph Smith, Jun.
Teachings of the Prophet Joseph Smith, Page 224

Said that if the people had common sympathies they would rejoice that the sick could be healed; that the time had not been before that these things could be in their proper order; that the Church is not fully organized, in its proper order, and cannot be, until the Temple is completed, where places will be provided for the administration of the ordinances of the Priesthood.

President Joseph Smith, Jun.
Teachings of the Prophet Joseph Smith, Page 237

And the communications I made to this council were of things spiritual, and to be received only by the spiritual minded: and there was nothing made known to these men but what will be made known to all the Saints of the last days, so soon as they are prepared to receive, and a proper place is prepared to communicate them, even to the weakest of the Saints; therefore let the Saints be diligent in building the Temple, and all houses which they have been, or shall hereafter be, commanded of God to build; and wait their time with patience in all meekness, faith, perseverance unto the end, knowing assuredly that all these things referred to in this council are always governed by the principle of revelation. (May 4, 1842.) D.H.C. 5:1-2.

Holy Ordinances of the Temple

President Joseph Smith, Jun.
Teachings of the Prophet Joseph Smith, Page 330

But how are they to become saviors on Mount Zion? By building their temples, erecting their baptismal fonts, and going forth and receiving all the ordinances, baptisms, confirmations, washings, anointings, ordinations and sealing powers upon their heads, in behalf of all their progenitors who are dead, and redeem them that they may come forth in the first resurrection and be exalted to thrones of glory with them; and herein is the chain that binds the hearts of the fathers to the children, and the children to the fathers, which fulfills the mission of Elijah. And I would to God that this temple was now done, that we might go into it, and go to work and improve our time, and make use of the seals while they are on earth.

President Joseph Smith, Jun.
Teachings of the Prophet Joseph Smith, Page 362

The declaration this morning is, that as soon as the Temple and baptismal font are prepared, we calculate to give the Elders of Israel their washings and anointings, and attend to those last and more impressive ordinances, without which we cannot obtain celestial thrones. But there must be a holy place prepared for that purpose. *** These must, however, be a place built expressly for that purpose, and for men to be baptized for their dead. It must be built in this central place; for every man who wishes to save his father, mother, brothers, sisters and friends, must go through all the ordinances for each one of them separately, the same as for himself, from baptism to ordination, washing and anointings, and receive all the keys and powers of the Priesthood, the same as for himself.

President Brigham Young
JD 9:317 July 13, 1862 SLC

The servants of God will officiate for the dead in the temples of God which will be built. The Gospel is now preached to the spirits in prison, and when the time comes for the servants of God to officiate for them, the names of those who have received the Gospel in the spirit will be revealed by the angels of God and the spirits of just men made perfect; also the places of their birth, the age in which they lived, and everything regarding them that is necessary to be recorded on earth, and they will then be saved so as to find admittance into the presence of God, with their relatives who have officiated for them.

The Utah War

Evil Reports Against My Holy Law of Priesthood Ignite Bitter Attack of Governing Power

Orson F. Whitney
Popular History of Utah, Page 118

The trouble [Utah War] was caused by false reports of a rebellion in Utah, and the sending of Federal troops to put down the alleged uprising.***

One of the main causes of the misunderstanding was a letter written by Judge William W. Drummond to the Attorney-General of the United States, charging that the Supreme Court records at Salt Lake City had been destroyed with the direct knowledge and approval of Governor Brigham Young; that Federal officers had been grossly insulted for questioning the treasonable act; and that a condition of affairs existed calling for a change of Governors and for military aid to enable the new Executive to perform the duties of his office.

These were grave charges; but even worse were made. Judge Drummond intimated that the murder of Captain Gunnison, the death of Judge Shaver, and the killing of Secretary Babbitt had all been done by the advice and direction of the leading authorities of the "Mormon" Church; and he asserted that all who opposed those authorities, in any manner whatsoever, were harassed, insulted, and even murdered, by their orders or under their influence.

President Brigham Young
JD 5:77 July 26, 1857 SLC

What is now the news circulated throughout the United States? That Captain Gunnison was killed by Brigham Young, and that Babbitt was killed on the Plains by Brigham Young and his Danite band. What more? That Brigham Young has killed all the men who have died between the Missouri river and California. I do not say that President Buchanan has any such idea, or the officers of the troops who are reported to be on their way here; but such are the newspaper stories. Such reports are in the bellows, and editors and politicians are blowing them out.

According to their version, I am guilty of the death of every man, woman, and child that has died between the Missouri river and the California gold mines; and they are coming here to chastise me.

Lies of Apostate and Government Agents Rebuked by Brigham Young

President Brigham Young
JD 5:56 July 19, 1857 SLC

There is another item that I will touch upon. Two weeks ago to-day, I mentioned the course of some individuals in this place who are writing slanders concerning us, stating that a man cannot live here unless he is a "Mormon," when at the same time they come here to meeting with perfect impunity. Some of them are in the meeting to-day, and are now preparing lies for their letters. A parcel of them clan together and fix up letters, and they write to the East how desperately wicked the "Mormons" are -- how they are killing each other, killing the gentiles, stealing and robbing, and what wicked, miserable creatures the "Mormons" are. And when any of them go from here, they report, "We have barely escaped with our lives: Oh! it was a very narrow escape that we made; but we did manage to get out of the place with our lives; yes, we did get away without being killed." They all safely escape to tell their lies.

They say that it is with great difficulty that they can live with the Saints, when at the same time no one has molested them during all the time they have been writing lies to stir up the wicked to destroy us. They pass and repass in our streets with the same privileges that other citizens enjoy; and there are professedly of our faith those who sympathize for them. May God Almighty let His curse rest on all such sympathizers.

President Brigham Young
JD 8:323 February 10, 1861 SLC

One of the most contemptible of characters we ever had here could swear falsely in Washington, and the Government could receive his oath, and make it a basis, with other lies, of sending an army here. William Drummond went to Washington and swore that we were treasoners, and to many palpable falsehoods; and King James could act upon that and send an army here at an expense of, probably, fifty million dollars. Says King James -- "Those lies are true." "What! receive a lie?" Yes, go and swear to a lie, and the Government can hear that and act upon it. *** What a reign is the reign of King James! It is enough to astound and throw into the shade the wisdom of all nations upon the earth!

Orson F. Whitney
History of Utah, Volume 1 Page 584

Several other letters found their way to Washington before or soon after Judge Drummond's resignation, and though some were of too late a date to have influenced the original action of the Government in sending troops to Utah, others arrived in ample time to contribute to that end, and all serve to show the feeling of hostility that inspired the movement, and shaped the policy of the administration toward the people of this Territory at that interesting and critical point in their history.***

Along with the Magraw letter, which was merely the preface to Judge Drummond's book of blood and horror, the foregoing documents were presented by President Buchanan to Congress in 1858. Possibly it occurred to some of those astute lawyers and statesmen to enquire, after reading the charges relating to the murder of Captain Gunnison, Judge Shaver and Secretary Babbitt, what manner of men these Mormons were, to be suspected (?) of killing their best friends, and allowing their worst enemies, such as Judge Drummond, ex-mail contractor Magraw, Indian Agent Hurt and others, to say nothing of the Craigs and Kerrs, the Hockadays and Burrs, "Gentiles of Salt Lake City," to be among them, still alive, or to slip through the fingers of that awful "oath-bound organization," and escape unmolested from the Territory.***

Other Federal officials, writing from Utah, or filing their affidavits at the national capital, also contributed to stir up prejudice throughout the east against the Mormon people. Among these were Associate Justice Stiles, who had had a difficulty with several local members of the bar, and accused the Saints of intimidating his court. Indian Agent Hurt found fault with Brigham Young, as Superintendent of Indian Affairs, for his policy in relation to the red men, and intimated that the funds appropriated for them by Congress had been improperly expended. Mormon proselyting among the native tribes was represented as being highly prejudicial. Others, whose only grievance was that they hated Mormonism and all things connected with it, had complaints more or less trivial to lodge against the Mormon leader. In one of these the absurd charge was made that he opened and read all the letters that came into or went out of Utah.

It was upon such allegations as these, most of them utterly false, and the remainder grossly exaggerated, that President Buchanan, in the spring of 1857, without taking time to investigate as to their truth or falsity, decided that a rebellion existed in Utah, appointed a successor to Brigham Young as Governor of the Territory, and ordered an army to march to Salt Lake City to forcibly install and maintain in office the new Executive.

President Brigham Young
JD 5:125 August 9, 1857 SLC

Almost every man that has come from the East of late is telling you the political feelings and desires of the Government towards this people. Brother Taylor has just related that a gentleman he met on the road remarked, "What! can you 'Mormons' fight the United States? Can you contend with them? You had better take a more specific policy than you have. Do not speak about the President, nor about any of the officials." We shall talk as we please about them; for this is the right and privilege granted to us by the Constitution of the United States: and, as ministers of salvation, we shall take the liberty of telling men of their sins.

I shall take the liberty of talking as I please about the President of the United States, and I expect that I know his character better than he knows it himself.***

I wish that Hickory Jackson was now our President; for he would kick some of those rotten-hearted sneaks out, or rather order his negroes to do it. If we had a man in the chair who really was a man, and capable of magnifying his office, he would call upon his servants, and order him to kick those mean, miserable sneaks out of the presidential mansion, off from its grounds, and into the streets. But the President hearkens to the clamour around him; and, as did Pontius Pilate, in the case of Jesus Christ, has washed his hands, saying, "I am clear of the blood of those Latter-day Saints. Gentlemen, you have dictated, and I will order a soldiery and officials to Utah." It is said in the Bible, that whosoever ye yield yourselves to obey, his servants ye are. The President has yielded himself a servant to cliques and parties, and their servants he shall be. And all that has been spoken of him by brother Kimball, in the name of Jesus Christ, shall come upon him.

Do you think that we shall be called treasoners, for rebuking him in his sinful course? Yes. Talk of loyalty to Government! Hardly a man among them cares for the Government of the United States, any more than he does for the useless card that lies on the table while he is playing out his hand. They disregard the Constitution as they would any old fable in any old school book. Scarcely a member on the floor of Congress cares anything about it.***

With regard to the present contention and strife, and to our position and situation, there are few things to be considered, and there is much labour to be performed. Let the Saints live their religion; let them have faith in God, do all the good they can to the household of faith and to everybody else, and trust in God for the result; for the world will not believe one truth about us. I tell you that the Government of the United States, and other governments that are acquainted with us, will not believe a single truth about us. What will they believe? Every lie that every poor, miserable, rotten-hearted curse can tell. What are we to do, under these circumstances? Live our religion. Are you going to contend against the United States? No. But when they come here to take our lives solely for our religion, be ye also ready.

Do I expect to stand still, sit still, or lie still, and tamely let them take away my life? I have told you a great many times what I have to say about that. I do not profess to be so good a man as Joseph Smith was. I do not walk under their protection nor into their prisons, as he did. And though officers should pledge me their protection, as Governor Ford pledged protection to Joseph, I would not trust them any sooner than I would a wolf with my dinner; neither do I trust in a wicked judge, nor in any evil person. I trust in my God, and in honest men and women who have the power of the Almighty upon them. What will we do? Keep the wicked off as long as we can, preach righteousness to them, and teach them the way of salvation.

Public Outcry Against Brigham Young in the United States Causes President Buchanan to Remove Him as Governor of the Territory

President Brigham Young
JD 4:41 August 31, 1856 SLC

I am still governor of this Territory, to the constant chagrin of my enemies; but I do not in the least neglect the duties of my Priesthood, nor my office as governor; and while I honor my Priesthood I will do honor to my office as governor. This is hard to be understood by the wicked, but it is true. The feelings of many are much irritated because I am here, and Congress has requested the President to inquire why I still hold the office of governor in the Territory of Utah. I can answer that question; I hold the office by appointment, and am to hold it until my successor is appointed and qualified, which has not yet been done. I shall bow to Jesus, my Governor, and under him, to brother Joseph. Though he has gone behind the vail, and I cannot see him, he is my head, under Jesus Christ and the ancient Apostles, and I shall go ahead and build up the kingdom. But if I was now sitting in the chair of state at the White House in Washington, everything in my office would be subject to my religion. Why? Because it teaches me to deal justice and mercy to all. I am satisfied to love righteousness and be full of the Holy Ghost, while all hell yawns to destroy me, though it cannot do it.

Utah Was at Peace While Government Was at Way of War

Orson F. Whitney
History of Utah, Volume 1 Page 612

Governor Young: -- "I deny that any books of the United States have been burned. All I ask of any man is, that he tell the truth about us, pay his debts and not steal, and then he will be welcome to come or go as he likes. I have broken no law, and under the present state of affairs I will not suffer myself to be taken by any United States officer, to be killed as they killed Joseph."

George A. Smith
JD 11:181 October 8, 1865 SLC

The administration of President Buchanan brought the power of the Government to bear against us. The traitor, General A. S. Johnston, was sent with what was then called by Secretary Floyd the best appointed army that was ever fitted ont [out] by this Government since its formation. General Scott issued orders to keep the troops massed and in hand, the supply trains to be kept with the main body of the army. The newspaper press of the country asserted that this army was to cause the blood of the Elders and Saints to flow in the streets of Great Salt Lake City. The mails being stopped, and the ordinary sources of communication closed, it was supposed the "Mormons" would be ignorant of the movements until the army came upon them like a thunder cloud. The Governorship was tendered to a number who were unwilling to come out with a formidable army, but were willing to come without. Benjamin McCullough, of Texas, declined the honor on the ground that a confirmed old bachelor ought not to interfere with polygamy. Colonel Alfred Cumming accepted the office, and his appointment was hailed with general acclamation by the enemies of Utah, as he was considered a man of desperate character, who had on one occasion compelled even Jeff. Davis to apologise. When Governor Cumming arrived here and investigated the matter, he was satisfied that the Administration had been duped, and he made official reports to Washington that the charges against the Saints were totally unfounded, and the Administration let the whole matter fizzle out, and Uncle Sam, the generous old gentleman, had to submit to his pocket being picked to the tune of about forty millions of dollars -- the cost of the Utah expedition.

President Brigham Young
JD 5:226 September 13, 1857 SLC

I have been in this kingdom a good while -- twenty-five years and upwards, and I have been driven from place to place; my brethren have been driven, my sisters have been driven; we have been scattered and peeled, and every time without any provocation upon our part, only that we were united, obedient to the laws of the land, and striving to worship God. Mobs repeatedly gathered against this people, but they never had any power to prevail until Governors issued their orders and called out a force under the letter of the law, but breaking the spirit, to hold the "Mormons" still while infernal scamps cut their throats. I have had all that before me through the night past, and it makes me too angry to preach. Also to see that we are in a Government whose administrators are always trying to injure us, while we are constantly at the defiance of all hell to prove any just grounds for their hostility against us; and yet they are organizing their forces to come here, and protect infernal scamps who are anxious to come and kill whom they please, destroy whom they please, and finally exterminate the "Mormons."***

On the 24th of July last, a number of us went to Big Cottonwood Kanyon to pass the anniversary of our arrival into this Valley. Ten years ago the 24th of July last, a few of the Elders arrived here, and began to plough and to plant seeds, to raise food to sustain themselves. Whilst speaking to the brethren on that day, I said, inadvertently. If the people of the United States will let us alone for ten years, we will ask no odds of them; and ten years from that very day, we had a message by brothers Smoot, Stoddard, and Rockwell, that the Government had stopped the mail, and that they had ordered 2,500 troops to come here and hold the "Mormons" still, while priests, politicians, speculators, whoremongers, and every mean, filthy character that could be raked up should come here and kill off the "Mormons." I did not think about what I had said ten years ago, till I heard that the President of the United States had so unjustly ordered troops here; and then I said, when my former expression came to my mind, In the name of Israel's God, we ask no odds of them.

I do not often get angry; but when I do, I am righteously angry; and the bosom of the Almighty burns with anger towards those scoundrels; and they shall be consumed, in the name of Israel's God. We have borne enough of their oppression and hellish abuse, and we will not bear any more of it; for there is no just law requiring further forbearance on our part. And I am not going to have troops here to protect the priests and a hellish rabble in efforts to drive us from the land we possess; for the Lord does not want us to be driven, and has said, "If you will assert your rights, and keep my commandments, you shall never again be brought into bondage by your enemies."***

Well, the enquiry is, "What is the news? What is the conclusion?" It is this -- We have to trust in God. I am not in the least concerned as to the result, if we put our trust in God. The administrators of our Government have issued orders for marching troops and expending much treasure, and all predicated upon falsehoods, while every honourable man would have first made an economical and peaceful enquiry into the circumstances. And even now, every honourable man would use all his influence to avert the present unjust and entirely groundless movement against us; but Captains, Majors, Colonels, and other subordinate officers have not the power. Wicked persons, solely for the accomplishment of their unhallowed schemes, have had the power to array the Government against us, through their lying and misrepresentation; but citizens, unorganized into cliques and parties, no matter how good their intentions and wishes, have not the power to avert the blow when the Administration of our Government is arrayed against us, unless they will also unite against the few well-organized scoundrels who are plundering our treasury and fast urging our country to dissolution. We have got to protect ourselves by the strength of our God. Do not be concerned in the least with regard to all the affairs that are before you; for we shall live and grow finely, as said a certain woman, who weighed but two pounds when an infant, and was put in quart cup. Upon being asked whether she lived, "O yes," she said, "I lived and grew finely." It will also be said of the Latter-day Saints, "They lived and grew finely."***

Do not be angry. I will permit you to be as angry as I am. Do not get so angry that you cannot pray: do not allow yourselves to become so angry that you cannot feed an enemy -- even your worst enemy, if an opportunity should present itself. There is a wicked anger, and there is a righteous anger. The Lord does not suffer wicked anger to be in his heart; but there is anger in his bosom, and he will hold a controversy with the nations, and will sift them, and no power can stay his hand.

The Government of our country will go by the board through its own corruptions, and no power can save it. If we can avert the blow for another season, it is probable that our enemies will have enough to attend to at home, without worrying the Latter-day Saints. Have faith, and all will be well with us. I would like this people to have faith enough to turn away their enemies. I have prayed fervently about this matter; for it has been said that the troops would come: but I have said that, if my faith will prevent it, they shall not come.

Message of Governor Brigham Young to the Legislature

President Brigham Young
Millennial Star 20:235 December 15, 1857 SLC

The members and officers of the last Legislative Assembly, familiar with the evils visited upon the innocent by the miserably bad conduct of certain officials heretofore sent here by Government, knowing that all republican governments -- which both our General and State Governments are, in form--are based upon the principle that the governed shall enjoy the right to elect their own officers and be guided by laws having their own consent, and, perfectly aware that, by the Constitution, residents in Territories are guaranteed that great right equally with residents in States (for Congress has not one particle more constitutional power to legislate for and officer Americans in Territories than they have to legislate for and officer Americans in States), respectfully memorialized the President and Senate to appoint officers for Utah in accordance with an accompanying list, containing the names of persons who were her first choice for the offices placed opposite those names; but, if that selection did not meet with approval, they were solicited to make the appointments from a list containing other and a larger number of names of residents, who were also the choice of the people; and if that selection was also rejected, to appoint from any part of the Union, with the simple request, in such event, that the appointees be good men. In this matter of appointment of officers, what more rights could the most tyrannical in a republican government ask a Territory to waive? Yet, up to this date, no official information concerning the action, if any, taken upon that memorial has ever reached us.

Time glided by, and travellers and newspapers began to confirm the rumour that the present Executive and a part of his Cabinet had yielded to the rabid clamour raised against Utah by lying editors, corrupt demagogues, heartless office-hunters, and the ignorant rabble, incited by numbers of the hireling clergy, and were about to send an army to Utah with the sole and avowed purpose, as published in almost every newspaper, of compelling American citizens, peacefully, loyally, and lawfully occupying American soil, to forego the dearest constitutional rights, to abandon their religion, to wallow in the mire and worship at the shrine of modern civilization and Christianity, or be expelled from the country or exterminated. Where now are constitutional rights? Who is laying the axe at the root of the tree of liberty? Who are the usurpers? Who the tyrants? Who the traitors? Most assuredly those who are madly urging measures to subvert the genius of free institutions and those principles of liberty upon which our Government is based, and to overthrow virtue, independence, justice, and true intelligence, the loss of either of which by the people, the celebrated Judge Story has wisely affirmed, would be the ruin of our Republic -- the destruction of its vitality. And ex-President James Madison, among other purposes, declared it to be the purpose of Government "to avoid the slightest interference with the rights of conscience or the functions of religion, so wisely exempted from civil jurisdiction."

Has Utah ever violated the least principle of the Constitution, or so much as broken the most insignificant constitutional enactment? No; nor have we the most distant occasion for so doing, but have ever striven to peacefully enjoy and extend those rights granted to all by a merciful Creator. But so unobtrusive and wise a course does not seem to please those who live and wish to live by office and those who make and love lies; and since those characters are numerous, and also powerful through well-disciplined organization, and since Utah has yielded right after right for the sake of peace, until her policy has emboldened the enemies of our Union, it must needs be that President Buchanan, if he has ordered an army to Utah, as reported -- for he has not officially notified me of such a movement by his order -- has at length succumbed, either of choice or through being overcome, to the cruel and nefarious counsels of those enemies, and is endeavouring to carry out a usurpation of power which of right belongs only to the people, by appointing civil officers known to be justly objectionable to freemen, and sending a so-called army under mere colour of law, to force those officers upon us at the point of the bayonet, and to form a nucleus for the collection and protection of every gambler, cut-throat, whore-master, and scoundrel who may choose to follow in their train. Such a treasonable system of operations will never be endured, nor even countenanced, by any person possessed of the least spark of patriotism and love of constitutional liberty. The President knew, if he knew the facts in the case, as he was in duty bound to do before taking action, that the officials hitherto sent here had been invariably received and treated with all the respect their offices demanded, and that a portion of them had met with far more courtesy than elsewhere would have been extended to them or their conduct deserved; he also knew, or had the privilege of knowing,

that the Memorial to the last Assembly, as already stated, respectfully informed him that Utah wished good men for officers, and that such officers would be cordially welcomed and obeyed; but that we would not again tamely endure the abuse and misrule meted by official villians, as were some who have formerly officiated here. Such being a few of the leading facts, what were the legitimate inferences to be drawn from the rumours that the President had sent a batch of officials, with an army to operate as their *posse*? That he had wilfully made the official appointments for Utah from a class other than good men, and placed himself, where tyrants often are, in the position of levying war against the very nation whose choice had made him its chief executive officer.

Fully aware, as has been justly written, that "patriotism does not consist in aiding Government in every base or stupid act it may perform, but rather in paralyzing its power when it violates vested rights, affronts insulted justice, and assumes undelegated authority," and knowing that the so-called army, reported to be on its way to Utah, was an undisguised mob, if not sent by the President of the United States, and if sent by him in the manner and for the purpose alleged in all the information permitted to reach us, was no less a mob, though in the latter event acting under colour of law, upon learning its near approach, I issued, as in constitutional duty bound, a Proclamation, expressly forbidding all bodies of armed men, under whatsoever name or by whomsoever sent, to come within the bounds of this Territory. That so-called army, or, more strictly speaking, mob, refused to obey that Proclamation, copies of which were officially furnished them, and prosecuted their march to the neighbourhood of Forts Bridger and Supply, (which were vacated and burnt upon their approach,) where it is said they intend to winter. Under these circumstances, I respectfully suggest that you take such measures as your enlightened judgment may dictate, to insure public tranquility and protect, preserve, and perpetuate inviolate those inalienable constitutional rights which have descended to us -- a rich legacy from our forefathers.

A civilized nation is one that never infringes upon the rights of its citizens, but strives to protect and make happy all within its sphere, which our Government, above all others, is obligated to accomplish, though its present course is as far from that wise and just path as the earth is from the sun. And, under the aggravated abuses that have been heaped upon us in the past, you and the whole people are my witnesses that it has more particularly fallen to my lot, and been my policy and practice to restrain rather than urge resistance to usurpation and tyranny on the part of the enemies to the Constitution and Constitutional laws, (who are also our enemies and the enemies of all republics and republicans,) until forbearance under such cruel and illegal treatment cannot well be longer exercised. No one has denied or wishes to deny the right of the Government to send its troops when, where, and as it pleases, so it is but done clearly within the authorities and limitations of the Constitution, and for the safety and welfare of the people: but when it sends them clearly without the pale of those authorities and limitations, unconstitutionally to oppress the people, as is the case in the so-called army sent to Utah, it commits a treason against itself, which commands the resistance of all good men, or freedom will depart our nation.

In compliance with a long-established custom in appointing officers not of the people's electing, which the Supreme Court of the United States would at once, in justice, decide to be unconstitutional, we have petitioned and petitioned that good men be appointed, until that hope is exhausted; and we have long enough borne the insults and outrages of lawless officials, until we are compelled, in self-defense, to assert and maintain that great constitutional right of the governed to officers of their own election and local laws of their own enactment. That the President and the counsellors, aiders and abettors of the present treasonable crusade against the peace and rights of a Territory of the United States may reconsider their course and retrace their steps, is earnestly to be desired. But, in either event, our trust and confidence are in that Being who at his pleasure rules among the armies of heaven and controls the wrath of the children of men; and most cheerfully should we be able to abide the issue.

Permit me to tender you my entire condence [confidence] that your deliberations will be distinguished by that wisdom, unanimity, and love of justice that have ever marked the counsels of our Legislative Assemblies, and the assurance of my hearty co-operation in every measure you adopt for promoting the true interest of a Territory beloved by us for its very isolation and forbidding aspect; for here, if anywhere upon this footstool of our God, have we the privilege and prospect of being able to secure and enjoy those inestimable rights of civil and religious liberty, which the beneficent Creator of all mankind has, in His mercy, made indefeasible, and perpetuate them upon a broader and firmer basis for the benefit of ourselves, of our children, and our children's children, until peace shall be restored to our distracted country.

BRIGHAM YOUNG.

The Army of Aggression of Illegal Sending Was of a Resistance to Enter the Capital City of Utah Territory by Territorial Governing Power

President Brigham Young
JD 5:210 September 6, 1857 SLC

On Friday evening, the 11th inst., two of the brethren who accompanied brothers Samuel W. Richards and George Snider from Deer Creek to 118 miles below Laramie, came in, and reported that soldiers and a heavy freight train were there encamped opposite to them and on the south side of the Platte. They could tell that they were soldiers, from the appearance of their carriages, waggons, tents, and mode of encampment. We did not learn anything very definite from these two brethren lately arrived.

Messrs. Russel and Waddle are freighting for Government, and some of their trains were scattered along to the Sweetwater. They have twenty-six waggons in each train, with a teamster and six yoke of oxen to a waggon. Some of those trains were on the Sweetwater when brother Samuel passed down, and quite a number of them are in advance of the soldiers. The brethren learned that Captain Van Vliet, Assistant Quartermaster, was coming on to purchase lumber and such things as might be needed for the army.

Last evening, brother John R. Murdock arrived direct from St. Louis. He left here with the mail on the 2nd day of July, and reached Independence in sixteen days, making by far the shortest trip on record, and in eighteen days-and-a-half from here landed in St. Louis. He tarried there till brother Horace S. Eldredge and brother Groesbeck had transacted some business, and then started up the river with a small train. On the 9th of August, brother Murdock left Atchison, K.T. Troubles were daily expected to break out in Kansas between the Republican, or Free State, and the pro-slavery parties; for which reason General Harney, with the cavalry, a portion of the infantry, and, I think, one or two companies of the Artillery, were detained there by orders from Washington, and Colonel Johnston ordered to assume the command of the army for Utah.

Some fifteen or sixteen hundred infantry started from Leavenworth; and when brother Murdock passed them, one hundred miles below Laramie, about five hundred had deserted, leaving, as he was told, about one thousand men on their way to this place. He passed a few freight trains, which were entirely deserted by the teamsters, and Russel and Waddle were not able to hire teamsters to bring those trains forward.

Brother Murdock did not think that they could get here this fall, unless we helped them in. Their teams are pretty good, but they are very much jaded. Their mule teams are in better condition, because they regularly feed them on grain.

From the time that I heard that the President of the United States had issued orders for soldiers to come here, they have had my best faith that the Lord would not let them get here. I have seen this people, when palsied with agues, fevers, and with various other diseases, hurled out of doors, driven away from their cellars full of potatoes, from their meal chests, from their cows, houses, barns, orchards, fields, and finally from their happy homes and all the comforts of life. I have seen that a good many times, and I pray that I may never see it again, unless it is absolutely necessary for the welfare and advancement of God's purposes on the earth. I want to see no more suffering. I will not use the word suffering, for I call it joy instead of sorrow, affliction, and suffering. If we live our religion and exercise faith, it is our firm belief that it is our right to so exercise our united faith that our enemies never can come here, unless the Lord in his providence sees that it will be for our good.

It is my faith and feelings that, if we live as we should live, they cannot come here; but I am decided in my opinion that, if worse comes to worst, and the Lord permits them to come upon us, I will desolate this whole Territory before I will again submit to the hellish corruption and bondage the wicked are striving to thrust upon us solely for our exercising our right of freedom of conscience.***

Orson F. Whitney
History of Utah, Volume 1 Page 631

At all events, no delay was now made in taking action calculated to convince the troops and the Government which sent them that Brigham Young and his people were in earnest, and that not without a struggle to prevent would they permit the army now east of the Wasatch Mountains to invade and occupy their valley homes. At the same time it was determined to shed no blood, to take no life if it could possibly be avoided. Such were the orders issued to the militia.***

It was a bloodless campaign that the Mormons were resolved upon, even against the armed force which they believed had been sent to kill or drive them from their homes, debauch their wives and daughters, and despoil them of all that life held dear. Moreover, the plan of that campaign had been matured in the leading councils of the Church at Salt Lake City, weeks before General Wells went to the front.

On the return of the messengers with Colonel Alexander's reply, they were invited to dine with the Lieutenant-General. During the progress of the meal he asked Major Lot Smith if he thought he could take a few men and turn back the Government supply trains that were on the way, or burn them?

"I think I can do anything that you tell me to," was the confident reply.

Pleased with the ready response, General Wells then said: "I can furnish you only a few men, but they will be sufficient, for they will seem many more to the enemy. As for provisions, none will be supplied, as you are expected to board at the expense of Uncle Sam."

Lot Smith understood the order, and the program laid out was much to his liking. Utterly devoid of fear, with a physique and a will of iron, he was admirably fitted for just such a daring and dangerous feat as the one proposed. Forty-three men were given him, Captain Horton D. Haight and Lieutenants Thomas Abbott and John Vance being his subordinate officers, and at 4 o'clock p. m. of October 3rd they set out toward Green River.

Orson F. Whitney
History of Utah, Volume 1 Page 638

Thus it was that Lot Smith burnt the Government trains. It was a daring act in itself, but not more daring than the order which directed it. If the Mormons were accused of treason before they had done anything affording the shadow of a basis for such a charge, and an army had been sent against them to suppress a rebellion which never existed, what would now be said and done in view of events that had actually taken place? But Brigham Young and his compeers were perfectly aware of the risk they were running. They had entered upon the campaign with their eyes wide open. An investigation, a hearing was what they desired. It had hitherto been denied them.***...President Buchanan, on finding that the Mormons were in earnest, and that in their efforts to maintain their rights they dared even burn Government property and paralyze for the time being the arm lifted to strike them, was finally constrained, after the first burst of indignation was over, to order an investigation into the Utah situation.

Brigham Young Meeting With Peace Commissioners June 12, 1858

President Brigham Young
History of Utah, Volume 1 Page 683

"I have listened very attentively to the Commissioners, and will say, as far as I am concerned, I thank President Buchanan for forgiving me, but I really cannot tell what I have done. I know one thing, and that is, that the people called 'Mormons' are a loyal and a law-abiding people, and have ever been. Neither President Buchanan nor any one else can contradict the statement. It is true, Lot Smith burned some wagons containing Government supplies for the army. This was an overt act, and if it is for this we are to be pardoned, I accept the pardon.

*   *   *   *   *   *   *   *   *

"What has the United States Government permitted mobs to do to us? Gentlemen, you cannot answer that question! I can, however, and so can thousands of my brethren. We have been whipped and plundered; our houses burned, our fathers, mothers, brothers, sisters and children butchered and murdered by the scores. We have been driven from our homes time and time again; but have troops ever been sent to stay or punish those mobs for their crimes? No! Have we ever received a dollar for the property we have been compelled to leave behind? Not a dollar! Let the Government treat us as we deserve; this is all we ask of them. We have always been loyal, and expect to so continue; but, *hands off!* Do not send your armed mobs into our midst. If you do, we will fight you, as the Lord lives! Do not threaten us with what the United States can do, for we ask no odds of them or their troops. We have the God of Israel-the God of battles on our side; and let me tell you, gentlemen, we fear not your armies.

*   *   *   *   *   *   *   *   *

"Now let me say to you Peace Commissioners, we are willing those troops should come into our country, but not to stay in our city. They may pass through it, if needs be, but must not quarter less than forty miles from us.

"If you bring your troops here to disturb this people, you have got a bigger job than you or President Buchanan have any idea of. Before the troops reach here, this city will be in ashes, every tree and shrub will be cut to the ground, and every blade of grass that will burn shall be burned.

"Our wives and children will go to the canyons, and take shelter in the mountains; while their husbands and sons will fight you; and, as God lives, we will hunt you by night and by day, until your armies are wasted away. No mob can live in the homes we have built in these mountains. That's the program, gentlemen, whether you like it or not. If you want war, you can have it; but, if you wish peace, peace it is; we shall be glad of it."

President Brigham Young
JD 5:337 October 18, 1857 SLC

Should we ever be obliged to leave our houses, the decree of my heart is that there shall naught be left for our enemies but the ashes of all that will burn. [The congregation responded, "Amen."] They shall not have my house nor my furniture, as they have had hitherto.***

We have sought for peace all the day long; and I have sought for peace with the army now on our borders, and have warned them that we all most firmly believe that they are sent here solely with a view to destroy this people, though they may be ignorant of that fact. And though we may believe that they are sent by the Government of the United States, yet I, as Governor of this Territory, have no business to know any such thing until I am notified by proper authority at Washington. I have a right to treat them as a mob, just as though they had been raised and officered in Missouri and sent here expressly to destroy this people. We have been very merciful and very lenient to them. As I informed them in my unofficial letter, had they been those mobocrats who mobbed us in Missouri, they never would have seen the South Pass. We had plenty of boys on hand, and the mode of warfare they would have met with they are not acquainted with.***

Colonel Alexander preached to me a little, stating in his letter, "I warn you that the bloodshed in this contest will be upon your head." But that warning gave me no thought. But if the blood of those soldiers is shed, it will be upon the heads of their officers.***

I wish the people to hasten and gather together and secure all that they have raised in the fields; and when this little skirmish is over, I am going to instruct the people to begin to prepare for going into the mountains, also to raise their grain another year, and to secure that which we now have by putting it where our enemies cannot find it.

You want to know where you can go. I know of places enough where I can hide this people and a thousand times more, and our enemies may hunt till doomsday and not be able to find us.

I do not know but we shall call upon the sisters to go into the fields and raise potatoes while their husbands go out to war; and if they can do that, then perhaps we will see whether they can go into the fields and raise wheat while their husbands are defending Zion. In such an operation we shall call for volunteers; we shall have no compulsion about it.***

The President of the United States, his Cabinet, the Senate, the House of Representatives, the priests of the various religious sects and their followers have joined in a crusade to waste away the last vestige of truth and righteousness from this earth, and especially from this part of it. Yes, they have joined together; and we have to maintain truth and righteousness, virtue and holiness, or they will be driven from the earth. With us, it is the kingdom of God, or nothing; and we will maintain it, or die in trying, -- though we shall not die in trying. It is comforting to many to be assured that we shall not die in trying, but we shall live in trying. We will maintain the kingdom of God, living; and if we do not maintain it, we shall be found dying not only a temporal, but also an eternal death. Then take a course to live.***

We are free. There is no yoke upon us now, and we will never put it on again. [The congregation responded, "Amen."] That is the way for every man and woman to feel.***

You hear a great many people talk about a virtuous life. If you could know what an honourable, manly, upright, virtuous life is, you might reduce it to this -- Learn the will of the Lord and do it; for he has the keys of life and death, and his mandates should be obeyed, and that is eternal life.

President Brigham Young
Millennial Star 32:577 July 25, 1870

I will just relate a little of the history of this people. When they commenced in the East the war of James Buchanan against the Latter-day Saints, they sent the flower of the army here, with the best outfit any army had ever had in this Republic up to that time. What for? To use the Saints up. The army and the hangers-on amounted to 17,000 men. We then said to the North, "give up," but did not say to the South, "keep not back." The North gave up. Every family was on the move; they marched through this city south. We calculated to march south to where our women and children could live and take care of our stock, and we would wait in the mountains, and burn everything. That was the watchword. Our tinder and every material that could be was got into the houses, so that a single match would burn every house in this city, and then continue on until they would cease to pursue us, and if they inhabited these valleys they should have them as naked as we took them. And the North did give up; they gave up willingly. They had good houses and good farms, and they were ready to cut down every green tree. You may say such a course was not necessary. It was not necessary for us to be forced to it.

President Buchanan Pardons Brigham Young

President Brigham Young
JD 11:322 February 10, 1867

We had to leave, and we have come here into these mountains, and do you think we are going to be swallowed up by our enemies? Why, they have already done their uttermost. "Could they not send a hundred thousand men here to destroy the 'Mormons?'" Yes; that is, they could try. In the winter of 1857-58, when the army was at Bridger, Col. Kane came here to see what he could do for the benefit of the people, and to caution and advise me. He was all the time fearful that I would not take the right step, and that I would do something or other that would bring upon us the ire of the nation. "Why," said he, "at one word there would be a hundred thousand men ready to come here." I replied that "I would like to see them trying it." Afterwards a calculation was made that, for men to come here.--tarry through the winter and get back the next summer, it would require four and a half oxen to carry the food, clothing, and ammunition necessary for each man. This was more stock than they could take care of, to say nothing about fighting. I was resolved that they would find nothing here to eat, nor houses to live in, for we were determined that we would not leave a green thing, and if I had time not one adobie should be left standing on another. I was satisfied that if Col. Kane could see what I saw, he would know that the weight of such an army would be so ponderous that it would crush itself, and it could never get here. It is just so now, too.

James Buchanan did all he could do, and when he found he could do nothing, he sent a pardon here. What did he pardon us for? He was the man that had transgressed the laws, and had trampled the Constitution of the United States under his feet. We had neither transgressed against the one nor violated the other. But we did receive his pardon, you know, and when they find out they can do nothing they will be sending on their pardons again.

President Brigham Young
JD 7:56 June 27, 1858 Provo

What is the present situation of affairs? For us the clouds seem to be breaking. Probably many of you have already learned that General Johnston passed through Great Salt Lake City with his command under the strictest discipline. Not a house, fence, or side-walk has been infringed upon by any of his command. Of course, the camp-followers are not under his control; but so far as his command is concerned while passing through the city, he has carried out his promises to the letter.

Crusade Against Celestial Plural Marriage

Congress Passes an Anti-Polygamy Act -- 1862

Orson F. Whitney
History of Utah, Volume 2 Page 59

But there was also another barrier to Utah's admission [into statehood], and probably at this period it was the main objection in the minds of the majority of congressmen. It was the Mormon practice of plural marriage -- polygamy -- which the Republican party, now in power, in its original platform had coupled with slavery and stigmatized them as "twin relics of barbarism." It was rather too much to expect that the Republicans, now in the overwhelming majority in Congress, and consequently having the power to invest Utah with statehood if they so desired, would use that power in her behalf, in view of their recent declaration against polygamy, thereby placing a cudgel in the hands of their political opponents from whom they had but just succeeded in wresting the reins of national authority. Had the Mormons been willing to abandon polygamy in 1862, thus meeting the Republican party half way, it is not improbable that Utah, in view of her loyal attitude, might have been admitted into the Union; provided of course that the bug-bear of an alleged union of Church and State, of priestly influence in the politics of the Territory, had not acted as a deterrent to those who, barring these considerations, professed to be friendly to her people.

Possibly it was to help solve this problem, -- to assist the Mormons to arrive at a conclusion to forsake the plural wife practice and "be like the rest" of the nation, as to monogamy, divorce, etc., that a bill was introduced in Congress in the spring of this same year, only a few weeks after the action of the State Convention of Deseret, to punish and prevent the practice of polygamy in the Territories, and, as afterwards appeared, to disincorporate the Church of Jesus Christ of Latter-day Saints. If this hypothesis be correct, the Mormons were to receive equal rights with and be treated like the rest of American citizens, if they would put away their Mormonism and thenceforth cease to be a distinct people. General Clark, at Far West, in 1838, had made them essentially the same offer.

The bill in question was introduced in the House of Representatives on the 8th of April, 1862, by Justin S. Morrill, of Vermont. It was read twice and referred to the Committee on Territories. Being reported back on April 28th with a recommendation that it pass, the bill -- H. R. No. 391 -- was again read.***

Orson F. Whitney
History of Utah, Volume 2 Page 61

The anti-polygamy bill, having passed the House, came up in the Senate on the 3rd of June.***

The yeas and nays were ordered, and being taken, resulted -- yeas 37, nays 2.***

So the bill was passed.

The title was amended so as to read, "A bill to punish and prevent the practice of polygamy in the Territories of the United States and other places, and disapproving and annulling certain acts of the Legislative Assembly of the Territory of Utah."***

In the House of Representatives, June 30, 1862 --

Mr. Granger, from the Committee on Enrolled Bills, reported as a truly enrolled bill an act (H. R. 391) to punish and prevent the practice of polygamy in the Territories of the United States and other places, and disapproving and annulling certain acts of the Legislative Assembly of the Territory of Utah.

President Abraham Lincoln Signs the Anti-Polygamy Act

It has often been stated that the anti-polygamy act of 1862, became law without the signature of President Lincoln. This is an error, as the following paragraph of the record already quoted from will testify:

"In the House of Representatives, July 2, 1862 --

"A message was received from the President of the United States, informing the House that he had approved and signed an act (H. R. 391) to punish and prevent the practice of polygamy in the Territories of the United States and other places, and disapproving and annulling certain acts of the Legislative Assembly of the Territory of Utah." The full text of this enactment was as follows:

The Morrill Bill

Be it enacted, etc.:

That every person having a husband or wife living, who shall marry any other person, whether married or single, in a Territory of the United States, or other place over which the United States have exclusive jurisdiction, shall, except in the cases specified in the proviso to this section, be adjudged guilty of bigamy, and, upon conviction thereof, shall be punished by a fine not exceeding five hundred dollars, and by imprisonment for a term not exceeding five years. *Provided nevertheless*, That this section shall not extend to any person by reason of any former marriage whose husband or wife by such marriage shall have been absent for five successive years without being known to such person within that time to be living; nor to any person by reason of any former marriage which shall have been dissolved by the decree of a competent court; nor to any person by reason of any former marriage which shall have been annulled or pronounced void by the sentence or decree of a competent court on the ground of nullity of the marriage contract.

And be it further enacted:

SEC. 2. That the following ordinance of the provisional government of the State of Deseret, so called, namely: "An ordinance incorporating the Church of Jesus Christ of Latter-day Saints, passed February eight, in the year eighteen hundred and fifty-one, and adopted, re-enacted, and made valid by the Governor and Legislative Assembly of the Territory of Utah, by an act passed January nineteen, in the year eighteen hundred and fifty-five, entitled "An act in relation to the compilation and revision of the laws and resolutions in force in Utah Territory, their publication, and distribution," and all other acts and parts of acts heretofore passed by the said Legislative Assembly of the Territory of Utah, which establish, support, maintain, shield, or countenance polygamy, be, and the same hereby are, disapproved and annulled: *Provided,* That this act shall be so limited and construed as not to affect or interfere with the right 'of property legally acquired under the ordinance heretofore mentioned, nor with the right' to worship God according to the dictates of conscience, 'but only to annul all acts and laws which establish, maintain, protect or countenance the practice of polygamy, evasively called spiritual marriage, however disguised by legal or ecclesiastical solemnities, sacraments, ceremonies, consecrations, or other contrivances.

And be it further enacted:

Sec. 3. That it shall not be lawful for any corporation or association for religious or charitable purposes to acquire or hold real estate in any Territory of the United States during the existence of the territorial government of a greater value than fifty thousand dollars; and all real estate acquired or held by any such corporation or association contrary to the provisions of this act shall be forfeited and escheat to the United States: *Provided,* That existing vested rights in real estate shall not be impaired by the provisions of this section.

Thus was passed the first direct Congressional enactment against the Mormon Church. As will be seen, the anti-polygamy act of 1862 remained, as predicted by Senator McDougall, a dead letter upon the statute books of the nation; only one conviction being secured under it in twenty years, and that of a man who, for test-case purposes, furnished the evidence which convicted him. That man was George Reynolds, of Salt Lake City. This law, however, was the forerunner of other acts of Congress, also directed against Mormonism, which have wrought, in these later days, great changes in Utah.

Utah Legislature Petition's Congress to Repeal the Anti-Polygamy Act

Orson F. Whitney
History of Utah, Volume 2 Page 173

In January, 1867, the Legislative Assembly memorialized Congress for the repeal of the anti-polygamy act of 1862. The reasons assigned for the request were: that according to the faith of the Latter-day Saints plurality of wives was a divine doctrine, as publicly avowed and proclaimed by the Church ten years before the passage of said act; that the doctrine had not been adopted for lustful purposes but from conscientious motives; that the enactment of the law whose repeal was desired was due, it was believed, to misrepresentation and prejudice, which the people of Utah had deplored and exerted themselves to the utmost to remove; that the Judiciary of the Territory had not tried any case under the anti-polygamy law, though repeatedly urged to do so by those who were anxious to test its constitutionality; *** The memorial stated that the Territory, as the fruit of plural marriages, had enjoyed an unexampled immunity from the vices of prostitution and its kindred evils, and for all these reasons Congress was asked to grant the prayer of the memorial, leave the people free to exercise their religion and its ordinances, and thus promote the peace and welfare of the country and frown down the insidious attempts that were being made to array the inhabitants of one section against those of another, because of differences in religious belief.***

At the same time a Representative to Congress for the State of Deseret was to be chosen, and the Constitution of the State, as amended, to be voted upon by the people. *** The amended Constitution of Deseret was adopted, and Hon. William H. Hooper was re-elected delegate to Congress, and chosen also Representative for the State of Deseret. The memorials for the repeal of the anti-polygamy act and the admission of Deseret into the Union, were soon afterwards conveyed to Washington.

The Wade Bill

Orson F. Whitney
History of Utah, Volume 2 Page 210

In this connection appropriate reference may be made to what is known as the Wade bill, which, although it never passed, was introduced and considered in Congress at the very time that militia companies from nearly all parts of the Territory were performing valiant and uncomplaining service against the savages. The bill takes its name from its parent, Senator Ben Wade, and its introduction, in June, 1866, created far less discussion than so radical a measure would have provoked during any other than the exciting times of the reconstruction period. The bill is worthy of note as embodying within itself nearly all the important items of special legislation since enacted in various Congressional laws affecting Utah affairs. It provided for the appointment by the Government of probate judges, the selection of juries and the service of process by the United

States Marshal, the regulating of the marriage ceremony -- which was declared to be a civil contract -- and the recording of certificates; it declared the illegality of church divorces or marriages; required the Trustee-in-Trust of the Mormon Church to annually make a full report of all Church properties, real and personal; held acknowledgment of the marital relation in prosecutions for polygamy to be proof of cohabitation; and aimed at the entire abolition of the prevailing militia system by giving to the Governor the power to select, appoint and commission all officers, either civil or military; to organize and discipline the militia in such manner and at such times as he might direct, and to make all rules and regulations for the enrolling and mustering thereof; it further declared that "all commissions and appointments, both civil and military, heretofore made or issued, or which may be made or issued before the 1st day of January, 1867, shall cease and determine on that day, and shall have no effect or validity thereafter." As a matter of history this much notice of the sweeping measure is interesting. To comment upon it, since it went into early obscurity, would be obviously unprofitable.

Letter Written by John Taylor in Response to a Speech Given by the Vice-President of the United States

Apostle John Taylor Defends Celestial Marriage Before the Nation in Letters to the Newspapers

President John Taylor
History of Utah, Volume 2, Page 339

AMERICAN HOUSE, BOSTON, MASS.
October 20th, 1869.

To the Editor of the Deseret Evening News,

DEAR SIR: -- I have read with a great deal of interest the speech of the Hon. Schuyler Colfax, delivered in Salt Lake City, October 5th, containing strictures on our institutions, as reported in the Springfield *Republican*, wherein there is an apparent frankness and sincerity manifested. It is pleasant, always, to listen to sentiments that are bold, unaffected and outspoken; and however my views may differ -- as they most assuredly do -- from those of the Hon. Vice-President of the United States, I cannot but admire the candor and courtesy manifested in the discussion of this subject; which, though to him perplexing and difficult, is to us an important part of our religious faith.

I would not, however, here be misunderstood; I do not

regard the speech of Mr. Colfax as something indifferent or meaningless. I consider that words proceeding from a gentleman occupying the honorable position of Mr. Colfax, have their due weight. His remarks, while they are courteous and polite, were evidently calmly weighed and cautiously uttered, and they carry with them a significance, which I, as a believer in Mormonism, am bound to notice; and I hope with that honesty and candor which characterize the remarks of this honorable gentleman.

Mr. Colfax remarks:

"I have no strictures to offer as to your creeds on any really religious question. Our land is a land of civil and religious liberty, and the faith of every man is a matter between himself and God alone; you have as much right to worship the Creator, through a President and Twelve Apostles of your Church organization, as I have through the ministers and elders and creed of mine; and this right I would defend for you with as much zeal as the right of any denomination throughout the land."

This certainly is magnanimous and even-handed justice, and the sentiments do honor to their author; they are sentiments that ought to be engraven on the heart of every American citizen.

He continues:

"But our country is governed by law, and no assumed revelation justifies any one in trampling on the law."

At first sight this reasoning is very plausible, and I have no doubt that Mr. Colfax was just as sincere and patriotic in the utterance of the latter as the former sentences; but with all due deference permit me to examine these words and their import.

That our country is governed by law we all admit; but when it is said that "no assumed revelation justifies any one in trampling on the law; "I should respectfully ask, what! not if it interferes with my religious faith, which you state "is a matter between God and myself alone?" Allow me, sir, here to state that the assumed revelation referred to is one of the most vital parts of our religious faith; it emanated from God and cannot be legislated away; it is part of the "Everlasting Covenant" which God has given to man. Our marriages are solemnized by proper authority; a woman is sealed unto a man for time and for eternity, by the power of which Jesus speaks, which "sealed on earth and it is sealed in heaven." With us it is "Celestial Marriage;" take this from us and you rob us of our hopes and associations in the resurrection of the just. This is not our religion? You do not see things as we do. You marry for time only, "until death does you part." We have eternal covenants, eternal unions, eternal associations. I cannot, in an article like this, enter into details, which I should be pleased on a proper occasion to do. I make these remarks to show that it is considered, by us, a part of our religious faith, which I have no doubt did you understand it as we do, you would defend, as you state, "with as much zeal as the right of every other denomination throughout the land."***

I have, sir, written the above in consequence of some remarks which follow:

"I do not concede that the institution you have established here, and which is condemned by the law, is a question of religion."

Now, with all due deference, I do think that if Mr. Colfax had carefully examined our religious faith he would have arrived at other conclusions. In the absence of this I might ask, who constituted Mr. Colfax a judge of my religious faith? I think he has stated that "the faith of every man *is a matter between himself and God alone.*"

Mr. Colfax has a perfect right to state and feel that he does not believe in the revelation on which my religious faith is based, nor in my faith at all; but has he the right to dictate my religious faith? I think not; he does not consider it religion, but it is nevertheless mine.

If a revelation from God is not a religion, what is?

His not believing it from God makes no difference; I know it is. The Jews did not believe in Jesus but Mr. Colfax and I do; their unbelief did not alter the revelation.

Marriage has from time immemorial, among civilized nations, been considered a religious ordinance. It was so considered by the Jews. It is looked upon by the Catholic clergy as one of their sacraments. It is so treated by the Greek Church. The ministers of the Episcopal Church say, in their marriage formula, "What *God has joined together,* let not *man* put asunder;" and in some of the Protestant churches their members are disfellowshiped for marrying what are termed unbelievers. So I am in hopes, one of these times, should occasion require it, to call upon our friend, Mr. Colfax, to redeem his pledge:

"To defend for us our religious faith, with as much zeal as the right of every other denomination throughout the land."***

But permit me here to return to the religious part of our investigations; for if our doctrines are religions, then it is confessed that Congress has no jurisdiction in this case and the argument is at an end. Mr. Webster defines religion as "*any system of faith and worship*, as the religion of the Turks, of Hindoos, of Christians." I have never been able to look at religion in any other light. I do not think Mr. Colfax

had carefully digested the subject when he said, "I do not concede that the institution you have established here, and which is condemned by law, is a question of religion."

Are we to understand by this that Mr. Colfax is created an umpire to decide upon what is religion and what is not, upon what is true religion and what is false? If so, by whom and what authority is he created judge? I am sure he has not reflected upon the bearing of this hypothesis, or he would not have made such an utterance.

According to this theory no persons ever were persecuted for their religion, there never was such a thing known.***

You say we complain of persecution. Have we not cause to do it? Can we call our treatment by a milder term? Was it benevolence that robbed, pillaged and drove thousands of men, women and children from Missouri? Was it Christian philanthropy that after robbing, plundering, and ravaging a whole community, drove them from Illinois into the wilderness among savages?

When we fled as outcasts and exiles from the United States we went to Mexican territory. If not protected we should have been at least unmolested there. Do you think, in your treaty with Mexico, it was a very merciful providence that placed us again under your paternal guardianship? Did you know that you called upon us in our exodus from Illinois for 500 men, which were furnished while fleeing from persecution, to help you to possess that country; for which your tender mercies were exhibited by letting loose an army upon us, and you spent about forty millions of dollars to accomplish our ruin? Of course we did not suffer; "religious fanatics" cannot feel; like the eels the fishwoman was skinning, "we have got used to it." Upon what pretext was this done? Upon the false fabrications of your own officers, and which your own Governor Cumming afterward published as false. Thus the whole of this infamous proceeding was predicated upon falsehood, originating with your own officers and afterwards exposed by them. Did Government make any amends, or has it ever done it? Is it wrong to call this persecution? We have learned to our cost "that the king can do no wrong." Excuse me, sir, if I speak warmly. This people have labored under accumulated wrongs for upwards of thirty years past, still unacknowledged and unredressed. I have said nothing in the above but what I am prepared to prove. What is all this for? Polygamy? No -- that is not even pretended.

Having said so much with regard to Mr. Colfax's speech, let me now address a few words to Congress and to the nation. I hope they will not object for I too am a teacher. And first let me inquire into the law itself, enacted in 1862. The revelation on polygamy was given in 1843, nineteen years before the passage of the Congressional act. We, as a people, believe that revelation is true and came from God. This is our religious belief; and right or wrong it is still our belief; whatever opinions others may entertain it makes no difference to our religious faith. The Constitution is to protect me in my religious faith, and other persons in theirs, as I understand it. It does not prescribe a faith for me, or any one else, or authorize others to do it, not even Congress. It simply protects us all in our religious faiths. This is one of the Constitutional rights reserved by the people. Now who does not know that the law of 1862 in relation to polygamy was passed on purpose to interfere with our religious faith? This was as plainly and distinctly its object as the proclamation of Herod to kill the young children under two years old, was meant to destroy Jesus; or the law passed by Pharaoh in regard to the destruction of the Hebrew children, was meant to destroy the Israelites. If a law had been passed making it a penal offense for communities, or churches, to forbid marriage, who would not have understood that it referred to the Shaking Quakers, and to the priories, nunneries and the priesthood of the Catholic Church? This law, in its inception, progress and passage, was intended to bring us into collision with the United States, that a pretext might be found for our ruin. These are facts that no honest man will controvert. It could not have been more plain, although more honest, if it had said the Mormons shall have no more wives than one. It was a direct attack upon our religious faith. ***

Do statesmen and politicians realize what they are doing when they pass such laws? Do they know, as before stated, that resistance to the law means force, that force means an army, and that an army means death? They may yet find something more pleasant to reflect upon than to have been the aiders and abettors of murder, to be stained with the blood of innocence, and they may try in vain to cleanse their hands of the accursed spot.

It is not the first time that presidents, kings, congresses and statesmen have tried to regulate the acts of Jehovah. Pharaoh's exterminating order about the Hebrew infants was one of acknowledged policy. They grew, they increased too fast. Perhaps the Egyptians had learned, as well as some of our eastern reformers, the art of infanticide; they may have thought that one or two children was enough and so destroyed the balance. They could not submit to let nature take its vulgar course. But in their refined and polite murders, they found themselves dwindling and decaying, and the Hebrews increasing and multiplying; and no matter how shocking it might be to their refined senses, it stood before them as a political fact, and they

were in danger of being overwhelmed by the superior fecundity of the Hebrews. Something must be done; what more natural than to serve the Hebrew children as they had served their own? and this, to us and the Christian world, shocking act of brutal murder, was to them simply what they may have done among themselves; perhaps more politely *a la Madam Restelle*, but not more effectually. The circumstances are not very dissimilar. When Jesus was plotted against by Herod and the infants put to death, who could complain? *It was law*: we must submit to *law*. The Lord Jehovah, or Jesus the Savior of the world, has no right to interfere with *law*. Jesus was crucified *according to law*. Who can complain? Daniel was thrown into the den of lions strictly *according to law*. The king would have saved him, if he could; but he could not resist law. The massacre of St. Bartholomew was in accordance with *law*. The guillotine of Robespierre of France, which cut heads off by the thousand, did it according to *law*. What right had the victims to complain? But these things were done in barbarous ages. Do not let us, then, who boast of our civilization, follow their example; let us be more just, more generous, more forbearing, more magnanimous. We are told that we are living in a more enlightened age. Our morals are more pure (?) our ideas more refined and enlarged, our institutions more liberal. "Ours," says Mr. Colfax, "is a land of civil and religious liberty, and the faith of every man is a matter between himself and God alone," providing God don't shock our moral ideas by introducing something that we don't believe in. If He does let Him look out. We won't persecute, very far be that from us; but we will make our platform, pass Congressional laws and make you submit to them. We may, it is true, have to send out an army, and shed the blood of many; but what of that? It is so much more pleasant to be proscribed and killed according to the laws of the Great Republic, in the "asylum for the oppressed," than to perish ignobly by the decrees of kings, through their miserable minions, in the barbaric ages.

My mind wanders back upwards of thirty years ago, when in the State of Missouri, Mr. McBride, an old gray-haired venerable veteran of the Revolution, with feeble frame and tottering steps, cried to a Missouri patriot: "Spare my life, I am a Revolutionary soldier, I fought for liberty, would you murder me? What is my offense, I believe in God and revelation?" This frenzied disciple of a misplaced faith said, "take that, you God d---d Mormon," and with the butt of his gun he dashed his brains out, and he lay quivering there, -- his white locks clotted with his own brains and gore on that soil that he had heretofore shed his blood to redeem -- a sacrifice at the shrine of liberty! Shades of Franklin, Jefferson and Washington, were you there? Did you gaze on this deed of blood? Did you see your companion in arms thus massacred? Did you know that thousands of American citizens were robbed, disfranchised, driven, pillaged and murdered? for these things seem to be forgotten by our statesmen. Were not these murderers punished? Was not justice done to the outraged? No. They were only Mormons, and when the Chief Magistrate was applied to, he replied: "Your cause is just, but I can do nothing for you." Oh, blessed land of religious freedom! What was this for. Polygamy? No. It was our religion then, it is our religion now. Monogamy or polygamy, it makes no difference. Let me here seriously ask: have we not had more than enough blood in this land? Does the insatiate moloch still cry for more victims?

Let me here respectfully ask with all sincerity, is there not plenty of scope for the action of government at home? What of your gambling hells? What of your gold rings, your whisky rings, your railroad rings, manipulated through the lobby into your Congressional rings? What of that great moral curse of the land, that great institution of monogamy -- *Prostitution?* What of its twin sister -- *Infanticide?* I speak to you as a friend. Know ye not that these seething infamies are corrupting and destroying your people? and that like the plague they are permeating your whole social system? that from your gilded palaces to your most filthy purlieus, they are festering and stewing and rotting? What of the thirty thousand prostitutes of New York City and the proportionate numbers of other cities, towns and villages, and their multitudinous pimps and paramours, who are, of course, all, all, honorable men! Here is ample room for the Christian, the philanthropist, and the statesman. Would it not be well to cleanse your own Augean stables? What of the blasted hopes, the tortured and crushed feelings of the thousands of your wives whose whole lives are blighted through your intrigues and lasciviousness? What of the humiliation of your sons and daughters from whom you can not hide your shame? What of the thousands of houseless and homeless children thrown ruthlessly, hopelessly and disgracefully upon the world as outcasts from society, whose fathers and mothers are alike ashamed of them and heartlessly throw them upon the public bounty, the living memorials of your infamy? What of your infanticide, with its murderous, horrid, unnatural, disgusting and damning consequences? Can you legislate for these monogamic crimes, or shall Madam Restell and her pupils continue their public murders and no redress? Shall your fair daughters, the princesses of America, ruthlessly go on in sacrificing their noble children on the altar of this Moloch -- this demon? What are we drifting to? This "bonehouse," this "powder magazine" is not in Salt Lake City, a thousand miles from your frontiers; it is in your own cities and towns, villages and homes. It carouses in your secret chambers, and flaunts in the public highway; it meets you in every corner, and besets you in every condition. Your infirmaries and hospitals are reeking with it; your sons and daughters, your wives and husbands are degraded by it. It extends from Louisiana to Minnesota, and from Maine to California. You can't hide yourselves from it; it meets you in your magazines and newspapers, and is disgustingly placarded on your walls, -- a living, breathing, loathsome, festering, damning evil. It runs through your very blood, stares out your eyes and stamps its horrid mark on your features, as indelibly as the mark of Cain; it curses your posterity, it runs riot in the land, withering, blighting, corroding and corrupting the life blood of the nation.

Ye American Statesmen, will you allow this demon to run riot in the land, and while you are speculating about a little political capital to be made out of Utah, allow your nation to be emasculated and destroyed? Is it not humiliating that these enormities should exist in your midst, and you, as statesmen, as legislators, as municipal and town authorities, as clergymen, reformers and philanthropists, acknowledge yourselves powerless to stop these damning crimes that are gnawing at the very vitals of the most magnificent nation on the earth? We can teach you a lesson on this matter, polygamists as we are. You acknowledge one wife and her children; what of your other associations unacknowledged? We acknowledge and maintain all of our wives and all of our children; we don't keep a few only, and turn the others out as outcasts, to be provided for by orphan asylums, or turned as vagabonds on the street to help increase the fearfully growing evil. Our actions are all honest, open and above board. We have no gambling halls, no drunkenness, no infanticide, no houses of assignation, no prostitutes. Our wives are not afraid of intrigues and debauchery; nor are our wives and daughters corrupted by designing and unprincipled villains. We believe in the chastity and virtue of women, and maintain them. There is not today, in the wide world, a place where female honor, virtue and chastity, are so well protected as in Utah. Would you have us, I am sure you would not, on reflection, reverse the order of God, and exchange the sobriety, the chastity, the virtue and honor of our institutions, for yours, that are so debasing, dishonorable, corrupting, defaming and destructive? We have fled from these things, and with great trouble and care have purged ourselves from your evils, do not try to legislate them upon us nor seek to engulf us in your damning vices.

You may say it is not against your purity that we contend; but against polygamy, which we consider a crying evil. Be it so. Why then. if your system is so much better, does it not bring forth better fruits? Polygamy, it would seem, is the parent of chastity, honor and virtue; Monogamy the author of vice, dishonor and corruption. But you would argue these evils are not our religion; we that are virtuous, are as much opposed to vice and corruption as you are. Then why don't you control it? We can and do. You have your Christian associations, your Young Men's associations, your Magdalen and Temperance associations, all of which are praiseworthy. Your cities and towns are full of churches, and you swarm with male and female lecturers, and ministers of all denominations. You have your press, your National and State Legislatures, your police, your municipal and town authorities, your courts, your prisons, your armies, all under the direction of Christian monogamists. You are a nation of Christians. Why are these things not stopped? You possess the moral, the religious, the civil and military power but you don't accomplish it. Is it too much to say, "Take the beam out of thine own eye and then shalt thou see clearly to remove the mote that is in thy brother's."

RESPECTFULLY, ETC.,

JOHN TAYLOR.

The Cragin and Cullom Bills -- 1870

Orson F. Whitney
History of Utah, Volume 2 Page 391

It was during the winter of 1869-70 that the measures known as the Cragin and Cullom bills were introduced into Congress.*** This was the beginning of a long series of such conspiracies by cabals of local anti-Mormons -- Federal officials and others -- with politicians at the nation's capital, to secure special Congressional legislation against the Mormon people. Here, indeed, was the virtual origin of the Utah "ring" -- child and successor of the Connor-Harding "regenerating" combination -- which obtained within the next ten years so much notoriety. The so-called "ring" was the head and front of the Gentile wing of the Liberal Party.

The sponsor of the Cragin bill was Senator Aaron H. Cragin of New Hampshire. He introduced his measure in the Senate early in December, 1869, but this, it seems, was its second presentation, it having been before Congress during the previous winter. It was a bill of forty-one sections, several more than were comprised in the Wade bill, which it resembled, though differing from it in some respects, and being deemed by the Mormons even more

odious and detestable. Said the *Deseret News* of Senator Cragin's literary protege: "With the exception that it does not inflict the death penalty, no edict more thoroughly hateful and oppressive was ever concocted against the Hebrew children by Nebuchadnezzar, or the followers of Jesus by Nero."

Section ten of the bill gave the Governor the sole right to select, appoint and commission all officers of the Territory, excepting constables elected or appointed under the Territorial laws.

Section twenty-one abolished trial by jury in a certain class of cases, in that it provided that all criminal cases arising under the anti-polygamy act of 1862, "as well as all criminal cases arising under this act" -- and it was made criminal for a Mormon to solemnize marriages, to counsel or advise the practice of plural marriage, or to be present at "the ceremony of sealing" -- should be heard, tried and determined by the district courts without a jury.

Section twenty-seven virtually made the Governor of the Territory the Trustee-in-Trust of the Mormon Church; at least it required the Trustee-in-Trust to report to the Governor annually the amount, description and location of all properties and monies belonging to the Church.

Section thirty-six provided that the United States District Attorney and Marshal should attend to all Territorial business in the district courts, in lieu of the Territorial Attorney and Marshal -- which offices were abolished -- and be paid for such services out of the Territorial treasury.

Section thirty-seven provided that for the purpose of holding district courts the United States Marshal might take possession of any court house, council house, town house or other public building in Utah and furnish the same in a suitable manner for holding court, at the expense of the Territory.

Section forty took away the functions of the Legislature in relation to the jails and prisons of the Territory and bestowed them upon the Governor, who was empowered to make rules and regulations for said prisons, and appoint and remove at pleasure the wardens and other officers thereof.

Section forty-one repealed all acts or parts of acts of the United States or of Utah Territory inconsistent with this act, and made it unlawful and a misdemeanor for the Legislature of the State of Deseret to assemble, or for an election to be held for any member of said legislature or any officer under said State government.

There were many other objectionable features to the bill, but these were the most formidable. The measure *in toto* was summarized by the *News* as follows: "No American citizen who is a Mormon has any rights -- he is not a free man but a slave, to be tried, convicted, fined, imprisoned, at the will of his masters -- to be made to pay taxes, but to have those funds spent by his masters in persecuting and torturing him, and enriching them for the service -- to wear the form of man, but to have none of the privileges of manhood -- to have no right to believe the Bible, practice its precepts, follow its examples, or to worship its God."***

Mass Meeting of Mormon Women

Some time before the latter event, here in Utah was enacted a scene upon which Gentile civilization gazed with wide-eyed wonder; a mass meeting of Mormon women assembling in the Tabernacle at Salt Lake City and protesting against the passage of the Cullom bill. Three thousand of the so-called "down-trodden women of Mormondom," alleged slaves and playthings of a "polygamic hierarchy," eloquently and earnestly declaiming and resolving against the striking off of those fetters with which Christian statesmen, orators and editors insisted that they were bound.*** Strange as it may seem, the Mormon women, quite as much as the Mormon men, have upheld plurality of wives as a divine principle and conscientiously insisted upon the right of their husbands and fathers to practice it.

But to the mass meeting and its proceedings. It occurred on the 13th of January, 1870, soon after the introduction of the Cullom bill into Congress. The weather was inclement, but the Old Tabernacle, where the gathering was held, and which would comfortably seat about three thousand persons, was densely packed with ladies of all ages.***

Resolved, That we, the ladies of Salt Lake City, in mass-meeting assembled, do manifest our indignation, and protest against the bill before Congress, known as "the Cullom bill," also the one known as "the Cragin bill," and all similar bills, expressions and manifestoes.

Resolved, That we consider the above named bills foul blots on our national escutcheon -- absurd documents -- atrocious insults to the honorable executive of the United States Government, and malicious attempts to subvert the rights of civil and religious liberty.

Resolved, That we do hold sacred the constitution bequeathed us by our forefathers, and ignore, with laudable womanly jealousy, every act of those men to whom the responsibilities of government have been entrusted, which is calculated to destroy its efficiency.

Resolved, That we unitedly exercise every moral power and every right which we inherit as the daughters of American citizens, to prevent the passage of such bills, knowing that they would inevitably cast a stigma on our republican government by jeopardizing the liberty and lives of its most loyal and peaceful citizens.

Resolved, That, in our candid opinion, the presentation of the aforesaid bills indicates a manifest degeneracy of the great men of our nation; and their adoption would presage a speedy downfall and ultimate extinction of the glorious pedestal of freedom, protection, and equal rights, established by our noble ancestors.

Resolved, That we acknowledge the institutions of the Church of Jesus Christ of Latter-day Saints as the only reliable safeguard of female virtue and innocence; and the only sure protection against the fearful sin of prostitution, and its attendant evils, now prevalent abroad, and as such, we are and shall be united with our brethren in sustaining them against each and every encroachment.

Resolved, That we consider the originators of the aforesaid bills disloyal to the constitution, and unworthy of any position of trust in any office which involves the interests of our nation.

Resolved, That, in case the bills in question should pass both Houses of Congress, and become a law, by which we shall be disfranchised as a Territory, we, the ladies of Salt Lake City, shall exert all our power and influence to aid in the support of our own State government.

This meeting of "the sisters" was but the initial to many such held in various parts of the Territory during the next few days, all protesting in a similar manner against the passage of the Cullom bill.***

The Cullom Bill Passes the House of Representatives

Orson F. Whitney
History of Utah, Volume 2 Page 426

The Cullom bill, shorn of some of its repulsive features, but retaining a sufficient number of them to make it a hideous enactment, passed the House of Representatives by a vote of ninety-four to thirty-two. The parts omitted were Section 11, making the lawful wife of an accused polygamist a competent witness against him; Section 14, providing that the statute of limitations should be no bar to a prosecution; Section 30, authorizing the confiscation of the property of persons convicted; Section 31, for the temporary relief of persons reduced to destitution by the enforcement of the act, and Section 32, authorizing the employment of forty thousand volunteers to assist in its enforcement.

The news of the passage of the act by the House, being telegraphed to Utah, created a profound sensation. There was no excitement, at least none of outward exhibition -- such would not have been characteristic of the Mormon people -- but to say that a deep and widespread sentiment of indignation if not of alarm was felt throughout the community, is but to state the simple truth. Mass meetings were held all over the Territory to protest against the action of the House, and appeal to the Senate to not permit the iniquitous measure to become law. ***

The Cullom Bill Dies in the Senate

Orson F. Whitney
History of Utah, Volume 2 Page 439

The result of all these movements was that the Cullom Bill, after its passage by the House of Representatives, died, like its predecessor, the Cragin Bill, in the Senate, to the infinite satisfaction of the friends of Utah everywhere, and the corresponding chagrin and disappointment of her enemies.

Brigham Young's Arrest and Imprisonment -- October 2, 1871

Orson F. Whitney
History of Utah, Volume 2 Page 589

It was the purpose, in short, to indict and try Brigham Young and other leading Mormons, not for polygamy, under the Congressional act of 1862, but for adultery, or at least lewd and lascivious cohabitation, under the laws of the Territory.

Orson F. Whitney
History of Utah, Volume 2 Page 592

It was late in the afternoon of Monday, October 2nd, 1871, that a warrant of arrest was served by U.S. Marshal Patrick upon President Brigham Young, at his residence in Salt Lake City. He was charged with lewd and lascivious cohabitation with his plural wives.*** Having been ill for several days, and at the time of his arrest being unable to leave the house, he was permitted by the kindness of the Marshal, who performed his duty in this instance in a delicate and gentlemanly manner, to remain in his own home, a deputy being left in charge of the distinguished prisoner.

Judge McKean's Remarkable Decision

Orson F. Whitney
History of Utah, Volume 2 Page 598

Finally on October 12th, [1871] Judge McKean rendered his decision, portions of which are here presented:***

It is therefore proper to say, that while the case at bar is called, *"The People versus Brigham Young"* its other and real title is, *"Federal Authority versus Polygamic Theocracy."*

The Poland Bill -- 1874

Orson F. Whitney
History of Utah, Volume 2 Page 738

On the 5th of January, 1874, Mr. Poland, of Vermont, introduced in the House a bill "relative to courts and judicial offices in the Territory of Utah." This was the nearest attempt to conform to the recommendations in the President's message, and as its provisions discriminated against the majority of the citizens of the Territory in various respects, it was vigorously opposed. The Legislature of Utah was now in session, and endeavored to ward off the proposed legislation by Congress. With this purpose in view, a memorial was unanimously adopted, denying the accusations of disloyalty made against the majority of the people of Utah and earnestly soliciting the sending of a commission of investigation, and the suspension, pending its labors and until it had rendered its report, of all action in the nature of special legislation toward this Territory.

This memorial was presented to Governor Woods for his signature, but on February 4th he returned it with a caustic veto message, accusing the legislators of the Territory of enacting improper laws. Said he: "To ask, or expect me to join you in condemning my own official acts, pronouncing them 'absolutely untrue,' and made 'with malicious intent,' is a sad commentary upon the judgment and good taste of those who ask it. That I cannot do so is certain."

The memorial, however, came before Congress, being presented by Delegate Cannon on the 16th of February. It doubtless had a measure of effect in the direction intended by the memorialists, although the House Judiciary Committee, on February 21st, expressed its opposition to the commission, and agreed to report the Poland bill. On March 2nd, Delegate Cannon introduced into the House a bill for an enabling act for the people of Utah to frame a State government.* [Footnote: This bill failed to pass, as did also one of a similar nature introduced into the House of Representatives on December 21st, 1875. The last mentioned was supported by a petition from the ladies of Utah. This bore 23,626 signatures, and in addition to the request that Utah be given statehood asked that Congress repeal the anti-polygamy law.]

Matters went along till May, with efforts for and against Utah, until, early in that month, Mr. Poland withdrew his proposed measure and presented one still further modified. This was amended and became a law on the 23rd of June. It repealed the laws of Utah respecting the Territorial Marshal and Attorney-General, and placed the powers and duties of those officers upon the United States Marshal and District Attorney. Certain judgments and decrees of the probate courts -- those already executed, and those rendered, the time to appeal from which had expired -- were confirmed, but the jurisdiction of such courts was thenceforth to be limited to the settlement of estates of decedents

and to matters of guardianship and divorce. The jurisdiction of justices' of the peace was slightly extended, and the appointment, by the Territorial Supreme Court, of United States Commissioners, authorized. Certain fees to Federal officials were made payable out of the Territorial treasury. Appeals were allowed to the United States Supreme Court in bigamy and polygamy trials, as well as in cases involving capital punishment, and the drawing of grand and petit jurors was placed in the hands of the Probate Judge and the Clerk of the District Court. This gave non-Mormons equal representation on the jury list with the Mormons, though the latter were greatly in the majority in the Territory.

President Brigham Young Imprisoned for "Contempt of Court" March 1875

The Ann Eliza Case -- Brigham Young's "Nineteenth Wife" Sues for Divorce

Orson F. Whitney
History of Utah, Volume 2 Page 757

On the 28th of July, 1873, a divorce suit had been planted in the court presided over by Judge McKean. The plaintiff was Mrs. Ann Eliza Webb Young, the alleged nineteenth wife of President Brigham Young, who was made the party defendant. Besides a decree of divorce and permanent support for herself and her children, the plaintiff asked for alimony and sustenance *pendente lite*, or during the progress of the litigation.***

In answer to the complaint the defendant interposed as follows. He denied that the plaintiff was or ever had been his legal wife, though he admitted that on the 6th of April, 1868, he had married her as a plural wife according to the rites of the Church of Jesus Christ of Latter-day Saints, of which they were both members. He had been advised since their marriage, though he was not aware of it at that time, that the plaintiff had never been divorced from her former husband, James L. Dee, whom she wedded on the 10th of April, 1863. Consequently the said James L. Dee, who was living, was still her lawful husband. The defendant further alleged that on the 10th of January, 1834, at the town of Kirtland, Ohio, he had been duly and lawfully married to Mary Ann Angell, who was still living and had ever since been his lawful wife.***

On August 25th of the latter year the defendant's answer was filed, and in September following arguments were made upon the motion to grant temporary alimony and counsel fees. It was not until the 25th of February, 1875, nineteen months after the filing of the plaintiff's petition, that the question of alimony *pendente lite* was ruled upon. On that day Judge McKean gave a lengthy decision covering the point, and on the ensuing day issued an order of court conformatory thereto. He directed that the defendant pay to the plaintiff the sum of three thousand dollars to defray the expenses of prosecuting her suit, and that he also pay to her for her maintenance and the maintenance and education of her children the further sum of five hundred dollars per month, to commence from the date upon which the complaint was filed. Ten days were given the defendant in which to pay the three thousand dollars, attorney's fees, and twenty days in which to pay nine thousand five hundred dollars, accumulated alimony for the period of nineteen months. Thereafter he was to pay five hundred dollars on the first day of every month during litigation in the case. An exception was taken by the defense, and on the 8th of March, ten days after the issuance of the order, an appeal to the Supreme Court of the Territory was perfected.

At the expiration of the time within which the defendant was required to conform to that part of the decision relative to the payment of the three thousand dollars, attorney's fees, no such payment having been made, the plaintiff's counsel obtained an order of attachment requiring the defendant to come into court and show cause why he should not be punished for contempt. President Young, on the morning of the 11th of March, appeared personally and by his attorneys in the District Court and made answer accordingly. The answer, which was read by Mr. P. L. Williams, stated that the respondent had been advised by his counsel that he was by law entitled to an appeal from the decree of the 25th of February, and that pending the determination of such appeal the execution of the court's order might be stayed; that an appeal to the Supreme Court of the Territory had been taken and perfected, and that his omission and failure to comply with the said order was owing wholly to his desire to obtain the benefit of his appeal.

The respondent disclaimed all intention or disposition to disregard or treat contemptuously any process of the court, and prayed that further proceedings in execution of the order relative to the payment of fees and alimony be stayed until the determination of the appeal.***

Judge McKean then wrote out and read the following order:

***It is therefore, because of the facts and premises, ordered and adjudged that defendant is guilty of disobedience to the process of the Court, and is therein guilty of contempt of Court.

And since the Court has not one rule of action where conspicuous and another where obscure persons are concerned; and since it is a fundamental principle of the Republic that all men are equal before the law; and since this Court desires to impress this great fact, this great law upon the minds of all the people of this Territory:

Now, therefore, because of the said contempt of Court, it is further ordered and adjudged, that the said Brigham Young do pay a fine of twenty-five dollars, and that he be imprisoned for the term of one day.

Done in open Court, this 11th day of March, 1875,

JAMES B. MCKEAN,
Chief Justice and Judge of the Third District Court.

President Young Spends One Day in Prison

As soon as the reading was ended Attorney McBride requested the court to so amend the order as to cause the defendant to be imprisoned until the fees were paid. The Judge replied that he would let the future take care of itself. The three thousand dollars were paid to the plaintiff's attorneys by Mr. James Jack, President Young's chief clerk, just after the rendering of the decision.

With the calm dignity so characteristic of him, particularly in the presence of a crisis, President Young received the sentence passed upon him by Judge McKean. The same quiet demeanor which he had worn all through the proceedings ending in the indignity so ungenerously put upon him, was manifested as he arose and left the court room in custody of U. S. Deputy Marshal A. K. Smith. Entering his carriage, which had remained in waiting, the President, accompanied by his guard, was driven to his own residence, where he ate dinner, supplied himself with bedding, clothing and such other articles as he might need while in prison, and was then conveyed through a heavy snow storm to the Penitentiary. Mayor Wells, Dr. S. B. Young and Mr. William A. Rossiter accompanied the President and Deputy Marshal Smith, and remained at the Warden's house over night. Many other friends of the prisoner drove out to the Penitentiary during the afternoon, and a small host of sympathizing adherents, awaiting the hour of his deliverance, found lodgings at every available place in the vicinity. The President was at first locked in a cell -- the only one that the institution afforded -- with murderers, thieves and other convicted criminals, or men awaiting trial for alleged crimes; but this was only until better quarters could be provided for his reception. In a short time he was transferred to a room adjoining the Warden's house, where he passed the night in comparative comfort. He received from his guard all the courtesies that could consistently be granted under the circumstances. Between twelve and one o'clock next day, Friday, March 12th, -- the brief term of imprisonment having expired -- the prison gates swung open, and the freed captive, surrounded by a multitude of friends, was escorted back to the city.

The Testimony of President John Taylor Concerning President Brigham Young

President John Taylor
JD 19:138 October 14, 1877 SLC

Before the Prophet Joseph departed, he said, on one occasion, turning to the Twelve, "I roll the burden of this kingdom on to you," and, on another occasion, he said their place was next to that of the First Presidency, and he wished them to take their place that he might attend to other duties, such as translating, etc. At the time he was taken away he was in the bloom of life and the vigor of health, and although his departure was sudden and unexpected our organization rendered it no difficult matter to decide who should assume the leadership of the Church. There was no difficulty in the matter; it was understood that the duty rested on the Twelve. Why? The revelation stated that the Twelve were to hold the keys of the kingdom in connection with the First Presidency, which were handed down under various circumstances. You will find in the history of the Prophet Joseph Smith, that this matter is made perfectly plain. He

said there was no authority or power of presidency over the Twelve except the First Presidency, and where he was not there was no presidency over the Twelve. Hence President Brigham Young said, when the Prophet Joseph was taken away, "Thank God the keys of the kingdom are not taken from us," and being head of the Twelve, he assumed his position and so acted on the authority he held and according to the rules laid down. Thus there was no scattering, confusion or difficulty that might otherwise have existed if the organization of the Church had not been perfect.

President John Taylor
JD 1:229 April 8, 1853 SLC

Who have we for our ruling power? Where and how did he obtain his authority? Or how did any in this Church and kingdom obtain it? It was first obtained by a revelation from the Lord of the Universe, by the opening of the heavens, by the voice of God, and by the ministering of holy angels. It is by the voice of God and the voice of the people, that our present President obtained his authority. Many people in the world are talking about mis-rule and mis-government. If there is any form of government under the heavens where we can have legitimate rule and authority, it is among the Saints. In the first place, we have a man appointed by God, and, in the second place, by the people. This man is chosen by yourselves, and every person raises his hand to sanction the choice. Here is our President, Brigham Young, whom we made choice of yesterday, who is he? He is the legitimate ruler among this people.

President John Taylor
JD 5:189 August 30, 1857 SLC

The kingdom is put upon the shoulders of President Young and this people to carry it out, and by whom? By the Lord God -- by him who holds dominion throughout the universe; by him who created all by the word of his power; by him who said, "Let there be light, and there was light;" by him who spake, and the worlds rolled into existence. By him you received rights that are not of this world -- rights that flow from the great Eloheim.

President John Taylor
JD 5:263 September 20, 1857 SLC

Well, then, we are taught our duty to our God by our brethren. And who are our brethren? The officers and authorities of this Church -- the servants of the living God. Who is President Young? The mouthpiece of God to this Church and to the world. Has God any other? Yes, lots of them appointed by him, but he is the head.

President John Taylor
JD 7:325 October 7, 1859 SLC

When you hear a man talk against the authorities of this Church and kingdom, you may know he is sliding down hill. He does not know what spirit influences him; he is ignorant that he is in the dark; and, unless he retraces his steps quickly, he will go overboard. You may set that down as a fact all the time. Why? Because, if this is the Church and kingdom of God, and President Young is the elect of God, and his Council and the Twelve and others are the elect of God, and you seek to injure them, you run a great risk, and will be found fighting against God; for Jesus says, "He that receiveth you receiveth me, and he that receiveth me receiveth him that sent me; and he that rejecteth you rejecteth me, and he that rejecteth me rejecteth him that sent me."

President John Taylor
JD 19:123 October 7, 1877 SLC

Brigham Young needs no factitious aid to perpetuate his memory; his labors have been exhibited during the last forty-five years in his preaching, in his writing, in his counsels, in the wisdom and intelligence he has displayed, in our exodus from Nauvoo; in the building of cities throughout the length and breadth of this Territory, in his opposition to vice and his protection of virtue, purity and right. These things are well known and understood by the Latter-day Saints, and also by thousands and millions of others. But, as with his predecessor, Joseph Smith, who had to leave, while we are called upon to mourn a President dead, angels announce a President born in the eternal worlds; he has only gone to move in another state of existence.

Chapter 3

Administration of President John Taylor

Defense of the Celestial Law of Holy Union

The Celestial Law Defended As a Constitutional Religious Right

President John Taylor
JD 20:317 October 6, 1879 SLC

I was asked, "Do you believe in obeying the laws of the United States?" "Yes I do, in all except one" -- in fact I had not broken that. "What law is that?" "The law in relation to polygamy." "Well, why do you except that one?" "Because," I replied "it is at variance with the genius and spirit of our institution; because it is at variance with the Constitution of the United States; and because it is in violation of the law of God to me." The United States Supreme Court, however, since that time has made it a law of the land, that is, it has sanctioned it; it was not sanctioned at that time, that question was not then decided. We are here to-day, gathered together according to the word and law of God and the commandments of God to us. "Gather my Saints together unto me," says one of the old prophets, "those that have made a covenant with me by sacrifice." "I will take you," says another, "one of a city and two of a family, and I will bring you to Zion, and I will give you pastors according to mine heart, which shall feed you with knowledge and understanding." Now, the servants of God in these last days have been sent out as they were in former days to gather the people, and the Lord has given us this law -- the [Celestial Law] -- among other things, and I know it before God and can bear testimony of it, if nobody else knows it. I know that it came from God, and that God is its author. But there are hundreds and thousands of others who have a knowledge of the same thing; but I speak of it in this wise to testify before God, angels and men, before this nation and all other nations that it came from God. That is the reason that I speak of it, that I may bear my testimony to you and to the nations of the earth. Now, then, about the result of it; that is with God and with the people. It is for us to do the will of God; it is for the Lord to bring about the results in his own way.

George Q. Cannon
JD 20:38 July 7, 1878 SLC

What is the crime of which the people of Utah are accused? It is that of marrying women! It is not that of seducing or debauching them. All the pains and penalties inserted in bills before Congress for the punishment of the "Mormon" people are affixed to the marriage of women. This is made a crime, and because of it, it is proposed to punish men. Not one word of condemnation, nor penalty of any character, is proposed for the seducer, or the vile betrayer of female innocence;***…but the man who marries women, and maintains them honorably and virtuously, sustaining family and parental relations in all purity and sacredness, is to be disfranchised and visited with other pains and penalties!

First Place of My Union Eternal Being Required to be of Full Exalting

Joseph F. Smith
JD 20:28 July 7, 1878 SLC

Some people have supposed that the doctrine of plural marriage was a sort of superfluity, or non-essential to the salvation or exaltation of mankind. In other words, some of the Saints have said, and believe, that a man with one wife, sealed to him by the authority of the Priesthood for time and eternity, will receive an exaltation as great and glorious, if he is faithful, as he possibly could with more than one. I want here to enter my solemn protest against this idea, for I know it is false.*** The marriage of one woman to a man for time and eternity by the sealing power, according to the law of God, is a fulfillment of the celestial law of marriage in part...*** But this is only the beginning of the law, not the whole of it. Therefore, whoever has imagined that he could obtain the fullness of the blessings pertaining to this celestial law, by complying with only a portion of its conditions, has deceived himself. He cannot do it.***

Saints Encouraged to Endure the Persecutions

President John Taylor
JD 25:87 February 10, 1884 SLC

The carnal mind knows not the things of God, and is not subject to the law of God, neither can it be. They form all kinds of opinions, even, with regard to our gathering. "Why don't you stop at home as other folks do?" Some say that it is an emigration scheme gotten up to make money, and that missionaries are sent out by us to deceive the weak and the ignorant, and to gather them together that they may be made merchandise of. That is one idea. You all know how far that is true, and how far it is false. Others say that we are gathered here for licentious purposes -- to carry out polygamic ideas, to corrupt, demoralize, and trample under foot the women who come and associate with us, and to destroy their virtue; whereas you know there is not a place in the world where women are better protected and their virtue more sacredly guarded than in Utah. They compare plural marriage to their whoredom, seductions, their social evils, and the many kinds of iniquity, corruption and rottenness that prevail among themselves. Reasoning from their own standpoint, they consider that we are a very wicked, corrupt and licentious people. But according to the statistics that we have pertaining to these matters, our immorality is twenty to forty times less than theirs here in our midst, without going any further. The crimes, iniquities and corruptions committed by the small minority of outsiders in our midst very far exceed, perhaps by twenty to thirty times, the crimes of the Latter-day Saints. This excess of crime on the part of outsiders is what might be reasonably expected; for we profess to be a better people, and we ought to be a better people than those who make no pretentions to be guided by divine revelation. Examine the records of our city jail, of the Penitentiary, of the county prisons, which have been published and are being published, and you will find a full statement in relation to these matters and the per cent of crime that exists between one and the other.***

Speaking of the doctrine of the plurality of wives, I remember talking with one of our Presidents -- I mean one of the Presidents of the United States -- on this subject in Washington, a number of years ago, as I have with others since on the same subject; but I remember some of the remarks made on that occasion. "Well," said he, after talking some little on politics, and one thing and another, "what about your polygamy?" "Mr. Pierce," said I, -- I can mention his name now as it is a thing of the past -- "it may be possible that some of us may have wrong ideas in regard to these things. We read about such a man as Abraham, who is described as 'the friend of God;' we read about such a man as David, who is described as 'a man after God's own heart:' we read about Jacob, who had twelve sons, whose names are to be written upon the twelve gates of the holy city. Who was Jacob? He was a man who had several wives, by whom he had these twelve sons. Then we read of Moses -- a man of God, a leader of Israel, and a law-giver. He told the people how they should treat their children whether by the first wife or by the second, and how all these matters were to be arranged. "Mr. Pierce," said I, "It is possible that we of the nineteenth century, have not been able to instruct the Lord very much in regard to these matters. Probably He knew just as much about them then as we do now, and that in regard to our marital laws, we have made some mistakes. "Well," said Mr. Pierce, "I cannot say." Of course he coul [could] not.

Crusade of Government Powers Against Celestial Law of Eternal Marriage During John Taylor's Administration

The George Reynolds Case
October 23, 1874 -- January 6, 1879
Declared Constitutional by the United States Supreme Court

Orson F. Whitney
History of Utah, Volume 3 Page 45

The opening of the year 1879 brought with it a very important decision from the Supreme Court of the United States. It was the final decree in the celebrated Reynolds case, involving the constitutionality of the anti-polygamy law of 1862. This was the first effectual move made by the Federal Government against what the Gentiles termed "the Mormon power." Though the immediate result was not momentous in a general way, the defendant in the case and those dependent upon him being the only ones seriously affected, it nevertheless had an indirect bearing upon the fortunes of the whole Mormon community, foreshadowing as it did a radical change in the policy of the Government toward Utah, and constituting a precursor of the great crusade inaugurated under the Edmunds law.***

Ever since the enactment of the anti-polygamy law, in 1862, the Mormon people and many others had considered it unconstitutional, being violative, as they believed, of one of the cardinal principles upon which the United States Government was founded, the principle of religious liberty. This opinion was held by some of the leading statesmen and jurists of America. The reader need not be told that the Constitution, in its first amendment, declares: "Congress shall make no law respecting an establishment of religion, or prohibiting the free exercise thereof." Nor is it necessary to state to those who have followed this narrative to the present point, that at the time Congress created the law in question, plurality of wives was a portion of the Mormon religion, and had been proclaimed as such, at the seat of government, ten years previously; Apostle Orson Pratt, in the year 1852, having taken a special mission to the city of Washington for that purpose. Consequently this law was looked upon, especially by the Latter-day Saints, as unconstitutional and therefore void. They believed that such would be the decision of the court of last resort, as soon as a case involving the principle at issue should come fairly and squarely before that tribunal. So confident were they in relation to this matter that many leading Mormons, including President Young himself, repeatedly expressed the wish that a test case might be passed upon by the Supreme Court at Washington.

The local representatives of the Government, despairing of accomplishing much toward the extirpation of polygamy, as the law and public sentiment in Utah then stood, were no less desirous that such a case might be brought. In the summer of 1874 negotiations were opened between the Mormon authorities and the United States Attorney, Mr. Carey, and it was arranged that the case should be provided. Mr. Carey and his assistants were preparing at this very time to launch a series of prosecutions for polygamy against prominent Mormons, who,

though it was known that they could not be legally convicted, -- their polygamous relations being of older standing than the law under which it was proposed to prosecute them, -- had nevertheless been singled out as targets for a vain though vigorous onslaught.

The District Attorney agreed that if a test case were furnished, these proceedings should all be dropped. This circumstance no doubt expedited the subsequent arrangement. It was stipulated that the defendant in the case should produce the evidence for his own indictment and conviction, and it was generally understood that the infliction of punishment in this instance would be waived. Only the first half of the arrangement was realized. The defendant in the test case, George Reynolds, supplied the evidence upon which he was convicted, but his action did not shield him from punishment; though it doubtless had the effect of mitigating the same. Such was the inception of the Reynolds case, which had its origin on the 23rd of October, 1874, when the first indictment was found therein.

Elder George Reynolds, the person selected to be the defendant in the celebrated case which bears his name, is at the present time -- 1896 -- numbered with the general authorities of the Mormon Church, being one of the First Seven Presidents of the Seventies. At the beginning of these proceedings, however, he was not so conspicuous a character, though a man of some repute among his people in an official and literary way. He had been the private secretary of President Brigham Young. An Englishman by birth, a native of the city of London, he had been a Mormon since May, 1856, and a resident of Utah since 1865. He was thirty-two years of age and the husband of two wives when he stepped to the front to become the defendant in this *causa celebre*. His first wife, Mary Ann Tuddenham, was married to him on the 22nd of July, 1865; his second wife, Amelia Jane Schofield, on the 3rd of August, 1874. These facts were communicated to the Grand Jury of the Third District at the September term of the last named year. The result was his indictment for polygamy, or, as the law styled his offense, bigamy, on the 23rd of October. Three days later he went before the District Court, surrendered himself a prisoner and asked to be admitted to bail. According to previous agreement between U. S. Attorney Carey and the defendant's counsel, J. G. Sutherland, the bond was fixed at twenty-five hundred dollars.

The trial took place in the spring of 1875, beginning on the 31st of March and ending on the 1st of April. Judge Emerson presided, Messrs. Carey and Baskin prosecuted the case and Messrs. Sutherland, Bates and Snow defended it. The jury was composed of seven Mormons and five non-Mormons, namely, Joseph Siegel, Jesse West, George M. Ottinger, Albert W. Davis, William Naylor, DeWitt C. Thompson, Joseph Peck, S. F. Nuckolls, Samuel Bringhurst, M. B. Callahan, W. C. Morris and James McGuffy.

Among the witnesses was Mrs. Amelia J. Reynolds, the defendant's plural wife, who admitted the fact of their marriage on the 3rd of August, 1874. The ceremony, she stated, took place***at Salt Lake City, President Daniel H. Wells officiating. The latter confirmed this statement, which was also conceded by the defense. The Judge having charged the jury, they retired to their room, but returned in about half an hour with the following verdict:

SALT LAKE CITY
April 1st, 1875.

We, the jury in the case of the People of the United States in the Territory of Utah *vs.* George Reynolds, indicted for polygamy, find a verdict of guilty, and recommend the prisoner to the mercy of the court.

SAMUEL BRINGHURST,
Foreman.

It was now discovered that the defendant, who had just been pronounced guilty, had not been arraigned before trial, and that the indictment had not been read to him. His counsel took advantage of this point, and moved an arrest of judgment and the setting aside of the verdict, preliminary to a motion for a new trial. The court granted the motion. Mr. Carey, though somewhat nonplussed, announced that he was ready to proceed immediately and re-try the case. This, however, was rendered unnecessary by the defendant, who waived the point and pleaded "Not guilty as charged in the indictment." Pending further proceedings Elder Reynolds was released in bonds of five thousand dollars. On the 10th of April the convicted man received his sentence, which was that he should

be imprisoned in the Utah Penitentiary at hard labor for one year, and pay a fine of three hundred dollars. An appeal was taken to the Supreme Court of the Territory, where, on the 19th of June, the decision of the District Court was reversed. The ground for reversal was the illegality of the Grand Jury which had found the indictment; it being composed of twenty-three instead of fifteen men, as required by law. Chief Justice Lowe by that time had arrived, and it was he, with Associate Justices Emerson and Boreman, who then composed the Supreme Court. Elder Reynolds was now released from his bonds.

During the progress and immediately after the close of the trial, the prosecution manifested considerable animus against the defendant. They even insisted that he be imprisoned pending his appeal to a higher court. Judge Emerson, however, would not yield to this demand. The reversal of the decision of the District Court served only to increase the bitterness of the prosecuting officers.

Elder Reynolds was again indicted in the fall of 1875, by a Grand Jury composed of seven Mormons and eight non-Mormons. The date of this indictment was October 30th. The witnesses upon whose testimony it was found were John and Mary Tuddenham, Daniel H. Wells, Amos K. Lucas and Arthur Pratt. The defendant was arrested on the 1st of November and was forthwith admitted to bail in the same sum as before. His second trial began on the 9th of December before Chief Justice Alexander White...*** The defendant having pleaded not guilty to the charge of bigamy, the trial began. It had become evident by this time that the U. S. Attorney, under the stress of anti-Mormon influence, had departed from his design to try the case purely as a test of the constitutionality of the law, and that it was the intention to fasten criminality upon the prisoner with a view to securing his punishment. Owing to this vindictive spirit, Mrs. Amelia J. Reynolds refused to appear as a witness, and was not found when the officers went in quest of her. The Court, however, permitted the prosecuting attorney to call the lawyers and other persons in attendance at the former trial, and accepted as evidence their testimony of what Mrs. Reynolds had stated at that time. The witnesses examined were John and Mary Tuddenham, Daniel H. Wells, Amos K. Lucas, John R. McBride, George R. Maxwell, Arthur Pratt, J. G. Sutherland, Hamilton Gamble, Orson Pratt, Sr., John Nicholson and John Sharp. The jury on the 21st of December found a verdict of guilty against the defendant, but recommended him to the mercy of the court. The judgment was that he be imprisoned at hard labor for a term of two years, and pay a fine of five hundred dollars. The defendant appealed to the Supreme Court of the Territory, where the case was heard on the 13th of June, 1876, Chief Justice Schaeffer then presiding. The decision of the lower court was unanimously affirmed.

As contemplated from the beginning an appeal was taken to the Supreme Court of the Nation, where, on the 14th of November, 1878, the case was argued, Messrs. G. W. Biddle, of Philadelphia, and Ben Sheeks, of Salt Lake City, appearing for the appellant, and Solicitor General Phillips for the Government. Two days were occupied by the arguments, and the case was then taken under advisement. The court's decision, which was unanimous, but for the non-concurrence of Associate Justice Field on a minor point, was delivered on the 6th of January, 1879. It was voiced by Chief Justice Waite. It confirmed the decisions of the lower courts, and declared constitutional the act of Congress making criminal the Mormon practice of plural marriage.

John Taylor with the Courage of Heaven

Orson F. Whitney
History of Utah, Volume 3 Page 50

A few days after the delivery of the decision a notable interview occurred between President John Taylor, the head of the Mormon Church, and Colonel O. J. Hollister, U. S. Collector of Internal Revenue for Utah, and correspondent of the New York Tribune. The meeting, which was solicited by Mr. Hollister, took place in the President's office at Salt Lake City, June 13, 1879. Besides the two principals, several prominent Mormons were present and took part in the conversation. Asked as to whether he took issue with Judge Waite's statement of the scope and effect of the amendment to the Constitution guaranteeing religious freedom, President Taylor answered in the affirmative. He then said:

PRESIDENT TAYLOR. A religious faith amounts to nothing unless we are permitted to carry it into effect. Congress and the Supreme Court are carrying out the same principles that were practised in the persecutions against the Huguenots in France, the Waldenses and Albigenses in Piedmont, the Non-conformists in England, and others who have been persecuted on account of their religion. *** They will allow us to think -- what an unspeakable privilege that is -- but they will not allow us the free exercise of that faith which the Constitution guarantees. Here is the injustice and the manifest breach of faith.

COLONEL HOLLISTER. Is it not true that marriage is the basis of society, that out of it spring the social relations, obligations and duties with which governments must necessarily concern themselves? And is it not therefore within the legitimate scope of the power of every civil government to determine whether marriage shall be polygamous or monogamous under its dominion?

PRES. T. I do not look upon it in that way. I consider that when the Constitution of the United States was framed and adopted, those high contracting parties did positively agree that they would not interfere with religious affairs. Now, if our marital relations are not religious, what is? This ordinance of marriage was a direct revelation to us through Joseph Smith the Prophet. *** You may not know it, but I know that this is a revelation from God and a command to His people, and therefore it is my religion. I do not believe that the Supreme Court of the United States nor the Congress of the United States has any right to interfere with my religious views, and in doing it they are violating their most sacred obligations.

COL. H. My idea of religion is this: -- that man acknowledges, loves, reverences, worships and gives thanks to God; that constitutes religion. Worship may take various forms of expression, but where did it ever, how can it, take the form of marrying and raising families -- either single or plural families?

PRES. T. Mr. Hollister, are you a believer in the Bible?

MR. PENROSE. Mr. Hollister's question is answered by the Bible, which plainly says that marriage is ordained of God, etc.

PRES. T. Now, Mr. Hollister, I have so far answered your questions, will you answer mine?

COL. H. In one sense I do. I believe that part of the Bible that my reason approves of.

PRES. T. It would not be of any use arguing with you on this subject then; but as my opinions are desired for the public, I will state that I believe in the Bible, and believing in it, I believe in those principles therein set forth.

COL. H. If marriage can be legitimately called religion, what human relation or pursuit may not be so called? And if everything is religion, and the state is prohibited from interfering with it, what place is there left for the state?

*   *   *   *   *   *   *   *   *

MR. P. That is easily answered. When one's religion assumes to interfere with the rights and liberties of others.

PRES. T. Whose rights do we interfere with? That is a question I was going to ask you.

COL. H. I consider that you interfere with men's rights and women's rights and children's rights.

PRES. T. How can we interfere with men's rights or with women's rights if all enter into it voluntarily?

COL. H. I think it interferes with the rights of men and women, because when a man marries a second woman, some other man must do without any.***

You believe that Mormonism will be universally received, but polygamy cannot become universal, because the sexes are born in about equal numbers. How can a principle, not of universal applicability, be philosophically sound, or sound in any sense?

MR. P. What need of going out of Utah?

COL. H. If you are going to defend polygamy as a sound philosophical principle, I don't see how you can avoid going out of Utah.

MR. P. But we only practice it as a part of our religion.

COL. H. But if it is a true principle it must be of universal applicability.

*   *   *   *   *   *   *   *   *

PRES. T. These theories are too visionary and too far in the future. It is well known that there are scores of thousands of women in these United States who cannot obtain husbands and the same also in England and other Christian countries. And furthermore, we regard the plural order of marriage as being voluntary, both on the part of the man and the woman. If there should be any disparity, as you refer to -- if there should not be two wives for one man, why then he could not get them.

*   *   *   *   *   *   *   *   *

COL. H. Viewed socially or philosophically, apart from all religious considerations, do you regard polygamy as worthy of perpetuation at the cost of perpetual antagonism between your people and their countrymen?

PRES. T. However we may respect the government and its institutions, I would respectfully say we are not the parties who produce this antagonism. *** Our revelation given in August, 1831, specifically states that

if we keep the laws of God we need not break the laws of the land. Congress has since, by its act, placed us in antagonism to what we term an unconstitutional law, and it now becomes a question whether we should obey God or man.

COL. H. But in taking that position do you not set yourselves up as the judges of the Constitution, whereas the laws (Sec. 709 R. S.) make the Supreme Court the judge of the constitutionality of the laws of Congress?

PRES. T. Without any interpretations from the Supreme Court, I take it that the words themselves are explicit on this point. *** When the Constitution says Congress shall make no law respecting an establishment of religion or prohibiting the free exercise thereof, we take it to mean what it says. Congress, indeed, can pass laws, and the Supreme Court can sanction those laws; but while they have the power, being in the majority, the justice of those laws is another matter.

COL. H. Viewed as above, do you regard polygamy as superior to monogamy as the form or law of marriage, and if so wherein?

PRES. T. I consider it altogether superior to the law of monogamy in a great many particulars. First, I base it upon the will and command of God both in ancient and modern times; second, I base it upon the natural results of monogamy. There is in all monogamic countries, the United States not excepted, a terrible state of things arising from the practice of monogamy, infanticide and foeticide prevailing to an alarming extent. *** Polygamy protects its offspring; monogamy does not. How many are there now in Washington, New York, Chicago, Philadelphia and other cities, that make it a practice to cohabit with other women, to whom children are born, the results of their adultery, whom they do not acknowledge, but who are turned out upon the streets to become waifs in the shape of newsboys, street-sweepers, etc., outcasts and pariahs of society, augmenting also the criminal classes and the paupers, leaving other people to provide for their illicit offspring! And it is not an infrequent thing for such children, while engaged sweeping the street crossings, to ask their own fathers for a penny, the child not knowing the father nor the father the child.

COL. H. Do you consider these evils the necessary concomitants of monogamy more than of polygamy?

PRES. T. These are the results of monogamy, whether necessary or not, and these are the evils associated with it. We acknowledge our children, we acknowledge our wives; we have no mistresses. We had no prostitution here until it was introduced by monogamy, and I am now told that these other diabolical deeds are following in its train. The courts have protected these people in their wicked practices. We repudiate all such things, and hence I consider that a system that will enable a man to carry out his professions, and that will enable him to acknowledge his wife or wives and acknowledge and provide for his children and wives, is much more honorable than that principle which violates its marital relations, and, whilst hypocritically professing to be true to its pledges, recklessly violates the same and tramples upon every principle of honor, which sits down and coolly and deliberately decides how many children shall be murdered and how many shall live. The one, Mr. Hollister, is a great deal better system than the other.

* * * * * * * * *

You say you think it wise for the government to endeavor to suppress polygamy. I think they should first manifest their antagonism to the practice of infanticide and foeticide and the prevailing prostitution, and instead of prosecuting and proscribing us, they should assist us in removing these contaminating influences from our borders. Furthermore, while Great Britain is a monarchial government she can tolerate 180,000,000 of polygamists [in India] and throw around them the protecting aegis of the law, while the United States, a republican and professedly a free government, is enacting laws prosecuting and proscribing so small a number as 150,000 in her Territory.

* * * * * * * * *

Polygamy is not a crime, per se; it was the action of Congress that made polygamy a crime. As before stated, the British government allows one hundred and eighty millions of their people to practice it, and by law, protects them in it. It is very unfortunate that our republican government cannot be as generous to its provinces as a monarchial government can to its colonies.***

COL. H. If you persist in the future as in the past in this practice, what kind of an ultimate outcome do you anticipate? Could you not consistently surrender polygamy on the ground that there is no prospect of changing the opinion and law of the country against it, and that nullification of the laws is sure to result disastrously in the end to the nullifiers?

PRES. T. Not so much so as the nullification of the Constitution.***

MR. MUSSER. I think the Lord could better answer that question.

COL. H. "The Lord" is a foreign power to this government, in the sense in which you constantly refer to Him.

PRES. T. I am afraid He is, and there lies the difficulty. When nations forsake God we cannot expect them to act wisely. In doing what they have done, they have opened the flood gates of discord to this nation which they cannot easily close. We are now proscribed, it will be others' turn next. Congress has assumed a most fearful responsibility in breaking down its Constitutional barrier.***

COL. H. You hold, then, that your church possesses the oracles of heaven exclusively, and that the condemnation of polygamy by all Christian nations is without reason and wisdom, and contrary to the spirit of revelation?

PRES. T. We most assuredly do.

* * * * * * * * *

COL. H. Is not, in fact, what you call revelation, the expression of the crystallized public sentiment of your people; and if a majority of them should desire to abandon polygamy, would what is called revelation deter them from doing so?

MR. CALDER. Mr. Colfax, when he was here, and as he was leaving, said to President Young," Mr. Young, you say Joseph Smith had a revelation instituting polygamy; my advice to you is to get a revelation to do away with it."

COL. H. My idea of revelation is embodied in my question. In your case I look upon it as the crystallized expression of the highest wisdom of your people, speaking through your organ, the head of the Church.

* * * * * * * * *

PRESIDENT JOSEPH F. SMITH. It is very unfair, Mr. Hollister, in you to even think that a people who have suffered as we have for our faith, having been driven five different times from our homes, and suffered even to martyrdom, should be insincere in our belief. Questions you have asked here repeatedly imply that we could get up revelations to suit ourselves.

* * * * * * * * *

COL. H. What effect, on the whole, do you apprehend Chief Justice Waite's decision will have on the question?

PRES. T. I don't know that it will have any effect, except to unite us and confirm and strengthen us in our faith.

As soon as the nature of the decision against Elder Reynolds became known, an effort was made to have the case reopened, on the ground that the sentence rendered included "hard labor," which was in excess of the law and the authority of the judge to pronounce. The Supreme Court refused to set aside the verdict and order the proceedings quashed, but on the ensuing 5th of May it issued a supplemental order to the following effect: "That this cause be and the same is hereby remanded to the said Supreme Court [of Utah Territory] with instructions to cause the sentence of the District Court to be set aside, and a new one entered on the verdict in all respects like that before imposed, except so far as it requires the imprisonment to be at hard labor." A mammoth petition, signed by over thirty-two thousand citizens of Utah, was now forwarded to Washington, setting forth the fact that the defendant's was a test case, and asking for his pardon by the Executive. President Hayes heeded not the petition.

On the 14th of June Elder Reynolds was re-sentenced, and two days later, in custody of Deputy Marshals George A. Black and William T. Shaughnessy, set out for the State prison at Lincoln, Nebraska, whither he had been ordered by the Department of Justice. He remained at Lincoln twenty-five days -- during which time he was given the position of book-keeper of the prison -- and was then brought back to Utah.

Arriving at Salt Lake City on the 17th of July, he was at once conveyed to the Penitentiary, where he was held in confinement; serving out his full term, barring one hundred and forty-four days remitted on account of good behavior. He was kindly treated by Warden Butler and the guards, and spent much of his time in prison writing for the press and in teaching a school attended by the other convicts. His example and instructions had such a salutary effect that the warden was wont to say: "Reynolds is worth more than all the guards in keeping order among the prisoners." Repeated efforts were made to secure his pardon, Delegate Cannon doing all in his power to obtain it, and Marshal Shaughnessy also interesting himself in the prisoner's behalf; but all in vain. The President was deaf to every appeal for clemency. The captive remained in prison until January, 1881, suffering the full penalty pronounced against him, except the payment of his fine, which was remitted.

George Reynolds Case Was of a Full Destroying of the Way of Constitutional Guarantee of Religious Freedom

Rulon Jeffs' Sermons 7:23 July 3, 1988 Sandy

The George Reynolds decision of 1879, when there was a deliberate case taken up

to the Supreme Court of the United States, decided the issue not on the language of the Constitution of the United States, which says, "Congress shall make no law respecting the establishment of religion or prohibiting the free exercise thereof." The object of that case was the Cullom Bill passed by Congress, against the Constitution of the United States, prohibiting polygamy in the territories of the United States. And the Supreme Court upheld the constitutionality of the Cullom Bill, but they ignored the wording of the Constitution and went to the mores, or moralities of the day, saying simply that polygamy was an abomination under the morality of the day. And as far as it being a religious belief is concerned, the court said: "Yes, you can believe anything you want, but when it comes to the practice of it, if it collides with the mores of the day, we must give way to it;" and compared polygamy, practiced by the Latter-day Saints, to that of a cult, or religion which believed in human sacrifice, which they would not stand for. The one destroys life, the other brings life.

Revelation of the Lord Jesus Christ Given to President Warren S. Jeffs Palestine, Texas Monday, October 3, 2011

1. Thus saith the Lord to the powers of government who uphold the ruling of the Supreme Court in the George Reynold's Case of 1879, wherein the laws against my Celestial Law of Celestial Plural Marriage were upheld:

2. I, your God over all, declare you continue to not uphold my inspired rule of law, the Amendment to the Constitution of the United States guaranteeing religious and faith freedom; even now you are of a illegal way.

3. You have allowed this evil and destructive ruling to be as a guide.

4. Now overrule that wrong court ruling; for it is not constitutional, nor just.

5. It is used wrongly by present courts, as though man's government can overrule

my revealed law of Celestial Eternal and exalting power; a pure holy law of my revealing through my servant Joseph Smith; only to be lived by pure men and women in my Priesthood, and not for the world.

6. You are of a breaking of righteous principles of freedom when continuing to uphold such a misruling of unjust way.

7. I revealed my holy law to be administered by my own revelations to my Keyholder of Priesthood in each of their administrations.

8. Now let there be a repealing of this unjust ruling, to be of true freedom of religion. Amen.

Anti-Mormon Measures Introduced into Congress -- December 1881

Orson F. Whitney
History of Utah, Volume 3 Page 165

When the Nation's law-makers met in December, [1881] a most bitter feeling prevailed against the Mormons almost universally. The Senate and House were fairly inundated with petitions from all parts, praying for speedy and effective action upon the Utah question. Early in the session several Anti-Mormon measures were introduced into both branches of Congress, among them the famous Edmunds Bill, which was destined to become law. It derived its name from Senator George F. Edmunds, of Vermont.***

President Taylor Explains the Importance of the Laws of God

President John Taylor
JD 22:229 June 26, 1881 Bountiful

Here is Brother George Reynolds, who is present, he was subject to the law. Did he fulfil the law? Yes, he did. Did he meet all its demands? Yes. And having met them, what more remains? If a law is made, and because we are conscientious before God, seeking to fulfil his law unto us, we violate such a law, and we are deprived of our liberty, by the help of God, his power and grace being with us to sustain us, we will bear the consequence. What can be asked then? We think we can fulfil the law of God and the law of man as near as they will let us; and if they wish to punish us for keeping the commandments of God, let them do it, and let them abide the consequence. And when we get through we will say, you Judge and Jury, who passed upon certain men, we have met your requirements, we now go to the Lord and say, Father, we have also met thy requirements; we could not barter away thy laws; we could not violate thy commandments, but, O God, we have been true to thee, and we have been true to our national obligations. And having done our best to promote peace, and having fulfilled the law of both God and man, we feel that we shall be justified by the Lord, and by all honorable, highminded, just and patriotic men. We are not the first who have been put to the test -- Daniel and the three Hebrew children had to pass through this ordeal, they met the consequences, as we propose doing. This was under a despotic government, but under our republican form of government, and with our free institutions, with a Constitution guaranteeing human liberty and the free exercise of religious faith, we have a right to expect a different action. But should this nation persist in violating their Constitutional guarantees, tear away the bulwarks of liberty, and trample upon the principles of freedom and human rights, that are sacred to all men, and by which all men should be governed, by and by the whole fabric will fall, and who will sustain it? We will, in the name of Israel's God. Of this the Prophet Joseph Smith prophesied long, long ago. This is the position we stand in. And if the Government of the United States can afford to oppress us, we can afford to suffer and grow strong.

Let us go to the law of God. We are here to build up Zion; and how ought we to feel?

President John Taylor
JD 11:223 April 7, 1866 SLC

Let us now go back to the action of Congress in relation to plural marriage, of which these eternal covenants are the foundation. The Lord says, "I will introduce the times of the restitution of all things; I will show you my eternal covenants, and call upon you to abide in them; I will show you how to save yourselves, your wives and children, your progenitors and posterity, and to save the earth from a curse.

Congress says, if you fulfill that law we will inflict upon you pains and penalties, fines and imprisonments; in effect, we will not allow you to follow God's commands. Now, if Congress possessed the constitutional right to do so, it would still be a high-handed outrage upon the rights of man; but when we consider that they cannot make such a law without violating the Constitution, and thus nullifying the act, what are we to think of it? Where are we drifting to. After having, with uplifted hands to heaven, sworn that they will "make no law respecting the establishment of religion, or prohibiting the free exercise thereof," to thus sacrilegiously stand between a whole community and their God, and deliberately debar them, so far as they have the power, from observing his law, do they realize what they are doing? Whence came this law on our statute books? Who constituted them our conscience keepers? Who appointed them the judge of our religious faith, or authorized them to coerce us to transgress a law that is binding and imperative on our consciences? We do not expect that Congress is acquainted with our religious faith; but, as members of the body politic, we do claim the guarantees of the Constitution and immunity from persecution on merely religious grounds.

What are we to think of a United States judge who would marry a man to another man's wife. He certainly ought to know better. We are told that she was a second wife, and, therefore, not acknowledged. Indeed, this is singular logic. If she was not a wife, then polygamy is no crime in the eyes of the law; for Congress have passed no law against whoredom. A man may have as many mistresses as he please, without transgressing any law of Congress. The act in relation to polygamy contemplates punishing a man for having more wives, not mistresses. If she was simply his mistress, then the law is of no effect; and the very fact of Congress passing such a law is the strongest possible proof, in law, of the existence of a marriage covenant, which, until that law was passed, was by them considered valid. If, then, she was not his wife, no person could be punished under that law for polygamy. If she was his wife, then the judge transgressed the law which he professionally came to maintain.

In relation to all these matters, the safe path for the Saints to take is, to do right, and, by the help of God, seek diligently and honorably to maintain the position which they hold. Are we ashamed of anything we have done in marrying wives? No. We shall not be ashamed before God and the holy angels, much less before a number of corrupt, miserable scoundrels, who are the very dregs of hell. We care nothing for their opinions, their ideas, or notions; for they do not know God, nor the principles which he has revealed. They wallow in the sink of corruption, as they would have us do; but, the Lord being our helper, we will not do it, but we will try to do right and keep the commandments of God, live our religion, and pursue a course that will secure to us the smiles and approbation of God our Father. Inasmuch as we do this He will take care of us, maintain His own cause, and sustain His people. We have a right to keep His commandments. But what would you do if the United States were to bring up an army against you on account of polygamy, or on account of any other religious subject? We would trust in God, as we always have done. Would you have no fears? None. All the fears that I am troubled with is that this people will not do right -- that they will not keep the commandments of God. If we will only faithfully live our religion, we fear no earthly power. Our safety is in God. Our religion is an eternal religion. Our covenants are eternal covenants, and we expect to maintain the principles of our religion on the earth, and to possess them in the heavens. And if our wives and children do right, and we as fathers and husbands do right in this world, we expect to have our wives and children in eternity. Let us live in that way which will secure the approbation of God, that we, his representatives on the earth, may magnify our calling, honor Him, and maintain our integrity to the end; that we may be saved in His celestial kingdom, with our wives, and children, and brethren, from generation to generation, worlds without end. Amen.

President John Taylor
JD 25:349 October 19, 1884 Ogden

I remember some little time ago a gentleman named Mr. Pierpont (who was Attorney-General under President Grant) called upon me. I was pleased to see him, and am pleased to see all honorable gentlemen.*** After talking further with him upon the subject I said, "Now, Mr. Pierpont, you are well acquainted with all these legal affairs. Although I have yielded in this matter in order that I might not be an obstructionist, and do not wish to act as a Fenian, or a Nihilist, or a Communist, or a Kuklux, or a Regulator, or a Plug Ugly, or a Molly Maguire, yet, sir, we shall stand up for our rights and protect ourselves in every proper way, legally and constitutionally, and dispute inch by inch every step that is taken to deprive us of our rights and liberties." And we will do this in the way that I speak of. We are doing it to-day; and as you have heard it expressed on other occasions, it looks very much like as though the time was drawing near when this country will tumble to pieces; for if the people of this nation are so blind and infatuated as to trample under foot the Constitution and other safeguards provided for the liberties of man, we do not propose to assist them in their suicidal and traitorous enterprises; for we have been told by Joseph Smith that when the people of this nation would trample upon the Constitution, the Elders of this Church would rally round the flag and defend it. And it may come to that; we may be nearer to it than some of us think, for the people are not very zealous in the protection of human rights. And when legislators, governors and judges unite in seeking to tear down the temple of liberty and destroy the bulwarks of human freedom, it will be seen by all lovers of liberty, that they are playing a hazardous game and endangering the perpetuity of human rights. For it will not take long for the unthinking to follow their lead, and they may let loose an element that they never can bind again. We seem to be standing on a precipice and the tumultuous passions of men are agitated by political and party strife; the elements of discord are seething and raging as if portending a coming storm; and no man seem scompetent [seems competent] to take the helm and guide the ship of State through the fearful breakers that threaten on every hand. These are dangerous things, but it becomes our duty as good citizens to obey the law as far as practicable, and be governed by correct principles.

I had some papers read over at the General Conference, giving my views in relation to some of these matters. They have been published, but I will have one or two extracts read for your information.

President Cannon then read as follows:

The distinction being made between Polygamy and Prostitution:

1st. Congress made a law which would affect both; and cohabitation with more than one woman was made a crime whether in polygamy or out of polygamy.

2nd. The Governor turned legislator, added to this law, and inserted in a test oath to officials, the following words regarding cohabitation, "in the marriage relation;" thus plainly and definitely sanctioning prostitution, without any law of the United States, or any authority.

3rd. The United States Commissioners, also without legislation, adopted the action of the Governor, and still insisted on this interpolation, in the test oath in election matters, and placed all polygamists under this unconstitutional oath, and released prostitutes and their paramours from the obligations placed upon others.

4th. The Prosecuting Attorney has sanctioned these things, and pursued a similar course: and while he has asked all the "Mormon" grand jurors certain questions pertaining to their religious faith in the doctrines of the "Mormon" Church, and challenged them if they answered affirmatively as to their belief in polygamy, he has declined to ask other jurors whether they believed in prostitution, or whether they believed in cohabiting with more than one woman or not.

5th. Chief Justice Zane when appealed to on this question, refused to interfere, or give any other ruling.

Thus a law was first passed by Congress, which has been perverted by the administration, by all its officers, who have officiated in this Territory, and made to subserve the interests of a party who have placed in their political platform an Anti-Mormon plank; and have clearly proven that there is a combination entered into by all the officers of state officiating in this Territory, to back up this political intrigue in the interest of party, and at the sacrifice of law, equity, jurisprudence, and all the safeguards that are provided by the Constitution for the protection of human rights.

Congress cannot be condemned for these proceedings. The law as it stands on the nation's Statute Books make no such distinction, so far as the qualification of jurors are concerned, between those who cohabit with more than one woman in the marriage relation, and those who do so outside of that relation. All the rest has been aided by officials here. The law reads: "Section 5: That in any prosecution for bigamy, polygamy, or unlawful cohabitation, under any Statute of the United States, it shall be sufficient cause of challenge to any person drawn or summoned as a juryman or a talesman, first, that he is or has been living in the practice of bigamy, polygamy, or unlawful cohabitation with more than one woman, * * or second, that he believes it right for a man to have more than one living and undivorced wife at the same time, or to live in the practice of cohabiting with more than one woman." It will thus be seen that the same questions can be properly put to both classes; and such was the evident, unmistakable intention of Congress. But the Prosecuting Attorney with red-hot zeal changes all this, in his religio-political crusade against the faith of the Latter-day Saints he insists upon his right to propound the question with the Governor's interpolation super-added, whilst he entirely ignores the other side of the case; hence those who cohabit outside of the marriage relation can go scot free, without interrogation or questioning, and when attention is drawn to this perversion of the law, he asserts that he has the right to propound what questions he chooses, and decline to ask those he has no mind to; in fact that the whole proceeding was a purely optional matter with him. Thus the whole weight of the law is unjustly and unrighteously thrown on the shoulders of those who believe and act in the marriage relation, and entirely removed from the others, who develop into the jurors, who are to indict, try and condemn the other and far more honorable class.

The People of Utah Petition Congress for a Commission of Investigation -- 1882

Orson F. Whitney
History of Utah, Volume 3 Page 180

On that very day [that the Edmunds bill passed the Senate] the Utah Legislature, which had been in session for several weeks, adopted a memorial praying Congress not to act hastily upon the extreme measures then pending before it, inimical to the people of this Territory, and asking for a commission of investigation.*** Later, another memorial, giving reasons why a commission of investigation should be sent, was drafted by a special joint committee of both branches of the Assembly, unanimously adopted and signed by the officers and members thereof, and a printed copy sent to the President of the United States, each member of his Cabinet, each Senator and Representative in Congress, and other government officials and prominent persons.

This memorial stated that for many years the people of Utah had patiently endured the misrepresentations and slanders of unscrupulous persons who had located at different times in the Territory, and who, from various unworthy motives, had formed themselves into political and religious cliques avowedly to represent the liberal and progressive element of the Territory, but really to vex and annoy the majority of the people and deprive them, if possible, of their civil, religious and political rights.***

This action of the people's representatives was supplemented by mass meetings of citizens in various parts of the Territory, and four mammoth petitions, signed respectively by men, women and the youth of both sexes, denying the falsehoods and detractions set afloat concerning them, and asking for a fair and full investigation of the charges, were prepared and sent to Washington. The signers of these petitions aggregated over sixty-five thousand souls.

Edmunds Bill Passes the Senate February 16, 1882

Orson F. Whitney
History of Utah, Volume 3 Page 180

Doubtless many who voted for the Edmunds Bill did so from choice, being in full sympathy with the measure. There were some, however, who supported it against their inclination, fearing it would displease their constituents if they listened to the dictates of conscience and regarded their oaths to sustain the Constitution. All were more or less influenced by the terrible rush and roar of the Anti-Mormon crusade; a hurricane of hatred and bigotry, before which statesmen, usually strong-minded and courageous, bent like willows in a storm. It was Thursday, the 16th of February, when the bill passed the Senate.

The Edmunds Bill Becomes Law March 22, 1882

Orson F. Whitney
History of Utah, Volume 3 Page 186

In the interim the Edmunds Bill, which had passed the Senate, was "railroaded" through the House of Representatives. The entire discussion occupied only two hours; little or no opportunity was given for amendments; speeches were limited to five minutes each, and every effort was made by the friends of the bill, who were in the majority, to prevent a full and free discussion of its provisions.***

The bill passed the House by a vote of 199 to 42; 51 members not voting. On the 22nd of March it received the signature of President Arthur and became a law of the land.

Arrival of the Utah Commission -- August 1882

Orson F. Whitney
History of Utah, Volume 3 Page 207

The summer of 1882 also witnessed the arrival in Utah of the five Commissioners [Utah Commission] provided for in the Edmunds Act and recently appointed by the President of the United States.*** Those duties, as defined in the Act creating the Commission, were:

First -- To appoint officers to perform each and every duty relating to the registration of voters, the conduct of elections, the receiving or rejection of votes, the canvassing and returning of the same and the issuing of certificates or other evidence of election.

Second -- To canvass the returns of all the votes cast at elections for members of the Legislature, and issue certificates of election to those persons who, being eligible for such election, should appear to have been lawfully elected.

Third -- To continue in office until the Legislative Assembly, so elected and qualified, should make provision for filling the offices vacated by the Edmunds Act, as therein authorized.

The Test Oath, Precluding Members of the Church to Vote

Orson F. Whitney
History of Utah, Volume 3 Page 228

TERRITORY OF UTAH, }
COUNTY OF . . . . } ss.

I . . . ., being first duly sworn (or affirmed), depose and say that I am over twenty-one years of age, and have resided in the Territory of Utah for six months, and in the precinct of . . . . one month immediately preceding the date hereof, and (if a male) am a native born or naturalized (as the case may be) citizen of the United States and a taxpayer in this Territory, or (if a female), I am native born, or naturalized, or the wife, widow or daughter (as the case may be) of a native born or naturalized citizen of the United States; and I do further solemnly swear (or affirm) that I am not a bigamist or a polygamist; that I am not a violator of the laws of the United States prohibiting bigamy or polygamy; that I do not live or cohabit with more than one woman in the marriage relation, nor does any relation exist between me and any woman which has been entered into or continued in violation of the said laws of the United States prohibiting bigamy or polygamy; and (if a woman) that I am not the wife of a polygamist, nor have I entered into any relation with any man in violation of the laws of the United States concerning polygamy or bigamy.

Subscribed and sworn before me
this . . . . . day of . . . . ., 1882.

Registration Officer,
. . . . Precinct.

How the People of the Church Regarded the Test Oath

Orson F. Whitney
History of Utah, Volume 3 Page 231

The Mormon people did not propose to sit supinely and allow any such discrimination to daunt them. With all polygamists disfranchised they were still in the great majority in the Territory, and, unlike their opponents, had no reason to fear the result of an election, if each party was given a fair field, "a free ballot and an honest count." The First Presidency, in an address to the members of the Church, dated at Salt Lake City, August 29, 1882, animadverted upon the Commissioners and their test oath, and counseled their own followers in this wise:

It has been with feelings of profound regret that we have seen the Commissioners, men of high position and bearing honored names, take this view of the law, and frame such an oath as this to be administered unto the people, yet on the other hand, it is with unmixed satisfaction we perceive that the oath draws the line so sharply and distinctly between marriage and licentiousness. By the attempt in the construction of this oath to shield from injury those who, by their illicit connections with the other sex, might, under the provisions of the Edmunds law, be disfranchised, the Latter-day Saints, who, in all sincerity and honor, have obeyed a revelation from God, are not reduced to their degraded level.

Our counsel, then, is to the Latter-day Saints, who can truthfully take this oath, there is no reason we know of in the Gospel, or in any of the revelations of God, which prevents you from doing so.*** Very many of you can take this oath with conscientiousness and entire truthfulness, as you could even if it were in a form which many of your traducers could not take without perjury; and yet there would be no impropriety, while you do take it, in protesting against it as a gross wrong imposed upon you.

* * * * * * * * *

In regard to your political arrangements, the Territorial Central Committee is an organization that has for its object the preservation of the rights of every citizen of this Territory, without regard to party or sect. They will doubtless issue such instructions, from time to time, as circumstances demand. It is in the interest of every patriot to faithfully observe and practically carry out the suggestions that they may make.

The Anti-Polygamy Laws Made Retroactive

The next act of the Commission was the issuance of an order prohibiting the registration of any person, male or female, who, at any time since the passage of the anti-polygamy laws of 1862 and 1882, had lived in bigamous or polygamous relations.

President Taylor Speaks of the Edmunds Bill and the Untruths Circulated

President John Taylor
JD 23:60 April 9, 1882 SLC

I give these statements of facts for the information of the brethren who are here from a distance; but, then, they know them as facts; that is, they know how these soi disant regenerators act, but many of them do not know what their civilization is here, and what is sought to be introduced among us, and the infamous statements circulated concerning us. We are ready, as I said before, to compare notes with them or the people of this or any nation at any time. And then again, we ought to be more pure and virtuous than they, for we do profess to be the Saints of the Most High God. With this view, when this Edmunds bill was being canvassed, and there was a prospect of its passing -- although we thought at first it was impossible that such a concern could pass through Congress; but when we saw the falsehoods that were being circulated, the furore that was being raised and fanned by religious fanatics and political demagogues, petitions were gotten up by the people here, one of them representing the male class, another our Relief Societies, another our young men, and another our young ladies' Improvement Societies. All of them represented that we were a virtuous people -- that polygamy was a religious institution; and the young people asserted that it had been taught to them by their parents from their youth up, and that the principles of purity, virtue, integrity and loyalty to the government of the United States had been instilled into their minds and hearts since their earliest childhood; and further, that they had been taught and understood that chastity was their greatest boon, far above jewels or wealth, and more precious than life itself. In a few days we had 165,000 [65,000] signatures, and they were forwarded to Washington. The request was that Congress would not act as the government had before -- first sent out an army and then send commissioners to inquire, but that they would send commissioners first to inquire into the facts of the case. But they did not choose to listen. In fact, there has been a great furore in the United States in relation to these matters, and that has originated to an extent through our Governor. Now I am very much averse to talking about official men; I do not like to do such things. They ought to be honorable men; the most charitable construction I could put upon his acts would be to say that his education had been sadly neglected, and that he was not acquainted with figures.

Annie Gallifant in Contempt for Failure to Testify Against Her Husband Before Grand Jury -- November 17th 1882

Orson F. Whitney
History of Utah, Volume 3 Page 275

A few months later occurred a sensational episode which, though isolated from the long series of raids and prosecutions that followed, was a precursor of what was approaching and gave token of some of the tactics that would be employed by the crusaders. It was the imprisonment of a young Mormon woman named Annie Gallifant. She was the alleged plural wife of John Connelly, a baker and confectioner. On the 17th of November, 1882, the young woman -- she was under twenty years of age -- was before the Grand Jury at Salt Lake City, where she was plied with questions the answers to which, it was supposed, would lead to the conviction of her reputed husband. One of the questions was a direct demand for the name of the person to whom she was married. She refused to answer, whereupon she was taken before Chief Justice Hunter, who informed her that the questions asked were proper, and that it was her duty to reply to them. Still she refused. The Judge then sentenced her to imprisonment in the Penitentiary until such time as she should be willing to answer.

The event created considerable indignation, which was not in any degree lessened when it became known that the young woman thus consigned to a felon's cell was about to become a mother. She was a frail little creature, and it was feared that a premature birth might result from the excitement attendant upon her incarceration, to be followed by the death of both mother and child.*** All fears, however, were set at rest regarding the imprisoned witness on the day following her incarceration. The Grand Jury having been discharged, she was released from custody and permitted to return to her home. Her child was born four days later. Subsequently, John Connelly, who proved to be her husband, was indicted for polygamy and in the fall of 1884 was tried and acquitted.*** [Footnote: Subsequently John Connelly was convicted of unlawful cohabitation and sent to the Penitentiary.]

Rudger Clawson's Arrest -- April 24, 1884

Orson F. Whitney
History of Utah, Volume 3 Page 278

Another year passed and then came the arrest and initial proceedings in the case of Rudger Clawson; the virtual opening, on the part of the courts, of the great anti-polygamy crusade. The defendant in this celebrated case was a son of Bishop H. B. Clawson and his second wife, Margaret Judd. He was a young man of exemplary habits, zealous for the cause in which he had been nurtured from childhood. His intrepid conduct at the time of the murder of his fellow missionary, Joseph Standing, in Georgia, has been dwelt upon. He was a firm believer in the principle of plural marriage, to which he owed his earthly origin, and had married, according to rumor, two wives. His first wife was Florence Dinwoodey, daughter of Henry Dinwoodey, the wealthy head of a large furniture establishment at Salt Lake City. His alleged plural wife was Lydia Spencer, daughter of Daniel Spencer; a name prominent in early Utah annals.

Rudger Clawson was arrested by United States Marshal Ireland on the 24th of April, 1884; the same day on which he had been indicted by the Grand Jury. Taken before U. S. Commissioner William McKay, he was placed under bonds in the sum of three thousand dollars and was then given his liberty.

Chief Justice Zane Arrives in Utah -- August 1884

Orson F. Whitney
History of Utah, Volume 3 Page 266

While all Utah was ringing with the dreadful news of the massacre of the Mormon missionaries and their friends in Tennessee, and just one day after the train bearing the bodies of the murdered Elders reached its destination, there arrived at Salt Lake City a man whose remarkable career in these parts as a representative of the Federal Government will form much of the matter of the remaining portion of this volume. That man was Hon. Charles S. Zane, late of Springfield, Illinois, who had recently been appointed Chief Justice of this Territory.

The wonderful changes following and in part flowing from Judge Zane's administration might induce in many the belief that he was an instrument of Destiny, and that he came to Utah with a special mission from the Government; a mission for which he had been carefully chosen and vested with extraordinary powers. Indeed, he was more than once styled "a mission jurist," and, like Judge McKean, whom he was supposed at one time to be ambitiously emulating, was charged with having as his object the overthrow of Mormonism as a religion.***

Judge Zane's Past Record and the Prospect Confronting Him

Judge Zane's appointment seems to have come in the ordinary course of events; no Jesuitical influence securing him the office, and no Star Chamber council at Washington instructing him how to discharge its functions. The case in a nutshell is this: The Government was determined to suppress the practice of polygamy in the Territories; a law had been passed by Congress to that end, and the Federal officials in Utah were under obligations to enforce it. A vacancy occurred in the Chief Justiceship of the Territory, and Charles S. Zane, being considered a proper man for the place, was sent to fill it. Not that the appointment came independently, without the usual intervention of powerful friends and their influence; but it came, according to his account, without his solicitation or seeking.

The Mormon Leaders Go into Exile

Orson F. Whitney
History of Utah, Volume 3 Page 344

The President [John Taylor] took his own counsel and retired from public view; an example speedily followed by his Counselors, the Apostles, and other leading men of the Church; with others less prominent but still liable to prosecution. From time to time the First Presidency communicated with their people by means of epistles read to them at their general conferences; but with the exception of a few intimate friends, including members of his family, who accompanied him in his secret journeyings from place to place, sharing his retirement and acting as guards or messengers for him and his fellow exiles, the Latter-day Saints never again saw President Taylor alive. The most persistent efforts were put forth for his capture, but all to no purpose. The friends whom he trusted were true, and coaxings, promises and threats were alike ineffectual in leading to his discovery.

There was no traitor, or what is almost as bad, no thoughtless, mischievous gossip in the ranks of the faithful souls surrounding the venerable exile during the few sad years remaining to him.

The United States Supreme Court Upholds the Edmunds Law -- 1885

Orson F. Whitney
History of Utah, Volume 3 Page 351

It was on March 23rd of this year [1885] that the Supreme Court of the United States rendered its decision in the case of Murphy *vs.* Ramsey, the effect of which was to establish the constitutionality of the Edmunds Law, but to nullify the test oath formulated by the Utah Commission,***

The Edmunds Law was declared constitutional; Congress having the right to enact it for the reason that the power of the Government of the United States over the national Territories was supreme.

Orson F. Whitney
History of Utah, Volume 3 Page 356

Meantime the Federal courts continued the prosecution of polygamous cases, and the United States Marshal and his deputies busied themselves in raiding the settlements and searching houses suspected of harboring men and women wanted as victims of the crusade. Early in April Marshal Ireland and several of his aids visited Logan, as did U. S. Marshal Dubois, of Idaho, and some of his subordinates; the unusual event of a general conference at that point inspiring them with the hope that some of those whom they most desired to apprehend would be found or heard of in Cache Valley at that time. They were doomed to disappointment, and returned empty-handed, and empty-headed -- so far as information of the whereabouts of the Mormon Presidency was concerned -- to their accustomed haunts in and around the capitals of their respective Territories.

Arrests of persons less notable went on, however, and well nigh the whole inter-mountain region was overrun by the emissaries of the courts, hunting with all the assiduity of sleuth-hounds, and with as little pity as would have been shown by such animals, men accused or suspected of violating the Edmunds Law. The officers, who usually traveled in squads, would suddenly pounce upon some small settlement at midnight or in "the wee sma' 'ours" [the wee small hours] between midnight and daybreak, rudely arousing the inhabitants from slumber, sometimes by discharging firearms at hastily decamping fugitives, and spreading general terror and dismay. Delicate women, fleeing from or frightened by the marauders, received injuries from which they never recovered, and more than one death lies at the door of these heartless disturbers of the peace of innocent and unoffending citizens. Even wise and brave men lost their judgment at times, and had their courage unstrung by this hateful system of harassment; so much more difficult to deal with, since the offenders were officers of the law, than if they had been thieves and trespassers, in which event many of them would undoubtedly have bitten the dust.

President John Y. Barlow Speaks Concerning the Edmunds Act

President John Y. Barlow
John Y. Barlow's Sermons [RTJ] 8:363 Nov. 23, 1947 SCA

We have been out of jail for two years. Whether they will release us yet, we do not know. If they do, we will be free from that score. But what is back of it? There is a law that has been made by the legislature of this State that makes it a felony, from one to five years in the penitentiary; and if we teach the commandments of God as is laid down, why, we are subject to that law.

When the Edmunds Law was made, we either had to go for the laws of God or the laws of the land, one of the two things. Every member of the Church either had to go to the laws of God or the laws of the land. Some preferred the laws of God, and some the laws of the land. Some will say, if we live the laws of the land, we are free, so far as the law of the land is concerned. If we follow the laws of God, then we can have eternal increase. But if we follow the laws of the land, that is the end of your kingdom, you cannot have an increase. That is what the good book says.

President John Y. Barlow
John Y. Barlow's Sermons [RTJ] 8:134 Aug. 25, 1940 SLC

When the higher ordinances of the Gospel were given to the people by the Prophet, only two percent of the people obeyed these ordinances.

Then what came? The Edmunds Law, and the people got scared and ran. Finally the Master said, "What have you done? Get up the young men and the middle-aged and go back and redeem My land."

Brothers and sisters, we are in that condition today. God has spoken, and He is going to come back here, and the people are going to redeem that land. I want to bear my testimony that God never gives any commandment unless He opens the way. It will take more than a Manifesto to ever stop the principle of Celestial Marriage.

The 1886 Revelation

Revelation of the Lord Jesus Christ Given to President John Taylor September 27, 1886

Priesthood Articles, Page 178

My son John, you have asked me concerning the New and Everlasting Covenant how far it is binding upon my people.

Thus saith the Lord: All commandments that I give must be obeyed by those calling themselves by my name unless they are revoked by me or by my authority, and how can I revoke an everlasting covenant, for I the Lord am everlasting and my everlasting covenants cannot be abrogated nor done away with, but they stand forever.

Have I not given my word in great plainness on this subject? Yet have not great numbers of my people been negligent in the observance of my law and the keeping of my commandments, and yet have I borne with them these many years; and this because of their weakness -- because of the perilous times, and furthermore, it is more pleasing to me that men should use their free agency in regard to these matters. Nevertheless, I the Lord do not change and my word and my covenants and my law do not, and as I have heretofore said by my servant Joseph: All those who would enter into my glory must and shall obey my law. And have I not commanded men that if they were Abraham's seed and would enter into my glory, they must do the works of Abraham. **I HAVE NOT REVOKED THIS LAW, NOR WILL I,** for it is everlasting, and those who will enter into my glory MUST obey the conditions thereof; even so, Amen.

The Lorin Woolley Statement

Priesthood Articles, Page 180

As further and ultimate proof of the existence of this revelation we quote a statement in extenso from Lorin C. Woolley, a bodyguard of John Taylor at the time the revelation was received, and who was given a copy of the same on the day it was written, as the statement indicates.

Statement of Lorin C. Woolley with reference to the revelation of 1886, on the subject of Celestial or plural marriage, given September 22, 1929:

There were present Lorin C. Woolley, Daniel R. Bateman, John Y. Barlow, J. Leslie Broadbent and J. W. Musser. Prayer was offered by John Y. Barlow.

Lorin C. Woolley related the following:

While the brethren were at the Carlisle residence (in Murray) in May or June of 1886, letters began to come to President John Taylor from such men as John Sharp, Horace Eldredge, William Jennings, John T. Cain, Abraham Hatch, President Cluff and many other leading men from all over the Church, asking the leaders to do something, as the Gentiles were talking of confiscating their property in connection with the property of the Church.

These letters not only came from those who were living in the plural marriage relation, but also from prominent men who were presiding in various offices in the Church who were not living in that relation. They all urged that something be done to satisfy the Gentiles so that their property would not be confiscated.

George Q. Cannon, on his own initiative, selected a committee comprising himself, Hyrum B. Clawson, Franklin S. Richards, John T. Caine and James Jack, to get up a statement or manifesto that would meet the objections urged by the brethren above named. They met from time to time to discuss the situation. From the White home, where President Taylor and companions stopped, after leaving the Carlisle home, they came out to father's. George Q. Cannon would go and consult with the brethren of the committee, I taking him back and forth each day.

On September 26, 1886, George Q. Cannon, Hyrum B. Clawson, Franklin S. Richards, and others met with President John Taylor at my father's residence at Centerville, Davis County, Utah, and presented a document for President Taylor's consideration.

I had just got back from a three days' trip, during most of which time I had been in the saddle, and being greatly fatigued, I had retired to rest.

Between one and two o'clock P.M. Brother Bateman came and woke me up and asked me to be at my father's home, where a manifesto was to be discussed. I went there and found there were congregated Samuel Bateman, Charles H. Wilkins, L. John Nuttall, Charles Birrell, George Q. Cannon, Franklin S. Richards and Hyrum B. Clawson.

We discussed the proposed Manifesto at length, but we were unable to become united in the discussion. Finally George Q. Cannon suggested that President Taylor take the matter up with the Lord and decide the same the next day.

Brothers Clawson and Richards were taken back to Salt Lake. That evening I was called to act as guard during the first part of the night, notwithstanding the fact that I was greatly fatigued on account of the three days' trip I had just completed.

The brethren retired to bed soon after 9 o'clock. The sleeping rooms were inspected by the guards as was the custom. President Taylor's room had no outside door. The windows were heavily screened.

Some time after the brethren retired and while I was reading the Doctrine and Covenants, I was suddenly attracted to a light appearing under the door leading to President Taylor's room, and was at once startled to hear the voices of men talking there. There were three distinct voices. I was bewildered because it was my duty to keep people out of that room and evidently someone had entered without my knowing it. I made a hasty examination and found the door leading to the room bolted as usual. I then examined the outside of the house and found all the window screens intact. While examining the last window, and feeling greatly agitated, a voice spoke to me saying, "Can't you feel the Spirit? Why should you worry?"

At this I returned to my post and continued to hear the voices in the room. They were so audible that although I did not see the parties I could place their positions in the room from the sound of their voices. The three voices continued until about midnight, when one of them left, and the other two continued. One of them I recognized as President John Taylor's voice. I called Charles Birrell [Footnote: Charles Birrell was also a bodyguard of the brethren and was to take the second shift in watching on this night.] and we both sat up until eight o'clock the next morning.

When President Taylor came out of his room about eight o'clock of the morning of September 27, 1886, we could scarcely look at him on account of the brightness of his personage.

He stated, "Brethren, I have had a very pleasant conversation with Brother Joseph (Joseph Smith)." I said, "Boss, who is the man that was there until midnight?" He asked, "What do you know about it, Lorin?" I told him all about my experience. He said, *"Brother Lorin, that was your Lord."*

We had no breakfast, but assembled ourselves in a meeting. I forget who opened the meeting. I was called to offer the benediction. I think my father, John W. Woolley, offered the opening prayer. There were present at the meeting, in addition to President Taylor, George Q. Cannon, L. John Nuttall, John W. Woolley, Samuel Bateman, Charles Wilkins, Charles Birrell, Daniel R. Bateman, Bishop Samuel Sedden, George Earl, my mother, Julia E. Woolley, my sister, Amy Woolley, and myself. The meeting was held from about 9 o'clock in the morning until 5 in the afternoon, without intermission, being about eight hours in all.

President Taylor called the meeting to order. He had the Manifesto, that had been prepared under the direction of George Q. Cannon, read over again. He then put each person under covenant that he or she would defend the principle of Celestial or plural marriage, and that they would consecrate their lives, liberty and property to this end, and that they personally would sustain and uphold that principle.

By that time we were all filled with the Holy Ghost. President Taylor and those present occupied about three hours up to this time. After placing us under covenant, he placed his finger on the document, his person rising from the floor about a foot or eighteen inches, and with countenance animated by the Spirit of the Lord, and raising his right hand to the square, he said, "Sign that document? -- Never! I would suffer my right hand to be severed from my body first. Sanction it -- never! I would suffer my tongue to be torn from its roots in my mouth before I would sanction it!"

After that he talked for about an hour and then sat down and wrote the revelation which was given him by the Lord upon the question of Plural Marriage (the text of which revelation is given above). Then he talked to us for some time, and said, *"Some of you will be handled and ostracized and cast out from the Church by your brethren because of your faithfulness and integrity to this principle, and some of you may have to surrender your lives because of the same, but woe, woe, unto those who shall bring these troubles upon you."* (Three of us were handled and ostracized for supporting and sustaining this principle. There are only three left who were at the meeting mentioned -- Daniel R. Bateman, George Earl, and myself. So far as I know, those of them who have passed away all stood firm to the covenants entered into from that day to the day of their deaths.)

After the meeting referred to, President Taylor had L. John Nuttall write five copies of the revelation. He called five of us together: Samuel Bateman, Charles H. Wilkins, George Q. Cannon, John W. Woolley, and myself.

He then set us apart and placed us under covenant that while we lived we would see to it that no year passed by without children being born in the principle of plural marriage. We were given authority to ordain others if necessary to carry this work on, they in turn to be given authority to ordain others when necessary, under the direction of the worthy senior (by ordination), so that there should be no cessation in the work. He then gave each of us a copy of the revelation.

I am the only one of the five now living, and so far as I know all five of the brethren remained true and faithful to the covenants they entered into, and to the responsibilities placed upon them at that time.

During the eight hours we were together, and while President Taylor was talking to us, he frequently arose and stood above the floor, and his countenance and being were so enveloped by light and glory that it was difficult for us to look upon him.

He stated that the document (referring to the Manifesto) was from the lower regions. He stated that many of the things he had told us we would forget and they would be taken from us, but that they would return to us in due time as needed, and from this fact we would know that the same was from the Lord. This has been literally fulfilled. Many of the things I forgot, but they are coming to me gradually, and those things that come to me are as clear as on the day on which they were given.

President Taylor said that the time would come when many of the Saints would apostatize because of this principle. He said "one-half of this people would apostatize over the principle for which we are now in hiding; yea, and possibly one-half of the other half" (rising off the floor while making the statement). He also said the day will come when a document similar to that (Manifesto) then under consideration would be adopted by the Church, following which "APOSTASY AND WHOREDOM would be rampant in the Church."

He said that in the time of the seventh President of this Church, the Church would go into *bondage both temporally and spiritually* and in that day (the day of bondage) the one Mighty and Strong spoken of in the 85th Section of the Doctrine and Covenants would come.

Among other things stated by President Taylor on this occasion was this, *"I would be surprised if ten per cent of those who claim to hold the Melchizedek Priesthood will remain true and faithful to the Gospel of the Lord Jesus Christ, at the time of the seventh president, and that there would be thousands that think they hold the priesthood at that time, but would not have it properly conferred upon them."*

John Taylor set the five mentioned apart and gave them authority to perform marriage ceremonies, and also to set others apart to do the same thing as long as they remained upon the earth; *and while doing so, the Prophet Joseph Smith stood by directing the proceedings. Two of us had not met the Prophet Joseph Smith in his mortal lifetime and we -- Charles H. Wilkins*

and myself -- were introduced to him and shook hands with him.

(Signed) Lorin C. Woolley

Excerpts from an Epistle of the First Presidency to the Church of Jesus Christ of Latter-day Saints -- April 8, 1887

The Mind and Will of the Lord, Page 177 Address 36

Due to the question over the legality of polygamy and the desire of certain federal officials to imprison, prosecute, and/or otherwise hound church leaders into compliance with questionable civil law, many of the Brethren, notably members of the First Presidency, were forced to go underground to avoid public appearances. Unable to attend the 57th Annual General Conference of The Church of Jesus Christ of Latter-day Saints, and in lieu of what they might have said had they been able to attend, President John Taylor issued the following epistle that was read to the conference by Bishop G. F. Whitney on April 8, 1887. As a number of the Brethren were experiencing the same difficulties with the law, it was thought advisable to hold General Conference in Provo, Utah, rather than in Salt Lake City as usual.***

Millennial Star, Volume 49 Page 292

From the day of the organization of the Church of Jesus Christ of Latter-day Saints, the adversary of souls has stirred up the wicked to accomplish its destruction. Various agencies have been employed to effect this purpose. Falsehood, tradition, deep-rooted prejudice, the learning, wealth and power of Christendom, mob violence, fire, fetters, the rifle and the sword, wholesale expulsion and military force having been tried in vain, a new crusade has been inaugurated in the form of legislative and judicial tyranny, prompted by Satan and carried on by cunning adventurers and reckless fanatics.

Perhaps the most shameful and unrepublican attempt of this character was the latest scheme devised by the local conspirators. What is known as the Edmunds law -- the act of March 22, 1882 -- was hoped to be broad enough in its intended scope to secure the political control of the Territory to the anti-"Mormon" voters. A large number of both sexes were by that act deprived of the franchise. That it did not wrench the control of the Territory out of the hands of the majority of its residents, is not to be credited to the absence of such a wish and design on the part of its authors and promoters, but to the overruling providence of the Almighty. The ground which those who favored this measure seemed to take was, that it was both praiseworthy and justifiable to violate the soundest political principles, and even the Constitution itself, to take the political control of the Territory of Utah from the "Mormon" majority and concentrate it in the hands of the anti-"Mormon" minority. Having gone thus far to accomplish this end, it was scarcely to be expected they would hesitate to make other and more outrageous attempts, when they found that the Edmunds law had not answered the full purpose for which it was intended. It appears to be one of the effects which follow a departure from sound republican and constitutional principles like the enactment of such a strange piece of legislation as the Edmunds Law, that every future attempt in the same direction will be more regardless of the settled principles of political liberty than its predecessor.***

With full confidence that the dense clouds which have darkened our horizon during the past two or three years will be soon dissipated by the bright rays of the sun of righteousness, and invoking the blessings that come through patient endurance of affliction and faithful adherence to the right, upon the Saints of God in all the world, we subscribe ourselves your fellow servants in the great work of the latter days,

JOHN TAYLOR
GEORGE Q. CANNON
JOSEPH F. SMITH

First Presidency of the Church of Jesus Christ of Latter-day Saints
April, 1887.

President John Taylor Died a Double Martyr

President Leroy S. Johnson
Leroy S. Johnson's Sermons 2:506 July 16, 1972 SLC

In the days of Joseph the Prophet, He was establishing His work in the earth and He instructed the Prophet Joseph Smith daily what to do and how to set in order His house. But through the unfaithfulness of the people, Joseph was not permitted to do all that the Lord wanted him to do. If we will go into history, we will find that there were very few men who stood by the Prophet Joseph continually and faithfully without accusation about his performance. But, because of the criticism and the unstable minds of men, he was not permitted to accomplish what he would like to have done.

After the Prophet Joseph passed, we can say the same thing of Brigham Young and John Taylor -- John Taylor, especially. Why John Taylor, especially? John Taylor was with the Prophet when he was martyred; and when it became his duty to rule over the saints, what happened? He was driven into hiding. He wasn't permitted, because of the unfaithfulness of his brethren, to do the things that he would like to have done. He was permitted to accomplish some things. He was permitted to set in order a movement that later on would eventually set in order the machinery to be used in the redemption of Zion. Today this machinery is operating.

President Leroy S. Johnson
Leroy S. Johnson's Sermons 1:61 Sept. 25, 1960 Canada

There are many ways we can improve ourselves day by day to measure up to the character of that great Being. One of the greatest responsibilities upon us today is to teach our children to become like God. If you can put into practice the things taught here, you will have a community here that will cease to worship golden calves; and they will worship our Father in Heaven. Joseph Smith tried to put this idea over; Brigham Young tried in his day; John Taylor also tried in his day, but he had to go into hiding and died a martyr because he didn't have friends enough to help him.

President Rulon Jeffs
Rulon Jeffs' Sermons 3:167 October 7, 1973 CCA

There were none closer to the Prophet than John Taylor, who once said, "I did not know who Joseph really was until that night in Carthage." And he was a witness and a testator for Joseph. All praise to his name, for he died a double martyr, going from house to house of his friends to avoid his enemies who would have destroyed him. And he was able, thus, to finish his work, the greatest part of which was in hiding.

President Rulon Jeffs
Rulon Jeffs' Sermons 5:508 Oct. 28, 1984 Sacred Grove

Jesus and Joseph came to John Taylor to

see that this great work was carried on, and responsible keyholders to follow, because the Church had given up the fullness of the Gospel and rejected the Lord. There were not very many men who would give the Prophet John Taylor succor and help as he was in hiding.

President Leroy S. Johnson
Leroy S. Johnson's Sermons 4:1276 Sept. 19, 1976 SLC

Every man, woman, and child that dares to say that Joseph Smith was a Prophet of God, takes their lives in their hands when they say it. They did in Joseph's day; they did in Brigham Young's day; and they did in John Taylor's day. John Taylor even had to go into hiding because he couldn't tell the people that he knew that Joseph Smith was a Prophet and be safe and know that he would be a live man after he said the words.

President Lorin Woolley Bears Testimony of President John Taylor by John Y. Barlow Account

President John Y. Barlow
John Y. Barlow's Sermons [RTJ 8:284] May 14, 1944 SLC

I knew Lorin Woolley, and he also told me things. I want to bear my testimony to the truth when he said that the Priesthood came on down from John Taylor, etc. Read the 90th Section of the Doctrine and Covenants, where it tells us that the keys of the Kingdom were given to Joseph Smith. Now I want you to find any other place in the Church where they say that. The keys came on down through John Taylor and the others. I was glad to hear my brother say that he got that testimony for himself. I want you to find out these things for yourselves.

Chapter 4
Administration of President John W. Woolley

**Revelation of the Lord Jesus Christ
Given to President Warren S. Jeffs
Palestine, Texas
Sunday, October 2, 2011**

1. Thus saith the Lord to all peoples, that my holy servant John Taylor was called to be my Keyholder of Priesthood; which keys of power I, your Lord, only place on a man of my holy Order Eternal.

2. Thus he was faithful in all his word and labors, in upholding every word of my giving, both through the Keyholders before him, and also my will through him.

3. I, your Lord, visited him in his time of hiding from government persecuting powers; having mine holy resurrected servant, Joseph Smith, with me as the authority I sent to teach John Taylor, and Brigham Young before him.

4. John Taylor was instructed to keep my Priesthood and Celestial Law of Plural Celestial Marriage alive and increasing on earth.

5. He was shown of the coming greater prosecuting powers of the United States government against my Celestial Law.

6. He was told to set apart six men as confirmed apostles of your Lord, and place them as men of silent labor, to only promote my Celestial Law among they who would receive in sacred trust my Celestial Plural Marriage Law in full plural and holy living.

7. When the governing powers pressured the President of the Church, who was not my Keyholder of Priesthood, even Wilford Woodruff, he gave in, notwithstanding I gave my own word to him beforehand to not make any compromises to the wicked concerning my Celestial Law.

8. He lost Priesthood, and was an instrument to lead astray many of my Church; until the leaders of that organization fully opposed my Priesthood, and sought to destroy the continuation of my Celestial Plural Marriage law from continuing on earth.

9. I called my servant John W. Woolley to be my holy and authorized Keyholder of all the sealing keys and powers of Priesthood after I took my servant John Taylor from the earth in his passing unto the spirit world, to await his resurrection.

10. John Woolley was fully pure, faithful, and noble in fulfilling my will.

11. He was a silent witness of the apostasy of the majority of the members of that branch called the Church of Jesus Christ of Latter-day Saints, which broke itself away from my Holy Priesthood, becoming gentile and of the apostasy of rebelling against God and His Celestial Law.

12. Now learn that my true Priesthood continued through John Woolley.

13. He was of full Priesthood authority.

14. He was faithful and abided my Celestial Law.

15. He was of a power to visit often the former Prophets.

16. He could see beyond the veil, and visit with my Priesthood of the full authority as he held.

17. He was led by revelation to test

the President of the Church, even Heber J. Grant; a man who fully opposed my Celestial Law when he was in the President position, and proved himself a traitor to Priesthood and my Celestial Law.

18. Thus, Heber J. Grant caused much persecution to come against my Priesthood during the days of my Keyholders of Priesthood, namely, in the times of John W. Woolley, Lorin C. Woolley, and John Y. Barlow.

19. These Keyholders, each in their time, stood faithful in continuing my Celestial Law of Plural Marriage.

20. Thus I reveal to all peoples that I, your Lord, guided my authority on earth to continue my Priesthood power and Priesthood law of Celestial Plural Marriage on earth.

21. Now learn that the Church calling itself the Church of Jesus Christ of Latter-day Saints is apostate and not of my Priesthood.

22. My true Church on earth, saith your Lord, is now of a naming to represent the upholding of all my laws of Celestial power to exalt unto eternal lives, even the Fundamentalist Church of Jesus Christ of Latter-day Saints; which Church continues as an organization of my full Priesthood authority now on earth.

23. This sacred revealing is to tell all peoples on earth I, your Lord, have continued my Church, Priesthood, and Kingdom on earth by preserving my Keyholders who lived fully my Celestial and Eternal laws of Priesthood, even my law of Celestial Plural Marriage.

24. Now learn that I, God, have done this.

25. Thus, all who speak against my Priesthood and against my Celestial Law are not of me, and shall not prosper, but shall be brought low, and be among the wicked.

26. My holy law is pure, holy, and purifies the obedient to my law unto an exalting throne in heaven of Godhood -- they who abide the fulness of my law through the Priesthood I authorize on earth.

27. Now be of an understanding that my Priesthood and my Celestial Law is on earth, and is governed by my will and holy power.

28. All who fight against my Priesthood and my Celestial Law of Celestial Plural Marriage are against God.

29. Therefore, they shall be of a full receiving of my judgments on earth, and in the eternal judgment that shall come on all peoples hereafter.

30. Know that my Celestial Law is mine, and is eternal, and cannot be done away; but continues with my keys of Priesthood on earth, even my servant in bondage at this time.

31. He is of full keys of my eternal authority and power of thy Lord.

32. All who fight against him fight against God.

33. Therefore, repent, and know my judgments of cleansing are nigh at hand.

34. Let my servant go free to do my will.

35. I, even Jesus Christ, the God over all peoples of every time of earth's history, speaketh.

36. So shall I preserve my Priesthood and Celestial Law.

37. Now let all learn that the present persecution through prosecution is not

of righteousness, but of evil; and all who thus participate shall feel my judgments of humbling.

38. Some shall be taken. Others shall be laid low of power.

39. I am God that saith my will to the persecution combination of government prosecuting and policing powers who have derided my holy law, and also to all peoples, that my holy way is not of the world, but of a Celestial eternal power and authority, not governed by earthly governing authority.

40. My law is pure. My pure people are commanded of their God to abide my law in purity.

41. Let them be freed who are in bondage, lest a more severe judgment increasingly come upon the land, saith Jesus Christ, the God over all. Amen.

Revelation of the Lord Jesus Christ Given to President Warren S. Jeffs San Angelo, Texas Monday, August 1, 2011

1. Let all know my pure way of Eternal Union Celestial power of Priesthood of my keys and authority was continued through a holy vessel of sacred worth of eternal power.

2. My holy and pure and named and ordained servant of continuing my Keyholder power, John Taylor, was of a martyr's crown Celestial; even to be of the holy and exalting power of ruling over all by my will of revealing saving truth to few in a day of falling away from truth, was John Woolley.

3. I revealed through John Taylor, September 26, 1886, my will, saith your Redeemer, Jesus Christ, to set apart five faithful apostles, to carry on my holy law of Celestial Marriage of Plural Order, who did so under my servant John Woolley; who also was a son of God, who was able to visit the heavenly power, able to dwell in thy Lord's own presence; having my power of full sealing power to bless all of my eternal power of holy, pure way; to be my power on earth to officially continue my holy pure way of Eternal Union of Marriage Eternal; to be of a holy way of noble doing, to be of silent way under a covenant to not let any know of my holy Priesthood authority on earth save I shall reveal.

4. Let him be of my noble and great ones, who, for forty-one years, was of noble way.

5. Let all now rejoice in John Woolley, and my holy way being of a continuation of every gift, power, authority, eternal keys of Melchizedek Priesthood on earth; there being only one man on earth at a time holding keys of sealing up into eternity, even being temple worker at times, when thy Lord would visit freely in holy places of my naming; even on street, in city, or in wilderness, or as I named; able to see beyond the veil to know greater truths.

6. Let his name be heralded to all my Priesthood to be preserved for an underground way of silent keeping all remaining among generation falling away from my Holy Priesthood.

7. Let him be known as an holy vessel of pure way of life eternal.

8. He was visited often by Joseph Smith, as well as thy Savior; and was led to accomplish the way of eternal covenant of Union Celestial, while all around him were men of apostate doing away with religious way of revealing; until he continued my law in hiding unto John Y. Barlow, remembering worthiness is discerning of character of all around

and among falling-away members who sold their Priesthood way for naught.

9. Let it be heralding to all nations John W. Woolley is my son of loyal integrity worth of Celestial power; who visits my servant on earth, who is of the power of Union Eternal of key power of eternal Priesthood in full; now an administering power to many.

10. Let him be among my sons of holy Godhood, eternity of pure holy power in him abiding; while the branch of being as a dead branch broke off when Wilford Woodruff sold his Priesthood rights and power by a way of ceasing my Order of Celestial Plural Marriage power in his own domain, and giving way to governing powers, thus not being Keyholder of sealing power.

11. John W. Woolley continued in the key position, teaching, expounding, advancing my work eternity of blessing power of Priesthood.

12. He was and is stalwart, immovable in ordinance preserving of holy way of Eternal Power Priesthood in all things. Amen.

Testimonies Concerning the Prophet John W. Woolley

President Leroy S. Johnson
Leroy Johnson's Sermons 4:1575 June 3, 1978 Canada

All the leaders that have come to the earth and taken their place among God's people were fore-ordained before they came here. They were given enough knowledge to guide them along the way before their time of administration came.

I was almost fifty years old before the Lord put His finger on me. He said He wanted me to get prepared for another work when He called me into the Apostleship. About four or five years before that, I visited Brother John W. Woolley who was then head of the Priesthood -- God's chosen servant in the earth. He was the first to hold the presidency after John Taylor in this line of Priesthood. My brother took me to

see him, introduced me to him. I sat down on the couch after shaking hands with Brother Woolley. He looked a hole through me for a moment. I thought, "Oh, this man is going to tell me of all the trials and tribulations I have had." He startled me by saying, "Get up, young man, and come over here. I want to feel your hand again." I don't know whether I was shaking or whether I wasn't. I know I had a feeling that I was being tested. He looked me in the eye and said, "My boy, you'll do. You'll do." He told me to go and sit down, and I did. He says, "Now I know that I am among friends." And he opened up and told me of the revelation of 1886 and the eight-hour meeting.

A few years later, a meeting was held at Brother Charley Owens' home.*** Two weeks later, I met my brother, Price, again. He says, "Well, Roy, what do you think about what you were told in that meeting at Brother Owens' the other day?"

Until that time, I had been having an argument in my mind, because I was a good follower in the Church. I had held many prominent positions up until that time, presiding in the Aaronic Priesthood, in the Sunday School, and so forth. But when my brother put the question to me, I felt the fire go through me. I said, "Price, every word that those men told us was true. If you and I don't do what they told us to do, we will be swept off with the wicked." I have never varied from that testimony. That was the testimony given to me of this work -- this order of things. And it has been since I joined up with this order of the Priesthood that I have come to understand how Priesthood works, the order of things from the beginning until now.

President Leroy S. Johnson
Leroy Johnson's Sermons 4:1606 August 20, 1978 SLC

If I understand the record correctly, the Prophet John Taylor was visited by the One Mighty and Strong as well as by another party from the heavens. They instructed the Prophet John Taylor to set men apart to carry on the work of the Priesthood until the Redemption of Zion. I believe that that order that was given to the Prophet John Taylor by those two men that night was the true order of things that we have today and that this priesthood is trying to carry on. If this be the case, it has been told to us by all of the brethren from time to time that John W. Woolley was the man that was set apart to see that this work was carried on from that time.

There was, for awhile after the death of John W. Woolley, a short time that Lorin Woolley carried the load alone. But the work had to go on, so the Lord sent John Woolley to his son and he told him who to call and set apart to carry this work along. And those men were called.

President Leroy S. Johnson
Leroy Johnson's Sermons 5:27 December 28, 1952 SCA

If the words of the Prophet Brigham Young are true and the Priesthood of God is out of the hands of the Church of Jesus Christ of Latter-day Saints, where is it? Where has it gone? Either it is somewhere outside of the Church, or Brigham Young is a false prophet. John W. Woolley filled a little niche in the line of Priesthood. He had to live in obscurity out of the lives of most people. There were only a few people that knew his position, and those who did find out his position had a hard time doing so. They had to be men of God and the Spirit of God would have to be upon them in order to find it out. Lorin Woolley stood alone in the capacity for some time, until the Lord came to him and told him to fill up the quorum, or call other men to his assistance.

President John Y. Barlow
John Y. Barlow's Sermons [RTJ] 8:216 Sept. 3, 1942 SLC

My brothers and sisters, I have been greatly edified and built up through the remarks of my brethren. Looking over the congregation now, I am wondering how many are here that were with us a few years ago. I can see a few faces here that were with us a few years ago. When we used to go up to Uncle John Woolley's and Lorin Woolley's, they would tell us of things -- how the Savior and Joseph Smith came to their place and what he told them to do to keep this principle alive. I have heard those men testify to that many times. I have been called into their Council and told of these things -- tutored up. I used to live just a little way from Uncle Lorin Woolley, and I knew Uncle John Woolley; and I heard the neighbors say that Joseph F. Smith used to go up and visit with him. They said that Joseph F. thought a lot of him, that he went up and pled with him and pled with him. Yes, he did -- he counselled with him, but he wasn't pleading with him as they thought he was doing.

President John Y. Barlow
John Y. Barlow's Sermons [RTJ] 8:169 May 25, 1941 SLC

My brothers and sisters, I have been greatly pleased with the testimonies that have been borne this afternoon. I know that this work is true. I know it only through the Spirit of God. When Brother Price Johnson was talking of Brother John Woolley, I thought many are the hours I have spent with him. Many things were showed to me then. We have seen many of those things literally fulfilled. I have seen these other men and know that they had the Spirit of God upon them. The Holy Ghost is the Spirit of prophecy.

There are a great many things that I would like to say this afternoon. One is concerning the keys. Brothers and sisters, those keys were conferred upon us brethren. None asked for them. All we can do is bear our testimony to you that these things are true, and that God has set us apart to see that these things are done.

D.& C. 132
45. For I have conferred upon you the keys and power of the priesthood, wherein I restore all things, and make known unto you all things in due time.

46. And verily, verily, I say unto you, that whatsoever you seal on earth shall be sealed in heaven; and whatsoever you bind on earth, in my name and by my word, saith the Lord, it shall be eternally bound in the heavens; and whosoever sins you remit on earth shall be remitted eternally in the heavens; and whosoever sins you retain on earth shall be retained in heaven.

President John Y. Barlow
John Y. Barlow's Sermons [RTJ] 8:330 April 1, 1945 SLC

Brethren, let us get a lineup on the Priesthood and find out what people are following the Priesthood of God. In the Doctrine and Covenants, Section 90 verse 4, it says that the oracles of God will be given through the Prophet Joseph. Find any other people that you can where the oracles were given through Joseph Smith. Can you find any others that have the line that comes from Joseph Smith to Brigham Young, from Brigham Young to John Taylor, to these men? Can you find any other line? I want to know the authority in the things I want. I have not heard of any other group that has been able to furnish an abstract deed as this group has in the line of the Priesthood. I just wanted to say these few words. We want you to get the testimony for yourselves. I had to get it for myself.

President John Y. Barlow
John Y. Barlow's Sermons [RTJ] 8:147 Dec. 31, 1940 SLC

In our day, when we stop to think of what has happened -- Elijah, holding all the power, came to the Prophet Joseph and gave it to him; and now here we are receiving it. Are we not blessed? Others are rejecting it.

Lorin Woolley used to keep telling us that his father, John Woolley, came to him quite a bit. I asked the Lord whether it was so, or whether it was not. Next time John Woolley came, I was in the room. He turned to me and said, "There is scarcely a man in this Church under ninety years old that is abiding this covenant." He gave me to understand that men out of the Church were abiding it, those who had been ostracized. (Lorin testified that I was there when his father came.)

Now, sisters, before Lorin died, he wanted to fill the Sanhedrin, and he told us that the Priesthood on the other side went from Canada to Mexico, and they couldn't find men to do it. What a condition. Talk about apostasy.

President John Y. Barlow
John Y. Barlow's Sermons [RTJ] 8:364 Nov. 23, 1947 SCA

Joseph Smith is the head of this dispensation and Joseph Smith is the One Mighty and Strong. John Woolley asked me if I knew who the One Mighty and Strong was. I said, "It is Joseph Smith." He said, "I know it, my boy, I know it. I am sure of it." Just a short time before that, he told us he expected the visit of some of the brethren. I said, "Uncle John, did they come and see you?" He said, "They sure did." The Doctrine and Covenants speaks of Joseph Smith. It speaks his name right out. The only thing we claim is this: God set us apart to see that all these laws and ordinances are kept alive.

Supreme Court Upholds Edmunds-Tucker Bill -- 1890

A Chronology of Federal Legislation on Polygamy

1890 April The United States Supreme Court sustained Edmunds-Tucker Bill, increasing the threat of total disfranchisement, wherein the Church would be dissolved and its property escheated. The Court held that "Congress may not only abrogate laws of the Territorial Legislature but it may itself legislate directly for the local government. Congress had a full and perfect right to repeal its [LDS] charter and abrogate its corporate existence." (United States Reports, Vol. 136, pp. 1-68. The late corporation of the Church of Jesus Christ of Latter-day Saints vs. United States, Nos. 1030, 1054.)

Law Against Plural Marriage in Utah

Constitution of the State of Utah 1896, Page 6

Article 3. Ordinance. The following ordinance shall be irrevocable without the consent of the United States and the people of this State: First: -- Perfect toleration of religious sentiment is guaranteed. No inhabitant of this State shall ever be molested in person or property on account of his or her mode of religious worship; but polygamous or plural marriages are forever prohibited.

Proceedings for the Confiscation of Mormon Church Property

Orson F. Whitney
History of Utah, Volume 3 Page 588

The day after the funeral of President Taylor, proceedings for the confiscation of Mormon Church property began, under the provisions of the Edmunds-Tucker Law. To this end, two suits were planted, at the instance of the United States Attorney General, in the Supreme Court of the Territory.***

Orson F. Whitney
History of Utah, Volume 3 Page 599

The Court's decision was delivered on the 5th of November. It was voiced by Chief Justice Zane and was a unanimous opinion. It sustained the position of counsel for the Government, and granted the motion for the appointment of a Receiver.

The Supreme Court of the United States Sanctions the Confiscation of Mormon Church Property -- May 1890

Orson F. Whitney
History of Utah, Volume 3 Page 740

On the 19th of May another sensation was created in Utah by the telegraphed announcement that the Supreme Court of the United States had that day rendered a decision adverse to the defendant in the great suit of the Federal Government vs. the Mormon Church; the issue in which was the confiscation of the Church property under the provisions of the Edmunds-Tucker Act. For more than a year the Court had had this case under advisement, the arguments therein having been made in January, 1889.

The Court's opinion -- voiced by Mr. Justice Bradley -- reasserted the constitutionality of the Edmunds-Tucker Act, and confirmed the decision confiscating the Mormon Church property. That Church, the Court said, was an organized rebellion, a contumacious organization, the distinguishing features of whose creed were polygamy and the absolute ecclesiastical control of its members. It wielded by its resources immense power in Utah, and employed those resources in propagating a practice offensive to civilization, and in constantly attempting to oppose, subvert and thwart the legislation of Congress and the will of the Government. Hence, Congress had the right to do as it had done. "We have carefully examined the decree, and do not find anything in it that calls for a reversal. It may perhaps require modification in some matters of detail, and for that purpose only the case is reserved for further consideration."

The Manifesto -- September 24, 1890 Plural Marriage Suspended by the Mormon Church

Orson F. Whitney
History of Utah, Volume 3 Page 743

The autumn of the year witnessed an event of supreme importance to Utah and the Mormon people. No event in the history of the Territory has caused more comment or been more prolific of results. It was the issuance by the President of the Church of Jesus Christ of Latter-day Saints and the unanimous acceptance by its members, of what is known as "The Manifesto," an official declaration in which the Mormon leader -- Wilford Woodruff -- made known his intention to submit to the laws of Congress enacted against the practice of plural marriage, and use his influence to induce his people to do the same.

Many Fall in Upholding Manifesto Against the Celestial Law

President Leroy S. Johnson
Leroy Johnson's Sermons 4:1357 March 20, 1977 SLC

And I guess one of the greatest stumbling blocks of all times was the signing of the Manifesto by President Wilford Woodruff. It caused more people to stumble and lose their way than anything I know of. Yet, the Lord has allowed stumbling blocks to be laid in the paths of the Priesthood as well. And many of the Priesthood have fallen away because of these stumbling blocks.

President Leroy S. Johnson
Leroy Johnson's Sermons 1:211 September 8, 1970 CCA

It was mentioned here today of the 1886 Revelation; and in that revelation it tells us that the way was prepared for the continuation of this Gospel through a wicked generation of people. In 1890 the Manifesto was signed by the President of the Church of Jesus Christ of Latter-day Saints; and not only did they sign away their privileges to the New and Everlasting Covenant, or the law of Plural Marriage, but they broke every other commandment that God has given. Why? Because God says: Break one of these commandments and you are guilty of the whole. Why doesn't every Latter-day Saint in the Church of Jesus Christ of Latter-day Saints back up the law of Plural Marriage and the Celestial Law in its fullness? Simply because they have signed away their rights to it.

The Priesthood in Hiding in the Days of the Persecution by the Power of Government

President John Y. Barlow
John Y. Barlow's Sermons [RTJ] 8:321 Dec. 24, 1944 SLC

I can well remember the underground days. I can remember men hiding at our home and women being taken across. I remember Uncle John Woolley telling of a case where he went to Grantsville with a woman who gave birth to a child on the way, and he had to attend to her himself. How many of you have read the pamphlet that Ellis got out? Get it and follow up the trials and tribulations they went through. We haven't gone through anything like that yet. What we will go through, I don't know. But I do know this -- if you are humble and prayerful, a door will be opened and we will be relieved.

Mormon Church Joins Law Enforcement in Prosecuting the Priesthood People; Presidents John and Lorin Woolley Suffer At the Hand of the Mormon Church

Testimony of Fred M. Jessop and Richard S. Jessop

Threats of prosecution were made to Lorin Woolley personally. Richard Seth Jessop, a friend and close associate of John and Lorin Woolley related, that Lorin Woolley attended a stake conference in 1922 and was told by a leading church official that, "your father has not suffered enough. We intend to put that old man away for 6 months."

April 1931 Deseret Evening News, Conference Report

At the April conference of 1931, President Heber J. Grant had pledged the resources of the Church and its members to the prosecution and imprisonment of all those adhering to the law of plural marriage, asking them to ratify the same by vote. He stated at this conference: "We have been, however, and we are entirely willing and anxious too that such offenders against the law of the State should be dealt with and punished as the law provides. We have been and we are willing to give such legal assistance as we legitimately can in the criminal prosecution of such cases."

Chapter 5
Administration of President Lorin C. Woolley

Revelation of the Lord Jesus Christ Given to President Warren S. Jeffs
Palestine, Texas
Wednesday, October 5, 2011

1. Thus saith the Lord unto all peoples, that my servant Lorin C. Woolley was next Keyholder of full Sealing Powers and keys after his father John Woolley passed on.

2. He stood alone bearing the apostleship for a time; I then having quorum called by him to receive the apostleship.

3. He was my son of witnessing his father's administration; and of witnessing the apostasy of most of my people when they persecuted my Priesthood as a Church, fighting against my Celestial Law of Celestial Plural Marriages; even that origination once of my Priesthood.

4. He, Lorin, was of the gift of receiving my own presence.

5. He is witness to eternal visions, visitations and visiting eternal powers Celestial while in the flesh; confirming him in knowledge of God in full exalting power.

6. He shall yet be on earth again as a son of full power of Priesthood holy power, in the governing of the earth during my holy reign of peace. Amen.

Revelation of the Lord Jesus Christ Given to President Warren S. Jeffs
San Angelo, Texas
Monday, August 1, 2011

1. My sole apostle on earth at a time of Priesthood in hiding was Lorin Woolley, a son of a Keyholder, and also next Keyholder of all full powers of Priesthood. He often met with thy Lord in wilderness, and in sacred temple places, was so pure, he could be of a conveying to peoples far away; to teach and bless.

2. Lorin C. Woolley continued as Keyholder, alone in apostleship holding until he was of an ordaining way of pure apostleship power upon a quorum of sons who he taught full key powers of Priesthood power; John Y. Barlow next to stand in my Keyholder position, able to also visit the Holy Priesthood on the other side of the veil.

3. He, Lorin Woolley, was a great Prophet, able to walk and talk with me, even momentarily as needing guiding to be preserving my Priesthood on earth, now a God of eternal power.

4. Let all rejoice in the mission and pure abiding power of Priesthood I bestowed upon Lorin Woolley, a son of God of eternal power of holy power Celestial. He was witness to his father's administrating all keys of Priesthood; and of power to visit places of needing Priesthood power.

5. Let my Holy Priesthood power be of resounding joy.

6. Let all know I shall preserve my holy way unto Zion, unto full power eternal. Amen.

Testimonies Concerning the Prophet Lorin C. Woolley

President Rulon Jeffs
Rulon Jeffs' Sermons 6:330 December 14, 1986 CCA
And this is a continuation; this work and this Priesthood, which we have with us, is a

continuation from that time through John W. Woolley, through Lorin C. Woolley, through John Y. Barlow, and Leroy Sunderland Johnson. The Lord set up that order of Priesthood, a continuation of it, in 1886, in contemplation of the Church leaving the Priesthood. The Church left the Priesthood and went into the wilderness and is now roaming around in darkness.

So, my dear brothers and sisters, you can see why I have to say what lies before me is awesome. But I testify to you that God is at the helm, and the work of God will continue according to His direction and His ways and His will.

President Leroy S. Johnson
Leroy S. Johnson's Sermons 4:1606 August 20, 1978 SLC

There was, for awhile after the death of John W. Woolley, a short time that Lorin Woolley carried the load alone. But the work had to go on, so the Lord sent John Woolley to his son and he told him who to call and set apart to carry this work along. And those men were called.***

So, the house of God is still in order. It is going along being led and directed by the same characters that visited the Prophet Joseph Smith, Brigham Young, and John Taylor. So, we are on our way. My dear brothers and sisters, we are on our way. Let us continue our preparation, for in all ages of the world men have had to be prepared for the great and glorious work the Lord had for them to accomplish. So, this work is going on. There is no discrepancy in the leadership that we have, for we have all been called under the same spirit and are being directed by the same spirit that directed the organization of the Church of Jesus Christ of Latter-day Saints, and the setting up of the Priesthood work. And it is going to go on. It is going to continue until the way is prepared for someone else to take over.

President John Y. Barlow
John Y. Barlow's Sermons [RTJ] 8:214 Aug. 9, 1942 SLC

I know this work is true, and I know these brethren sitting by me today have the authority that they say they have. I know that. Many of the other brethren here have been with them and

know wherein they spoke it was true. When I was set apart in this work I said, "Are you doing this because I am your friend?" He [Lorin C. Woolley] said, "I had nothing to do with it whatever. God told me to set you apart." I want to bear my testimony to you that I did go to the Lord as I was told to do, and I got my testimony. God did set these brethren apart to do this special work, and to see that these principles were kept alive. God never reveals in any day or age non-essentials. When God reveals a law, He gives it to you because it is essential.

President John Y. Barlow
John Y. Barlow's Sermons [RTJ] 8:149 Jan. 3, 1941 SLC

Hail to the Prophet ascended to heaven. Let me tell you something here, that the Prophet Joseph has ascended to heaven, and there are times he comes down to earth. I had the privilege of seeing him come from heaven, and he told me he wanted a man, and he wanted him quick. I told the brethren that it was Brother Isaac Carling, that he was wanted on the other side. We don't know any day when the Lord will say, "We want them up there and want them quick." I have heard Brother Lorin tell when he was very sick -- I miss him -- Lorin Woolley told Brother John, "Brother John, I make that promise to you, that you will do a great and mighty work in the Kingdom of God here on the earth;" and I want to say that every man that has been called of God by revelation is doing a great and mighty work upon this earth today.

President John Y. Barlow
John Y. Barlow's Sermons [RTJ] 8:216 Sept. 13, 1942 SLC

When we used to go up to Uncle John Woolley's and Lorin Woolley's, they would tell us of things -- how the Savior and Joseph Smith came to their place and what he told them to do to keep this principle alive. I have heard those men testify to that many times. I have been called into their Council and told of these things -- tutored up. I used to live just a little way from Uncle Lorin Woolley, and I knew Uncle John Woolley... .

Chapter 6

Administration of President John Y. Barlow

Revelation of the Lord Jesus Christ Given to President Warren S. Jeffs
Palestine, Texas
Sunday, October 2, 2011

1. I, your Lord Jesus Christ, the God over all, now reveal concerning my servant John Y. Barlow; that he was my full and pure Keyholder of Priesthood after my servant Lorin C. Woolley passed on.

2. Let it be known that John Y. Barlow continued my keys of Priesthood and my Celestial Law of Celestial Plural Marriage, and all the laws of Priesthood on earth, faithfully.

3. He was imprisoned for living my Celestial Law.

4. He was faithful to the end.

5. He called twelve brethren of the apostleship to be faithful, ordaining seven of them himself by my appointing.

6. He was of the full receiving of all keys of Elijah of sealing power.

7. He was of the receiving of revelations, dreams, visitations of former Prophets, to guide him of me, saith your Lord.

8. Now receive my word:

9. John Y. Barlow continued my Priesthood and Celestial Law on earth by my word and full Priesthood authority.

10. He is of they who returneth and helps to govern the nations during my reign on earth of the Millennial time of peace soon at hand.

11. Now learn that the wicked persecuted John Y. Barlow unto the end, he being as a holy and pure martyr for my cause; and shall be a witness against the people of the Church of apostate persecuting power, and against governing powers of the nation, in a time of full judging of thy God upon this wicked generation. Amen.

The Prophets Speak About Persecution

President John Y. Barlow
John Y. Barlow's Sermons [RTJ] 8:265 Feb. 6, 1944 SCA

Brigham Young said, "Be careful how you persecute this people. God will hold men responsible for every act against the Latter-day Saints."

We have been preaching to get the Spirit of God and keep it. Brothers and sisters, we are going to need it. We have got to be more humble; we have got to let the things of this world go by and bring our minds and our souls and everything under God. If we don't, we are going to be in a trap. If we do it, God will open up a door, and just as men think they have us caught, Uncle Lorin told us, if we will exercise the right kind of faith, a door will open and we will go through.

Supposing some of us are put in jail. What difference does it make? The Prophet Joseph never was convicted in law. Why was he ever arrested? Because of the prejudice of the people. Every history that we have of the saints of God on earth is just like we are getting today. You hear them say, "Why, it is against the law of the land." Who made the laws? Men did. They aren't the laws of God. Those are the things we are looking for. When Daniel was told not to pray because it was against the law of the land, Daniel prayed just the same. It wasn't against the laws of God. They threw him into the lions' den, but he had the Spirit of God around him and those lions couldn't touch him. The Three Hebrews were cast into the fiery furnace, and the fire couldn't hurt them.

The servants of God have been trying to get before the people of the world for a number of years now, the truth of the everlasting Gospel as it was given to the Prophet Joseph Smith for the salvation of the human family. And what is the reaction? I first got acquainted with this work in 1934. Since that time, we have seen four raids come in because the people were afraid that we were going to get too strong. They tried to whip us on conspiracy to teach lewd and obscene doctrine to the people through the mails. But it didn't go. Why? Because the Lord would not let it. His doctrine is not lewd and obscene, but it pertains to the eternal salvation of man. That didn't suit them. They sent some of our men to jail. They came out with the same spirit that they had before. They would not give up. Then they tried it again, but they did not succeed -- in 1935, and in 1941. In 1944, they took us in for conspiracy. In 1953, they came in and took all of us out. They took the men out and put them in jail, then they came in and loaded their families and took them away.

1935 Raid in Short Creek, Arizona

President Leroy S. Johnson
Leroy S. Johnson's Sermons 4:1256 August 8, 1976 CCA

...in 1934, President Barlow, Price Johnson, and Carling Spencer were arrested and brought to trial. At this time, I had already had the privilege of hearing the brethren speak and I believed what they had to say sufficient that I commenced to get on my armor and began to fight for the rights of the Priesthood. Since that time, we have gone through several other raids in which I was personally involved to some extent.

President Leroy S. Johnson
Leroy S. Johnson's Sermons 5:350 October 6, 1963 SLC

...he [the prosecutor] was in Short Creek holding court over President Barlow *** [the defense] entered a demur in the case, on the ground that the warrants were based upon belief and not on knowledge. The Justice of the Peace acknowledged the demur and dismissed the case. So, while Brother Bollinger was getting his papers ready for a new arrest based on knowledge, we slipped the prisoners out of the road and put them on their way. Brother Barlow's case was dismissed entirely, so he got out of it. The other two men had to flee for their lives.

Arizona Authorities Assisted By Mormon Church in Arrest of President Barlow

President John Y. Barlow
December 18, 1935, Letter to the Saints, Short Creek, AZ

No doubt you have heard or read of the trial and will say that in it all, the testimony showed that it was backed by those of the Church, and things that had been done in the High Councils of the stakes were taken as evidence. This is just another testimony that will stand against the leaders, and fulfills the scripture which says "They that lead thee cause thee to err and turn from the truth." We had for witness against them, a Stake president, a Bishop, and men who were born thru this Law.

Government Power Raids Priesthood in 1944 in Utah, Arizona, and Became Persecutor of Religion

President Rulon Jeffs
History of Priesthood Succession, Page 199

At six o'clock in the morning on March 7, 1944, officers arrested sixty people in three states all at the same time.***

In the course of the morning, after having been docketed in the county jail, we were taken over to the Federal Building on 4th South and Main Street to be arraigned before the U.S. magistrate. The charges were conspiracy to put into the United States mail lewd and lascivious matter, like the Truth Magazine. Our charges on the state level were conspiracy to teach the practice of plural marriage and unlawful cohabitation.

President John Y. Barlow and Fourteen Other Men Go to Prison in May 1945

History of Priesthood Succession, Page 205
[Truth 11:26]

The Supreme Court of the United States denied the petition for rehearing in the cases involving the unlawful cohabitation charges. Accordingly, the defendants appeared before Judge Van Cott on May 12, [1945], and were committed to the custody of the sheriff to carry out the sentence. Immediately, attorneys for the defendants served notice of petition for writ of habeas corpus, and they were retained in the county jail pending hearing of the petition in the court of Judge J.

Allan Crockett. He heard the arguments April 14 and 15, and denied the petition for such writ.

The fifteen***have been incarcerated in the state penitentiary for an indeterminate period not to exceed five years.

The hearts of all honest and truth-loving people go out to these men and their families, who are called upon to make this sacrifice for the sake of the Gospel.

The Entity Called The Church of Jesus Christ of Latter-day Saints Assists Government

President John Y. Barlow
John Y. Barlow's Sermons [RTJ] 8:278 April 6, 1944 SLC

The government is against us, but we do know that it is being run by those at the head of Main Street [the Mormon Church]. We know that this has all been fixed up by a man now made president of a European mission, and we do know that it was a bishop who put the law forth. Are we going to get mad? Let us let the Lord take a hand in that, and say within ourselves, "God, forgive them, for they know not what they do." Let us let the Lord take a hand in it. I do know that every man who raises a hand against these laws of God will sooner or later feel the power of God upon them. The Lord says to forgive all men, and He will forgive whom He will. If they can stand it, then we can. The only way we can get out of this is by fasting and praying to the Lord. I saw this over a year ago, and said if we would be humble and prayerful, that there would be a door open in the wall.

President John Y. Barlow
John Y. Barlow's Sermons [RTJ] 8:334 April 7, 1946 SCA

My brothers and sisters, I cannot tell you how thankful I am. I cannot tell you how I love this people here. Yes, we knew you had prayed; we knew a lot of other things, too. We knew there were others fighting, and we knew that some were praying, and knew that God was hearing and answering prayers. The first time I went before the board of pardons, they were just as bitter as could be (I should say parole board). I went home and fasted and prayed; and in a week I went back again, and he said, "You can go and stay as long as you want to, and just let us know when you want to come back." I know that God touched their hearts.

President John Y. Barlow Goes to Prison; One Man Rule Upheld

President Rulon Jeffs
Rulon Jeffs' Sermons 7:489 February 26, 1949 SLC

The grandest example we have in this life are the sacrifices of the Lord Jesus Christ. They were many. As He made one sacrifice after another, He gained strength. But think of the power He had to go and stand with His Father,

Fifteen imprisoned in 1945, John Y. Barlow front row, second from right.

         Chapter 6 -- Administration of John Y. Barlow

and lay hold on eternal life, brothers and sisters, after He made the last great sacrifice.

Brother Johnson and Brother John and others made the sacrifice, and don't you think that after coming out of prison, that their strength and power is greater now than it was? They now have power over their traducers, those who have striven to take their lives. How can we go before the Lord and have confidence that He will answer when we know we are doing some wrong? Let us resolve to clean up our lives. "If ye love Me, keep My commandments."

President Rulon Jeffs
Rulon Jeffs' Sermons 7:525 January 1, 1950 SLC

And let no man set upon the name of any who preceded John Y. Barlow, and John Y. Barlow himself; for I would stand between him and you, if you would. I want to tell you, John Y. Barlow was a servant of God. ***

No one can destroy this Priesthood or the principles of the Everlasting Gospel, and though I lay down my life for it, it will go on. It will take the best blood of this generation yet. I would consider it a privilege and honor to give mine, if it would be needed. Let us see to our knitting.

President John Y. Barlow
John Y. Barlow's Sermons [RTJ] 8:286 May 28, 1944 SLC

2 Timothy 3

12. Yea, and all that will live godly in Christ Jesus shall suffer persecution.

Connect that up with this group that are being fought against. Find out about them. God said, I believe to Nephi, that He never commanded a people to do a work except that He opened a way to do it. Now the laws of the land come up and say if you do live the laws of God, you will be sentenced. I, among others, am being sentenced, and they want to put us in jail and make it hard for us to keep out. I do not know but what it will be a good thing for some of us. It will humble us. I do not want to go if I can get out of it, but if they do put us in, I hope the Lord will give me the strength to go on. As Brother Snow said, "Though I go to prison, God will not change the laws of marriage." This people should know by this time that Mormonism, if one of its leading principles is wrong, because it is from God, all God's laws are wrong. Some of us know that that thing is right. We know what is coming, that we have a fight on our hands.

The whole thing is not plural marriage. It is the Priesthood of God and who has the right to it. It is not long before that stone is going to roll, and when it starts it will not stop; and as the consumptive decree will be sent out there, it will put an end to all nations. There is not any of us that needs a Prophet of God to see what is coming. It is before us.

I say to all you men and women, get behind the laws of God.

John Y. Barlow's Testimony of Celestial Plural Marriage Unto This Generation

President John Y. Barlow
John Y. Barlow's Sermons [RTJ] 8:256 Dec. 12, 1943 SLC

Nothing less than eternal salvation will satisfy the immortal soul. We were put on this earth to live a Celestial Law. If we fail to live these commandments, then we will be thrown back. How will we feel when we think that we might have gone on? It is this law that is going to exalt us.

President John Y. Barlow
John Y. Barlow's Sermons [RTJ] 8:156 Feb. 23, 1941 SLC

Are we obeying it? Are we keeping it? I tell you what is going to happen to us if we don't obey the voice of the Lord. President Young says the only people that will be exalted will be those that are living the Celestial Law. John Taylor said that God has given a revelation that will exalt us in the eternal worlds, and we do not intend to have it kicked out, whether in the Church or not.

President John Y. Barlow
John Y. Barlow's Sermons [RTJ] 8:162 April 6, 1941 SLC

My brothers and sisters, I have been greatly edified by the words that have been spoken today. I heard a man say the other day, "Is it in this life that plural marriage first came into existence?" Do you expect to get into the Celestial Kingdom? That law was taught in the beginning. Adam had to live it, and he had to beget spirit children in that law before he came here to earth. That law was taught and practiced in that time as well as it is now. Then we, no doubt, understand it before we came to this life. Remember, this law, plural marriage, is not a law of the people; it is a law of the holy Priesthood. It was taught to Joseph Smith and some of his friends, and he had twenty-seven wives sealed to him before it was made known to the people. It was taught to him in 1831, but it was not until 1843 that it was made known to others. The people of the Church never accepted it until 1852, and in a special Conference here in Salt Lake, they adopted the principle, and sent Brother Orson Pratt to Washington. It was taught as a law of the Church, and in 1890, it was rejected. Then the Priesthood picked it up again and it was never rejected; and God saw that it went on and sent His Son Jesus Christ and Joseph Smith here to earth to see that this law was continued. Why? Because you and I cannot be Gods without it. There is a law irrevocably decreed upon which every blessing is predicated.

President Leroy S. Johnson and President Rulon Jeffs Bear Testimony of the Prophet John Y. Barlow

President Leroy S. Johnson
Leroy S. Johnson's Sermons 8:180 February 22, 1953 SCA

The name of John Y. Barlow will someday be heralded as one of the greatest Prophets of this time, and one of the greatest leaders of this time, because he lived in a time when the Priesthood of God came out of hiding. He not only bore testimony to the truthfulness of the Priesthood, but he suffered imprisonment, he suffered persecution, and he died a martyr to the cause.

President Rulon Jeffs
Rulon Jeffs' Sermons 1:13 December 8, 1946 SCA

John Y. Barlow, the President of the Priesthood upon the earth, is the mouthpiece of God. I know it as I know I live. He, along with his co-workers, are God's servants.

President Rulon Jeffs
Rulon Jeffs' Sermons 1:21 September 14, 1947 Widtsoe

I know that this is the work of God, and John Y. Barlow is the mouthpiece of God on the earth today. I know I bear the Priesthood of God, and that I am an Apostle of Jesus Christ. I can't believe that unless I believe that John Y. Barlow holds the keys of the Priesthood on earth today, because I got mine from him. Let us stand shoulder to shoulder.

Chapter 7
Administration of President Leroy S. Johnson

Revelation of the Lord Jesus Christ Given to President Warren S. Jeffs Palestine, Texas Sunday, October 2, 2011

1. I, your Lord, speak to all peoples, that my son of faithful and peaceful way, even Leroy S. Johnson, was of the full Keyholder power and authority of my Eternal Priesthood after John Y. Barlow passed on to his reward.

2. Leroy S. Johnson held keys of Priesthood from the time of John Y. Barlow's passing; I, your Lord, giving him those keys of power, to continue mine authority on earth, as also mine holy Celestial Law of Celestial Plural Marriage, and all my Priesthood laws.

3. Thus, he was also persecuted.

4. In 1953, a raid of the government came upon him and my community in Short Creek, Arizona, carrying away all women and children, even mothers with their children; the government announcing they were going to adopt out all the children, trying to destroy my Celestial Law and Priesthood.

5. I led my servant, Leroy S. Johnson, to overthrow this government attack, and to gather back all my people who were taken.

6. Thus did I overthrow this attack, and preserved my Priesthood and the Celestial Law on earth.

7. He is among the Gods in eternal power, and shall also be among the governing Celestial powers that are on earth guiding my Priesthood in Councils of full governing authority during my Millennial Reign of Peace, now soon to burst forth upon all nations.

8. He is my son of suffering power, suffering unto a full reward as a God of full power. Amen.

1928 Meeting with John W. Woolley

President Leroy S. Johnson
Leroy S. Johnson's Sermons 4:1575 June 3, 1978 Canada

I was almost fifty years old before the Lord put His finger on me. He said He wanted me to get prepared for another work when He called me into the Apostleship. About four or five years before that, I visited Brother John W. Woolley who was then head of the Priesthood -- God's chosen servant in the earth. He was the first to hold the presidency after John Taylor in this line of Priesthood. My brother took me to see him, introduced me to him. I sat down on the couch after shaking hands with Brother Woolley. He looked a hole through me for a moment. I thought, "Oh, this man is going to tell me of all the trials and tribulations I have had." He startled me by saying, "Get up, young man, and come over here. I want to feel your hand again." I don't know whether I was shaking or whether I wasn't. I know I had a feeling that I was being tested. He looked me in the eye and said, "My boy, you'll do. You'll do." He told me to go and sit down, and I did. He says, "Now I know that I am among friends." And he opened up and told me of the revelation of 1886 and the eight-hour meeting.

A few years later, a meeting was held at Brother Charley Owens' home. I heard Brother Zitting, Brother Kelsch, Brother Joseph Musser declare that John Y. Barlow held the keys of the Priesthood. I knew that Brother John W. Woolley had passed away, and that was all I had heard about it. I never saw Lorin Woolley. I never had the privilege of seeing Leslie Broadbent. Until that time, I had never met John Y. Barlow. My nephew, Isaac Carling, was the man that took me out to this meeting at Brother Owens' place. My brother, Price, was there, too. Two weeks later,

I met my brother, Price, again. He says, "Well, Roy, what do you think about what you were told in that meeting at Brother Owens' the other day?"

Until that time, I had been having an argument in my mind, because I was a good follower in the Church. I had held many prominent positions up until that time, presiding in the Aaronic Priesthood, in the Sunday School, and so forth. But when my brother put the question to me, I felt the fire go through me. I said, "Price, every word that those men told us was true. If you and I don't do what they told us to do, we will be swept off with the wicked." I have never varied from that testimony. That was the testimony given to me of this work -- this order of things. And it has been since I joined up with this order of the Priesthood that I have come to understand how Priesthood works, the order of things from the beginning until now.

I bear testimony to you that Joseph Smith was a prophet of God; and this is his work continued, and nobody elses. It is the work of Joseph Smith continued in the earth. In other words, this is the work of Jesus Christ, the Church and Kingdom of God continued in the earth; and anyone who fights against this order of things will be sloughed off, and be damned, for the Lord has said so. It does not make any difference what our relatives say, or those who are near and dear to us by the ties of nature. It is the same. If we don't keep the commandments of God as they are given to us through this order of things, we will be sloughed off and destroyed.

1953 Raid on Short Creek

What Really Happened at Short Creek, by an Eye Witness

Fred M. Jessop, December 1953
History of Priesthood Succession, Page 256
(Truth 19:193-198)

They knew the raid was coming, but plans for commemorating the advent of the coming of the pioneers had been made. They celebrated gravely and with mingled feelings. Observing the 24th, consisted of cannon salute and flag ceremony at sunrise. Men and boys were up unusually early to participate. Several World War II veterans maneuvered and gave a rifle salute as those present signified true patriotism. Among those present was one venerated by a life of honesty and candor for 84 years, his flowing beard yielded manifestly in the cool morning breeze, the performing ex-soldiers who had seen foreign action for freedoms cause, seeing this from the corner of their eye, bowed their homage in spirit to their superior patriot grandfather, standing bare-headed, slightly bent with faithfulness over so many snows, while Old Glory was drawn up to be kissed by the first rays of sunrise at the public square.

Celebration programme was for all day.

Preparations for lemonade stand, playground and entertaining facilities used up the time of well organized crews of younger men and boys. The yard had been previously raked clean of trash and anything unsightly that would mar the enjoyment of the day.

At ten o'clock people gathered from every quarter. Work had been suspended. Pickups, cars and trucks loaded with families, boys and girls cleaned up specially, all eager eyed chattering exuberantly in anticipation, unloaded at the school ground. The rig that had been dispatched to Cedar City, seventy miles distant to bring the ice cream, was the last to come, just in time for every one to be crowded into the auditorium for the program, where appropriate songs and speeches imbued the hearts of all present with genuine gratitude for pioneer sacrifices, and carefully adjusted attitudes to appropriately celebrate. The program concluded with a humble benediction and a blessing on the food. A corps of busy efficient women under the direction of the general committee had by this time prepared a dinner and facilities to serve the congregated 500 towns folk and visiting people a wholesome dinner, forty at a time, on roast chicken, mashed potatoes, green salad, corn bread, buttermilk, raisin pie and ice cream.

No one felt the burden of so fine a spread because it was beforehand planned, the expense having been taken care of from the general treasury, into which all had pooled their earnings. Men from the sawmill, timber crews, fence building crews, fruit pickers, farmers, gardeners, mechanics, and carpenters, took pride in realizing this was their treat to their great happy community family. Children frequented the lemonade stand and joined the *games intermittently. All was free, activities well organized and supervised. No one was hurt, no one offended. Thoughtful people carried trays of food home to those not able to attend the dinner.****

Social relations at a pitch almost out of this world attained by careful guidance, willing and diligent practice.

Tired and happy children went to bed that evening while adolescents and grown ups gathered for the final celebration social. Despite the gravity in the minds of the oldsters over the impending possible disaster, genuine smiles were exchanged from behind beards and beneath bonnets in keeping with the theme of the pioneer character ball they were attending.

Religious -- in work and in play, devotion is never neglected. After a prayer for propriety to characterize the social co-mingling, music began, and the well practiced dancers forgot their worries in wholesome decorum. As the larger hours presented, the celebration's 'finale' was rendered by selected home talent in a chorus anthem, *"Grant us peace O Lord, and we will serve Thee", "Let all who fight Thee be confounded, let the Righteous dwell in peace." "In all Thy holy mountains let peace abide forever, Grant Thou our prayer."* Tenors, altos, sopranos, basses, in ecstatic harmony filled the atmosphere with melody and penetrated every listening heart. Fired them with determination to stand true, to the commandments of God given to the early founders, enjoining faithful compliance upon all those seeking salvation. *Every accountable heart knew the history, when the birth of this nation guided by the hand of providence became a haven for the religiously oppressed -- knew God made obligatory the practice of ancient orders by which to seal earth to heaven -- knew that in course of time political debauchees had steered legislative enactments against the Mormon exiles. Knew that the faithless of the banished people predominated over the stalwarts, and succumbed their commonwealth to the persecutions, fearing man more than God. Knew that since that time those who braved salvation's pathway did so at the peril of infractions of the law. Knew as Jesus knew that the resurrection was beyond Gethsemane -- and resolved to accept the inevitable, yet hoping with every American corpuscle that "we hold*

these truths, (our God-inspired Constitution) to be self-evident, that all men are created equal, that they are endowed by their Creator with certain inalienable rights, that among these are life, liberty and the pursuit of happiness. That to secure these rights governments are instituted among men, deriving their just powers from the consent of the governed. That whenever any form of government becomes destructive of these ends, it is the right of the people to alter or abolish it, and to institute new government laying its foundations on such principles and organizing its powers in such form, as to them shall seem most likely to effect their safety and happiness."

It was midnight......twenty-four hours elapsed......I heard the dynamite blasts that warned the townspeople that the raid was coming on, and to get up and be dressed. Saw a pickup shuttle through the village giving the call to assemble at the schoolhouse. In record time they gathered. One of the fellows hurried across lots and started the generator. The people went inside. The long converted barracks building had been carefully set for worship. Men and women took their places quickly and without comment, while the elders went to the stand, grave faced but perfectly composed, two sat and one stood at the pulpit, perfect attention was given to "Uncle Roy" a genial father by nature, solid and prophetic befitting his leadership responsibility, his steel grey eyes and vibrant voice sweetly and willingly respected, he wore an overcoat and was a little hoarse but undaunted and fearless, explained the reasons for "our calling you together." "We want to be ready when they come." He called for the chorister -- hymn books quickly whisked through the audience, then in calm unmistakable voice declared that "We will use 'Brigham's' weapon, the songs of Zion," page announced, prelude ended, and the congregation again responded accurately, swelled the building with harmonic, ecstatic determination. I heard the patriarch dedicate *"this people to the Lord"*, I saw the elders beckoned outside to receive the whispered report of intercepted radio conversation of the tattler and the invaders. Breathless, heard the report and resounding admonition to *"stand true to God," "this has not come upon us because we have failed to keep God's commandments or broken any moral law, but because the Lord has found a people willing to be made an example of,"* *"let us rid our hearts of all dis-unity or ill feelings toward one another, we are all in His hands."*

Further songs of prayer and praise were interrupted by a runner from the hill top as he stumbled in, fatigued and gasping intelligence of the long line of blacked out police cars moaning along in the last dim light of the eclipsed moon. People moved outside into a little tight knot on the lawn.

All eyes turned toward the horizon as husbands held tight handclasps to their wives and the few children not left in the houses were huddled close and told not to cry, "we must be brave" and "God will take care of us". The low moan of the sirens and flashing red lights and sweeping spotlights moving like a stealthy serpent in upon the waiting community, filled every heart with unmistakable apprehension -- this is it!! Some one rang the bell -- the elder called "sing" and the taut nerves of the compact little group then responded to the patriotic resignation produced by "America" sung to full resounding volumes in early morning darkness. A veteran soldier led in a unison pledge of allegiance to the flag almost before it reached the top of the mast. By this time the county sheriff's car leading the cavalcade was in front of the schoolhouse. The sheriff, with a trace of tension in his voice, called out through a radio speaker, *Stay where you are. Stay where you are."* "This is Sheriff Porter. We have warrants for your arrest. Stay where you are." No sooner had the first word sounded than the police cars bristling with artillery filled the streets, every officer covered by another officer. *Immediately the little knot on the lawn was literally corralled by armed officers with their hands only inches from their undrawn guns -- all was poised to handle a dirty mess -- BUT THERE WAS NONE.* "Uncle Roy" in fearless but not unkind voice sounded out clear above the tumult, *"Why have you come here? We're bothering no one. Why don't you let us alone? We're not giving up if it costs the blood of every man of us! Why don't you clean up your own places? You are a bunch of cowards to come so upon us."* This said as he strode from officer to officer who formed the stockade. *There I saw a man whom the world calls brave -- one who has braved many a hole, taken his life in his hands to take a desperado, armed with all*

the paraphernalia to render his prey helpless and lifeless at the quickest instant -- stand mute before that lion of the Lord [President Leroy S. Johnson] as he stood bare handed and bare headed before that officer, snatching a frightened child from her mother presenting it to the gallant officer armed to the teeth covered in the darkness with machine-guns and tear gas and scores of riflemen prepared to quell a riot, saying, "Have you the heart to take this screaming child from its mother? Have you?" I saw and heard the octogenarian [Joseph Smith Jessop] virile with the experience of a life-time of rectitude step forward, his voice booming over the foray say, "If it's blood you want take mine, I'm ready!" Saw two Korean frontlinemen standing on the perimeter declare their utter disgust at such gestapo tactics, dismayed at such a homecoming, and over a dozen other veterans identify themselves as having served in foreign theaters for freedom, asking why such preposterous un-American proceedings.

Officers in charge all but fought back the pressmen by the hundreds, who previously invited, had come especially to cover the synthetic news; representatives of local, county and state newspapers and leading magazines from California, Denver, Chicago, New York, London and Paris, until official photographs were taken. Daylight found the little group still corralled. A few conspiring stooges were brought forth to identify the principle men and to attach names to faces now seen in the early grey light of a desecrated Sabbath day.

The well ordered chapel room was quickly converted into court chambers. Officials and henchmen smoked and littered in the Sunday School room. One adjoining room, guarded on every side, served as the jail. The line of demarcation was drawn, men were hailed into court and thus incarcerated. Women and children with none to counsel or advise them, save those who wiley sought the downfall of their homes, milled wantonly about the schoolyard forbidden to leave. (One woman sought leave to go home to her baby but was restrained; she insisted a gentleman would not detain her.)

By this time the whole town was under a type of martial law, every home had been invaded, literature, deeds, documents, books, bibles and effects taken by police, officers, investigators and welfare agents. Women and children were rounded up to attend court, charged like their husbands with conspiracy to commit rape, bigamy, adultery, white slavery, etc. Detachments from the National Guard with all the gear for occupation, set up radio station, field kitchen, road blockades, medics station, Welfare, and officers quarters.

Breakfast was hours belated, the community mercy sister entreated for the privilege to go home for bread for a delicate woman and to take nursing mothers to relief, but was denied. Men from the chow march to the field kitchen in a pasture a quartermile distant, waving smiles and greetings to their companions and anxious children, heard the governor's radio speech as he sat securely in the Capitol padded by the colossal conspiracy of aggregated press and propaganda machinery, set up for a planned political parade, droning out the news almost before it happened, promising that though the men were already enroute to the county jail, the children would be provided for and be granted "happiness of their own choosing". The children looking back, knew they were loved, wanted, planned for, yet bewildered, heard horrid threats that the bonds of their honorable fathers and virtuous mothers, ordained and approved by God, would be nullified and their homes abated, deported themselves as only well bred children can. And this because of complaints that tax money from cattle grazed on Government free used land begrudged the education of children whom God had sent -- children whose lives and calibre the State authority has not the power to produce but disconcerted to guarantee to them their freedoms.

Leave taking came. It was by dint of heroic manhood in certain humane officers that one man and a venerable old patriarch were escorted to their homes to take leave of a sick wife and change to more appropriate clothing respectively. Good-byes were waved to singing "sisters" as the prisoners were directed into cars for the parade of "captured polygamists" to jail. Having spent that long hot July day in the Sunday School room, men had fanned themselves intermittently with hymn books -- some few they carried with them to jail, there serving to cheer the prisoners and to prompt prayers for deliverance and perhaps entertain the passers-by with the balanced harmony renditions, or to annoy the other 'criminals' downstairs, as the case may be.

For a week the occupation continued obnoxious in the erstwhile quiet little valley divested of its providers and protectors, where cattle had grazed contentedly, where evening breezes vivified the growing things that strove against the bright and burning daytime sun. Where the children's play and musical voices were now transformed to whispers and apprehension. Obnoxious for the disruption dealt the daily labors of the chore boys, and because of added anxiety to heroic mothers keeping vigil, going unrewarded of deserving sleep necessary for physical fortitude to keep inviolate the sanctity and dignity of their American homes. *Obnoxious occupation because, with all the admitted 26 months of planned prosecution, the children, not all processed through shameful juvenile hearings, were all loaded unwillingly into five large buses to be transferred to appropriate (?) homes 450 miles distant. Loyal mothers heroically refusing to be separated from their own flesh and blood would have rather submitted to extinction in these United States in preference thereof, accompanied them. From Sunday to Saturday the awful strain continued then when the few older boys left to take care that the dumb creatures (the cows) lactating, suffer not, watched the caravan make off with the political kidnap of their loving mothers and dear little brothers and sisters, stood courageously by in a downpour of rain wept graciously from heaven to cleanse the evacuated little hamlet of the stench of tobacco smoke and the more intolerable intrusion, influences of people of vile lives, prejudiced minds and evil intents, come to clean up the mess where real delinquency only existed on legal (?) documents and in the minds of bitter antagonists.* The boys fatigued from so gallant a stand for a week were soon lost in the reverie that brings all men peace. Strangely true, at this juncture the bailed out 31 men and nine childless women and grandmothers arrived home by truck. No lights shone in the village, all was quiet and still, the air was sweet and fresh from the rain. One by one the men alighted from the truck took his hat and jacket in hand, and entered in at his own gate, found overturned playthings left on the pathway, his house dark and quiet, no light shone in the window, no loving companion heard his foot falls nor welcomed him home. The rooms littered, showed a hurried leave the children's beds were all empty. His house left desolate. He was alone.

Doubtless the pen has never been touched able to describe the feelings that coursed through the heart of every man as he realized his situation. In his mind saw expectancy, as the woman in travail with the dragon before her, leering greedily in wait to devour her child as soon as it was born -- thusly his unborn given of God to be seized at its birth by the State with a ban on its heritage, his parental endowment adjudicated as naught. Mentally saw and heard infant children kneeling, lisping sweet prayers for their father, saw mothers preoccupied by the formidable prospects of piloting alone the bark of life upon which her orphaned family was thrust. *Re-echoed the Governor's boast guaranteeing 'Happiness of their own choosing', wondering what manner of sophistry had crept into places of political trust. Reviewing the past long week of experience, saw how the 'political', boisterous and bombastic all but run amuck hatefully disregarding the very basis of its origin -- the 'ecclesiastical'. Watched unhallowed polity break the rules, felonize the citizenry, kidnap community and run for a judicial touchdown, while bought-off referees wagged their impious heads and said, "how unfortunate", as half those in the grandstand rose and ignorantly cheered to the dismay and disgust of the other half. Saw by the vision of the ages, the great umpire rise and gather his principals, saw the regents summon the people and move to correct the ill-gotten score. Puzzled, fatigued, but undaunted resigned himself to God knowing that his heart harbored no malice -- smiled determinedly and wearily slept.*

Fred Jessop.

Test on the Mormon Church, the Government, and the Priesthood

President Leroy S. Johnson
Leroy S. Johnson's Sermons 1:62 Sept. 25, 1960 Canada
God can fight the battles better than we can. In 1953, Governor Pyle made a notorious speech to the world that he had stopped a great insurrection, wiped out a city, put the men in jail, and was going to adopt the children out so that in two years their identity would be lost. David O.

McKay, on the radio, told the people that he and the Latter-day Saint Church were in full harmony with the State of Arizona and what they did.

Brigham Young said, "If the time ever comes that this Church strikes hands with the wicked, know ye then that the Priesthood is lost from them." Whether we know it or not, the Lord is giving us another chance to align ourselves with His work, or He will raise up another people. He could easily do it if you don't get on the ball and take hold of His work. The Lord may do it another way to carry off His work, but scriptures tell us that He will carry off the Kingdom. If we want to be partakers of this blessing, we must hasten. See that we don't sleep with feelings in our hearts against our neighbors, wives, or husbands. See to it that we don't harbor any feeling of enmity or jealousy or whatever and keep it.

President Leroy S. Johnson
Leroy S. Johnson's Sermons 3:1081 July 20, 1975 SLC
We will bring it down now a little closer. After a little time the Saints were driven from their homes. They had to find a new place to live, so they came to this goodly land upon which we live today thinking that they would come out of the world and be able to live and obey the laws that would save them from another great destruction. But soon after they arrived here, the leadership was lowered into carnal security; and through the promises of great wealth and great security, they gave up the Celestial Law.

I am going to bring it down now to my day -- my experiences in this work. In 1944 two great wars started. To put it in the words of the prophet Joseph W. Musser, "Today war was declared in the east, and today war was declared in the west." When war was declared by the United States against Germany in the Second World War, the same day war was declared against the Celestial Law in this goodly land in which we live. Since that time, we have been persecuted, driven, pulled out of our homes, and our wives and children have been taken out and held captive.

In 1953, that great day when the army came in and took over the city of Short Creek, it started to rain a gentle rain. The Lord told the people at that time that the heavens wept. This is not the only time that the heavens wept. You can go to the Book of Moses and find out what was done in the days of Enoch. The heavens wept. The heavens did not stop weeping in 1953 until after the enemy had accomplished its work. They took the men out and put them in jail. Then they ravaged their homes, took their wives and children, loaded them on buses and took them away. It took a week's time to accomplish all this, but they did it. When they were going out, there was so much mud on the roads that the buses had to be helped until they got to Fredonia, a distance of about forty miles, till they got on the oiled roads. So, the heavens wept because of what was taking place. Was it altogether because of what was taking place? Was it altogether because of the taking away of wives and children and men? No. It was another great test that had to be accomplished, and this was the way the Lord had of accomplishing it. He had to know again how the Church of Jesus Christ of Latter-day Saints felt toward the Celestial Law. So, this is what happened: Soon after these people landed in Phoenix, Arizona, there was a quarterly conference held in Mesa, Arizona. President David O. McKay was in that conference, and he made this statement, "I want the people to know that the Church of Jesus Christ of Latter-day Saints is in full harmony with the actions of the state of Arizona in the Short Creek episode."

President Leroy S. Johnson
Leroy S. Johnson's Sermons 4:1390 May 22, 1977 SLC

In 1944 when the government made a raid upon this order of the Priesthood, the Federal government joined in with the state and made war against this people -- this order of things. And at that time, the Church of Jesus Christ of Latter-day Saints was tried. I am going to tell you what happened at that time.

An attempt had been made prior to this to do away with the Doctrine & Covenants by printing a little book called Commandments of More Enduring Value. Some two hundred sections or parts of sections of the Doctrine & Covenants had been taken out and this little book was printed to take the place of the Doctrine & Covenants. But at that time the people rejected it. There was only one edition made and put out to the public. I have, in my possession, one of the publications which I value very dearly because it is good evidence of what took place.

At the same time, one of our Apostles was haled before the courts and the man that wrote the book -- or the revision of the Doctrine &

Covenants was the star witness against him. He appeared on the witness stand and took the oath that he would tell the truth and nothing but the truth, but before he was on the stand long enough to answer any questions to amount to anything, he fell over. He was carried out and in a week or so he was laid away.

In 1953, the state of Arizona raided this order of the Priesthood and carried away the women and children. They first put the men in jail and then raided their homes while they were yet in jail, and carried their wives and children away to Phoenix, Arizona. After a week's time, the day the buses left Short Creek, Arizona, with the women and children, the men were released from prison in Kingman, Arizona, and came home -- to empty homes.

Again the Church was tried. They answered to the tune of $50,000 to assist the State in carrying away the women and children of this people. They haled nine men into court and placed them on parole for a year. They had to report to the court every month for a year for their actions. And while this was going on we were fighting for our deliverance from the hands of the enemy of righteousness. But soon after the raid was made, at a Conference in Mesa, Arizona, President David O. McKay made this remark. He said, "I want the world to know that the Church of Jesus Christ of Latter-day Saints is in full harmony with the actions of the State of Arizona in the Short Creek episode."

When I read this piece in the paper, I said to my wife, who was then in a detention home where I went to see her, I said, "This is the turning point. The key is turned now and from now on we will win the battles of the Saints." Which we did. The Lord had preserved us up to that time, and soon after that they started their adoption of the children -- or tried to. But the Lord told us where to find the necessary law to stop it. And He spoke through my mouth. He said, "In your law book there is a clause that reads something like this, `No child can be adopted out without the consent of the parents.'" They said if it was there they would find it, and they started to work to find it. The next morning the lawyers called me in. "I want to read to you what I found. 'No child can be adopted out without the written consent of the parents.' So, we will see what happens." So, the lawyer called the Attorney General and told him to get Statute number such and such and turn to a certain page. Now read clause such and such. And our lawyer read it over the phone to him. He says, "When we meet you in court today, we are going to stand on this point of the law." There was a short hesitation and then the Attorney General said, "This case will be continued until we study the law." Our lawyer shut up his book and says, "That's it. We have won the case. You won't have to bring your children in for adoption."

However, the Governor of Arizona, at the time of the raid or before, asked J. Edgar Hoover, the head of the F.B.I., to send men to help take part in the raid. J. Edgar Hoover, before he would answer the Governor, called the Federal Judge in Phoenix and asked him for his opinion on whether or not they should take part in the raid on the Short Creek people. The Judge says, "It's my opinion that if we take part in this raid they will beat hell out of us. So let's keep out of it." So the F.B.I. kept out of it.

Establishing My "One Man Rule" Among the Church and Kingdom of God

President John Taylor
JD 6:25 November 1, 1857 SLC

If there cannot be a people anywhere found that will listen to the word of God and receive instructions from him, how can his kingdom ever be established? It is impossible? What is the first thing necessary to the establishment of his kingdom? It is to raise up a Prophet and have him declare the will of God; the next is to have people yield obedience to the word of the Lord through that Prophet. If you cannot have these, you never can establish the kingdom of God upon the earth.

What is the kingdom of God? It is God's government upon the earth and in heaven.

What is his Priesthood? It is the rule, authority, administration, if you please, of the government of God on the earth or in the heavens; for the same Priesthood that exists upon the earth exists in the heavens, and that Priesthood holds the keys of the mysteries of the revelations of God; and the legitimate head of that Priesthood, who has communion with God, is the Prophet, Seer, and Revelator to his Church and people on the earth.

When the will of God is done on earth as it is in heaven, that Priesthood will be the only legitimate ruling power under the whole heavens; for every other power and influence will be subject to it. When the millennium which we have been speaking of is introduced, all potentates, powers, and authorities -- every man, woman, and child will be in subjection to the kingdom of God; they will be under the power and dominion of the Priesthood of God: then the will of God will be done on the earth as it is done in heaven.

This places man in his true relationship to the Most High; and while others are boasting of their own intelligence, powers, authority, rule, greatness, and might, our boast, glory, might, strength, and power are in the Lord.

President Rulon Jeffs
History of Priesthood Succession, Page 313

In the fall of 1979, President Johnson became very sick. I had a visit with him. He was laying on a couch in the front room in Lincoln Street. After talking some matters over, I got up to leave, and he called me back. He said, "Brother Jeffs, I and you must establish once and for all the one man rule," according to Section 132.

President Rulon Jeffs
Rulon Jeffs' Sermons 6:258 August 10, 1986 CCA

It is my testimony to you that Leroy Sunderland Johnson was designated by John Y. Barlow to receive that position, and I have been busily engaged, since this split and this crisis that has come to this work, in trying to establish, as Brother Johnson told me I was to do; he said in the fall of 1979, "Brother Rulon, I and you must re-establish the one man rule in the holy Priesthood," referring to Section 132 verse 7. I have been busily engaged in doing just that ever since, and I hope to continue.

President Rulon Jeffs
Rulon Jeffs' Sermons 5:374 March 18, 1984 Sandy

As one of the speakers indicated here, and I have told you I think before, in late 1979, President Johnson, when I was visiting him, had confirmed some marvelous items of truth, which he confirmed to me. As I was about to leave him he said, "Brother Jeffs, I and you have the responsibility of establishing once for all the one man rule as set out in Section 132 verse 7,"*** There is only one man, the head, who is to receive revelation and commandments for the people."

Summary Teachings of President Leroy S. Johnson:

Strong Warnings of Preparation for the Redemption of Zion and the Whirlwind Judgments

President Leroy S. Johnson
Leroy S. Johnson's Sermons 7:251 Sept.7, 1975 Canada

We're entering into one of the greatest scenes of bloodshed the world has ever seen, so said the Prophet Joseph Smith. So great was the scene, said he, "I could not look upon it any longer. So I asked God to close the scene from before my eyes."

Zion must be redeemed. The Lord has said so. It doesn't matter what happens on this earth, Zion will be redeemed. Who is going to redeem Zion? The Lord said, "I will take the young and middle-aged and redeem Zion." We're here in the midst of the work of God. We're here to work out our salvation in fear and trembling before Him. Every man and woman that desires to be crowned with a celestial crown must be able to stand under the pressure of whatever name or nature it might be. It was hard for the Prophet to look upon the scene; it will be hard for you and me to witness it, but we are about to witness something that the world has never seen before. We have seen the bloodshed and all this and that, and men have been wiped completely off this earth, so the record tells us, but the Lord told the Prophet Joseph that never again will the Priesthood be taken from the earth.

When I read Third Nephi, I believe the words of the Savior, when He said the remnant of Jacob would walk through the Gentiles if they wouldn't repent, and tread them down, and none could deliver. "I'll throw down their strongholds, destroy their chariots, destroy their cities, their orchards," and so forth.

So it's going to be terrible, and great famines will be upon the land, but we have one thing, one thread to hang to -- and no other people have it. It is that God has said that He would protect His saints if He had to send fire from heaven to do so, and He's a man of His word. He did it when Christ visited the Nephites upon this continent. The record tells us that all the wicked were killed and only the more righteous were saved. So He has ways and means of protecting His saints.

We should go down the road with our heads up and our minds clean and free from turmoil and confusion. We should have a prayer in our hearts continually to the God of heaven to protect us from the evil doer.

President Leroy S. Johnson
Leroy S. Johnson's Sermons 7:353 February 12, 1984 CCA

We will see the judgments of God poured out more and more from this time forth until this part of the earth is empty of its inhabitants -- those who are not able to say, "I am clean every whit," and have the Lord call us up. So we are working under a great handicap, my dear brothers and sisters. If this people that I am speaking to today don't hasten to lay away their sins and their wrong-doings and come clean before the Lord, they are going to find the Lord is not pleased with them, and they will have to go down with the wicked.

Now, I pray that God's blessings will be upon us, because He has granted us a few days more to clean up our lives and get down on our knees and pray night and day for deliverance as He has said. This is the time we will have to begin that practice. God bless you, amen.

President Leroy S. Johnson
Leroy S. Johnson's Sermons 4:1361 March 27, 1977 CCA

Think about it, you young boys and girls. We are living in a time when we have got to be prepared -- when the Lord is trying to prepare a people that He can use, not only in the heavens but on this earth for a thousand years. And those who are partakers of that great blessing will have to be clean every whit, so says the Lord. And that means clean up our minds, clean up our bodies and keep ourselves clean and free from the destroying elements that are abroad upon the earth today, not only in the minds of the people but in the minds of our educators, our legislators, and our rulers. The whole world has rejected the Celestial Law.

We have a little pamphlet called, "The Coming Crisis and How to Meet it." The coming crisis and how to meet it is upon us. The crisis is here now. The thing we have to do is learn how to meet it, how to clean up our minds, our bodies and our determinations, not only in our thoughts but in our actions and in our everyday life. Let your light so shine that the world might wonder what is going on. Let us be prepared, everyone of us, to be counted worthy of being called upon when the time comes when our names are called, that we can come up and be counted worthy members of that great Kingdom called Zion. For Zion is the home of the pure in heart.

President Leroy S. Johnson
Leroy S. Johnson's Sermons 7:394 June 24, 1984 Canada

The Lord has said, "Stand ye in holy places and watch the arm of the Lord made manifest." The only holy places we have are our dedicated homes. The Lord is very angry with the Church of Jesus Christ of Latter-day Saints for the way it has acted and operated throughout the last hundred years or more. Since the days of Brigham Young, they have rejected the Celestial Law. Not only that -- when Wilford Woodruff signed the Manifesto, he not only signed away his rights to the Celestial Law, but he signed away his rights to the Priesthood, also. That being the case, what priesthood have they been operating under? They claim they have been operating under a priesthood. Read "The Coming Crisis and How to Meet it." It will tell you exactly who they have been serving and what has transpired in the last few years.

It is our place now to clean up our minds and get the Spirit of God and keep it, because the Spirit of God is the only protection that we will have. The scriptures tell us that there will be two working at the mill; one will be taken and the other left. Two will be working in the field; one will be taken and the other left, and so forth. This is true. We will have to have the Spirit of God upon us enough to be caught up when the judgments of God go over the earth, then we will be let down again. That is the only way the Lord can protect His people. He says He will protect His saints if He has to send fire from heaven to do so; and this, He will do.

First Two Great Commandments Must be Lived to Be Part of Zion and the Holy United Order

President Leroy S. Johnson
Leroy S. Johnson's Sermons 6:386 November 16, 1969 SLC

If we labor all our days, if this Priesthood Council labors all their days and they can bring up a people that can learn to keep the two great commandments -- Love the Lord thy God with all thy heart, might, mind, and strength; and the second is like unto it, Love thy Neighbor as thyself; if we can bring a people up that can keep those two commandments, we will be ready for the United Order.

President Rulon Jeffs
Rulon Jeffs's Sermons 6:487 January 10, 1988 CCA

So let us unite. Let us be one. God will not be able to accomplish His work unless He has such a people, and I know He will have it, this people. I pray the Lord to be with us always, dear brethren and sisters. Learn to love. The first law of heaven is obedience. The first commandments to be obeyed are to love the Lord our God with all our heart, might, mind, and strength; and the second is like unto it, thou shalt love thy neighbor as thyself. If we would but carry out these two commandments, all other things would follow: unity, become one people, become a power in the hands of God to go forward and redeem Zion. The thing that I loved about Uncle Roy was his vision of preparing a people to redeem Zion.

President Leroy S. Johnson
Student Star Vol. 17, Page 384 Dec. 29, 1963 Sunday School

The Lord cannot look upon sin in the least degree of allowance. You can't do anything evil without paying a penalty for it. We must be kind and honest to one another and not hold feelings. The first great commandment is: Love the Lord with all your heart, might, mind, and strength, and the second one like unto it: Love your neighbor as yourself.

President Rulon Jeffs
Rulon Jeffs' Sermons 6:47 May 17, 1985 Sandy

The greatest lesson you can teach your children, my dear sisters -- and the great responsibility rests upon you, as Brigham Young said -- is to teach them obedience, obedience to the first two great commandments which covers all the rest: Thou shalt love the Lord thy God with all thy heart, might, mind, and strength, and thy neighbor as thyself. Disobedience to these two great commandments shows up in the lives of our children, and it comes and extends largely from the example of their parents.

President Rulon Jeffs Bears Testimony of the Prophet Leroy S. Johnson

President Rulon Jeffs
Rulon Jeffs' Sermons 4:390 October 8, 1978 Sandy

I testify to you that President Leroy Johnson is our Prophet, our head, the mouthpiece of God, and that he has given us continually the truths of heaven by the Spirit of revelation day in and day out, month in and month out.

President Rulon Jeffs
Rulon Jeffs' Sermons 3:28 August 6, 1972 Sandy

Now, dear brethren, you heads of families, draw near to the keyholder, as Heber, as Brigham, as John and the others drew near to Joseph, which assured them an inheritance with him in Zion. They set the glorious example. Others have followed since, and we have as our head, Leroy Johnson, our advocate with the Father, the keyholder by which we must come up to see the face of God, if we ever do. These brethren who lead us, dear brothers and sisters, these fathers in the Priesthood, are the ones by whom we must pass to see the face of Joseph, and Jesus, and Father. Talk about the love of brethren. I love the attributes of God as they exist in these my brethren -- Leroy Johnson, John Y. Barlow. These I must pass by, and the others before them, before I see Joseph, Jesus, and the white locks of Father Michael; and you must do likewise.

President Rulon Jeffs
Rulon Jeffs' Sermons 4:123 April 10, 1977 Sandy

So we have a great deal going for us, this people; and we have a true representative of the Lord Jesus Christ as our President and head -- a Christlike man, Leroy Johnson, who stands at the head of all. And we of this generation will have to account to him. He stands in the same position among us as Joseph did to the saints in his day -- the mouthpiece of God through whom all things must be revealed for the Church and Kingdom of God.

President Rulon Jeffs
Rulon Jeffs' Sermons 5:266 November 10, 1981 SLC

I know God is at the helm through this great and faithful man, Leroy S. Johnson. He is the keyholder of the holy Priesthood and of the sealing powers. He is the mouthpiece of God, and he is the fountainhead through whom the Holy Spirit of God is dispensed to the people who come under his presidency and direction. I know this by the Spirit of God, and I testify of it to you...

President Rulon Jeffs
Rulon Jeffs' Sermons 4:483 May 6, 1979 CCA

President Johnson is a man I love with all my heart, and I want to tell you why. The love of brethren transcends any other in life but the love of the chosen of God, for the chosen of God has to come in the same way as we love God. I love God because of the perfection of His attributes and character. That is what I worship in God -- the perfection of His character and attributes; and that is what I love in Roy Johnson. He is the most Christlike as any man I know, and stands in the position that God has called him to fill before he came here. Like Joseph Smith said, he was called by the Council before he came here to fill his position; and Brother Johnson is his legal successor. I say, though there are other Apostles, they come under the direction of the head, the chief Apostle, who leads us today; and that is the place I desire to be. I desire to be an advocate for him and to build him up, and we should all be doing the same thing. Why? Because he holds the keys, the means to obtain the mind and will of God; as Brigham Young said after the death of Joseph Smith, when Sidney Rigdon and others came to try and take charge. He has the means to obtain the mind and will of God for us, and all revelation must come through him for the people.

President Rulon Jeffs
Rulon Jeffs' Sermons 7:390 September 7, 1992 Sandy

Those remarks concerning President Johnson, I realize I am to carry on for him, as to the redemption of Zion.***

He said when he was in his last days there, "I want you to know that I am going to be there," at the redemption of Zion. That is what I pledged when I took over, that I was to carry on exactly as he has, build on the foundation he has laid. He is a grand and great Prophet, thirty-seven years at the helm of the Kingdom of God. Only John W. Woolley exceeded him in time, forty-one years, all that time in hiding.

He went to visit John Woolley, Uncle Roy did, a few months before he died. He and his brother Price went to visit with him, and after a very fine interview, as Uncle Roy was about to leave, Uncle John summoned him back. He took his hand and said, "My boy, you will do." I have had much the same association with Uncle Roy. As you know, he turned you all to me.

Chapter 8
Administration of President Rulon Jeffs

Revelation of the Lord Jesus Christ Given to President Warren S. Jeffs
Palestine, Texas
Sunday, October 2, 2011

1. I, even Jesus Christ, reveal that my servant Rulon T. Jeffs was of full Keyholder power of my giving him keys of sealing power in full, keys of the holy Eternal Union authority.

2. He continued my Holy Priesthood in fulness on earth, by my holy will guiding him.

3. He continued my Celestial Law of Celestial Plural Marriage; also my other laws of Priesthood.

4. I caused him to file Corporation Sole legal papers for the recognition of my true Church on earth to be named the Fundamentalist Church of Jesus Christ of Latter-day Saints, my continued Church under my Priesthood authority.

5. I restored my Priesthood first in the sending Peter, James, and John to Joseph Smith to receive my fulness of the Melchizedek Priesthood as an apostle of Jesus Christ; thereafter did I establish on earth again, through Priesthood, my Church on earth.

6. That Church organization rejected both my Priesthood and also my Priesthood Celestial Law of Celestial Plural Marriage.

7. Therefore, it became as a dead branch connected to my Priesthood tree of life, and broke itself off fully as they persecuted my Priesthood.

8. Thus, even now that apostate gentile organization labors, both in public and in secret labor, against my Priesthood and Celestial Law, and are not of me; though the name of their organized and legal corporation bears my name.

9. I, your Lord, reveal to all peoples that my Church of Jesus Christ of Latter-day Saints is now of the name Fundamentalist Church of Jesus Christ of Latter-day Saints, meaning my Church upholds all the fundamental laws and principles revealed through my servant Joseph Smith; none of which can be done away.

10. All my Celestial laws must be in my Church to be my Church, and must be guided by my Priesthood of full keys of Priesthood.

11. The revelations of my will always uphold my previous revealed will of eternal principles.

12. I cannot do away with a Celestial eternal law.

13. Rulon Jeffs is of full power of Priesthood, and is among they who cometh with me in the clouds of heaven at my glorious appearing.

14. He shall assist governing nations through the guiding of my Priesthood on earth by my revealing.

15. He is of full Priesthood power of Eternal Power Celestial as a witness against this now most wicked generation ever to be on earth.

16. He is a Judge in Israel. Amen.

Labor to Prepare a People of God for Zion

President Rulon Jeffs
Rulon Jeffs' Sermons 6:360 April 5, 1987 CCA

If we can go on now, dear brothers and sisters, in this great common cause to prepare a people to redeem Zion, to build a great city and the temples of the Most High God, we will realize the glorious desires of God for us, which existed also in the heart and the mind and the being of President Leroy Johnson. And I am committed, dear brothers and sisters, to carry on that work which he has so gloriously commenced and laid the foundations for us to go on down the road with him. And we are yet going to have him with us as we go down that road. The great ambition which I have, to the glory of God and the accomplishment of His purposes, with this people, is to find that group of five hundred Elders of Israel, which shall be the heart's core of the great work of the redemption of Zion, and going on that journey.

And as I have said before, dear brethren and sisters, we must have the spirit of Zion in our hearts, here and now! And regardless of whether there be those around us who don't have it, it is up to us to get it, if we want to be in that great concourse of Priesthood which will go down the road.

President Rulon Jeffs
Rulon Jeffs' Sermons 3:196 January 6, 1974 Sandy

We are being constantly reminded that this people is supposed to be prepared to redeem Zion, a people raised up out of the heart's core of the people of the Church of Jesus Christ of Latter-day Saints -- for this is what we are -- that they might become the nucleus of the great Millennium, and usher it in by redeeming Zion.

I was struck by the thought that in the redemption of Zion a people must be prepared. The Lord tried to get enough faithful men under Joseph Smith in the formation of what we call Zion's Camp to go back and redeem Zion. In calling for five hundred men, and finally settling for one hundred, who would go up under Joseph and not murmur and follow their commander, their leader, as one man under God, they could have redeemed Zion.***

This is what President Johnson and all of our Priesthood fathers have been telling the saints from Joseph on down, trying to prepare a people to redeem Zion.

In order for us to redeem Zion, if this may help us, we must first have Zion in our hearts; create a Zion in our families. Zion is not only a place. And by the way, the whole of America is Zion. The center place is Jackson County, and all of the other places will be stakes of Zion. This is the place. But Zion is also a condition, a condition of the heart and of the mind, of the spirit. Until we have Zion in our hearts, the Zion of the true and the faithful, the Zion of our God, with a pure love of Christ, charity, with knowledge, perfect faith, with justice, and mercy, and judgment, and truth -- until we are filled with these, which are the Holy Ghost, and become one, we cannot go there and accomplish that great objective of the last dispensation of the fullness of times, which has fully come.

President Rulon Jeffs
Rulon Jeffs' Sermons 7:51 August 28, 1988 CCA

What I have uppermost, as I see the will of God concerning this people, is to prepare for Zion, the redemption of Zion. That was the burden of Uncle Roy's remarks and his labors, to prepare a people. We have heard so very well here today how that preparation can be made.

Testimony of Priesthood Keyholders

President Rulon Jeffs
Rulon Jeffs' Sermons 6:106 October 6, 1985 Sandy

I am impressed more and more all of the time by the conditions under which we obtain faith, and hope, and charity -- meek and lowly of heart. I think too few of us understand the meaning of that. We are so wrapped up in our own opinions and traditions. And I would to God we all understood Priesthood. I would to God we all understood Jesus Christ when He said, "I am meek and lowly in heart." He was simply asking us to become like Him. He is our God and Savior. And Joseph Smith is the Witness of the Father and the Son, and stands in the office of the Holy Ghost as a man. The Holy Ghost is a Personage of Spirit, which centers in the Father and issues forth from Himself to His children through one man, His representative upon the earth. It has ever been so eternally, and ever will be so. What do you suppose the Lord meant in that parenthetical matter when He said, "There is never but one man upon the earth at a time upon whom this power," this sealing power, "and the keys of the holy Priesthood are conferred"?

Training on Principles of Priesthood

What Is Priesthood?

President John Taylor Millennial Star 9:321

What is Priesthood? Without circumlocution I shall as briefly answer that is the government of God, whether on the earth or in the heavens, for it is by that power, agency, or principle that all things are governed on the earth and in the heavens, and by that power that all things are upheld and sustained. It governs all things -- it directs all things -- it sustains all things -- and has to do with all things that God and truth are associated with. It is the power of God delegated to intelligences in the heavens and to men on the earth.

President Brigham Young
JD 2:139 December 3, 1854 SLC

When we talk of the celestial law which is revealed from heaven, that is, the Priesthood, we are talking about the principle of salvation, a perfect system of government, of laws and ordinances, by which we can be prepared to pass from one gate to another, and from one sentinel to another, until we go into the presence of our Father and God. This law has not always been upon the earth; and in its absence, other laws have been given to the children of men for their improvement, for their education, for their government, and to prove what they would do when left to control themselves; and what we now call tradition has grown out of these circumstances.

President Brigham Young
JD 11:249 June 17, 1866 SLC

The priesthood of the Son of God in its operations comprises the kingdom of God, and I know of no form of expression that will better tell what that priesthood is than the language given to me by the Spirit, namely, that it is a pure system of government. If the people who subject themselves to be governed by it, will live strictly according to its pure system of laws and ordinances, they will harmonize in one, and the kingdom of God will steadily move on to the ultimate triumph of truth and the subjugation of wickedness everywhere on this earth.

President Brigham Young
JD 10:320 July 31, 1864 SLC

Our religion is founded upon the Priesthood of the Son of God -- it is incorporated within this Priesthood. We frequently hear people inquire what the Priesthood is; it is a pure and holy system of government. It is the law that governs and controls all things, and will eventually govern and control the earth and the inhabitants that dwell upon it and all things pertaining to it.

President Brigham Young
JD 7:202 July 31, 1859 SLC

The holy Priesthood is a system of laws and government that is pure and holy; and if it is adhered to by intelligent man, whom God has created a little lower than angels, it is calculated to preserve our tabernacles in eternal being; otherwise they will be resolved into native element. Nothing is calculated to satisfy the mind of an intelligent being, only to obtain principles that will preserve him in his identity, to enable him to increase in wisdom, power, knowledge, and perfection.

President John Taylor
JD 1:224 April 8, 1853 SLC

Perhaps it may be well, at this stage of my remarks, to give you a short explanation of my ideas on government, legitimacy, or Priesthood, if you please. The question, "What is Priesthood?" has often been asked me. I answer, it is the rule and government of God, whether on earth, or in the heavens; and it is the only legitimate power, the only authority that is acknowledged by Him to rule and regulate the affairs of His kingdom. When every wrong thing shall be put right, and all usurpers shall be put down, when he whose right it is to reign shall take the dominion, then nothing but the Priesthood will bear rule; it alone will sway the sceptre of authority in heaven and on earth, for this is the legitimacy of God.

President John Taylor
JD 5:187 August 30, 1857 SLC

Some people ask, "What is Priesthood?" I answer, "It is the legitimate rule of God, whether in the heavens or on the earth;" and it is the only legitimate power that has a right to rule upon the earth; and when the will of God is done on earth as it is in the heavens, no other power will bear rule.

In doing this, among other things, he [Abraham] found he had a right to the priesthood. I need not stop to tell you what that is, you Latter-day Saints. You understand it is the rule and government of God, whether in the heavens or on the earth, and when we talk of the kingdom of God we talk of something that pertains to rule, government, authority and dominion; and that priesthood is the ruling principle that exists in the heavens or on the earth, associated with the affairs of God. Hence, we are told in the Scriptures that Christ was a priest forever after the order of Melchisedec. Then of what order was Melchisedec? A priest for ever after the order of the Son of God, for if Christ was after the order of Melchisedec, Melchisedec must have been after the order of Christ, as a necessary consequence. Very well. Now, then, in relation to that priesthood it was something that ministered in time and through eternity; it was a principle that held the keys of the mysteries of the revelations of God, and was intimately associated with the Gospel, and the Gospel, wherever it existed, was in possession of this priesthood; and it could not exist without it. It always "brought life and immortality to light."

Only One Man at a Time
Holds the Keys

President Leroy S. Johnson
Leroy S. Johnson's Sermons 7:352 February 12, 1984 CCA

There is only one man at a time, and that is the way it has been throughout all the history of God's dealings with people, both in this world and the world before this one, and the world before that one. Only one man at a time holds the keys and power of the sealing power, and those who act during his administration are only acting under a delegated authority.

President Rulon Jeffs
Rulon Jeffs' Sermons [LSJ] 7:302 August 17, 1982 Creston

Brothers and sisters, there is one thing that Brother Johnson has laid upon me, and that is to establish the truth of Section 132, verse 7; and there's more in this section.

(Doctrine & Covenants, Section 132:7-8)
"And verily I say unto you, that the conditions of this law are these: (Pertaining to the new and

everlasting covenant which was instituted for the fullness of His glory.) *All covenants, contracts, bonds, obligations, oaths, vows, performances, connections, associations, or expectations, that are not made and entered into and sealed by the Holy Spirit of promise, of him who is anointed, both as well for time and for all eternity, and that too most holy, by revelation and commandment through the medium of mine anointed, whom I have appointed on the earth to hold this power (and I have appointed unto my servant Joseph to hold this power in the last days, and there is never but one on the earth at a time on whom this power and the keys of this priesthood are conferred), are of no efficacy, virtue, or force in and after the resurrection from the dead; for all contracts that are not made unto this end have an end when men are dead.*

Behold, mine house is a house of order, saith the Lord God, and not a house of confusion."

These keys and powers are conferred upon one man. The keys of the power of sealing and of the Holy Priesthood are conferred upon one man. By whom? It's all right here.

(132:45) "For I (God speaking) *have conferred upon you* (speaking to Joseph) *the keys and power of the Priesthood, wherein I restored all things, and make known unto you all things in due time."* (The same is done for those who are appointed in his stead by God Himself.)

President Rulon Jeffs
Rulon Jeffs' Sermons 5:316 November 25, 1983 CCA

Brethren, can't we draw near to our head? Draw our families near with us, that we may be called together in one place to prepare a people for the redemption of Zion, under President Leroy S. Johnson, who is holding the keys of the holy Priesthood. Priesthood is God; God is Priesthood. The Holy Spirit centers in the Father, as Brigham Young told us, and from it goes throughout all of His dominions, and through this one holding those keys. He becomes the fountain head of that Holy Spirit to those under his dominion, being the mouthpiece of God to us.

President Rulon Jeffs
Rulon Jeffs' Sermons 6:298 October 19, 1986 SLC

I desire above all, as I stand before you to have you know that I am four-square, one hundred percent with President Johnson, and I want, above all things, to enjoy his confidence. I cannot think of a more devastating thing that could come to me if I were to find that I had lost his confidence. I have full confidence in him, and I love him with all my heart. I desire to obey the commandments of God which he gives to us. I know he is a Prophet of God, called at this time and anointed of the Lord to lead this people and prepare this people to redeem Zion.

I used to say he is as Enoch to us; he is as Moses. And it is my testimony that he has been raised up as one like unto Moses, as Section 103 tells us, to lead us to Zion under the Lord Jesus Christ and the Prophet Joseph Smith, who is at the elbow of President Johnson all the time. I testify to you that he is full of the Holy Ghost and has the Spirit of revelation to deliver to this people. He is the mouthpiece of God. He is the keyholder and President of the holy Priesthood. And the Holy Ghost, being the power of the Priesthood, which centers in the Father, is dispensed to us through this man and the power of the Priesthood which he has. That is how I feel about him, brothers and sisters, and the only way we are going to accomplish what he wants to accomplish -- as the Lord wants him to accomplish -- is for us to draw near unto him, and he will draw near unto us. The Lord says this, "Draw near unto me, and I will draw near unto you." But this man is a representative of God upon the earth, the greatest man on earth to guide and direct a people to come back into the presence of the Lord Jesus Christ and our Father, Michael. He has said to us on different occasions that we have not made much progress in lo, these many years.

President Rulon Jeffs
Rulon Jeffs' Sermons 1:544 July 3, 1966 CCA

I think there is nothing more foolish or foolhardy than for a man and woman to come to this Priesthood and get blessings, the ordinances of the holy Priesthood, and then refuse to follow its counsels and dictates, becoming a law unto themselves. There is nothing more foolish. I know that all my life and light and wisdom must come from the Holy Ghost, which was administered through the power of this Priesthood through the key man, Leroy S. Johnson. I cannot get it in any other way. Heber C. Kimball spoke the truth when he said, "How will you get the Holy Ghost except through us?"

speaking of Brigham and the leading brethren holding the holy Apostleship. I don't expect to get it in any other way.

The power of my Priesthood is ineffective; the power of your Priesthood, brethren, is absolutely ineffective save it be in concert, and in following the leadership and counsel and direction of President Johnson. I tell you this in the name of the Lord. I cannot see any other way to get back to Father Adam except through those whom He has called and chosen, and who administer everlasting lives through the ordinances of the holy Priesthood. There is no other way.

Purity in the Family Order of Heaven

President Rulon Jeffs
Rulon Jeffs' Sermons 7:533 February 12, 1950 SLC

Let us set a worthy example and be pure above all things. The Spirit of God cannot dwell in us unless we are living humble, pure lives, and I mean sexual purity. I mean it. The law of plural marriage is set forth by the Gods because it calls for purity, and it makes Gods and Goddesses of us.

President Rulon Jeffs
Rulon Jeffs' Sermons 4:49 November 21, 1976 Sandy

The world and the doings of satan is so full of satanic and devilish things, that we little recognize them when they are presented before us, brothers and sisters; and these things are doing terrible things to the minds of our children. The suggestive things that are thrown in advertising, even in the newspapers and magazines, all of these things are very suggestive and clutter up our minds. We must clean them up from these things and create an atmosphere in our homes where the Spirit of God can dwell. These are the things that pollute and destroy. Immorality, practices that are destructive of the very life and soul of men and women, and of children, are among us. To be pure means to be sexually pure. This is the cardinal sin in the world today, the terrible immorality that is all around us. So we must clean up in this way and abide the laws of chastity in our families and in all of our doings. We must be clean every whit.

I love the proverb in which is spoken, "Come to the Lord with clean hands and pure hearts," clean hands and pure hearts. We must present ourselves in that condition before He can bless us and own us, and before we can be one. So, a part of the process of becoming one is to clean up our minds and bodies, our hearts, and live in love together, in our families and as a people. Until we come to this point, brothers and sisters, the Lord will not own us and bless us; and I pray that we may indeed come to this condition with full purpose of heart.

President Rulon Jeffs
Rulon Jeffs' Sermons 2:402 January 17, 1971 Sandy

We obtain this, my dear brothers and sisters, by getting and keeping the Spirit of God, the Holy Ghost, if you please, which is the power of the Priesthood that administers everlasting life unto us. We cannot get it except through that channel. Sisters, I repeat again, you cannot get and keep the Spirit of God, except you keep the channel clear through your husband who bears all the Melchizedek Priesthood, without which he cannot hold you, and without which he cannot administer to his family. Authority, my dear brothers and sisters, is all -- authority from Almighty God, which He restored through Joseph the Prophet and on down till this present day, to that one man standing at the head. "Draw near to Me," God says, "and I will draw near to you." How can we draw to Him? Through His Priesthood. Draw near to your husbands, sisters. And brethren, draw near to those who administer eternal lives unto you.

The Inspiring and Exalting Nature of My Celestial Law

President Rulon Jeffs
Rulon Jeffs' Sermons 2:351 September 6, 1970 Sandy

I am impressed with the great importance of our becoming like God. This is the burden of the Gospel of Jesus Christ. This is the burden of the laws of the holy Priesthood, brothers and sisters, which are designed specifically to make us like God if we will only abide those laws. Truly, the initiatory ordinances of the Gospel are the foundation for these things -- faith, repentance, baptism by immersion, and the laying on of the hands of the Priesthood for the gift of the Holy Ghost; the reception and the magnifying of the holy Priesthood by the brethren and their wives and their children -- all of these things together, abiding in the crowning principles and laws of the Holy United Order and Celestial and Plural Marriage, the Family Order of Heaven. These laws were given to us specifically to make us

like God, for it is His work and His glory to bring to pass the immortality and the eternal life of His children. It is His glory that we become like Him, that we might receive of those things that He has and is.

Revelation of the Lord Jesus Christ Given to President Warren S. Jeffs Eldorado, Texas Saturday, July 23, 2011

1. I, your Lord, speaketh to every nation on earth; to now prepare for my power eternal of full governing power, even my Holy Priesthood, to be among you as my governing authority on earth, to be my holy power eternal dwelling among you, to be my holy representatives among your peoples; to administer my will, to make known my full Power of Union of Celestial Power of my holy Union authority.

2. Let my power eternal be your guiding light.

3. Let all be of my holy way; to know a governing power of my sending from the eternal power of Celestial, pure, holy power shall be the power of peace and holiness among all nations; to be the New Era of Union Eternal on earth; to have among all peoples my knowledge of truth, even eternal truth, that exalts the soul unto eternal life; learning my order of pure holy union.

4. Let it be a way of peace in every land.

5. Let it be my order of revealing through my Holy Priesthood how to live a full law of Celestial power of my giving full way of pure holy truth unto the full way of salvation for all who receive me and my Father's power of Union Eternal.

6. I am Son Ahman, who is Jesus Christ, the Son of my Eternal Father of redeeming and atoning power. I am

Eternal; Endless and Holiness is my name.

7. I am above all by the power of pure and holy Celestial power of the Godhood of full Priesthood power over all things.

8. My love shines forth upon all creation, giving all things their existence.

9. I am a full power of Eternal Godhood over Michael, who is my Son of Creation.

10. My Father is Elohim, of the Council of the Gods of Creation, Eloheim.

11. My Father is over all, and I am the God of Creation over the earth upon which you dwell, as a probationary orb of testing in a mortal condition, to see your worth of becoming of the way of Union Celestial, in eternal realms of power of my giving to faithful sons of Priesthood holy authority; which is always my holy love extant, ruling all things in a perfect way of order, peace, light eternally, and with power of increase.

12. Let my Church on earth be sanctified. Let my domain of each people in every land be ready to acknowledge me as King of kings, Lord over all peoples at my appearing in the power of Priesthood of Godhood over all.

13. Let all people now be ready to be of the knowing I am among you on earth, in Zion, unto my full work being revealed in building my governing City, even New Jerusalem on the center place in America.

14. Let it be my holy place.

15. Let the people of the nation of United States of America now prepare.

16. Let peace, purity, kindness, love of God, truth, and justice proper be your way of life; for I shall cause a great cleansing power to come forth, to prepare my land for New Jerusalem soon at hand.

17. Be ye clean and holy, that you may dwell on my holy land and perchance visit New Jerusalem unto your salvation on earth and in heaven.

18. I shall bring with me eternal knowledge, to lift up all people to a greater love for eternal truth, which comes to you by my Spirit of truth abiding in you.

19. Let all now be of pure and holy walk in the daily labor of their individual places of abiding, of working, of habitations.

20. Let my holy order of peace be my holy order among you, all nations, peoples, tongues, and all kindreds.

21. Let all now be the pure way of Celestial power.

22. My time of whirlwind judgments is at hand, to bring all peoples to the knowledge I have spoken from the heavens, and shall fulfill my word of eternal salvation, to be given at the time I appear in my glory unto my people being of a pure, holy, Celestial oneness.

23. Let all now be of purity, so as to abide my power and glory in a more pure way; to be ready to receive Celestial power in every land, to be governed by my Priesthood in righteousness and in truth.

24. My Priesthood is being readied to receive, to receive their Lord in honor before Him and His heavenly host coming to earth, in the pure holy power of Eternal Union; to govern the earth; to be my spokesmen unto your nation and people.

25. Violence must stop in every surviving land.

26. The spirit of murder is in most lands.

27. When I appear in my glory, I

shall abolish all such evil, even to be my full judging on murder of innocence in children unborn, being destroyed by their own parents; to now be an abolished practice among all nations.

28. I shall fulfill this, my will, among every nation, kindred, tongue, and people on every land.

29. Prepare ye, prepare ye, for all of this is nigh at hand.

30. I am the Giver of all good, the Governing Power over all peoples, nations, tongues, and kindreds. Come unto me, your Lord, to gain eternal life. Amen.

Historical Attacks Against the Priesthood During the Administration of Rulon Jeffs

Lawsuit Filed in Federal Court by Apostates

President Rulon Jeffs
Rulon Jeffs' Sermons 6:468 December 13, 1987 CCA

Another assault is being made on the United Effort Plan. It is being made according to the pattern that we have in the times and life of the Prophet Joseph Smith -- by apostates. A massive lawsuit has been filed in the United States District Court in Salt Lake City. The complaint is a hundred pages long, eighty pages of complaint and twenty pages of exhibits.***

I would like to speak on the nature of this United Effort Plan. In 1942, after the United Trust operation was attempted here in Short Creek, and failed because of the selfishness and aspiring nature of some men, the United Effort Plan was brought together and formed under the inspiration of God, and brought into being on November 9, 1942, under the scrutiny and direction of President John Y. Barlow, Joseph Musser, and Leroy Johnson. They, with Brother Hammon and myself, were made Trustees in the original Trust agreement. We knew not then what God had wrought, as we are now seeing this great assault that has been made time and time again against this great document which God inspired and directed in the minds of

John Y. Barlow and Joseph Musser and Leroy Johnson.***

Five days later this action was filed in court, Salt Lake District Court of the federal government. We haven't been served yet. We are having to go and get copies of the complaint ourselves to know what is going on. The press knew about it before it was even filed.***

Well, we just felt like reporting this to you, and I just want to emphasize one thing. This is a religious common-law Trust, with members. No one on United Effort land is a beneficiary under the common understanding of Trusts. Surely they could be revoked. But this is a religious Trust with members, and a religion can excommunicate its members.

President Rulon Jeffs
History of Priesthood Succession, Page 366

As everyone who has lived upon land in Colorado City and Hildale (Short Creek) knows, according to the articles, where there are transgressors or those acting inimical to the interests of the Trust, they may be removed. Everyone has understood when they built improvements upon the land that was assigned to them, housing and improvements attached to the land remain with it. And they are "tenants-at-will" of the trustees of the United Effort Plan.

President Rulon Jeffs
Rulon Jeffs' Sermons 6:491 February 7, 1988 Sandy

We are under attack. We are laboring now with the large firm of attorneys in answering the complaint of some thirty-five plaintiffs who have attached their names to the document; which is an attack, as Brother Truman has said, against the United Effort Plan and against the Priesthood. It has been brought to my attention that the principal party engaged in getting that complaint filed and getting it together expects to see the United Effort Plan destroyed.

President Rulon Jeffs
Rulon Jeffs' Sermons 7:287 December 16, 1990 Sandy

Well, the Lord has spoken through these brethren as I have prayed for each of them, and I don't feel there is any more to add at this point except this: God Almighty is governing and is overruling in this court action. It is in His hands, as to the enemy and as to the judge. I just want to express my gratitude to the Lord for these great blessings that have come to us. There is more to go through, but God is at the helm. Let us stand as one man, and God will deliver the enemy into the hands where they belong. We are dealing with apostates. Just read what the Prophet Joseph had to say about them. And we will make no agreements with them.

They proposed in a settlement that we give them ten-year leases, renewable and assignable. Uncle Roy said, "I want you to get discouraged and leave," and they have got to agree to leave before we can go any further. Zion must be made clean and pure. We are building a Zion where we are, dear brethren and sisters. Each of us in our hearts must have Zion, and as a whole, one people acting as one man, preparing to live that holy order. The enemy is trying to destroy it, but God will be our "Right-hand Man".

No Compromise With the Apostates

President Rulon Jeffs
Rulon Jeffs' Sermons 7:294 February 17, 1991 Sandy

I feel impressed to talk a little about apostasy and apostates. We are having to deal with so many of them in this lawsuit, but all of the apostates are not on the lawsuit; and by the word of God, through Uncle Roy, they must leave our community. During the past two months, the opposition lawyers approached our lawyers and asked that they consider a settlement out of court. They are tired of the case. They know they don't have a case. But they started it and they have got to finish it.

Training on Keeping the Spirit of God Through the Prophet Rulon Jeffs

"Keep Sweet" Is Our Only Protection

President Rulon Jeffs
Rulon Jeffs' Sermons 7:316 May 26, 1991 CCA

The Gospel of Jesus Christ is the plan of God unto salvation. If we want our salvation we must pay a price, the price of obedience. Be sweet. "Keep sweet," as Uncle John always said, and which I can't help but repeat every day in talking to people. Keeping sweet means keeping the Holy Spirit of God. That is the grand, all-powerful influence, and power of the Gods, and by which we become like God, to have a fullness

of that Holy Spirit in us. Seek for it and live by it, I pray in the name of Jesus Christ, amen.

President Rulon Jeffs
Rulon Jeffs' Sermons 7:368 December 6, 1991 Sandy

I want you all to understand the continual use of the two words "keep sweet," means keep the Holy Spirit of the Lord, until you are full of it. Only those who have it will survive the judgments of God which are about to be poured out without let or hindrance upon the earth, beginning at the House of God, where the Mormons are. I mean the Mormon Church, which is now apostate completely, and will never be set in order. We have the true and living Church of Jesus Christ of Latter-day Saints under our administration. And we add the word "Fundamentalist" in order to distinguish the true Church of Jesus Christ of Latter-day Saints from the name of the one that now is a complete gentile sectarian church. The Lord has rejected it.

President Rulon Jeffs
Rulon Jeffs' Sermons 7:385 June 7, 1992 Sandy

The Lord has surely answered my prayers, giving the messages that I wanted given here. It has been marvelous. I want you all to know I love you, and I want to save you, by the power of God. My sermon is: Keep sweet. It is a matter of life or death. The remnant spoken of will be those who are full of the Holy Ghost. May we all be there, I pray in the name of Jesus Christ, amen.

President Rulon Jeffs
Rulon Jeffs' Sermons 7:402 December 4, 1992 Sandy

Just these brief words, dear young people. I love you, and I want to save you in the Celestial Kingdom of God. So, if you will keep the grand teaching that we are trying to get over: Keep the Holy Spirit of God. KEEP SWEET! It is a matter of life or death.

You have had the teaching regarding what is required in order for us to survive the judgments, sufficient of the Holy Spirit of God that we can be lifted up and then set down after it is over. That will be the remnant which will go to redeem Zion. The wicked will be swept off from the face of this land. The wicked are they who come not unto Christ. There is only one people who comes unto Christ, and that is this people under His servant.

President Warren S. Jeffs' Testimony Concerning His Father, Rulon Jeffs

President Warren S. Jeffs
Warren S. Jeffs' Sermons December 20, 1998 Sandy

President Rulon Jeffs holds the Priesthood after the order of the Son of God, and his right-hand Man is the Lord God Himself. And on his side stand the hosts of heaven and all the Prophets who looked forward to the accomplishment of the promised work that they were given.

Upon whom do the Prophets Isaiah, Jeremiah, Moses, Abraham, Isaac, Jacob, Father Adam -- all the Prophets of old -- who do they look to, that their work will not fall to the ground unheeded? They look to this Prophet, President Rulon Jeffs, in preparing a people who can survive the great judgments and go into the Millennium establishing Zion; a people who will build a beautiful city that God Himself will visit, who can receive the ancient Prophets into their living rooms and be taught of them; a people who will meet Enoch as he descends and they rise. And in all these great events ahead, President Rulon Jeffs will be in the midst of it. He will receive the Prophet Joseph, who is the One Mighty and Strong, visiting this Prophet on earth. The Prophet Joseph, a Celestial, glorified being covered with light, will come to his legal successor, President Jeffs. He will be told by revelation who from among this people are worthy to go back and redeem Zion in the new Zion's Camp. And this Prophet, to accomplish these great events, will be renewed and restored, strengthened, taking those of his family and this people who are prepared.

I testify to you, dear brothers and sisters, this work is just beginning for the obedient. Press forward in your preparation. Success is within reach through your faith unto repentance; purifying your life so you can be filled with the Holy Spirit of God. It comes to you through your love and obedience to this Prophet, President Jeffs, and you know it. You know the evil powers are trying with their might to stop you from placing your whole confidence in the words and teachings of our Prophet. It is taking the greatest battle of faith that you have ever fought to press forward and perfect your lives as our Prophet teaches you. This is a witness that you must go forward with all of your might. Do not lighten up. Stand fast and know that God is with this Prophet.

This is my testimony to you this day, that though individuals might be taken, or fall, there will be sufficient from among this people for our Prophet to use; and they will become the nucleus of the great Millennium. Nothing can stop this work -- the work the Lord has given the Prophet Joseph and continued in the life of our Prophet, President Jeffs. Draw near and the Lord will give you this testimony, for you will be buoyed up -- lifted up in your hearts and feelings. With greater energy do all the good possible within your reach.

I yearn that we will be encouraged, that whatever we are called to go through, it will be worth it. The blessings that await that prepared people are so great. Do not be cast down because you cannot see it all right now. This is your test of faith. Press forward and the Lord will be with you as you are with President Jeffs.

President Warren S. Jeffs
Eldorado, Texas
Thursday, July 21, 2011

A son of God of Eternal Union of full keys of sealing power of the Holy Priesthood of Melchizedek was given to my father by our Lord. Ordained an apostle in April 1945, he was an holy inspired Prophet of Priesthood truths, always perfectly loyal to the Keyholder of the Priesthood over him. He was as a little child in obeying the Prophets over him.

His love for God and the Holy Priesthood was a full love loyalty of perfect sweetness.

God chose this Prophet to finish their preparing for Zion's mission of the order of pure Priesthood principles taught and lived. His power of heavenly-empowered Priesthood power was felt. He loved the saints, suffering unto death for the Priesthood and for our Heavenly Father.

He gave, of the Lord, the Godhead training, teaching who God is and how to become like Him. He was a God in humanity and is like God, and is one of the Gods of eternity under Christ our Lord, and under our Father in heaven. Let all rejoice in the Lord for Rulon Jeffs and his perfect walk before God and all men.

Having a perfect understanding of Priesthood, he was a loyal apostle to John Y. Barlow and Leroy S. Johnson, and was a full power of Priesthood keys and authority on earth over all men. The majesty of his Priesthood was felt increasingly; and he gathered a people to be taught the key to be Zion, even to keep sweet, and be filled with the Spirit of God.

John Y. Barlow said of my father, Rulon Jeffs: "You are sweet and sound." He labors now in the heavenly Kingdom with God and the Prophets in behalf of the saints whom he loved, as a guiding, perfect father, only desiring the will of God. His guiding light was to read, learn, and teach of Joseph Smith the Prophet; and was able to declare his oneness with God through Joseph Smith and the Keyholders before him, as he, with them, declared: "I have only taught what Joseph Smith taught."

Thus, the work of God through Joseph Smith was carried on through each Keyholder of Priesthood, as did my father, Rulon Jeffs. He taught us the correct understanding of Priesthood,

saying -- "God is Priesthood; Priesthood is God with us and among the people." He fulfilled the Lord's directive to him by the Prophet Leroy S. Johnson, "to help establish once and for all the One Man Rule" of the Keyholder of Priesthood, even God's rule through His chosen servant on earth, who is ordained by God Himself to hold the full sealing powers of Elijah, unto the full ordinances being performed unto eternal life, by our Lord's will revealed. He and all the Keyholders were foreordained to hold the key position of Priesthood power, even before the earth was made. He is one of the sons of God, continuing on to do our Lord's will.

My testimony of Priesthood, given of me of the Lord through my father, is that the correct understanding of Priesthood is: God, through His Keyholder of Priesthood, has the right to rule in every area of our lives; and we, the people of God, have the right, duty, and privilege to love to obey God through His Keyholder of Priesthood.

"He that receiveth my servants receiveth me," said the Lord. "Obey the Priesthood of God to obey God" is his life's example of a pure and holy walk before God, and before all men. The Lord guided him and gave him revelation up to his passing moment. God and my father did and do right, is my testimony of them, which I give in the name of our Lord Jesus Christ. Amen.

Chapter 9

Administration of President Warren S. Jeffs

**Revelation of the Lord Jesus Christ
Given to President Warren S. Jeffs
Palestine, Texas
Sunday, October 2, 2011**

1. I, the Lord over all people, who is God in the power of full governing, reveal to all people my holy and eternal way.

2. My Holy Priesthood of full keys of sealing power is among men on earth.

3. Let all know I have a son of Priesthood who is of my order of keys of power, to bless all who will receive me and my plan of salvation; to administer the will of God to them; to be a full power of my authority and eternal gifts of exalting power; to bless on earth that which I shall uphold eternally in heaven.

4. Thus is your Lord to soon appear, to cause all to know, even they in the world of departed spirits, as well as all on earth, of my eternal Gospel of salvation; always of my Priesthood of the Eternal Union authority of my revealing and guiding.

5. I am He who has suffered for all men; who hath conquered death; who shall resurrect all people unto a judgment of eternal and full reward for all their deeds done in the flesh while on the earth.

6. My plan is of a full authority by all Celestial and eternal power of my Godhood over all.

7. Let all come unto me through my servant Warren Jeffs, as he is called to receive my will to all peoples.

8. Now know I am giving my will to all peoples to know I am soon of a full revealing of my power of cleansing all peoples; to prepare for my holy and pure governing powers to be on earth for a thousand years; after which cometh the end of the time of this earth's preparation; to be of a complete cleansing by eternal fire, consuming all dross; to Celestialize the earth unto a power of heaven; a sea of glass as a Urim and Thummim of revealing to all who dwell on the Celestial orb, truths of all kingdoms of a lesser power, to govern those kingdoms.

9. Let all know of my revelation of the degrees of glory in my holy word called Doctrine and Covenants, even that Section 76 therein, to know of my redeeming power; to know of the degree of glory yet to be given every person as their spirit of their keeping shall be given them in fulness; even to be as they chose on earth.

10. Let all be repenting, therefore, and be of the increase of my holy power, which is the gift of the Holy Ghost given by the laying on of hands of my Priesthood; to be the light of my power dwelling in the obedient who are of my baptized and preparing people of covenants unto eternal life.

11. Now prepare ye, all ye people of the earth, for my message of full power unto salvation; as I appear and preserve all who can receive my glorious way unto eternal life. Amen.

Thus Saith Jesus Christ, a Holy Revealing, of Evil Powers Seeking to Destroy My Celestial Power of Priesthood

Revelation of the Lord Jesus Christ Given to President Warren S. Jeffs
Palestine, Texas
Wednesday, October 12, 2011

1. Thus saith the Lord to all peoples of all nations: Having bestowed full Priesthood powers of keys of Elijah on my servant Warren Jeffs, I led him to perform sealings, and to begin a work of the Redemption of Zion mission.

2. He was led by me to find lands. He called people to my holy labor.

3. A holy house was built.

4. A people of my own order, unto my purposes being fulfilled, have now been laboring to be worthy of my presence.

5. Now learn that evil powers have combined with one another to seek to hinder or even destroy my Zion's mission.

6. A secret order was given evil revealings of lies, pure evil intent, to bring my servant Warren Jeffs into a place of harm, even in their surmisings, wanting to take life.

7. Let it be known this combination of evil is in full working, desiring to destroy him and my Priesthood.

8. Now I say, as God over all, my work shall triumph; my Priesthood shall be preserved; my Zion is increasing on earth through my will, unto New Jerusalem soon to rise; notwithstanding the evil combinings of the apostates and the government powers who have received of a similar dark spirit as apostates, when believing their lying ways of pure evil intent.

9. Thus have they lied, even in book publishings designed to turn this generation away from my holy authority.

10. Let it be known the falsehoods now believed by government officials are no longer to be heard nor of a following; for I reveal that Dan Fischer, a wicked man who once lived Celestial Plural Union of Marriage, turned bitter, and has actively used his riches to pay the way of persecution; helping to embitter other former and now apostate members of my Priesthood to fight against my Priesthood.

11. My Priesthood, Church, and Celestial Law of Celestial Plural Union of Marriage are pure.

12. All who fight against my law of pure holy Union Celestial are of evil corrupt ways, unto the spirit of murder in their hearts.

13. This shall be truth learned as government authorities take upon themselves lies against my servant, against my Priesthood and law of pure holy way.

14. I am God. My way of Priesthood law is pure, holy, noble, godly.

15. Only they who obey my law know of the purity required to live my law in pure holy way.

16. These apostates became immoral, and lost my power, and are darkening more each day.

17. Let all heed them not.

18. They are traitors against me and my holy way.

19. Now let their own lives be examined to see they are corrupt.

20. Let governing authority be of a labor to examine these false witnesses, who only have a lying spirit, twisting truth

with lying zeal, as though good is seen through unenlightened eyes as evil intent.

21. Thus, government courts, investigators, powers of legislative labor, governors, all have taken on the false way of these lying former saints, now darkened; who only look upon life through darkened minds; yielding themselves to persecute innocence unto imprisonment, robbing of lands, houses; and also seeking the virtue of my Priesthood to be destroyed, in promoting false authority, or full adulterous and Sodom sins; apostates losing all ways of pure holy living, following after the evil way inspired by Lucifer to thus harm in every way my holy people now preparing for my own power to dwell with them in New Jerusalem soon to come forth.

22. Thus, this man helped other apostates to file false charges.

23. Thus courts have been of a persecuting labor.

24. Now know my authority, though being of a way of past fearful and wondering way as great attacks came against him; yet I am with my servant, and reveal, through my grace, my own will, for I have him in my hands; and he gives my pure will to all peoples, by my pure revealing.

25. Now let him be about my full labor as my servant, to lead my Church.

26. Let all governing powers cease prosecuting work, lest my judgment of greater power come upon all who oppose my Priesthood.

27. Let Judge of present labor against my servant recuse herself completely from all cases pertaining to my Church.

28. Let all witnesses be examined in their lives.

29. Let this secret combination of apostate, with governing powers, fully be of a overthrow.

30. You shall reap my full way of power of judgment if you continue thy false way. Amen.

Warning of Judgment of Pure Justice

Revelation of the Lord Jesus Christ Given to President Warren S. Jeffs Big Lake, Texas Wednesday, March 23, 2011

2. For how can I, the Lord, uphold you as a nation when you continue the greater evils within your borders, even the murder of unborn children, of Sodom and adultery, licentious and corrupt ways; of persecuting an innocent religious minority who abide my laws of a Celestial, eternal nature; who persecute them to the taking of their lands and houses and hindering their advancement in my cause of Zion.

16. Hasten to correct these evils, or you shall begin to experience workings of destruction within thine own borders in a greater manner than before; for heretofore I have been merciful upon thee when my peoples have cried for mercy, and for the purpose of mine elect to be preserved on my land of Zion.

Motion of Jesus Christ in Court Proceedings in the Trial of My Servant

Revelation of the Lord Jesus Christ Given to President Warren S. Jeffs San Angelo, Texas Sunday, July 31, 2011

1. Let motion for my holy dismissing be of my doing, to be of a recusing of this judge to be of no longer a way of persecution, to have a way of no power

over present doing of the attack of the power of the enemy who seek to destroy purity of my doing in full law of eternal power.

2. Let it begin with the way of the court of usual titling, with my own word to be in content of the writing to show my rule is above all as an holy way to recuse, to allow all to know God is in the labor of this and other labor of pure way of truth, having full way of knowing what is in the heart of each person who is on my holy way of pure doing, to let them see I am the Doer of my delivering for my Order of Eternal Union of the holy noble way of my most pure way of pure abiding my law powering of pure holy labor in a full labor of my holy way being of Celestial power of my revealing truth.

3. Let all now hear my will of pure, holy truth as I show my way of justice by my power of truth of Celestial light, by which I know the way to discern and judge with eternal power; a light of my holy power pertaining to court abuse of power against my Church of Jesus Christ to be my holy way of pure revealing unto the true way known of motion to be of a removal by law, having performed illegal way of using Judicial power to be of a way to be of a unjust and corrupting work against innocence of children, loss of sacred and pure trust of religious and noble revealings pertaining to holy temple, now being a defiling of your way of ruling against my call to stop such injustice, yet not heeding my will of pure holy call to be a just and righteous upholder of justice in a nation that has constitutional guarantee of religious freedom; yet allowing my holy religious and sacred temple to be as no holy worth, not to be of government interference by right of pure principle of religion to be of greater protecting than the legal way of man; wherein my holy way is of heaven, saith Jesus Christ, the Lord of all, to Barbara Walthers, present Judge over case of unjust way; having allowed my holy way to be deriding before all people, even after my own will was of a giving; yet unheeded by you for no other reason than your own judging; not considering I told thee to cease this unjust and intrusive way against a holy, pure way of religion on earth, to be of salvation for all people who learn truth of my holy way of being ready for my holy coming.

4. Learn now thy transgression has been child abusing when you caused my innocent children to be carried away into the hand of your appointed and government agency people who were of the way of taking children into evil places of their bondage from family protection, into homes of corrupt, immoral way of upbringing; to have some be abused unto loss of virtue by workers in the caretaking homes, not monitoring the moral and unholy way of such who are of the world in conduct; yet my innocent ones, thrust into way of corrupting, were touched, handled, abused, even morally in their innocent unprotecting way of living, that my vengeance of eternal power shall be upon all such who destroy innocence, virtue, purity of morals.

5. Such was the truth of your intent to remove my holy way of life from children born and brought up in a most holy way of pure living, where prayer, moral discipline, worship of their Lord -- who now speaketh to thee; even to where I cause you to see your abuse by testimony of other caretakers of temporary helping, who later testified about abuse of the children, both mental and physical, in not

allowing loving mother of each child to be the watch-care over innocence; thrust into homes of no moral training, thus exposed to corrupt ways of living, unto some being of an abusing by wicked and immoral and deceiving, lying agents of your order way of social and unholy and unjust doing.

6. I, your Lord, say to you, I shall bring to light your evil intent now, before all people, to destroy my Church on earth by allowing sacred and private trust to be heralding over all nations; as you continue to allow prosecution of unjust way to be as a desecrating of sacred law of pure, holy religion of revealing from heaven, by a God of holy, pure, just way of abiding in eternal power, guiding His authority of heavenly power to be as watchman over my law of holy power of exalting way; unto all being of a more and a greater standard of moral purity, requiring a moral way above the way of those not of my holy religious way.

7. Thus you have abused me and my Church unto a desecrating of holy and sacred religious way of exalting my people to be my elect of pure religion from heaven revealing of my giving; to now be of a greater condemning way of thy Lord than before, when I called on you to cease proceedings of unjust rulings; allowing my holy house to now be as non-religious defiling of sacred place of holy labor of Priesthood and eternal blessings administering, as unto life everlasting of my holy way of pure, noble, righteous power of eternal power.

8. I am to now recuse you from this case.

9. Let your heart be open to the way of your now being before all nations, to know you would not preserve religious freedom, nor religious sacred trust, while you could thus do a labor of just way, of noble trust of a governing power to hold sacred to all, a religious principle dear to most faiths; to not defile sacred trust of holy place of my temple; now as a defiling that cannot be undone; as you now become a hiss and a by-word among all people, because you allowed my Church to be abandoned to ridicule unjustly, only having the intent to display my holy way before all people without any just cause, save to allow your will to be done; even when I had my Mouthpiece voice my warning of my own word declare you to Stop! Cease!, and thus be just in rulings that could be upon correct principle of keeping sacred to all peoples their religious edifices; now setting a way of defiling any religious sacred building; as though constitutional protection of religious faith and living is of no value; unto you now being an enemy to all religious and pure-faith way of worship.

10. This you did not consider as I sounded my voice and will in the proceedings before many; now heralding unjust way against sacred and religious way in every nation.

11. Hear my now judging of you as an unholy way of pure defiling of holy way; now to recuse yourself from present case; to now be of honor and step away from this abuse of power against a religious and pure faith in the Lord; who now is Judge of you, through my servant now voicing my will; to now be of honor to step away from these unjust doings, and no longer be of a Judge over religious way of worship of your Lord, who shall be of a soon appearing to my Church and people of every nation who remain after my power of pure, holy cleansing removes the evil off my land where my holy place shall be a

refuge of pure worship of God and way of my administering my holy law of Celestial Union of holy and noble way of living, unto pure honoring sons and daughters who abide a purity of living my Celestial Marriage holy Union of my revealing.

12. Let thy mind now turn to the truth of my will; and be of an honorable way, to step away from present case and not again rule against a holy way.

13. This from your Lord who hath bought all people with the price of His own suffering, to redeem all people unto life, to be judged for deeds and desires in the flesh, unto eternal judgment and just and pure truth revealing each heart; all things being revealed unto the knowing of all peoples their hidden way, none being exempt from my eternal power of judging all people.

14. Let this be a sober way of thy thinking; to now do as I direct, even Jesus Christ now revealing thy mind, as you sat before court contemplating ruling, you were to be of a just thought of ruling in favor of religious protection; yet you allowed a fear to enter in that my Church was not of a pure way; you thus did a private way of judging God and His revealing of laws eternal of Plural Celestial Union of my administering.

15. I fear you not, and shall show you as a worker against pure religious freedom by my own will being of a publishing to all people of your unjust way of adjudicating cases against my Church and principle of Union Eternal, thinking your court could deter practice of my faith and holy principle of eternal power of Priesthood guiding of members' lives in a way of abiding Celestial law, not of the earth, but of me, your Lord, who is Ruler over all.

16. Now sign order to recuse thyself; and allow this proceeding to stop; to now be reversed by your own doing of ruling mistrial, then recusing from case, and any other you have allowed to come against my elect, who some are suffering from thy way of court doing in family and brotherhood ties broken as fathers and faithful, religious and principled men, imprisoned for religious motive practice, living as I, their Lord, command; being of thy persecuting way, need also delivering.

17. I append this, my motion, with a new will of God revealing thy work soon to be a publishing to all people; to know of thy way of unjust and unprincipled ruling in a case where you could be of a just way for religion being protecting of thy court power; now defamed by your power to extol your way before all people; yet now being of an justice defiler way.

18. This is my judging, to be of public knowing now in court assembling, to be published by my will to all people.

19. Let it now be your doing to hear this writing, to now do honor to true justice abiding way of honorable removing thyself from case now before the court.

20. Let my servant sign his name as my holy and noble authority on earth to deliver my will to all nations, peoples, tongues, kindreds, and governing powers, saith Jesus Christ, whose right it is to rule over all, who shall bring true just and holy way of governing power with Him in my appearing over all peoples as King over all the earth, God over all; who shall be as a Rewarder of pure judging to all peoples, eternal in power, pure and holy in exalting

power unto salvation for all who come unto me through repenting of sin, and doing justly to all who are of the more righteous among all nations.

21. I, the Lord, have spoken. Amen.

Jesus Christ's Holy Will to Court of Unjust Way During Trial; Read in Record of Court to Tell All of My Way of Pure Holy Power Being of My Power Authority, and to Call Court to Cease Unjust Attack Against Me and My Holy Order of Pure Religion Revealed From Heaven

Revelation of the Lord Jesus Christ Given to President Warren S. Jeffs
San Angelo, Texas
Thursday, August 4, 2011

1. I your Lord who reigns over all my world of probationary and testing condition of pure holy creating power; even your Lord and God over all things, yea, He who spake, and the world was made, the God of my servant now dwelling in an unjust holding, to face thy unholy attack against all I have him perform unto my purpose of Zion being of a real place, kingdom, power, people, and ruling governing power over all nations; look at thy sin now of a heightening tower ready to fall with Babylon, the unholy way of persecuting power, now in a supposed court of law; to be of a unholy way of unjust attack in court, allowing prosecuting way to accuse me, the God over all, who is the power of you being of a power on my world of holy way of Celestial abiding, which world shall be my only way of salvation for all who have and will dwell thereon; to be of a heaven to all who live a Celestial Law, not of man, but of my revealing unto him who is Mouth on earth at this time to all people; of the way of my giving truth through revealing through authority of my holy calling; not of man's appointing; but of thy Lord, who is over all nations; who is of the authority of Godhood, who can see all in true judging of hearts to be just in holy and pure ways.

2. Let this court now be just, to cease letting my holy way of Celestial Law be as a dishonor among they of my power of governing authority be derided, mocked, as a way of accusing my holy way, thus accusing me, your Lord, of being not of noble pure way of doing.

3. I am God, and send thee my word: Cease! Do not present my holy way as a thing of naught; lest judgment come to a full measure to be cleansing powers sent to be a judging of all of my holy and pure power attending your evil intent.

4. Hear my warning as a full awakening unto repenting of your attack against pure religion Celestial, only for they of purity of life in religious way of eternal authority of my Priesthood.

5. Let my holy way be of freedom; to have my people be of my holy way.

6. Let my word now be of an awakening to all, that I, your Lord Jesus Christ, still speak from revealing of eternal and pure holy power to all on earth, through him you have caused to be as a witness against no justice given in the way of civil governing power, misjudging a servant of my sending, as a full attack of thy doing against thy Lord and His authority of noble pure way of Celestial and Priesthood law revealed from heaven; to be my authority among men to prepare my people of Celestial power for my holy coming.

7. I am soon to fulfill my will of cleansing the land of Zion, North and South America, by whirlwind judgments.

8. Let all prepare.

9. Let court cease this attack, is the will of thy Lord Jesus Christ who now reveals your own lives are as a light now turning to darkness by thy own choosing; to be persecuting power against innocence, that standeth firm in revelations of my giving; to abide more pure and holy judging than is known to man, who are not enlightened in my Celestial way of truth. Amen.

Jesus Christ Calls on Court to Cease Unjust Proceedings, to Have Recusal Hearing for Removal of Judge of Unjust Use of Power

Revelation of the Lord Jesus Christ Given to President Warren S. Jeffs
San Angelo, Texas
Tuesday, August 2, 2011

1. I who reign on high speaketh to court of present judication:

2. Cease this aggression against my own true Church, which I, your Lord, have established to perform the labor of final preparing of a pure and sacred labor of my inspiring; to have upon them the requiring way of eternal purity of purpose, of faith, of the nature of Celestial Law abiding in pure Celestial performing; to be my pure religion of perfect way of holy religion; guaranteed freedom of performing religion without government intervening, according to constitutional law of guarantee of all religion of pure purpose.

3. Verily I say unto you who now are of the legal work of deriding my sacred law of pure holy way, to cause the naming of your own will as if I were subject to you whom I, the God over all, have created and give place on my own domain of my creating, to have life, the ability to prove thyself, whether each son or daughter would obey law eternal that exalts unto salvation earned by a pure way of abiding law of pure way, in a giving of obeying to a just and holy Father of eternal power; able to exalt thee unto life and have place in my eternal domain of Celestial exalting.

4. Now receive ye my word, even from thy Lord through my servant now being of a labor to be of a witness against this unholy way of unrighteous labor against my holy revealing of pure noble way, of my own eternal authority being of a victim of government attack because of the way of my sending my own law of Eternal Union to earth, through revelation of my own will unto him who is my Mouthpiece to the world; to receive their Lord's own mind and way unto eternal life, by abiding in Celestial revealing of my own purposes, fulfilling all required way to become a son of God in realms eternal, a daughter of holy and pure Celestial Union with a son of God who can be able to dwell in realms eternal; by living law of that Celestial and eternal way, revealing my own purposes, fulfilling the measure of thy creation, of Him who is able to exalt thy soul unto my own eternal power.

5. Let the present course of this ruling judicial power now be of a postponing of proceedings.

6. Let transcript of sessions be given time to be preparing to be presented to a recusal hearing, lest the court perform a labor of unrelenting zeal of persecution against innocent way of eternal life lived in ordinances of my holy way, requiring the obedience to Celestial, holy, pure law, to earn the reward of faithful and righteous children unto the Father over all.

7. I who reign over all speaketh:

Let this proceeding stop, lest there be unjust way of thy doing that is harmful to innocent people, not having right to religious and holy law and Celestial power attending, now being of a deriding by present and unholy way; not having foundation at all to allow the presentation of the holy and sacred doing of God with a work of full intent to interfere with my holy way being the full law of a pure kingdom to rise on earth through the living of Celestial Plural Marriage, now having been of a law of eternal power from eternity; not to be done away by the prejudice of man, nor by earthly law that does not exalt the soul.

8. Let these realities awaken present judge to see the treading on my holy law is to turn to legal way of greater persecution against my holy way, even my pure way of exalting sons of God, daughters of holy and pure way, unto life eternal.

9. This from the Lord, even thy Creator, now sending His own will to present court, to know that my will shall be fulfilled in the end; whether it be by thy consent and righteous ruling in protecting religion of pure holy power of a way of my giving; or by my intervening by almighty power of judging this people of present dwelling on my land of my soon power of governing power on earth in Zion; to be my holy abode on earth as I dwell among men, to be the governing power of my holy eternal power of governing authority over all who will acknowledge me, your Lord and Governor over all, Jesus Christ, who will be my elect of the way of Celestial power eternal; to be my only way of pure holy abiding on earth for a thousand years of peace; to rule over all nations extant, in dominion of Celestial power, not allowing unjust way of religion

being of a persecuting way by governing power in the way of hindering their freedom of abiding law and way eternal of my own revealing unto all lands; a holy way of pure holy doing unto my coming among my people who are of the law of Celestial pure way; even my law of Celestial Marriage and my other holy law of the full Celestial way of Holy Order of Eternal Union of full sacred way of having all things common, a way of requiring my faithful to live pure in every way of their dwelling among my Holy City Zion; soon to be built by faithful and obedient children of my calling and empowering, to prepare for my own presence.

10. Let this court now rule in favor of postponing until recusal hearing can be properly prepared for in having court transcript preparing for review, to show unjust way of ruling against my holy Priesthood, Church, people, and Celestial Law of eternal and holy way, saith Jesus Christ, unto thy being forgiven as you do such just way; to preserve my holy way unto a full doing of holy and pure raising of a people unto thy God for salvation to be administered unto my Israel, to be gathered unto my land, Zion, even the land upon which you now dwell.

11. If thou do it not, know that innocence shall be harmed, and defiling of pure holy way become a way of government infringement on a pure holy faith of my own keeping to be a God of Creation.

12. Let all now be of the way of just and righteous judgment, to have as my will being performed; to have the nation now be of free exercise of religion in reality and in truth.

13. I, the Lord, have spoken it. Amen.

Jesus, Your Lord, Giveth His Word to Governing Power; Also My Will to My People to Prepare for My Full Power of Holy Power of Zion to Come Forth Among Nations of the Earth; Judgments Soon to Cleanse the Land

Revelation of the Lord Jesus Christ Given to President Warren S. Jeffs
Eldorado, Texas
Sunday, July 24, 2011

1. Let all now learn of their Lord, His will of my pure holy way of my full labor to redeem Zion unto New Jerusalem being built by power eternal soon to happen; to have my Church be the instrument of pure revelation on earth to know my will of Zion from heaven coming to earth; to be a pure and perfecting and, in time, lifted-up dwelling of the holy Order of Union Celestial.

2. Verily I say unto you, I called on my servant, each Priesthood Keyholder, to be as my holy will to my people who would hear my will; to teach how to become pure in all holy way and pure living; to be a people filled with my holy love in the keeping all my holy will; to love eternal, pure, holy, and exalting way of uplifting more noble laws of God that exalt unto Zion being only pure.

3. I have led my servant in each full giving of my word, even my Keyholder of full sealing key power of my Holy Priesthood; each one being of full way to seal marriage and other blessings of Celestial power sent by your God, to have the labor of sealing Celestial Marriage of holy pure abiding; unto all my people having a labor of true hope for a holy resurrection of their Lord, according to their walk in this probation of testing, to be my proving all -- who will abide Celestial Law of exalting way.

4. Thus have I sent each Prophet to lead my chosen people who would receive my holy way, by revelation and commandment from your God.

5. They are my people, sent by your Lord to build up my Church in abiding law Celestial, to earn my Zion to come forth in fulness.

6. Let all now be of my holy way, to be part of Zion soon to be on my holy way of Celestial power on earth; for I shall come in the cloud of my holy will being performed in all full power of pure eternal power.

7. Let all people learn of my holy way.

8. Let my Church be pure in all holy and inspiring, righteous, exalting, noble way of pure living.

9. Come out of Babylon to be my pure holy generation to build New City of Holiness, even Zion.

10. Let my people be free to dwell on my holy land of pure abiding, even Zion, the land of my coming, both North and South America; for I shall cleanse the land of all wicked and corrupt and impure way of their following the carnal, sensual way of evil doing.

11. All must now be of a warned and preparing way, to be surviving my cleansing power of God's own will being done in judgment of my power of pure judging; to hold every man of his own conduct unto there being no excuse for sin, when I have sent my own will to all peoples, nations, kindreds, tongues; and holy way of living have I taught all peoples.

12. Let my Spirit be your power of holy living.

13. Pray always in your minds and hearts until my appearing, to be ready; for

when I come, a setting in order shall take place, to purge all corrupt and ungodly from among them; to have full power to perfect their lives unto a Celestial way, that I may be to them a God, and they to me a pure people to be Zion, who are the pure in heart.

14. Love your God, because He is love, even with all your heart, might, mind, and strength; and love your neighbor as yourself in all holy and pure way, to be the holy people who can ask to be of a full deliverance unto my Kingdom being a preserving unto Celestial eternal powers dwelling among them for a thousand years, while I come and go as I will.

15. I have spoken it. Great are the soon coming events just when I am to cleanse the land of Zion in full measure.

16. I am now purifying the few elect who are seeking unto me through my servant on earth at this time, who is in my hands, though held by my children of governing powers in a bondage because he only seeks to do my will to establish Zion on earth by my holy will revealing who is to be of eternal power of Celestial Union in my Church.

17. Let him go to do my holy will, is the call of thy Lord and Redeemer.

18. Let his brethren be free, each one imprisoned by false way of using man's law to afflict my Church in marriage sent of God.

19. Let all now know I will be as a full Judge upon all powers of man.

20. Let all know I will preserve my Holy Priesthood, though tried in the sieve of persecution resulting from lying and deceiving witnesses who were of my Church, then left because they were of a non-compliance to my holy way themselves in their own personal living; turning as the dog to his vomit and the sow of cleansing to the mire, after being cleansed by my Gospel of pure holy way.

21. Let my people be free.

22. Return their lands and houses taken by unjust rulings inviting the open enemies of my people to dwell in my houses that were a consecration of my people unto their God, now taken and used to persecute and deprive my faithful from having all things mine in their holy, pure living of Celestial laws of my holy will revealing, to be my Zion.

23. Now awake to the day of cleansing. I am soon to sweep the wicked out of every land of every nation who continue in immoral and violent, murderous way, of sinning against life, even they who also love Sodom, as well as the murder of unborn children; which evil is corrupting the way before your Lord; having to cleanse all peoples of these evils by judgments eternal, even Celestial power of my sending the cleansing and destructive powers; for you are ripened in iniquity to be only of a condition to be removed from the land of my holy coming, who are of these evils, whether in practice, or by toleration, by assenting to such practices.

24. You then become a spiritually-dark people, seeing not your own evils of immoral way of corrupting yourselves and your habitations and families in way of ungodliness and in traditions of fighting against the way of life.

25. Cleanse yourselves and let my people live my holy pure way, by my revealing the power of my holy way of my Holy Priesthood, to administer my

Celestial Law of Plural Celestial power of Union Marriage.

26. Let my people be my preserving of pure holy way of living on earth, to become my holy, pure, and enlightened vessels, who shall be sent to surviving peoples, nations, kindreds, tongues in every land and nation, that my Gospel of salvation may be my holy will being as a saving way unto eternal life.

27. I have now called upon you, the court of oppression, to be as a delivering power for my servant Warren Jeffs and his brethren, with this, my own will, being revealed as the testimony of pure, eternal truth given to you and all people of the nation; which testimony is of your Lord of pure will manifest.

28. Let them be free.

29. Let all now know I am to soon reward all liars and hypocrites who have sought to destroy my people with a judgment of their being overthrown in every way, where they who joined with them who have sought my people's destruction, I shall turn it upon their own heads, to purge all corrupt way of following and loving a lie from the people of the land of Zion.

30. Let all nations beware.

31. I have sent my word of final warning of great judgments at hand.

32. Let no one be found against me, lest you become the unwise and be left outside my city New Jerusalem to dwell with they who have fought against Zion on earth, to no longer be a power to oppose the rise of Zion on earth.

33. Now be of a doing.

34. Let him, my servant, go, to do my will among my chosen people; and if you will be of truth, free my sons of my Holy Priesthood now unrighteously and unjustly held in bondage.

35. Let the witness of main testimony herself be examined.

36. She is a liar, a traitor to truth she once held dear, and turned from my law of Eternal Power, and is in darkness, used by prosecuting authority; willing to lie about the purity of my holy way she once said was her delight; now wallowing in sin herself of immoral way.

37. Let there be the work of witnessing of one of the law and of the profession of the police way who has had intimate way with the one who is of the chief witness against my holy law, to learn of a connection unclean pertaining to the cases of unjust imprisonment; as well as the corrupt, immoral ways of apostate witnessing.

38. Look into their lives to know they themselves are of an unclean way of immoral doing; who then accuse my pure way of unclean and evil intent; judging others according to the way of darkness within themselves.

39. Such do the wicked who once upheld my holy way as the only way to salvation in eternal life with your God, who is only holy, pure, righteous, exalting in all ways of holy power eternal; who now speaketh to present governing power to examine motive of false testifying against my pure and innocent ones, who only live my holy law of Celestial authority and pure Priesthood way by my command.

40. Now know that I shall be a deliverance unto my people.

41. I shall be as a power to reveal secret and wicked joining of the false witness and governing powers.

42. Let my people be free, lest my revealing shows you who prosecute and defame my holy way to be known in your corrupt way.

43. Let all now be pure before your God, who sees and knows all things, who shall reward all for how they receive my holy will; who are of the way of unbelief; who deny eternal truths of my revealing as they sin away the day of their final preparing, as my judgments of cleansing power are soon to be upon all peoples; to prepare for my glorious coming nigh at hand, saith your Lord, even Jesus Christ, who speaketh to all peoples through my servant in this time of final warning and preparing for the whirlwind judgments I shall soon send forth. Amen.

How to Labor Instant by Instant in the Increase of the Holy Spirit, the Gifts and Powers of Enlivening Joy, Perfecting Godliness in Your Natures Through Exalting Powers in Eternal Life, Even From That God Who Created You

Revelation of the Lord Jesus Christ Given to President Warren S. Jeffs Eldorado, Texas Thursday, May 5, 2011

1. Thus saith the Lord who reigns on high, in a manner of your understanding, laboring through my servant and with Zion's mission, my inspired love-giving to you, sustaining you day by day in life unto eternal life:

2. Thus must be your living awakening within you, wherein you possess lively hope unmeasured, filling your soul with enlightening Celestial glory; for this is the reality of the increase of my heavenly light within your nature as you abide Celestial laws in the spirit of your calling, not in an empty manner, not in an empty wondering; coming alive in the reality of my Spirit burning in you, known as a gentle peace of enlivening and enlightening joy, the joy of your Lord as your guide instant by instant.

3. Repent ye of thinking you are qualifying for my mission of Zion wherein you continue in a manner having times of darkness and then light, then the darkness.

4. Thus saith the Lord: It is not so. Overcoming must take place. Thereby do you learn to dwell in the increase of my light in the joy of your Lord, Him visiting you with continual flow of exalted thoughts and desires, willing to give all in a manner only to please your God, though it take your life; knowing you have a greater hope beyond this life unto eternal life with your eternal and loving Father who dwells in eternal burnings of everlasting glory, an earth like unto that orb shining upon thee giving thee daylight, Celestial planet of governing power, for thus it is.

5. And this I reveal to your sacred keeping, you on the mission of Zion's redemption where my Land of Holiness has upon it all things being prepared for the elect to be gathered.

6. Thus, faith is known by the continual increase of my Spirit; for this is faith, this power of the Spirit of God in action, my righteousness revealed, exercised through my giving power -- not of thy choice alone, but of the increase of thy Lord to thee, which always brings an acknowledgment of rejoicing in Him as you feel the thrill of joy, the witness of gentle peace and enlivening truth that exalts, as a witness that I am hearing and answering prayers.

7. Prayers will be answered in my time,

according to my will and thy continued faithful walk before me.

8. Thus, you are my Zion as you live in the spirit of your callings, thus described in this, my revealing, some needing more explanation, and not assuming righteousness or faith or hope.

9. And my holy love extant is not an empty doing that comes and goes, as it were, in some people's lives, where they feel a darkness at times because they choose to hearken to the whisperings of a dark power, and set upon by the memory of the past, in particular, as a great weakness in Zion's mission.

10. Look not back to a dark power when I remind thee of that which was in the past. There is a lifting-up power, enlivens your soul to remember the good.

11. And when evil is remembered, particularly personal sins or weaknesses that have been repented of, I lead thee to repent further, wherein you may be continuing in pleasure in unrighteousness in looking back, or being reminded how blessed you are at this time to continue in Zion's mission and among my Priesthood.

12. Thus I give you this detailed training of righteous living, all you on my Land of Holiness.

13. Have faith, the witness of gentle peace of enlivening and enlightening joy.

14. Be ye one on Zion's cause, is my love-giving message to you, my Zion's mission this day, called to the most holy work, sent from above from the God of Creation who reigns over thee.

15. And as the enlivening joy and enlightenment of mind of exalted and noble thoughts and feelings awakens your soul to a lifting-up above that which has troubled thee in the past, walk forward with that power, a confidence that as you thus receive, that power can continue with thee through thy continued rejoicing gratitude, never looking back in a downcast or worried or fearful way, walking hand in hand with thy Lord through the Spirit of peace of gentle nature, that enlivening enlightening to the soul.

16. When you still hear the whisperings of darkness when my light whispers to you there is further repenting; yea, and even times required atoning, whether it be a power I send, intervening for thee, upon one of atoning authority; whether it be humbling, justice satisfied -- the loss of my Spirit, feeling a darkness, a spiritual groping, waiting for deliverance and salvation until my Spirit returns to awaken you that you cannot choose darkness -- any degree of excuse, whether it be pleasure in evil, or fearsome worry you hang on to, to no effect, troubling thy soul, receiving, in return, emptiness; thus awakening thee to further repenting needed, turning to thy God in joyous lays, lifting-up happiness when He restores His Spirit, uplifting nature into your soul.

17. Let these details of laboring in the spirit with thy Lord, Him being your very real Heavenly Father, dwelling in eternal burnings on a Celestial orb of governing power, who sees and knows all things and can read and understand your minds, thoughts, and desires of your hearts and souls, an immediate return of the result of your choice; even whispering where to repent and improve instant by instant, not having to go a long time without that light burning in you -- instant return to Him when a dark power attempts to deride and disturb your soul --

18. Take these truths into thy exertion of your mind in faith, using the gifts and powers of my Spirit, which is always

a feeling of holy love extant, perfect kindness, undisturbed in nature, lowliness of heart, rejoicing in thy Lord, the Author of all good and righteous doing, all creation, and in thy individual thinking and feelings, which needs of an exalting nature increased more fully, all on Zion's mission.

19. This is my revealing: All must improve and not continue in a manner of dwelling on that which does not exalt, in a bothered or continued feeling downcast and disturbed way in your life, saith the Lord Jesus Christ, who sees and knows all things and has all power to lift thee up above the whisperings of darkness in a moment of need; yea, instant by instant, until your character is perfected in every form of godliness, revealed from my heavenly habitation, from the Father, to be called in Priesthood covenants to abide the Order of Eternal Union inspired love-giving. And I am with thee.

20. My presence comes among thee, even making known to thee heavenly powers are around thee, angels from Celestial and eternal glory whispering to your minds: "Pray now. Do this." Heed my warning of improvement, deliverance from that which can harm, perfection needed further -- always a greater humbling to depend completely on the whispering power of salvation of my Holy Spirit, which lifts you up in the real and holy way of life that can be discerned, delicious to the soul.

21. Thus it is a gift of my giving, causing you to acknowledge thy God in all things with rejoicing gratitude, the necessary element of the prayer of faith always abiding in thee as a witness of my Spirit, that power of faith by which you labor instant by instant unto the perfecting of Zion within you.

22. And I am with you who stay constant unto me in that joyous-gratitude prayer of faith, visited at times with a testing, a lessening of that heavenly light, witnessing to you a greater need to be more fervent and diligent in my cause of Zion, and in thy further preparing in this manner I am now revealing through my servant of a needed gift of enlightenment, truth from above your understanding -- the immediate applying, adding to your immediate prayer of faith at this time, that your worrisome fears may be obliterated out of your nature concerning past sins or present weaknesses or feelings downcast, saith your Lord.

23. Be of an enlivening power among your fellows, both men and women, even children, to be of the prayer of faith extant, not abiding in a lonesome, wearied, or withdrawn manner.

24. None of you need abide a lesser light on Zion's mission, for my house of holiness dwells ready for a people to receive the ordinances of mine house, yet empty at this time, waiting the final preparing of mine elect, soon to be gathered.

25. Faith is a certainty of soul, not the wandering of the mind in wonderment, leading to doubts and fears that cause that darkening for an instant.

26. Turn unto me. The whispering is real, gentle and peaceful, enlivening with an enlightenment joy where you know I am a God at hand to whisper to the purer mind the full flow of exalted thoughts and feelings.

27. This is the Holy Spirit in your life, preparing you to be my Zion, perfecting your lives unto godliness, Godhood and Goddesshood, those who are well prepared.

28. Heed my word and holy sacred

revealing, giving you the details of how to be perfected in the gifts of my Holy Spirit instant by instant.

29. You need not spend moments searching for your Lord, wondering if He is near.

30. My Spirit is extant, filling all in all through all creation, giving all creation its form, appearance, and nature.

31. Thine own creation is an organized spirit and body together, a son and daughter, each one as the offspring of God.

32. This is my revealing to you.

Declaration of My Revealed Will of Warning to the President of the United States, Along with the Proclamation to All Government Officials

Revelation of the Lord Jesus Christ Given to President Warren S. Jeffs Eldorado, Texas Thursday, July 21, 2011

Jesus Christ, Your Lord and King Sendeth His Own Will to You of the Governing Power on the Land of America, and to all People of the Earth; and to Know My Holy Pure Way Is on Earth to Be a Way of Zion Soon Coming Forth -- and a Call to Let My People Go Free as My Work of Cleansing Shall Be in Full Measure Soon. Hear Ye My Will and Soon Promises to Be Fulfilled.

1. Thus saith the Lord to the people of this present and most unworthy of all people who have ever inhabited my chosen land of Zion where New Jerusalem shall be in full as the Celestial authority, to be as the governing power over all nations; who are of the power to be of pure way; who shall learn eternal way and living in Zion; unto my Church and Kingdom, even Jesus Christ, who giveth my own will to you now dwelling on my land; to yet be of a full purity and cleansing by judgments of my sending, to cleanse all wickedness from off the whole land; to prepare for New Era of holy, pure way of eternal power to govern the whole earth as a Celestial power of my giving; is as a fire of all purity and holy enlivening: I am soon to be of a pure and full labor of my full power of judgment on all people in every land.

2. Let all now hear my will: I am Son Ahman, who is Jesus Christ, the God over all the world; who shall be as a full power Celestial; to govern all nations who remain from Jerusalem of my New Order of Eternal Power, as New Era of my holy power comes to my earth, to be the holy power of my right to be your Ruler and King; to dwell among all of Zion in full power of my new way of pure giving life and holy work of Celestial Eternal Union.

3. I reveal my Celestial Law of Marriage is a most holy way, and can only be lived by my pure people of my holy and pure Priesthood who are of obeying all my holy will; not for the wicked nor unbelieving who are not receiving of my Church and will.

4. Let all now be of the witness of my law being holy, pure, sacred, righteous; and of my giving and revealing through my Keyholder of Priesthood authority, who is my servant Warren Jeffs, being of the way of captivity for doing my way and holy will.

5. Thus is he being of a power to give my will, to make known that I am soon to purge my land of my New City of Holy Celestial Power to be the governing power over all peoples, nations, tongues, and kindreds on all lands; to have my

holy will known that my love is to be of a power of eternal, holy governing; to be my full way of pure governing of you, my sons of Israel, and all peoples.

6. For I am the Holy One of the Order of Endless Power, who was God from before the earth was made; who was born on earth among men, rejected by my own, sacrificing all for my Father's will to be fulfilled, even for full salvation to be given to all who are of obeying eternal law of my revealing, unto pure dominions of eternal power in never-ending increase. I am He who was of your needed delivering from death, all to be raised unto life in the power of the Redemption; to be as a full Order of Eternal Power. I am He who sendeth these words of warning --

7. Let my people go! to be of my holy Order of Eternal Power in living Celestial law of pure holy way, of pure religious love-giving unto God, to do His revealed way.

8. I have decreed a famine to soon come on the land where my New City of holy and pure power shall soon rise.

9. Many shall perish in the dearth that cometh.

10. Repent ye, repent ye, all of my believing and receiving people, who can be of my Church on earth, unto the purifying their lives unto becoming mine holy nation of Kings and Priests unto God, Queens and Priestesses of pure way; in living my Celestial Law of holy eternal power of Priesthood; who are to be as pure holy Saviors on Mount Zion; to be as holy pure vessels of my saving unto eternal life.

11. I shall soon send an overflowing scourge, a full cleansing of my land of new holy and pure dwelling; when only mine holy pure Israel who gather to Zion shall remain on the land.

12. I shall be your holy and pure power of redeeming power, to be of the way of the holy pure law of Union Eternal, to be my Church of Celestial Power, to be a full order of my new era of holy love, bringing peace to all nations; to be the pure holy vessels of holy way in eternal power; of my power unto my holy pure way being thy way, to be the people of Zion who are in the way of life in a full way of my power Celestial.

13. Such shall be my holy power on an enlightened people who obey my will, to learn ways Celestial in every way of pure holy power, the holy power of eternal full and noble way of my pure giving; to receive the full way of my holy new era of Zion to dwell on earth.

14. Let all now be of a final way of pure holy way of living, saith your Lord and Holy Savior, even Jesus Christ, who is of the full power of pure and holy way; to be the Life of all, the Light of all; the Judge of all people unto eternal life for the more faithful of all people; and a judgment of eternal decrease and sorrow, of weeping unto everlasting regret upon those who seek the way of the fallen and unclean who seek evil; who will only be of a way of a lower gift in the eternal realm of Jehovah.

15. I am He. Come unto me. Obey my voice, saith your God to this people on earth who will not abide my law of salvation; who is now of the way of unbelief and derision against my Celestial Law, who have no desire for my holy way; who persecute my people.

16. Let my people be as a free and pure holy way, to bless all other of my Israel, and of all nations of surviving on earth; for I come and bring with me my holy way; to recompense to every man that which he has measured to his fellow

man unto eternity and full measure of reward what thou hast done in the flesh, according to the light given while in the way of this earth, to have all things of a full giving as thou hast performed unto your fellow sojourners on earth.

17. With my holy way now being on earth, you know I am soon to come to mine holy pure vessels of pure way.

18. Be ye pure to be of a surviving unto Zion, the pure way to redeem all peoples, nations, tongues; and faithful obedient people who will be my holy Order of Celestial Power in my New Jerusalem.

19. Let my holy order be one in pure, holy law of my revealing.

20. Let my will be read to all people in every land on earth, to know what is soon to take place on earth, even judgments of full power to cleanse all nations of the ungodly. Amen.

Revelation of the Lord Jesus Christ Given to President Warren S. Jeffs Huntsville, Texas Saturday, August 20, 2011

4. One Dan Fischer was giving bribe money to legislators in states prosecuting my servant.

5. Now trace this money, to know moneys of bribes being paid to prosecute my servant.

6. Let this now become a public outcry.

7. Let money be shown as political pressure to attack my Church.

8. Let judge of unjust way also be known as not being of honor, who would not defend religious freedoms guaranteed by Constitution of nation.

9. Let it be shown she hath commanded this full attack from the beginning; should recuse herself, and cease such evil.

Your Lord Jesus Christ Declareth Unjust Ruling of Prison Sentencing

Revelation of the Lord Jesus Christ Given to President Warren S. Jeffs Huntsville, Texas Saturday, August 20, 2011

1. Thus saith the Lord to the governing power that performed work of no justice; but did a labor of destroying freedom of religion and worship, by allowing an open and notorious presenting of all lying and use of that which is preserved for religious governing, to be of a presenting before all peoples; as though my holy pure way is not holy, pure, noble, righteous, exalting, inspiring.

2. I heed you not.

3. You have only destroyed religious protection.

4. You are a fallacy of justice.

5. You shall be overruled.

6. Your determined, open, and full attack against pure holy way of my revealed religion shall soon be heralded to all as false and base.

7. All who joined with government shall be of a foundering, to know their foundation is on conspiracy of falsehood told over years of apostate lies being enhanced; until my Priesthood answers them nothing.

8. They are from the lying spirit of the devil. Money is their god. They shall fall.

Revelation of the Lord Jesus Christ Given to President Warren S. Jeffs
Palestine, Texas
Tuesday, October 11, 2011

1. I who is over all speaketh to the whole world, your Lord who is of the Power of Eternity, now of a full labor to now be the holy order of Celestial authority governing all people:

2. Let all now be preparing for my holy power over all lands, to be of the full power of my Celestial holy eternal governing authority; to be your holy and Eternal Lord, King, and Redeemer; even my holy power now being revealed.

3. Let kings, rulers of nations, government over nations, be of a cleansing of all their ways of power; to be of the just way of righteous and peaceful way.

4. Let all people of the calling of my holy way be of a full purity; to dwell in my Zion. Let this be as a full holy, and authorizing call, to be ready. Amen.

We, the members of the Church called Fundamentalist Church of Jesus Christ of Latter-day Saints, give our names as witness, that all this publishing of the word of God through His servants, His chosen Prophets and Priesthood leaders of Keyholder position; also the histories herein told by they called to thus keep or have history recorded, in their day of being of knowing history, are all of truth; even the writings of Priesthood of pure witnessing; and that there is shown in this publishing many illegal, even violent actions of evil powers, and that the government of the land, even the national power, has for over one hundred years persecuted the saints of the true Church of God.

Thus, this publishing is a testimony against this nation; and also tells of our Lord's intervening to preserve His Church; His eternal authority of Priesthood on earth through Keyholders of pure holy authority; an authority placing them in position before God as judges over all peoples in their time; the very God of heaven guiding, authorizing; empowering them to be His representative, witness, and legal administrator, each in their time of Keyholder position. Amen.

_____

31 October 2011

Vaughan E. Taylor

Patriarch in the Fundamentalist
Church of Jesus Christ of Latter-day Saints

_____

10-31-2011

John M. Barlow

Counselor in the Bishopric of the Fundamentalist
Church of Jesus Christ of Latter-day Saints

Appendix A

Warnings of Previous Sending To Leaders of the Nation

A Warning to the Nation

A Petition to the President of the United States of America

Revelation of the Lord Jesus Christ to the Peoples of the Nation of the United States of America and to the Peoples of the Earth Through My Servant Warren Jeffs

A Petition to the President of the United States of America

Revelation of the Lord Given to
President Warren S. Jeffs
Draper, Utah
Thursday, October 7, 2010

1. To the honorable President of the United States of America now as standing at the head of this nation:

2. I who dwells on high, even your Lord and Savior, who redeemed all mankind by the shedding of His own blood, and who is over all and has all power, send to you my word.

3. Cause that my servant who presides over my Church now be delivered by thy hand.

4. Let my servant go, that he may perform his mission to prepare my people for My Coming.

5. Cause that the prosecutors, now cease their attack upon my servant Warren Jeffs.

6. Cause that this nation now restore to my people the consecrated land taken from them.

7. Cause that there be remuneration given them for the loss of the homes that are occupied illegally by the enemies of my people who are in the Colorado City, Arizona and Hildale, Utah area.

8. Cause that the attack against my people in Texas be stopped.

9. I, the Lord, shall cause my judgments to be withheld as you thus perform this work.

10. Otherwise, let this nation know I am with my people, and shall sweep the wicked from off the face of the Land of America.

11. Thus shall I perform my work by my Almighty power.

12. This from your Lord, even Jesus Christ, who shall subdue all His enemies under His feet.

13. Even as I have spoken, so shall I fulfill. Even so. Amen.

Revelation of the Lord Jesus Christ to the Peoples of the Nation of the United States of America and to the Peoples of the Earth Through My Servant Warren Jeffs

Reagan County, Big Lake, Texas
Saturday, February 5, 2011

1. Thus saith the Lord unto the nation of the United States of America: I, the Lord, am soon to send the shaking of the earth in a place in thy land not known as a usual place of violent shaking, unto the loss of many lives.

2. Let it be known, I, the Lord, have sent my message to government officials to free my servant Warren Jeffs, to cause my people to receive back their lands and houses, and you heed me not.

3. Thus I shall cause a great destruction in the land of Illinois, to the loss of life and to your awakening, that when I, the Lord, speak, let my word be fulfilled, lest you become as a people only worthy to be swept off my land of Zion;

4. For verily I say unto you, this earth is mine, and I have caused my people to receive a preparation work for my glorious coming on earth to establish my Zion, and they are my people. Let them go! For you shall now feel the wrath of an Almighty God in the place of my naming in a soon to happen event.

5. Though you deny me, know that I, the Lord, have spoken, and I send to you my word at this time, to receive my word that I

shall cause my servant on earth to deliver to thee a message of warning, that I, the Lord, will no longer uphold thee as a nation, corrupting your way before me, having in your midst legalized murder of unborn children, thus shedding innocent blood before the heavens, and allowing the sins of Sodom and immoral practices among you by legal consent; yet you persecute my people who abide by my will and my governing principles of purity, required of them by me.

6. No longer consider I shall preserve thy land as you continue to allow him, whom I have chosen to receive and give my word to the peoples of the earth, to remain in bondage; when he only is seeking to fulfill my will, saith the Lord, in preparing my people to establish on my holy land my Zion, a place of peace; which you know is among them, having illegally carried away innocent children, examining my people, knowing they are free from the corrupting influences of this wicked generation by your own examining.

7. Though you accuse them of corrupt practices and evil motives, they are my people, saith the Lord Jesus Christ, who sendeth this message to you: Let my people go! or you shall reap a whirlwind of judgments in near future sending, such as you have not seen; for I am God, and I speak from the heavens through him whom I have anointed.

8. Though he received testing, fearing for a time, yet I, the Lord, have raised him up and delivered him and am guiding him -- Now step forth and deliver my word to all peoples:

9. Repent ye! Repent ye! My day of judgments upon all the earth is at hand.

10. Send forth my word of warning to all peoples, beginning with this nation, and hereafter shall I cause a greater sounding of my warning voice, which, if you heed me not, shall be fulfilled in fulness; for I shall appear in the power of my might in the clouds of heaven, to make myself known to all peoples my right to rule; and nothing can hinder the progress of my Zion rising in fulness;

11. For though you stretch forth your hands to persecute mine elect on the earth, who have received exalted ways in pure, religious motive and practice; yet you believe traitors who are themselves corrupt, partaking of a spirit of outward prosecution, condemning that which is holy because thine own hearts are corrupt before me; accusing mine elect of wicked motives who only receive my laws of Celestial Plural Marriage, and my Economic Order of Heaven, a United Order of religious practice by my word, by the revelations of my will.

12. And this is my Church upon the earth, living laws that you know are of scriptural record among you; yet you condemn that which I, the Lord, have established for the salvation of the earth.

13. Verily I say unto you, let there be an immediate stop to the prosecution and governmental interference against my servant and against my people, lest you incur mine anger unto the fulfilling of what I have named, that I now send to you in a writing of your understanding.

14. And though false witnesses stand forth seeking to brand guilt upon innocence, I, the Lord, shall defend my people in a manner of deliverance to thine eternal regret and condemnation, as you stand before me in the day of judging, having lifted your hand against your God who created you.

15. Receive my word of warning, and know that I, the Lord, have spoken from the heavens at a needed time when you can respond to my word.

16. And as a testimony this is my word, I shall send forth a great storm in the land, crippling thy nation again, which I have been sending in increasing power since you allowed an unjust judge to confine my servant still, and other court actions in thy land against the holding of property where my people dwell; in that place in the Hildale, Utah and Colorado City, Arizona area,

illegally, by your own laws, interfering with a religious trust by governmental intervention.

17. Now this country of the United States of America shall go down, as she does not defend innocence, religious organization of pure religious intent.

18. I, the Lord, have spoken it. Hasten to respond to my word, as I send my word again to you, lest mine anger be kindled unto the fulfilling of all my promises against a wicked generation in a manner you have not seen before.

19. This from your Lord and Savior Jesus Christ, who hath redeemed all mankind, who will respond to my message of salvation; which shall go forth again to all surviving nations, they who will respond to my word and preserve my people who shall go among them to deliver my message of salvation in a day soon at hand.

20. And nothing can stay mine hand, saith the Lord, for all nations shall know I have spoken it.

21. And as my word is fulfilled, though the wicked among you deny me still, I shall preserve mine elect and establish my Zion until all nations shall know I am doing my work on the earth as I have promised.

22. Receive ye my word to thy understanding, and I shall preserve thy land as you execute equity and justice, not allowing the persecution of an innocent people who are only seeking to do the will of their God -- a revelation of my giving in the law of Celestial Plural Marriage, and revelations of my giving in the Law of Consecration of Stewardships, called the Holy United Order among my people.

23. These laws are of me, saith the Lord, and are of ancient record, that record being in your hands, by my faithful Apostles and Patriarchs of old, by prophets and kings and rulers who lived laws of my revealing in their time, which must be lived in purity, with no corruption among them, or they cannot be my people, saith the Lord.

24. And though you condemn my law, my law shall triumph over all opposition, all opposing powers, though all the world combine; for these laws are of me.

25. My people know that they must needs abide these laws to be my people; thus, they have suffered persecution, lo, these many years, rather than surrender eternal, exalting laws from their God.

26. And this is why they continue the living of my revealed, eternal laws, seeking salvation of souls for themselves and all others who would come unto me through my authorized representative on earth, each in their time; yea verily, my Prophets, upholding my law as revealed through my servant Joseph Smith, Jun.; as he was instrument in mine hands to restore my Gospel of salvation and mine authority to administer my laws upon the earth; which authority continues in the person of my servant Warren Jeffs, whom I have preserved, though tried, and he continues to receive my word.

27. And verily I say unto you, my judgments are soon to be poured forth upon all nations that forget their God, who will not heed my word and purify their lives before me, in righteous principles known to all peoples, if you corrupt your ways before me, in licentious and immoral practices that lead to the shedding of innocent blood, in most nations where murder of unborn children is allowed by legal consent; and this stench can no longer continue, for I shall stretch forth mine hand and all peoples shall know I have spoken.

28. Repent ye! Cease these evil practices immediately!

29. Change your laws that allow this evil practice, and other evil immoral practices that lead to the murder of the unborn; or you shall rise in the resurrection unto a buffeting worthy only for murderers who consent to this practice, even a whole generation upon the earth led astray by wicked men of evil practice themselves among you.

30. Thus is my word boldly given to you and sent to you in a manner of thy receiving, with no confusion involved, for this is a pure giving from the heavens unto you through my Church of Jesus Christ of Latter-day Saints upon the earth, known among you -- separating themselves from that branch that broke away from my Priesthood on the earth, to be known as upholding the original revelations and principles I revealed to my servant Joseph Smith, known as the Fundamentalist Church of Jesus Christ of Latter-day Saints, of a legal Corporation Sole among you, which I, the Lord, have now set in order, revealing the name of my servant as President of this Corporation Sole; which legal entity should be allowed by the courts to receive my consecrated lands;

31. But an unjust court illegally resolved to change the articles thereof to allow the taking away of my lands and houses belonging to me, saith the Lord, out of the hands of those appointed officers who answered you nothing because they only answer to the Lord their God for their religious responsibility before me; and you knowing the government, court, or authority in your land has no right to interfere with a religious trust of full religious intent, which I, the Lord, caused to be established to preserve my people in an organized labor, to live a law of eternal nature earning them a salvation in the Kingdom of heaven.

32. And they abide my law in a pure walk before me, which can only be administered by inspired religious leadership, not of governmental appointing.

33. And thus you have interfered in my Church, and I name this to you, O ye governmental officials of this nation -- Repair this, for you have sinned a sin against the God of creation who made you, in interfering with my Church, taking away my lands and houses, consecrated by religious giving by a people baptized and confirmed as members of my Church upon the earth,

and though knowest it; and you have been convinced by apostate and wicked people who thus persecute my people, though it be by outward show of legal authority.

34. And through your own corruptions among you, then you accuse my people of wicked intent -- and how can it be, when they give their all and are willing to suffer at thine hands, even imprisonment, rather than give up in their lives their religion, which I, the Lord, have commanded them that they must live to earn a place with me in the heavens?

35. I, the Lord, reveal this much to you -- that you have interfered, through your legal procedures, with the Lord your God and His work of bringing forth a righteous people who receive Him in His glory, whose only purpose in living these exalted laws is to glorify their God and bring salvation to a corrupt world; that I shall cleanse by my power as I descend in the clouds of heaven to my land of Zion; and also to my old Jerusalem, to gather mine Israel, which promises are in sacred writings among you.

36. I now step forth and cause my servant on earth to declare my word to you:

37. Let my people go! or suffer the judgments of a just God, and in eternity, the damnation of your souls, knowing that religious freedom should be guaranteed in every nation -- which you labored for; yea, for many, save for my people; having prejudiced your minds against them as though I, the Lord your God, was not guiding my Church.

38. Now receive my word and my promise of a judgment soon to come of thy knowing, and respond; for my almighty power shall be shown as a beginning of the cleansing of my land of Zion, known to you as North America, where my New Jerusalem shall be built, and extending to South America, saith the Lord God of heaven;

39. My land of Zion, appointed by me, before thy nation ever inhabited my land, to

be the place of a glorious kingdom, revealed from heaven unto an obedient and pure people on earth, which revelations have been among you since I restored my Priesthood and my revealed word through the Prophet Joseph Smith; and this generation has rejected my word.

40. And I am a God of truth and shall fulfill my word, saith the Lord God of heaven, Jehovah Christ, the God of Abraham, and of Isaac, and of Jacob, and of mine Apostles, who came to earth and suffered on the cross, that all men may be raised unto life and receive an eternal reward for their deeds and desires in the flesh.

41. And all things are known unto me, as I reveal your hearts, even this wicked generation upon my land of Zion, for you are a murderous and adulterous generation, legalizing a slaughter of innocence among you.

42. For verily I say unto you, you are like unto Herod of old, who sought to destroy my life when but a youth, in the slaughter of children, in the city of my begetting through a pure virgin.

43. Thus you slaughter innocence like unto him, by legal consent, which must now be cleansed off the earth before my glorious appearing, saith the Lord God of heaven.

44. And this I reveal to you through him whom I have appointed to send my message unto all peoples.

45. Though you listen not, in the trembling of the earth, some shall begin to awake.

46. And as the storms roll forth of more violent nature in thy land, some shall begin to awaken and wonder what is taking place;

47. And now you know I have spoken it.

48. Receive ye my word; and if you heed me not, prepare for my word to be fulfilled, warning you through him whom I have appointed.

49. This is the word of the Lord thy God, who created all things, who preserves all nations in their place, until they prove themselves so corrupt before me, I cause the dissolution of the wicked; yea, they who are ripened in iniquity, as you, the people on my land of Zion, who persecute my Church upon the earth, have now become.

50. And though you deny my record, revealed through the Prophet Joseph Smith -- my holy record named as the Book of Mormon -- like the Jaredites and Nephites of old, ye shall be swept off my land, saith the Lord, as you continue in your corrupt ways as did they of old; who followed these same practices in their lives, until I, the Lord, did not allow it any longer.

51. This from Him who reigns on high and who shall render eternal justice upon all -- a reward of eternal life for the pure and the righteous among you, and the reward of a damnation unto suffering for the wicked; who knowingly sin away the day of grace, knowing mine own word hath been sent to all peoples as delivered by mine ancient Apostles, my Gospel spreading over the earth and being restored anew through the instrumentality of Joseph Smith, my servant; who was martyred among you; whose murder is yet an event to be avenged by me, saith the Lord, upon this wicked nation; and the driving of my people and murdering of my people since the days of the establishment of my Church upon the earth in thy land; whose innocent blood was shed, still cries from the ground for vengeance against this nation.

52. Thus shall I be justified, at thy receiving my warning, to send forth greater judgments, until justice is satisfied; for you reek in the shedding of innocent blood as a nation, allowing this great evil among you, destroying life of my sending, of perfect innocence, unable to defend themselves; for your immoral practices have led you to this murderous work which I have named before you, as worthy only to be swept off my land of Zion.

53. This is the word of the Lord. Heed

my word, lest I send my judgment upon you.

54. And in a time the more wicked step forth to further hinder my work, my judgments shall be poured forth without let or hindrance, to leave the wicked neither root nor branch of an inheritance upon my land of Zion, as I, the Lord, have foretold, my word being revealed through my servants, the Prophets.

55. And like the days of Noah, only those I preserve shall remain upon my land of Zion.

56. Thus you shall know thy God hath spoken, both on earth, and as you plead for deliverance in the day you dwell in the world of departed spirits, suffering justice until you have paid the debt for your evil ways upon her, before I can raise you up to a degree of glory, according to the law you lived on earth.

57. And those who shed innocent blood commit an unpardonable sin.

58. Though they shall be raised from the dead, they shall yet suffer for their evils, resulting from immoral practices among you.

59. How can you continue this corruption, O ye people of the earth, fighting against the laws of life, your own life preserved only by my grace and power, saith the Lord your God who created you; though you deny that gift for others through interfering with the gift of life in their coming forth?

60. Such legalized murder corrupts all peoples in your land, consenting thereto by allowing it to continue among you.

61. Yet you persecute my people, who have none of these evils among them, but are careful to preserve life that I send forth, and raise up children in principles of an exalting nature; which is known among you now as you carried away my innocent children from among my people in a raid that was unjust, having broken none of your laws that are just, accusing them of being abusive to children simply because they seek to live my

high and holy and pure law, required by me, the Lord your God, for eternal exaltation to be earned; which my people know as the pure religious motive in their lives, willing to suffer at the hands of injustice to abide an eternal law and earn salvation in the Kingdom of heaven.

62. Let my people go! for my Zion shall rise from among them, notwithstanding all the opposition against my Church upon the earth.

63. I, the Lord, have caused this understanding now to be given in plain language.

64. I, the Lord, have spoken it; thus shall I fulfill to the sorrow of the wicked, to the rejoicing of mine elect.

65. Though they suffer at the hands of the wicked, they shall be delivered unto eternal salvation who stay faithful to my cause of Zion.

66. Thus, I record this on this day of giving mine own word from the heavens unto this wicked nation, which shall be known yet as I send forth more of my word, until all peoples know that I am a God of power and know all things.

67. I am a just God and a merciful God also, to those who repent and remove these evils from among them.

68. Now put it on record, saith the Lord, there shall now be a shaking in the place I have named, in a manner that government officials shall know beforehand that it would be so, which shall awake a few, denied by most unto their eternal condemnation, knowing my word, and would not heed my word.

69. And when they find more of my word has been given, they shall be among those that curse God and die, not caring for their own lives, let alone the lives of others.

70. Thus are they a murderous and a wicked and immoral generation, adulterous in nature, having pleasure in unrighteousness unto the murder of innocence.

71. And though I cause this to be on

record, they heed me not until the sign of judgments, of removing the wicked from my land of Zion, takes place.

72. Then they shall know, in the world of spirits, to a degree, some of their sin; for the evil powers there will promote lies, deceiving many, until they sin away every day of grace I have granted them.

73. And thus this record on earth is being made in a time I, the Lord, have reached for this generation to repent and earn a salvation, yet they would not; which causeth the heavens to mourn; yet they shall not mourn longer; for soon my justice shall be satisfied, and there shall be a cleansing; then mercy shall reach for those who repent and come unto me for salvation, saith the Lord Jesus Christ.

74. I shall cause a soon happening that shall humble many people to their awakening, that my word is coming forth with exactness, and I fulfill my word, to humble my Priesthood people; many of whom shall hasten to prepare, knowing I have spoken unto public knowing among this nation; for thus it shall be advertised and mocked and scorned until the time of fulfilling.

75. Then some few shall heed, while others shall mock more: "What else hath he said?" they will declare.

76. And when he steps forth to deliver more, and I thus fulfill, the mocker shall mourn, many taken in the holocaust of the several judgments I shall send; yet still in the spirit world, in their choosing darkness when my light was offered them, many will continue to deny me until every opportunity of salvation is rejected.

77. And when their memory is restored of once dwelling in a Celestial world, with their eternal God, who is their Father, that is the day of weeping and wailing and gnashing of teeth of eternal disappointment, that they turned against their Father who only loveth them; yet they would not heed every warning given.

78. Thus is the fate of the wicked who deny me, saith the Lord, put on record on earth at a time my Gospel of salvation is among them; yet they persecute my servant and my people, and decry against them falsely; though all they desire is the salvation of souls through abiding eternal laws that exalt, even those who abide these laws in a pure way before me.

79. Let go of this wicked generation, saith the Lord.

80. Seek not after it, or you will partake of this sin of consenting to murder and adultery, to Sodom and other licentious practices.

81. Such are the people raised up in honor among the wicked, even many rulers partaking of these licentious and corrupt practices, some even of murder of the unborn, which lawmakers uphold the laws.

82. Though some publicly oppose, this wicked generation allows it, and all are tainted thereby who do not actively do battle against these unjust laws.

83. Thus I, the Lord, shall reward all according to their deeds and the desires of their heart.

84. Justice shall be satisfied, my work shall triumph, my Zion is rising as I cleanse my people, and deliver this my word to you.

85. Let there also be this sent to those government officials in the Canadian state, a nation also corrupted before me by their own choice of murderous and adulterous and immoral practices.

86. I shall cleanse my land Zion, and nothing can stay my hand.

87. Oh, this wicked generation and unbelieving and corrupt people who will not heed even common sense of truth, for how can you murder an unborn child and think you do right? Thus shows the corruption of their nature.

88. Thus saith the Lord Jesus Christ to this most wicked generation, guilty of child-murder in the destruction of the unborn, an immoral and corrupt and

adulterous generation, like unto previous generations that have inhabited my land of Zion, who were swept off the land when fully ripe in iniquity -- I, the Lord, have spoken.

89. Therefore, LET MY PEOPLE GO! And no longer allow these evil practices destroy your souls; for I am a just God and shall reward every man and woman, and children of age, according to their deeds done in the flesh.

90. Thus, I give my word to this nation as a final warning; and if you do not respond to my word, saith the Lord, I shall send the judgment named to awaken you, that when I, the Lord, speak, so do I fulfill.

91. This from your Lord and Savior, the God over all the earth, even Jesus Christ, who hath all power to discern the mind and heart of each and every son and daughter sent to mine earth, for nothing is hidden from me.

92. Let there be an awakening of this wicked generation against the day that my whirlwind judgments shall be poured forth.

93. Let there be an acknowledgment of my word sent by those of governing powers of this nation, that you will thus respond to my word -- to him whom I have revealed to thee is my Mouthpiece, even your Lord Jesus Christ, calling my servant Warren Jeffs to that work upon the earth, that I may know you will now fulfill my word, lest this judgment come upon you, and mine other judgments, as I have promised through the mouths of all my holy Prophets, known to thee in sacred writ.

94. This is my word to this generation: Repent ye. I, the Lord, have spoken it, and so shall I fulfill.

95. I, the Lord God, am eternal and my judgments are just. I see and know all things.

96. Let this generation be warned, by this my message sent, that my day is at hand when wickedness must be swept off my land of Zion, and my New Jerusalem shall be

built, and I shall come in my glory as I have promised, and none shall remain who are unclean before me.

97. Let there be an awakening in government officials of an eternal judgment that shall come upon them from the God who made them, if they allow the continuation of these wicked practices of the destruction of innocence; of which I shall hold you eternally accountable, desiring life thyself, yet denying it, through legal consent, to unborn children, as though thou art God.

98. Let there now be an instant repeal of those laws that allow this wickedness among you, lest my judgments be hastened, having innocent blood upon your skirts, as it were; now having come up before your God, notwithstanding your professions of justifying nature.

99. I, the Lord, shall reveal more to this generation through my servant Warren Jeffs.

100. Hearken to my word, ye rulers of nations, lest your lands be left desolate in my day of greater judgments upon the earth; for I shall be known among all nations, and my power and righteous government shall be known, for I shall reveal to all peoples my message of salvation on earth, who remain.

101. And all shall hear me; for I am God, thy Redeemer, doing the will of my Father, unto the salvation of souls of those who will receive me through my Priesthood authority upon the earth; which I have restored and preserved, which Gospel of salvation has been among you, O ye people of the earth.

102. Seek unto Him who created you, and receive His message of salvation that I may own and bless you, yea, with an eternal salvation unto those who receive my Gospel through my authorized Priesthood authority among you.

103. And those who receive my Gospel of salvation on earth shall earn an eternal reward with me and with my Father; for mine atoning blood shall reach those who

purify their lives in abiding the laws of my Church and Kingdom revealed among man on earth.

104. O ye people of the earth, repent ye, repent ye! My day of judgment is at hand and my word shall be fulfilled that I have spoken through the mouths of all my holy Prophets.

105. Attaint your wicked and corrupt ways. Come unto me, thy Lord and Savior. I, the Lord, have spoken it. Amen.

We, the undersigned, Lyle S. Jeffs and Vaughan Taylor, Officers in the Fundamentalist Church of Jesus Christ of Latter-day Saints, do witness before all peoples that this is the word of the Lord received and revealed through His servant on the earth, even Warren Jeffs, and declare to all peoples our testimony that this is verily the word of God to this generation.

_____
Lyle S. Jeffs
Special Counselor to the President of the Fundamentalist
Church of Jesus Christ of Latter-day Saints

_____
Vaughan Taylor
Patriarch in the Fundamentalist
Church of Jesus Christ of Latter-day Saints

Fundamentalist Church of Jesus Christ of Latter-day Saints

P.O. Box 840459
Hildale, Utah 84784

Thus Saith Son Ahman, Even Jesus Christ, the God Over All Creation, to the President of the United States of America

Revelation of the Lord Given to President Warren S. Jeffs

Eldorado, Texas
Tuesday, April 26, 2011

1. Thus saith the Lord Jesus Christ unto you, the leader of the nation of the United States of America, even the President of this nation:

2. I address you, as the God of Creation, even Jesus Christ, who gave His life for the salvation of all mankind and is able to raise all in the resurrection and judge all for their deeds done in the flesh.

3. Righteous is my name; Endless and Eternal is my name.

4. When I speak, I fulfill.

5. I have sent to you mine own word to let my people go, and release my servant from bondage, and allow them freedom of worship in Celestial Laws of my revealing.

6. I have warned this nation and the leaders of this nation by sending mine own word to overthrow those laws that allow murder of unborn children, the gross immorality of Sodom and adultery; promotion of which is allowed by legal consent, even in entertainments and music and social ways throughout your land.

7. As the leaders of this nation allow these great evils to continue, I shall bring you to judgment.

8. Thou sayest you promote peace among nations and religious freedom, the freedom of expression; yet, since the days of my servant Joseph Smith receiving my Gospel of salvation, restored from heaven to earth, upholding my word in Old and New Testament, the words of all the ancient Prophets, my people have been a driven people.

9. And government powers of this nation of the United States of America have used their civil powers to prosecute and persecute my people of my Church of Jesus Christ of Latter-day Saints; which Church has continued under my Priesthood eternal authority revealed from heaven to Prophets since Joseph Smith's time, now known among men as the Fundamentalist Church of Jesus Christ of Latter-day Saints, known as upholding all the laws of my Gospel revealed through Joseph Smith, of their Lord.

10. But I will support and sustain and preserve my people, even through great whirlwind judgments that I prophesied of, as you can read in New Testament Record.

11. I refer you to Matthew 24 specifically, one of mine Apostles of old who heard my word and recorded my word.

12. I send you this, my word, calling upon you who leads this nation to promote true justice and religious freedom for my people; for they are of peaceful nature and only desire the salvation of all peoples.

13. They are seeking to build my Zion, prepare for my glorious appearing;

14. And if you will heed my word, blessings shall come upon this nation; else there shall come judgments to make room for the rise of Zion on this, the American continent, which is my land of Zion where New Jerusalem shall be built, as described by John the Beloved in the Book of Revelations in New Testament record; and I refer this to your reading, knowing of my Bible record.

15. My servant on earth is in bondage through unjust laws aimed to destroy my Priesthood, Church, and Kingdom upon the earth;

16. For I am the God of eternity, and the laws of my Church are revealed from heaven and guided by your Lord; and my people in thy land, of my Church and Kingdom, have rights of religious worship and religious freedom; and my Celestial Law is pure and only promotes happiness and salvation among the pure in heart.

17. My Zion shall rise through the principles of the laws of my Church and Kingdom upon the earth, revealed from heaven.

18. You can peruse these laws in my sacred writings through Joseph Smith in Doctrine and Covenants.

19. You can read of My Coming among a former people that dwelt on this land, and my prophecies to them concerning these days -- of this nation coming upon this land.

20. My record is extant and witnesses of my glorious coming, both ancient scripture and modern revelation, as is known among men.

21. And these are the motives of my Priesthood and my servant and my servants in my Church and Kingdom, who seek to live pure and eternal laws of salvation, which I require of them in this mortal existence on earth to prove worthy of an eternal salvation;

22. And this is the motive of their lives, notwithstanding the persecuting zeal of those who come against them, promoted by the lies of former members who have apostatized because their own lives were full of sin, accusing my Priesthood, Church, and Kingdom of unrighteous domain.

23. Come to understand the truth of these realities among you, and free my servants who are in bondage because of their religious beliefs and practices in obedience to my eternal laws, the revealed religion from heaven.

24. As I spoke concerning the destruction of Jerusalem and the scattering of the Jews, and thus fulfilled my word, so have I spoken concerning the judgments of God -- even of your Lord who sendeth this word to you -- upon this nation and the nations of the earth, if you continue to promote these great evils among your peoples, and allow the persecution and prosecution, which is an injustice against my Church, people, and Kingdom upon the earth.

25. And if you heed me not, you leaders of this nation of the United States of America, you shall feel the chastening hand of a just God; and

all my promises and prophecies of judgments upon the gentile nations shall be fulfilled in full measure.

26. Heed my word, that the more righteous among you may be preserved; and if you do not, and the peoples of this nation oppose the rise of Zion, I must needs come out in judgment to cleanse my land of Zion.

27. I shall come in my glory to establish righteous domain, a just and equitous government of eternal power, to rule over all nations, and nothing can stay mine hand, being the God of all creation over all nations.

28. Thus I send my word to you again, according to the understanding of men, in simple language, that you may see truth revealed by your God, which truth you can understand by simple perusal of the scriptures revealed through Joseph Smith, my servant, continued on earth in my Church and Kingdom.

29. I have declared to you that if these evils continue among your people and this nation, that I have named in many messages I have sent, the judgments I have promised shall take place, for wickedness shall not reign.

30. There shall be a thousand years of peace under my righteous rule, saith Jesus Christ, the Beginning and the End, who has all power and authority and right to rule, in heaven and on earth.

31. As you see a great storm of paralyzing nature over many parts of thy nation, and also an earthquake of damaging nature and the loss of lives in a place of unusual happening, as I have named, let your heart be touched that thy God hath spoken; and when He speaks, He fulfills His word.

32. My Coming in glory is nigh.

33. I send you my word through my authority of Priesthood on the earth.

34. I, the Lord, reveal to you, the leader of this nation, the formation of that which is of a secret combination among rich businessmen and some leaders of this nation, disturbed by thy policies of economic practices, using government powers, some of whom have joined with organized crime, plotting thy destruction.

35. This I reveal to you, to be careful in thy movements.

36. There are some of them determined to overthrow your influence, thinking your

policies are destroying this nation in economic power, fearing that political means may not be sufficient in their power to bring another into that presidential position in future election.

37. Let there be an investigation, of careful means and ways, into the organization of business leaders of banking industry combining with the political arm that is promoting free trade, opposing thy policies of increased debt that are joined with authorities from China, to which this nation has depended on investment into treasury and other stocks to bolster this economy, which organization is of the policy of free trade without restrictions, wanting to set aside governmental restrictions to allow economic growth without government hindrance, wherein the policies of this nation presently limit some exports to nations considered in human rights violations; yet this organization desires free trade, notwithstanding the policies of this government today.

38. Look well into organized crime in Chicago connecting with rich businessmen of an organization seeking free trade, and also having made some connections with foreign powers who also seek economic benefit by changing of laws and rules, in trade and commerce, the laws of this nation, seeking to get gain thereby.

39. I, the Lord, reveal this much, that the fears of this secret combination are -- they will lose their wealth if you promote certain policies in government concerning economic development.

40. I give you this, my word, saith the Lord, that you may know I see and know all things; can reveal my word and preserve life as I will.

41. I have named judgments to come upon this nation if they continue these most wicked practices of murder of unborn children, and Sodom, and the immoral wickedness that promotes these sins against innocence and against life;

42. Yet, if you will heed my word and now promote the repeal of those practices now upheld by law, I, the Lord, shall cause this nation to continue as they allow freedom of religion of my Church and Kingdom.

43. And if the leaders of this nation heed me not, my full judgment shall come to thy knowing; for I am the God of glory and fear no man, and shall come to earth in my glory to reign a thousand years in righteous dominion and government over all nations.

44. This is my word to you. Heed my word and promote principles of righteous government.

45. And thus this message is to the leaders of all bodies of government over this nation, to promote righteous principles that preserve life and purity and religious freedom.

46. I tell you these things beforehand for thy good.

47. Do not be taken in a snare by rich businessmen in promoting thy attending a business conference in Chicago of soon naming.

48. Excuse thyself that you may be preserved, is the word of the Lord to you.

49. Promote no longer war against other nations, save for self-defense.

50. Do not be the originator of attack against any nation, that this nation may be justified before your God as you also remove these great evils I have named from among thy peoples, which are allowed by legal consent in this day.

51. I, the Lord, have spoken it. Give heed to my word, and know that I shall repay all peoples, according to the measure they have measured to their fellow men, an eternal judgment, being the God over all creation, who came to earth among mortal men and suffered more than man can suffer, conquering death, hell, and the grave, to raise all peoples up in the resurrection to stand before the judgment bar of God, which tribunal shall render an eternal judgment upon all peoples -- happiness and eternal life for those who measured justice, righteousness and equity, and purity of life toward their fellow men and in their own lives; and promoting a great and eternal punishment upon those who would seek the destruction of life and of innocence, whether openly by legal means, or in private.

52. I have warned the leaders of nations to remove these great sins from among their peoples before my glorious appearing by sending forth my word.

53. And I shall be justified in cleansing the more wicked out of every nation on earth before my glorious appearing, preserving the more righteous who will receive my message of salvation and a righteous government power, even of thy Lord, on earth for a thousand years, a Millennial reign of peace, as I have promised.

54. My Coming is nigh at hand. Let my people go, to worship me in the freedom guaranteed by the laws of thy nation, my revealed religion

from heaven promoting pure and holy principles unto eternal life for those who obey my religious laws, that should be protected by the laws of thy land, yet have not been protected for many years -- legal prosecution and persecution coming against my people in many ways in this nation.

55. I send you my word to help you overcome the inward prejudice held by many lawmakers against my true Church and religion upon earth.

56. Peruse my policies of government in my recent sending of my publishing to thee, with the warnings to this nation and other nations.

57. I say to you lawmakers and government officials in this nation and in every state: My time of coming is at hand.

58. Turn to righteous principles that promote life and virtue and innocence, and protect the same, for I shall hold you accountable, saith the Lord God of heaven and over the earth.

59. Righteous and Holy is my name. Endless is my name. Eternal is my name, even Jesus Christ.

60. This earth is mine.

61. I have given man his agency to choose. Both good and evil are present before all peoples.

62. Choose to promote righteousness.

63. A heavenly power is coming to earth to govern the nations of the earth on my land of Zion, and my power shall be among them; and this is revealed in the scriptures of holy writ in thine hands.

64. I am a God of truth, and I have spoken my word through all the holy Prophets, and shall fulfill. Amen.

We, the undersigned Elders of Israel in the Priesthood of God, in the Fundamentalist Church of Jesus Christ of Latter-day Saints -- that Church restored through the Prophet Joseph Smith, known by this name, upholding all the laws of the Gospel of Jesus Christ in fulness, seeking the rise of Zion in these last days through heavenly laws lived -- we put our names before all peoples as witnesses that this is verily the word of God, who is Jesus Christ, Jehovah Christ, even Son Ahman. And this we know is true, giving our names to all peoples, this testimony.

_____

4-26-2011

Vaughan E. Taylor

Patriarch in the
Church of Jesus Christ of Latter-day Saints

Ben E Johnson

April 26, 2011

Ben E. Johnson

Counselor in the Bishopric of the
Church of Jesus Christ of Latter-day Saints

Exact copy of letter sent to the President of the United States

Fundamentalist Church of Jesus Christ of Latter-day Saints
P.O. Box 840459
Hildale, Utah 84784

Thus Saith Son Ahman, Even Jesus Christ, Your Lord and Savior Who Hath Redeemed All Mankind, Whose Right It Is to Rule Over the Heavens and the Earth, A Just God Who Sees and Knows All Things, and Shall Recompense to Every Man That Which He Has Measured to His Fellow Man, According to the Light and Knowledge They Have Received: Thus I Speak to the President of the United States of America, Now in Power, and Also to the Peoples of This Nation -- This Message of Warning of the Doctrine of Eternal Judgment Upon Thee, Even Upon All Peoples, Being the God of Eternal Power, an Eternal God Who Shall Bring All to Justice; Whose Mercy Shall Claim Those Who Repenteth in a Manner to Earn the Benefit of My Atoning Power -- Even Him, a God of Atoning and Redeeming Power, Who Suffered on the Cross and Was Raised From the Grave Unto Eternal Power to Judge All Mankind According As Their Works Are:

Revelation of the Lord Given to President Warren S. Jeffs

Eldorado, Texas
Tuesday, May 3, 2011

1. Let there be written my word, saith the Lord, in a manner of correspondence to the leader of this nation of the United States of America, a word of warning and counsel -- even Jesus Christ, who reigneth over all, empowering this nation to be a free nation since its creation, I guiding forefathers of the revolutionary battles wherein they broke away from the mother gentile nation from which they emanated.

2. And I, your God, inspired leaders of this nation to establish the Constitution of the United States, and the Bill of Rights, as it is called, guaranteeing religious freedom, even freedom of worship in a land of plenty at that time.

3. Thus saith the Lord to those who thus murdered Osama bin Laden:

4. You have transgressed greatly, turning to murder in a manner of seeking to retaliate against one in another land, not using the government powers where he dwelt to apprehend him safely, which could have easily been accomplished had you thus stepped forth and acted on correct principles.

5. But in thy glory-seeking and in thy violent nature, yea, to the celebration of millions in thy nation, you hath murdered a man who could have been apprehended peacefully, were attempts made therein by the governing power of the nation where he dwelt, being near the capitol city and power of authority of that nation in Pakistan.

6. I, the Lord, rebuke thee for thy murderous intent, turning to violence when peaceful means, or the governing powers over that place of residence, could have been used to apprehend and take in custody one accused of crimes.

7. And if you continue this practice, your murderous intentions shall turn upon thine own peoples, and mob rule shall ensue throughout thy land; murder and rapine, robbery and violence one against another, showing thy murderous intent and nature of the people of this nation, proving to thy God you are not worthy to remain on my land of Zion, but would have to be swept clean by just, yea, by justified judgments of God, to send thee to the world of departed spirits where you transgress no more in this mortal existence of probationary testing; which I, the Lord your

God, have sent all mankind to be tested, allowing good and evil to be placed before all, sending my Spirit -- which is only good, of the inspiring unto good -- to the mind and heart to every man, woman, and child who would receive and listen to what they call their conscience unto righteous works, choosing good, eschewing and casting off evil.

8. And thus all have their agency as they come to mature years, more especially, even the age of accountability; yea, even by the age of eight years old, a child knows good from evil.

9. Thus saith the Lord: As you continue in the spirit of murder of unborn children, and then become aggressive when peaceful means could be used -- I command thee to repent!

10. I am the God of Creation.

11. Cease these murderous ways.

12. Cease your military actions in nations who have not thus attacked thee.

13. I, the Lord, command thee to repent unto a bringing forth of a change of policy and intent, and even justice served upon leaders of nations, thus saith the Lord, within each nation by their lawmaking bodies, and not think that you can transgress the borders of another nation aggressively and perform murder -- thine own pride satisfied, and not correct principle of law-abiding and just ways being followed.

14. Thus I send this corresponding of mine own words to the leader of this nation, to his Cabinet, to lawmakers of high standing.

15. I reveal my word to thee: Repent of thy murderous and immoral ways, the leaders of this nation as well as the peoples of this nation, for you have offended thy God, the great numbers in millions celebrating in their hearts the murder of a soul who could have been taken peaceably, and tried before the courts in the jurisdiction appointed, and of justice, by the nation that could have apprehended him.

16. Thus saith the Lord: Let this wicked generation repent speedily, lest my cleansing process sweep them off my land of Zion and leave them neither root nor branch -- in earthquake, tornado, storm and windstorms, pestilence, hail, and famine, the overflowing scourge and desolating sickness promised this wicked generation if they repent not.

17. For I am the God that made you. You are sons and daughters of God sent to a probationary earth to be tested what you will choose.

18. And when leaders of nations choose wickedness, I, the Lord, execute judgment upon them through righteous justice administered, even overthrowing leaders of nations, removing them from power, and, at times, sweeping the wicked of a nation off the earth, where they can further repent, if they will, in the world of departed spirits; I being a God of love, laboring for the salvation of all, whether on earth, whether they be spirits yet unborn who shall be sent to this probationary earth, preserving their lives unto those who can beget them unto correct principles, just and righteous, to earn an eternal salvation; and also among those in the world of departed spirits.

19. My Gospel message shall go to all on this earth and in the world of departed spirits, now and in the future giving.

20. And I shall be called justified as every knee bows and every tongue confesses that Jesus is the Christ, a God over all creation, and He ruleth righteously, and He hath done right toward all peoples, nations, kindreds, and tongues.

21. This shall be declared in future time as truth is revealed and all secrets are made known.

22. And thus saith the Lord to leaders of this nation and all nations: All your secret acts and intentions of the heart shall be revealed in the Millennial Reign of Peace, in the government of God in Zion, and sent forth to the nations, and in the day of judgment when you stand before a just God in the resurrection;

23. For I am the Resurrection and the Life, and the God that shall judge thee, appointed by my Father, Elohim, even Ahman; for I am Son Ahman, to perform that work of judging all mankind.

24. You shall stand before me.

25. I shall unlock thy mind, which shall reveal all the secrets of thy life, and nothing hidden; and you shall be judged by a just and holy God, even your Lord and Redeemer, Jesus Christ, who speaketh these words to the leaders of this nation through mine authority on earth.

26. Thus saith your God to thee: You shall be judged, and wickedness shall be punished with that degree of buffetings and suffering requisite for justice to be satisfied upon every person who repenteth not, even a full justice;

27. For my atoning power and suffering can only be a benefit to those who repent and accept my Gospel of salvation; yea, my message of salvation I shall soon send to every nation of the earth, both before my glorious appearing, to

prepare many peoples, and a greater degree after my glorious coming to New Jerusalem, which shall rise in this generation.

28. This is my revealing to you at this time of a needed message to be given to the leaders of this nation of the United States of America, for you have offended your God in following wicked and unjust and corrupt principles, even unto murder, not having placed the accused before a tribunal, which you do in your own land for any criminal thus apprehended, of general policy, save those secret combinations which the leaders of this nation have sometimes followed in destroying life secretly in murderous intent.

29. Thus have the people of this nation offended their God, in glorying in murder, which could have been avoided.

30. The wicked shall slay the wicked, even in mob violence in thy land, if you heed me not; if this spirit of glorying in the loss of life, instead of mourning when one who is wicked passes on unprepared for salvation -- thus should all peoples do, understanding the purposes of thy God of Creation over thee, in bringing thee forth in this life of probationary and testing time to prove thy characters, whether or no you will love life and eternal principles that exalt, or transgress against the principles of life and earn a never-ending judgment of sorrow, not being exalted to be with the God who made thee.

31. And in the resurrection there shall be added to your mind the memory of having been born to a God of Creation, well-prepared; to know the purpose of this mortal life, forgetting previous existence as a test, yet having my Spirit of light and life in thee at birth, and in thy growing years, to teach you good from evil, prompting you in what you call your mental conscience unto better works.

32. I am the God of Creation whose Spirit of light and life shineth upon all creation, to give all creation its existence.

33. I am a God of love that blesseth all.

34. And as death passeth on all, sending their spirits inhabiting their mortal bodies, the body lying in the grave, the spirits going to a world of living, a place of departed spirits where my Priesthood labors to administer the message of my salvation to all of every nation, kindred, tongue, and peoples; verily, I reveal to you, murderers hath no forgiveness.

35. If you take on the spirit of that sin and consent to this evil in the conduct of any person, you shall also have the same degree of judgment according to thy crimes in the flesh -- crimes against thy God, and eternal, exalting principles; crimes against thine own knowledge; for all shall be judged according to the light they received in this mortal existence, saith the Lord God, who administers life unto eternal life to those who love and obey laws that exalt, ways to their greatest ability to understand according to the light they receive; yea, even a God who can exalt thee unto eternal life, those who live laws of progression unto eternal life, of my message, and Priesthood, Church and Kingdom, of salvation powers that are now on the earth, preparing the way for the rise of Zion in fulness, a New Jerusalem built on the continent where the United States of America dwells at this time; and nothing can stay mine hand;

36. For I shall sweep the more wicked off the earth and preserve the more righteous unto my reign of righteousness, which shall be for a thousand years of my dwelling among men, to their knowing, in my power and glory in Zion; and the Kingdom of heaven coming forth to earth as the governing power over all nations.

37. Heed my word.

38. Repent of your murderous and immoral ways, which leads thee to a murderous way;

39. For thus are the corrupt in heart not able to govern themselves, being blinded by their own corruptions, justifying their murderous ways.

40. I, the Lord, shall bring them to justice, even in the eternal duration of time, feeling the wrath of a just God, who hath given them His Spirit in their minds and hearts as a conscience to know good from evil.

41. Let the policies of thy government cease this practice, is the command of thy Lord in this correspondence of needed message to thee. Amen.

42. Thus saith your Lord and Savior Jesus Christ, further, to the people of the nation of the United States of America:

43. Repent ye! Repent ye! for my day of my glorious coming is nigh at hand.

44. Heed my word.

45. I have sent many warnings to the leaders of this nation, and to the peoples of this nation, of recent doing.

46. You must heed my words, lest there be upon you a greater judgment than you can bear, to leave you neither root nor branch of posterity upon the earth.

47. There are the sins of the shedding of innocent blood of unborn children legalized in this nation; the sins of corruption, of secret combinations to get gain by evil means, even of murder, upon this land and among your peoples, even among the leaders of this nation, which I, the Lord, reveal openly, and shall reveal more in a time soon to come;

48. For you cannot hide from a God who seeth all things, and is just and holy and righteous, and who shall judge all men according to their deeds done in the flesh.

49. Thus saith the Lord: Let there not be a celebration of thy peoples again of any man's being murdered, yea, his death.

50. Mourn over the loss of life when they go to the world of departed spirits, not having my message of salvation, unprepared for a glorious salvation, losing the same because they would not hear my word sent forth by testimony and holy writ.

51. Let not this people of this nation again glorify themselves in murder, wherein a man whose known location in another nation could have been apprehended by the authorities of that nation and placed before a tribunal, and not taken in death.

52. Thus saith the Lord: Let this cease in your natures.

53. Violence covereth this land, even in the spirit of the people of this nation.

54. Thus saith the Lord: I am the God of peace.

55. I will sweep those off the land where thy nation resides, in every nation on that continent, yea, on the North American continent who have violence in their nature.

56. For Zion is a place of peace, and my Zion shall rise, even New Jerusalem in the Center Stake of Zion, in Jackson County, Missouri, as I have proclaimed; and nothing can stay mine hand.

57. Thus I have sent this warning to the leader and peoples of this nation to repent, and know that My Coming is nigh at hand. Amen.

We, the undersigned, bear witness to all peoples, this is verily the word of our Lord and Savior, Jesus Christ, given by His authority on earth; verify the same by giving our names as witnesses.

_____

3 May 2011

Vaughan E. Taylor

Patriarch in the
Church of Jesus Christ of Latter-day Saints

Ben E Johnson

May 3, 2011

Ben E. Johnson

Counselor in the Bishopric of the
Church of Jesus Christ of Latter-day Saints

Fundamentalist Church of Jesus Christ of Latter-day Saints

P.O. Box 840459
Hildale, Utah 84784

Thus Saith Jesus Christ, Who Is Son Ahman, to the Leader of This Nation of the United States of America, and All the Leaders of This Nation in Their Several Governing Appointments and Powers; and Thus to the Peoples of This Nation, Mine Own Word from the Heavens; Even the God of Glory Who Speaketh Thus to Your Understandings -- A Call to Heed My Word, Even I Who Am Soon to Come in the Powers of Heaven to Dwell Among Men, a Governing Power Over All Nations of the Earth -- Hear My Words:

Revelation of the Lord Given to President Warren S. Jeffs

Eldorado, Texas
Thursday, May 26, 2011

1. Thus saith the Lord Jesus Christ, Son Ahman, the Creator of heaven and earth, who is Jehovah Christ, the Great I AM, even the Beginning and the End, who reigns in the heavens eternal, a Creator over this earth, sending forth the children of the Father to this probationary world for their time of testing, being given their agency to know good from evil, left to choose, yet being born with enough of my holy light to know good from evil from birth, yea, to be agents to themselves --

2. I, who created all things, speaketh from on high as one crying in the wilderness, a light that reigns over all, yet the inhabitants of the earth, dwelling in gross darkness, discern not the light that came among them in the meridian of time as the sacrifice of atoning power to conquer death and raise all in the resurrection to be judged by a just God for the deeds and desires in the flesh;

3. Yea, I speaketh, saith your Lord who created you, again, to the leader of the nation that now inhabits my land of Zion where my New Jerusalem shall be built, that you have heeded me not.

4. Though I have sent mine own word, my revealed word to thee, and have spared thy life as the God of Creation over thee, who giveth life to all who dwell upon the earth, who enlightens the mind to more noble thoughts and works; thus have I sent my words to you.

5. And you have gloried in thy doings wherein I have reproved thee and this nation, of which you, the President of the United States of America, officiate over by my grace, in that executive branch of earthly governing power, having influence over many peoples.

6. And how shalt thou stand in the day of judgment when the resurrection is brought forth in thy behalf before a just God, knowing the word of God has been given you, warning thee to bear influence to cease the murder of innocent unborn children in this nation, and bear influence in other nations to do the same?

7. And I have reproved thee and the leaders of this nation by mine own words revealed from the heavens for thy aggressive acts toward other nations who have not attacked thee, not being justified in thine aggressions, which shall clip thy power; as I have weighed thee in the balance and found you and the leaders of this nation wanting.

8. And as I have spoken judgments against thee and this nation, if you heed me not, so shall I fulfill.

9. And you have witnessed, even by personal traveling to see the destruction of the windstorms I have sent, that I warned thee of in my previous communicating, saith the Lord, Jesus Christ;

10. Thou hast seen the power of thy God

humble this nation in allowing windstorms and flooding, as an example that when He speaketh, He fulfilleth His word.

11. My word is sure, unto an eternal duration of the consequence of the choices made in every man's life being returned upon them -- a just recompense of reward -- that as they measure to their fellow man, so shall I, their God, measure an eternal judgment upon each one favored to come to the age of accountability.

12. Thus saith the God of heaven: My time is at hand.

13. My chastening hand is upon this nation and upon the nations of the earth, and I have sent forth mine own word through my servant, my Mouthpiece I have appointed and ordained on earth.

14. And my word has now gone forth to the leaders of all nations to cease their wars and draw their military and armies into their own borders, to only be used for defensive needs, save I, the Lord, shall command; for in my glorious appearing, I, your Lord and King, shall be the governing power known among all nations to humble all peoples who continue in a violent nature and in murderous and immoral ways.

15. I am the God of glory who giveth and taketh life as I will; and I doeth the will of the Father, performing a work to bring forth a thousand years of peace under a reign of a governing power sent from heaven, known among men as the Kingdom of God, yea, the Kingdom of Ahman, my Father;

16. For I am Son Ahman and doeth the will of the Father in all things, to the redeeming of all mankind from the grave and judging all in the resurrection.

17. And nothing shall be hidden, and all secrets shall be revealed, and the wicked shall tremble before me, a just and holy God who must soon send forth His message of salvation to all surviving nations; for this murder of unborn children, and Sodom, and violent and unjust ways, and immoral and corrupt ways cannot stand.

18. And I have sent forth my word to be justified before the heavens to send forth the cleansing powers to sweep the more wicked out of the lands of every nation on earth, to preserve the more righteous, who shall know of my ways of Zion and of New Jerusalem, that shall be built in that Center Stake appointed, of Jackson County, Missouri; and nothing can stay mine hand.

19. I have caused you to be warned of an assassination plot among the rich of this nation. Heed my word and I shall preserve thy life, to the performing of the works of overcoming these great outward evils I have named -- of legal consent in thy nation, upholding those evils to exist among thy people.

20. I have allowed you to know of mine own words coming forth, showing thee and the leaders of this nation, and the leaders of all nations, that I, the God of Creation, who brought forth this earth and caused the peopling thereof, am able to speak from the heavens; yet few will heed my words and accept my Gospel of salvation, having pleasure in unrighteousness;

21. Yet I, the God of glory, who am just and holy, shall reward all, and wickedness cannot reign.

22. A righteous government of heavenly power cometh to earth as I caused mine apostles in the meridian of time to preach the same, which record, known as the Bible, though it has been altered by wicked men in parts, yet it testifieth many truths of my coming, and the building of New Jerusalem, which is on the land known as North America, as I have named -- my land of Zion -- as I shall cleanse, as a whirlwind coming upon them, which example you have recently seen in the sweeping of life off certain places of thy land with the whirlwinds, of such destructive nature that should humble all peoples that the God of power and of glory speaketh.

23. Yet they heed me not, in overcoming their own evils, needing to cleanse the inside of the platter, as it were, in your own nation; for your laws are corrupt that uphold these great sins I have named, which sins shall be swept off the earth, saith the Lord Jesus Christ, out of every nation in the great judgments of a just God soon at hand.

24. And if you would seek the blessings of thy God who created thee, act on these true and correct principles to favor life, virtue and purity, honesty, lest my judgments humble you to the dust, and thy power be so clipped, you rise not again as leaders of a nation that could have done the works of righteousness, yet only promote the justifying of thy peoples in ways opposing the plan of life established by the God

who created thee; which the murder of unborn children and sodomy and adultery and immoral ways promote that sin of corruption of immoral ways that promotes the destruction of life of unborn children.

25. How canst thou not be touched by the flagrant and outward attack on the principle of life?

26. Yea, thy God speaking to the leader of this nation and all the leaders within this nation:

27. Awake! This sin of gross darkness shall blight thy soul unto an eternal damnation, you having been warned in this mortal and earthly existence by thy God sending His own word unto thine understanding, and you heed me not; I being justified now to send forth more judgments upon this nation -- earthquake, more storms of destructive nature, to thy knowing I have warned thee.

28. And as thou continuest warring against nations and supporting other nations in their wars against other nations, when those nations that are attacked by thee and thine allies, yea, thy NATO allies, not having attacked thee first, you become the aggressors in the sight of heaven and are promoting violence and war among nations, that, if you do not withdraw your violent ways, shall erupt in a conflict that shall absorb nations in that prophesied war that my servant John, my Beloved, recorded, seeing in vision these last days before my glorious appearing, to establish peace once again upon earth among all nations by establishing my New Jerusalem, my Zion on my land of Zion in full power from heaven.

29. Thus I send my word again to the leaders of this nation, and I fear thee not; for thy power can only exist of governing ability by the grace of God who created thee.

30. And as I predicted, during my ministry among mine apostles, the destruction of the Jewish nation and the scattering of that people, so shall it be with this nation -- a sweeping of this nation clean who oppose my Zion and my righteous rule soon to come, by opposing my Priesthood, Church, and Kingdom upon the earth, imprisoning and persecuting my people who are established by the revelations of their God, even Jesus Christ, who speaketh these words unto thee and sendeth them to thee by my Priesthood and eternal authority now dwelling upon the earth, my people being prepared for my glorious appearing, to build my Zion, even New Jerusalem, to receive their Lord in His glory.

31. Thus my people have been a persecuted people since the days of Joseph Smith, my servant and Prophet, whom I used, saith Jesus Christ, to restore my Church, Priesthood, and Kingdom upon the earth.

32. I have sent forth my policies of governing power in my publishings, mine own word revealed from heaven, that the governing power in New Jerusalem and in Zion shall administer justice and equity, and pure and noble ways of living.

33. Study the same, correct thy laws, and remove these greater outward evils from being upheld by legal consent.

34. Warn thy people of coming judgments soon at hand -- the sea heaving beyond its bounds, great cities swallowed up in the earth, disease, the overflowing scourge with no cure being sent forth upon this people who will not heed my word, but continue in their gross wickedness and corrupt ways.

35. Oh, that you would heed my word!

36. For the heavens weep over the wickedness now dwelling in the hearts of the children of men in this nation and in all the nations of the earth; yet I must do my will, declared from the heavens, the will of the Father, whose perfect way and will I do, saith Son Ahman.

37. And this earth shall know one thousand years of peace, my Zion the ruling city, the capitol city of governing power over the earth, raised up by the visitation of the heavenly powers to earth.

38. As recorded in holy writ, verily it shall be so.

39. And because you are my children on earth, having your agency, I, your just and holy God, who loveth all, send forth the warning voice that you shall reap as you have sown.

40. And my day of greater judgments are soon at hand.

41. And I loveth the salvation of souls through righteous works, who promote life and purity of life unto their own salvation and the salvation of the generations ahead.

42. There shall not be a prolonging much further of my merciful hand of warning.

43. My judgments have begun to cleanse my land of Zion, to preserve mine elect who will heed my words.

44. Mine Israel shall be gathered from all nations under heaven unto New Jerusalem and inherit their promised lands -- both my land of Zion and that land of old Jerusalem.

45. I shall humble this nation through a judgment they have not expected -- of a large city mostly destroyed, which city the inhabitants thereof have continued in gross wickedness for many years, having been warned since the days of my servant Joseph Smith, yet they will not repent.

46. And I being a just God, shall fulfill my word.

47. I have allowed my servant to be in the hands of bondage, and now make known that my word is coming forth to the leaders of all nations, and to thy peoples in every nation, that you may know I, a just God, am able to speak from the heavens and deliver my word to be justified to cleanse wickedness off the earth and preserve the more righteous, who uphold the ways of life and virtue, justice and equity.

48. With blessings unmeasured shall the more righteous be favored -- with knowledge from heaven and the blessings of a just and holy God upon them, who sees and knows all things, and nothing is hidden.

49. And verily, upon the ungodly, who delight in violent ways, and murder and immoral and corrupt ways, sudden judgment and a sweeping off the earth shall take place.

50. And I send you my warning voice again, that I may be justified, as a just and holy God, to perform this work of cleansing the earth and my land of Zion, to prepare the way for a righteous government of heavenly power coming to earth to rule over all nations, even by their consenting, seeing the noble and exalting ways of a Celestial heavenly power, and desiring the ways of Zion in their own lives, yea, those who remain upon the earth.

51. Now heed my word:

52. If you would reap the blessings, through repentance, from thy Lord, to preserve thy peoples in more righteous ways, and to receive my Zion without obstruction, without persecuting zeal against them -- either by prosecution or by mob rule, as has been done against my people in days gone by, even in this nation that professed religious freedom, driving my saints from that Center Stake of Zion in Missouri, never having made reparation to my Church and my Kingdom, which testimony cometh up before the heavens, justifying thy God to clip the power of this nation and bring them low, as I have done other wicked nations in ages gone by, when they rose to the height of corruption; for this nation is ripened in iniquity to overflowing in the eyes of heaven.

53. And I have declared that this land of Zion shall be reserved for a righteous people who serve the God of the land, even Jesus Christ.

54. I am He, your Lord and Savior, that speaketh these words, which you shall know in the day of judgment and resurrection that thy God hath spoken, and shall hold thee accountable, the leader of this nation and the leaders of this nation, in the several offices and government positions, for your conduct; for the judge on earth shall be judged of a just Judge in heaven.

55. Behold the earth, the heavens, the perfection of the bringing forth of life upon earth in every form and nature, the mysteries of which are only known by a God of Creation.

56. I am He who created this earth and peoples this earth by sending forth spirits to dwell in earthly bodies, giving them their life.

57. And this gross crime of the murder of innocence, of unborn children, is the powers of darkness working on the selfish will of those of immoral nature, to have pleasure in unrighteousness and not meet the responsibility of their own actions, thus destroying life before it is born, depriving spirits appointed this earth from the heavens to come to this earth and prove themselves, through their agency, whether or not they would choose good and eschew and cast off evil;

58. For my plan of salvation is extant, and shall reach all mankind -- past, present and future.

59. And I am the God of heaven that shall cause my Gospel of salvation to spread to every nation on earth in the day of the thousand years of peace, as I come to earth in my glory and cause my Kingdom of God, Council of Fifty, to be the ruling body over all nations, having representatives therein sufficient to maintain the rights of religious freedom and other freedoms thy God bestoweth upon His children to work out their salvation, without intrusion upon other peoples and their religious ideas and ways and tenets.

60. Therefore, know that the God of glory cometh, and hath warned the people of this nation and the leaders of this nation of greater judgments soon at hand, such that you have not witnessed before in your lifetimes nor in thine history as a nation;

61. For I have preserved this land to be a land of freedom where religion would be protected by law, yet my people have been a persecuted people by the falsehoods promoted by those of aspiring power and apostate and wicked intent, darkened by their own sins to persecute an innocent people.

62. And only by the grace of the God of heaven has my Church and Kingdom continued on earth;

63. Yea, verily, only by my grace do all nations keep their place; and all leaders of all nations shall soon be held accountable to the God of heaven, who cometh to earth in His glory, to their knowing I have come to earth.

64. And in that accounting, justice shall be satisfied where murderous and immoral ways have been promoted to gain power and to increase in power of governing nature.

65. Great Babylon, yea, spiritual Babylon, of which this nation is a part, soon falleth; and my Zion shall rise; and I shall preserve those who can be representatives of righteous living in the Zion of our God coming forth in fulness.

66. I, the Lord, have spoken it; and as I have spoken, so shall I fulfill.

67. And though the heavens weep over this most wicked generation that has ever been on my land of Zion, I must fulfill my word; for I am a God of truth, and nothing is hidden from before mine eyes.

68. And though I have been long-suffering, I shall send my fire from heaven to purify my land of Zion of all wickedness, and raise up a more righteous generation of mine Israel, and other peoples that shall be brought to my land of Zion, and receive my message of salvation unto their eternal lives being earned, and the blessings of many souls upon the earth unto eternal life; and also, the blessing of many souls who dwell in the world of departed spirits awaiting the blessings and ordinances of salvation through the Redemption of Zion;

69. For I, the Lord, have organized this earth to fulfill the purpose of its creation, and I send forth children to earth to prove themselves.

70. And there is a day of judgment beyond this life that pertains to this life of your earthly existence, when all secrets shall be known and nothing hidden from all.

71. Thus, awake! Awake!

72. Repent ye! Repent ye! is the call of thy just God, even your Lord and Master, who ruleth over all things, soon to come in the clouds of heaven in the power of His might to visit the righteous and to sweep the wicked off this land of Zion and in many lands of the earth. Amen.

73. I, who reigns on high, speaketh further -- He who has all power:

74. Though no man knoweth the hour or the day of my glorious appearing, it is nigh at hand.

75. And these, my words, being sent to the leaders of this nation, and mine other words revealed to the leaders of all nations, sent forth by my Church and Kingdom upon the earth, the sending forth of my word is witness that my coming is nigh at hand, to justify thy Lord in what He must do to preserve Zion -- a city of righteousness, of peace and holiness, wherein all who dwell therein shall be called holy.

76. Let none oppose my Zion, or I shall send forth the judgments of a just God upon thee, saith the Lord to this nation and all peoples of the earth.

77. And that nation that raises their hand against my Zion shall be laid low and lose power and influence on earth;

78. For my judgments are just, and all peoples shall stand before me in the day of the resurrection and know that thy God who created thee, who redeemed thee from the grave, hath done right.

79. And the wicked shall tremble at my appearing and stand afar off.

80. How oft I would have gathered you into the arms of my redeeming love, O ye peoples of the earth, and you heed me not.

81. Yet those who mock their God shall mourn and know that He fulfilleth His word, all being accountable to a just God for the conduct through their agency on earth.

82. I, your Lord Jesus Christ, call upon the leader of this nation and those who are of influence in Congress to heed my word:

83. Be peacemakers among nations.

84. Overthrow these wicked laws that allow murder of unborn children, and of Sodom and adultery in thy land; for you are like the people

in the days of Noah, with evil continually in your minds, and violence throughout thy land and in thy natures; and of a sudden, my whirlwind judgments shall come upon thee, even this nation on my land of Zion, and other nations on this land where my New Jerusalem shall rise.

85. While the governing powers are in thine hands, O ye leaders of this nation, do well.

86. Let deliverance and protection come for my people, for my servant and my servants in bondage.

87. And as my servant Daniel of old saw the destruction and upheaval of nations until Michael, mine Archangel, shall be sent to give the governing powers unto the hands of my saints, there shall be unrest and overthrow of nations until only my Zion remaineth on my land of Zion.

88. War shall come to thy borders. Millions shall flee to the center of thy land and fill the mountains.

89. A great famine shall be among those who flee, and where the war taketh place on thy borders, because you heed me not.

90. How can I favor thy nation above others in continued protection if you allow these gross evils to exist among you, and allow the persecution of my Church and Kingdom upon the earth, whether by persecuting zeal of outward prosecution of government powers against my Church and Kingdom, or whether it be persecuting zeal of a secret nature, seeking the lives of mine elect in a day of greater violence soon to come among the people of this land? which shall disrupt governing powers, unable to control thine own peoples, the unrest increasing, notwithstanding your supposed military might in the world today -- a day when all people shall fear, when brother shall rise up against brother, mother against daughter, and daughter against mother, father against son, as I predicted, revealing these truths of coming events to mine apostles of old, which shall take place in this nation, being a nation of supposed freedom, which I have favored with great power and influence on earth; yet, if you continue in these most wicked ways, my justice and full judgment shall fall upon thee.

91. Oh, that you would heed my words and turn thy lives to righteousness, and turn thy governing powers to justice and equity.

92. You depend upon thy God who created thee for the breath of life, for health, for the preservation of all you have, for the sun that shineth, and the rains that bringeth water of life to thy crops and fields and orchards, that allows peace in thy borders and in the hearts of the children of men, mine own heavenly Spirit sent forth to touch people's minds and hearts to be of a peaceful way if they would receive the impressions of good, of kindness and peace in their souls.

93. And as they labor with the children of men, giving them their agency, I am a just God who intervenes in the lives of those who do what is right in the sight of their God.

94. And my Gospel of salvation has been published and sent to the nations of the earth lo, these many years, both in that holy writ known as Bible printing, and also in the revelations of your God, even Jesus Christ, through my servant Joseph Smith, Jun., which has been published to all peoples, nations, kindreds, and tongues.

95. And therein my word declares of my glorious appearing to preserve the righteous, who remembereth thy Lord in His ways, who rejoice in His coming and glory in His redeeming love, applying His Gospel of salvation of righteous principles, yea, eternal principles revealed from heaven to their individual lives.

96. Thus shall be the favored lot of those who heed my word.

97. In my holy love, I send forth these words of warning to the leaders of this nation of the United States of America in plain, understanding language; a God of eternal power speaking, inviting thee, the leaders of this nation and the peoples of this nation, to be of an influence of more righteous ways, and preserving my people in their freedoms to establish Zion in their midst;

98. For I shall reward all peoples according to the blessings offered, yet, through their own actions and words and desires, reject blessings that could promote life, yea, and also eternal life for those who would receive my message of salvation, saith your Lord.

99. And in my glory coming to earth, I shall heal the surviving nations and make known to them the mysteries of all ages of time; and truth shall be told concerning every nation, people, tongue of every age of time. Even so. Amen.

We, the undersigned witnesses, bear testimony that these are verily the words of our Lord Jesus Christ, declared by His authority on earth from the heavens, knowing that as the God of heaven speaketh, so does He fulfill His word, yearning only for the salvation of souls of all peoples through the great majesty and redeeming power of our Lord and Savior Jesus Christ, the Creator of this earth, whose right it is to rule, having redeemed all mankind from the grave, and who cometh to earth to reign a thousand years among men, a righteous government revealed from heaven, whose coming is well prophesied of in holy writ. Amen.

_____

26 May 2011

Vaughan E. Taylor

Patriarch in the
Church of Jesus Christ of Latter-day Saints

_____

John M. Barlow

May 26, 2011

John M. Barlow

Counselor in the Bishopric of the
Church of Jesus Christ of Latter-day Saints

Fundamentalist Church of Jesus Christ of Latter-day Saints
P.O. Box 840459
Hildale, Utah 84784

Thus Saith Jesus Christ, Son Ahman, Unto the Leaders of the Nation of the United States of America, and to the Peoples Thereof, Warning and Continued Call to Prepare for Great Day of Final Judgments, Who Saith:

Revelation of the Lord Jesus Christ
Given to President Warren S. Jeffs

Huntsville, Texas
Thursday, August 18, 2011

1. Verily, verily, thus saith the Lord, even Jesus Christ, the Great Power over all peoples; who is the power of Eternal Union of all other powers; who spake, and the world was made; who came in the day of the way of Redemption; who suffered and atoned for all peoples; who hath conquered death; who is Resurrection and Life to all;

2. Verily I say to all peoples of the entire world, by the Mouthpiece of my sending: Ye are of fully ripening in iniquity.

3. Soon, yea, very soon cometh the entire cleansing I have given in many warnings, and by Isaiah, Jeremiah, and other Prophets, as testimony of my holy word being fulfilled.

4. The evil powers are as a blinding power over all mankind, though my language is given to your understanding; though you can read in a worldwide accepted language; yet you heed me not.

5. I, the Creator over all things, have not been silent.

6. I have given to national powers what must be done to survive my day of full cleansing power of whirlwind and destructive power.

7. My holy scriptures are full.

8. My time is nigh.

9. I shall burn my holy land of Zion of all evil, to prepare for a holy city to rise, even Zion, New Jerusalem; telling all peoples before what I shall do; that all may know thy God hath fulfilled His word, and shall continue to speak and fulfill.

10. Let now the storm of great power soon come to be as a full measure to humble this nation.

11. Know I held off this judgment to see if you would heed my word, in preparing for my coming; in cleansing thy evil laws of evil power, to be just; to preserve virtue, life; and also to send forth deliverance for my Mouthpiece; yet you heed me not.

12. Does not the loss of life mean anything to the rulers of this land?

13. Do they not see wickedness rules over the land -- putting innocence in prison now, even mine elders of obedient doing to Celestial Law of religion of my own revealing?

14. I am God, and all shall know my will.

15. Now cometh a shaking on thy land to humble thousands; yea, all the nation shall feel the result.

16. Let the people of my Church go free, lest I needs continue to pour out judgments on the land, like I did unto Pharaoh and the Egyptians, until they no more could oppose my right to rule.

17. I am Jehovah, even Jesus Christ, Son Ahman, the Full Governing Power of Celestial Priesthood power over the earth; yea, over the nation boasting great power on earth; yet now being but a waning power, none to console her, as nations turn from thee in the great fall of power of money system.

18. I alone have held thee in place.

19. Only I, your Lord, can preserve any of all peoples.

20. Let it be known a great heavenly body cometh, unseen by your technology; I able to blind your way until I take away the covering.

21. Know it shall be of a happening within new year's coming; an event of such magnitude, all peoples shall wonder.

22. I tell not exact time, whether one or two years of my giving a warning; yet some heavenly bodies of larger size shall soon strike the earth to the amazing thoughts of many; which shall begin to disturb the protective atmosphere layer, to cause men on earth not of my protecting, to suffer greater burnings on their bodies, as my servant John Beloved recorded; caused by heavenly bodies increasing to disturb the protective atmosphere layer.

23. Judgments shall be felt in the rising up of the people of Turkey, and cause many other people to falter in European stability.

24. NATO has lost credibility; has become spread far; is now an aggressive alliance.

25. Let all know I warned all of the fall of earthly powers.

26. Now know Israel shall step forth and be of an aggressive way when threatened.

27. Then shall my people know I have spoken, as I preserve the nation; though many perish because they also heed me not; do not cleanse their own peoples; nor do the peace labor I have named.

28. Libya is now a full way of aggression by countries never attacked by that nation.

29. Example of fear of aggression shall unite other nations to fight NATO nations.

30. Disunity shall absorb thee.

31. The economy of your lands shall wither. United States is a power of soon instability in own economic instability.

32. The holy law of retribution for aggression is upon her.

33. I am God. I hath spoken truth. She will not free him, my servant.

34. She shall feel my wrath soon. Then shall come to pass mine elect be preserved, while the wicked shall tremble and be no more a power against Zion rising.

35. O ye people of my earth, awake to catastrophe you are bringing upon yourselves.

36. I must fulfill the purpose of this earth.

37. Your temporary ways cannot overrule the eternal purposes of a God of power.

38. You are my creation.

39. Humble thyselves, to be of a receiving of some degree of life and salvation, from your Lord, Jesus Christ, who speaketh, as a voice from the wilderness -- from the wilderness because you seeth me not; my voice being my Spirit of truth, which toucheth every pure, honest mind with a witness of truth, in a gentle peace.

40. My holy way shall soon be known unto all peoples.

41. Receive ye my next warning; from thy God who loveth all, yet despiseth evil; to guide all here and hereafter to repentance, lest full eternal judgment cometh upon the soul who dies in their sins; to rise in never-ending sorrow for turning from me, your Redeemer; thus choosing death.

42. I am the Light, Life, Happiness, Peace, Truth, and Hope of all peoples.

43. I am your Savior, which speaketh.

44. Seek unto me through my Priesthood to receive my will; to benefit nations, peoples, individuals in soul-raising powers unto earthly and eternal salvation; through the full way of pure holy religion being my authority of heaven, now on earth.

45. Let the wicked of false testifying have one soon reveal their lying; to now show the world prosecuting power followed a scheme of lying combination of years of maturing; to imprison my servant.

46. Their falsehoods shall become a blot on their lives not able to be borne, even before all peoples.

47. Let the governing powers cause the illegal governing work of fighting a holy religion, clouded over by blinding legal and unjust attack of falsehoods, now to be a catalyst to be of a

fulfilling all my will concerning my own word to leaders of this nation, and other nations.

48. I am God who lendeth you breath; who upholds all powers of every kingdom to exist; to test all; to now be judged.

49. Let all receive my will, and hasten to be repenting, lest all my full judgments of full power of pure way be sent forth, to be testimony of my almighty power to all peoples of every nation.

50. I cometh quickly. Amen.

We, the undersigning witnesses, bear testimony to all peoples of the earth that these are verily the words of our Lord Jesus Christ; warning only truth; giving our names to all to witness the same unto Him, our Lord Jesus Christ, being the God of redeeming love. Amen.

18 Aug 2011

Vaughan E. Taylor

Patriarch in the
Church of Jesus Christ of Latter-day Saints

August 18, 2011

John M. Barlow

Counselor in the Bishopric of the
Church of Jesus Christ of Latter-day Saints

Fundamentalist Church of Jesus Christ of Latter-day Saints
P.O. Box 840459
Hildale, Utah 84784

Thus Saith Son Ahman, Your Lord Jesus Christ, to All Peoples of the Earth Unto Your Salvation if You Heed Me, Saying Thus:

Revelation of the Lord Jesus Christ
Given to President Warren S. Jeffs

Huntsville, Texas
Friday, August 19, 2011

1. Verily, saith your Lord, come unto me, all ye people who have the power to repent, lest sore affliction soon overtake you, in a manner you think not; in an awakening the soul from deep sleep spiritual; in bringing all to hear my way of salvation eternal, saith Jesus Christ.

2. I am your Advocate with the Father.

3. I have overcome, and sit at the right hand of the Father to bring all unto Him who will receive the message of salvation of souls.

4. Let all hear my will.

5. I am now to send a sickness upon the land of my coming, even in power upon all the earth, to be known of all peoples thy God of glory reigneth!

6. Let all now be of the order of endless and eternal lives, of the people of the promise of Israel being gathered unto Zion, as I confided in Peter, James, and John would take place in power in the days of wickedness, when I would be of the power of gathering all who have the blood of Israel of the pure seed of my holy family of the flesh, when I was on earth; with eternal power as thy Lord.

7. I was with men with the full power of Priesthood.

8. I could raise the dead, heal and bless by the power of Godhead in my own possession, of the Father, doing His will in all things.

9. Thus, am I your Advocate with the Father, to bring all unto salvation to all who heed my word unto character of God becoming your natural way, of my Spirit; through thy faith always exercised.

10. Let all be of the way of improving.

11. Let all be of truth.

12. Let all be of receiving my own way, saith the Light of all men.

13. Let my light of pure holy way enlighten thy daily walk unto overcoming evil.

14. I am only Just, Holy, True, Righteous; Governing Power; Equitous, Noble, Exalting, and the Rock of Salvation for all to build on.

15. Let all come unto me, your Lord, who saith to all nations of the earth -- come to me.

16. Be ye clean to survive my holy power of cleansing judgments upon all nations.

17. Let my love shine in you. Forgive all peoples.

18. I shall repay in a just judgment.

19. Let the Holy Priesthood be purged.

20. Let my Church be cleansed.

21. Let all now live my Gospel of peace. Amen.

We, the undersigning witnesses, bear testimony to all peoples of the earth that these are verily the words of our Lord Jesus Christ; warning only truth; giving our names to all to witness the same unto Him, our Lord Jesus Christ, being the God of redeeming love. Amen.

August 19, 2011

Vaughan E. Taylor

Patriarch in the
Church of Jesus Christ of Latter-day Saints

August 19, 2011

John M. Barlow

Counselor in the Bishopric of the
Church of Jesus Christ of Latter-day Saints

Jesus Christ Speaketh to the Nation of the United States Solemn Warning Again, Mine Own Word from the Heavens, to be Heeded Lest Judgments Follow Upon Those Who Heed Me Not, Saith the Lord, Even Son Ahman

Thus Saith the Lord Jesus Christ to the Leaders and Peoples of the United States of America, My Holy Word of Continued Warning of Final Judgments Soon at Hand, Heed My Word, Which Saith:

Revelation of the Lord Jesus Christ Given to President Warren S. Jeffs

Tennessee Colony, Texas
Sunday, September 25, 2011

1. I who reign on high speaketh, even Jesus Christ, through my servant on earth to the nation of the United States of America: You have transgressed and not kept my word, though I have sent mine own word to you in sacred revealings and publishings, yea to leaders of nations.

2. My warning voice has been sounded. I am the God of Creation which speaketh. My servant is in bondage. You yet hold him from my people.

3. My Zion shall rise, and I shall intervene in a judgment that you shall soon feel, and it shall continue until opposition is removed.

4. Thus saith the Lord to the leaders and peoples of this nation: Though my voice has been sounded often to you and sent forth, and you heed me not, I shall fulfill my word, and you shall know at the removing of those in power to their everlasting regret for not heeding my word when sent to them.

5. And I give my word to you as a witness that thy God can speak from the heavens and communicate in preparing those who will heed my word for my coming; for I shall have a people in every nation that survives to come to Zion and receive of the greater light coming forth of my revealing.

6. And I, the Lord, give to this nation and this people a warning, to be justified in the cleansing that must take place if they heed not the God who created them;

7. For I am God, Son Ahman, and I do the will of the Father, who is Ahman.

8. And thus saith the Lord: The will of the Father is being done, for you have seen increased storms, flooding, even more than you have witnessed before in areas where it has not taken place before.

9. You shall witness further, as I have named, until you are humbled.

10. O that you would heed my word and receive my word; and I send my word to you again, that hearts can be touched who will heed my word, both of the leaders of this nation, of states, counties, places of governing power, and also among the population of thy people, for the cleansing shall be of such a nature that only that which can be of a purification remain.

11. I have named many places that shall be cleansed entire, and as you witness this, a memory of my word shall hearken in your souls that thy God reigneth; and if you are of the ability to repent, your hearts shall be touched.

12. Yet my word shall be fulfilled, as I spoke before I was taken upon the cross to be sacrificed, saith the Lord Jesus Christ, even that word that among the wicked in the last days, when judgments come, many would lift up their voices against me, cursing God and perishing because they would not heed my word, having their hearts set on wickedness and pleasure in unrighteousness.

13. Repent ye of the great sins I have named that are among your people, for the murder of unborn children is a stench of corruption that causeth all thy works to be of the way of ignoble shame, the very heavens seeing your works limiting the coming forth of spirits to earth, appointed to receive tabernacles and prove their worthiness before the Lord.

14. Your practice of this murder of children yet unborn shall be answered upon thy souls in

the day of eternal judgment, with a suffering of soul that you would be of an assenting or agreeing to this sin and would not stop it among your peoples.

15. Your adulterous ways are the motive for this sin that must be obliterated of my judgments coming upon all who will not receive my word and change their ways from this terrible crime against innocence, purity, and life.

16. I, your God, have spoken it.

17. Let the laws be changed if you would be of a repentance, else full judgment shall come upon thy peoples, and you shall know it.

18. You have also persecuted my Church and Kingdom and allowed my leadership to be in bondage, when I have called upon thee to let my people go to their worshiping and laboring, having their houses and lands restored to them of legal appointing, being of an illegal way in removing them from their homes, who have thus been ruled against in courts of law.

19. Heed my word: Let my servant go.

20. And let there be a changing of your laws to purify thy peoples, lest there be full judgment of the removing of this nation from this land, of whirlwind nature, that I have promised in all my holy scriptures through my servants, the Prophets, whom I have sent -- in particular, Joseph Smith, Jun., in revealing my word to this generation.

21. There shall come upon the nation that inhabits this land, yea, each nation, a full judging, a cleansing, to only allow there to remain those who can endure the presence of God in Zion, New Jerusalem being built in that Center Stake appointed on the land called United States of America; that Center Stake being Jackson County, Missouri, well-appointed, and nothing can stay mine hand; for I shall claim my lands purchased by my Priesthood in former times, taken from them by mobocracy and driving and killing in the days of my servant Joseph Smith.

22. Heed my word: I shall recover what belongeth to me, and New Jerusalem shall rise, and nothing can stay mine hand.

23. Though you oppose me, and pass laws, and have thy people rise up against innocence, against my Church, I shall be of a defending nature, and you shall know that I have preserved my people against the day of my coming in my glory, as I have promised mine apostles in the meridian of time when I was upon the earth and after I was resurrected, angels revealing to them my glorious coming in power in the clouds of heaven.

24. This is in sacred holy writ, which you can peruse.

25. My coming is soon, and there cannot be these sins and corruptions on my land where I shall appear unto an elect people who have kept Celestial laws, holy laws of eternal revealing.

26. My law is pure, and you have attacked my Law of Celestial Plural Marriage and other laws of my Priesthood as though it was of a corrupt way. It is not so.

27. My law is pure and of my governing through my revealed authority, my Priesthood, my servant on earth, not to be given to general populous among your peoples, only to those who are pure and holy.

28. Thus you have imprisoned men who are holy and pure, of pure religious motive, not desiring harm to anyone; and your prosecuting zeal is of a crime against my Priesthood, Church, and Kingdom that shall be answered upon thy people and governing powers if you heed me not.

29. Let them go, saith the Lord. Amen.

We, the undersigned, bear witness to this generation that this is verily the word of the Lord Jesus Christ to the peoples of the United States of America and the leaders thereof. And we bear witness that we know, by the inspiration of heaven to our souls, by the grace of God, that these are verily the words of God and shall be fulfilled upon this generation. Amen.

(signature)

September 25, 2011

Vaughan E. Taylor
Patriarch in the Fundamentalist
Church of Jesus Christ of Latter-day Saints

John M. Barlow

September 25, 2011

John M. Barlow
Counselor in the Bishopric of the Fundamentalist
Church of Jesus Christ of Latter-day Saints

Appendix B

Appendix of My New Word of Pure Power
Printed in This My Proclamation to All
Peoples on All Lands Referencing Pages
To Find My Word in This Publishing

Appendix of My New Word of Pure Power
Printed in This My Proclamation to All Peoples on All Lands
Referencing Pages to Find My Word in This Publishing

Thus Saith Son Ahman, Jesus Christ, to the Power of Governing in the Court of Prosecuting Labor, and to the Leaders of National Power -- Let My Word Be Heard in Your Several Placings of Your Influencing and Governing Power, Even This, My

Warning to Not Abuse My Innocent People, But Maintain Their Rights of Governing Protecting of Religious Way of My Holy Order of Union Celestial in My Holy Church on Earth. Let There Cease to Be the Continued Way and Idea You Can Be of a Prosecuting Labor Against My Holy Way of Eternal Lives of Celestial Union Power Above All Peoples and Their Claims of Power to Rule Over All the People in Their Lands of Man Organizing Power. Thus Am I Now Giving My Will to Be Known Among All Surviving People on Earth. Hear Thou My Way of Truth by This, My Revealing to All:

Son Ahman Gives Truth of Eternal Power to Joseph Smith, A God of Power

Let Brigham Young Be Upheld as a Prophet of Power, Who Also Sought Celestial Power of Holy Way of Union Celestial

Son Ahman, Your Lord, Speaketh of the Pure Governing Power of All Nations of Millennial Time of Holy Pure and Authoritative Governing of Celestial Power; My Holy Power of Eternal Celestial Authority:

Son Ahman Saith Thus to the People of the Earth, of Full Way of Knowing I Am Continuing My Law of Celestial Union on the Land of Zion. Amen.

APPENDIX C

DOCUMENTS SHOWING THE LEGAL AND RELIGIOUS ESTABLISHING AND CONTINUING OF THE FUNDAMENTALIST CHURCH OF JESUS CHRIST OF LATTER-DAY SAINTS AMONG MEN ON EARTH, THY LORD ESTABLISHING HIS CHURCH APRIL 6, 1830, THROUGH JOSEPH SMITH, CONTINUED ON EARTH THROUGH MY PRIESTHOOD; NOW A LEGAL ORGANIZATION ACCORDING TO LAW OF LAND AMONG MEN, SAITH JESUS CHRIST, YOUR LORD

149512

ARTICLES OF INCORPORATION

FOR

THE CORPORATION OF THE PRESIDENT

OF

THE FUNDAMENTALIST CHURCH OF JESUS CHRIST OF LATTER-DAY SAINTS INC.

STATE OF UTAH	)
	: ss.
COUNTY OF SALT LAKE	)

I, RULON T. JEFFS, having been duly chosen and appointed President of The Fundamentalist Church of Jesus Christ of Latter-day Saints, in conformity with the rites, regulations and discipline of said Church, being desirous of forming a corporation for the purpose of acquiring, holding and disposing of Church or religious society property, for the benefit of religion, for works of charity and for public worship, hereby make and subscribe these Articles of Incorporation for a corporation sole pursuant to the provisions of Sections 16-7-1 et seq. of the Utah Code Annotated (1953, as amended).

ARTICLE I

The name of the corporation shall be THE CORPORATION OF THE PRESIDENT OF THE FUNDAMENTALIST CHURCH OF JESUS CHRIST OF LATTER-DAY SAINTS.INC.

ARTICLE II

The object of the corporation shall be to acquire, hold, or dispose of such real and personal property as may be conveyed to or acquired by said corporation for the benefit of the members of The Fundamentalist Church of Jesus Christ of Latter-day Saints, a religious society, for the benefit of religion, for works of charity, for public worship, for the establishment of schools and for the advancement of both religious and secular education, and for all other lawful purposes necessary or incident thereto. Such real and personal property may be situated, either within the State of Utah, or elsewhere (including foreign countries), and this corporation shall have power, without any authority or authorization from the members of said Church or religious society, to grant, sell, convey, rent, mortgage, exchange, or otherwise deal with or dispose of any part or all of such property.

ARTICLE III

The estimated value of property to which I hold the legal title and which I desire to place in this corporation for the purpose aforesaid, at the time of making these Articles, is the sum of $568,000.

ARTICLE IV

The title of the person making these Articles of Incorporation is "President of The Fundamentalist Church of Jesus Christ of Latter-day Saints.*INC.'*

ARTICLE V

In the event of the death or resignation from office of the President of The Fundamentalist Church of Jesus Christ of Latter-day Saints, or in the event of a vacancy in that office for any cause, the First Counselor of the First Presidency of said Church (or in the event such First Counselor shall not then be living or shall be disabled, the Second or next subsequent Counselor in the First Presidency as the President shall have designated prior to his death or disability) shall, pending installation of a successor President of The Fundamentalist Church of Jesus Christ of Latter-day Saints, be the corporation sole under these articles, and the laws pursuant to which they are made, and shall be and is authorized in his official capacity to execute in the name of the corporation all documents or other writings necessary to the carrying on of its purposes, business and objects, and to do all things in the name of the corporation which the original signer of the articles of incorporation might do; it being the purpose of these articles that there shall be no failure in succession in the office of such corporation sole. At the time of signing of these Articles, the First Counselor in the First Presidency of said Church is Parley J. Harker, and the Second Counselor is Fred M. Jessop. The President shall have authority to designate new counselors in the First Presidency of said Church, or to change the office of existing counselors, as he shall see fit.

ARTICLE VI

In the event of the winding up or dissolution of this corporation, after paying or adequately providing for the debts and obligations of the corporation, the remaining assets shall be distributed to a nonprofit fund, foundation or corporation, which is organized and operated exclusively for charitable, educational, or religious and/or scientific purposes.

ARTICLE VII

This corporation shall exist perpetually unless sooner dissolved by law.

DATED this 6th day of February, 1991.

Rulon T. Jeffs
Rulon T. Jeffs, President
The Fundamentalist Church of Jesus
Christ of Latter-day Saints
3611 East 9400 South

Sandy, Utah 84092

STATE OF UTAH)
              : ss.
COUNTY OF SALT LAKE)

I hereby certify that on this 6th day of February, 1991, personally appeared before me Rulon T. Jeffs, who is known to me to be the person whose name is subscribed to the foregoing instrument as President of The Fundamentalist Church of Jesus Christ of Latter-day Saints, and duly acknowledged to me that he executed the same as such president.

Patricia B. Birch
Notary Public
Residing in Salt Lake City, Utah

My Commission Expires:

7/10/92

AMENDED AND RESTATED ARTICLES OF INCORPORATION

OF

THE CORPORATION OF THE PRESIDENT

OF

THE FUNDAMENTALIST CHURCH OF JESUS CHRIST OF LATTER-DAY SAINTS

Pursuant to Utah Code Ann. § 16-7-14, The Corporation of the President of the Fundamentalist Church of Jesus Christ of Latter-day Saints, Inc., amends and restates its Articles of Incorporation to read in their entirety as follows:

ARTICLE I

The name of the corporation shall be "THE CORPORATION OF THE PRESIDENT OF THE FUNDAMENTALIST CHURCH OF JESUS CHRIST OF LATTER-DAY SAINTS."

ARTICLE II

The object of the corporation shall be to acquire, hold, or dispose of such real and personal property as may be conveyed to said corporation for the benefit of The Fundamentalist Church of Jesus Christ of Latter-Day Saints, a religious society, for the benefit of religion, for works of charity, for public worship, for the establishment of schools and for the advancement of both religious and secular education, and for all other lawful purposes necessary or incident thereto. Consequently, this corporation has not been organized for the purpose of making a profit. Such real and personal property may be situated, either within the State of Utah, or elsewhere (including foreign countries), and this corporation have power, without any authority or authorization of the members of said Church or religious society, to grant, sell, convey, rent, mortgage, exchange, or otherwise dispose of the same, or any part thereof; however this corporation is prohibited from declaring or paying dividends.

ARTICLE III

The corporate seal shall contain the words, "President FLDS Church, Corporate Seal," and an impression thereof is hereto affixed.

ARTICLE IV

In the winding up and dissolution of this Corporation, after paying or adequately providing for the debts and obligations of the Corporation, the remaining assets shall be distributed among legal entities of similar objectives, that is, to a non-profit fund, foundation or corporation, which is organized and operated exclusively for charitable, educational, religious and/or scientific purposes and which has established its tax exempt status under § 501(c)(3) (or its successor) of the Internal Revenue Code.

ARTICLE V

The estimated value of property to which I hold the legal title and which I desire to place in this corporation for the purpose aforesaid, at the time of making these Articles, is the sum of $1,000.

ARTICLE VI

The title of the person making these Articles of is "The President of The Fundamentalist Church of Jesus Christ of Latter-Day Saints."

IN WITNESS WHEREOF these Amended and Restated Articles of Incorporation are adopted by The Corporation of the President of the Fundamentalist Church of Jesus Christ of Latter-day Saints.

Rulon T. Jeffs
Rulon T. Jeffs, President and Corporation Sole

STATE OF UTAH)
         :ss.
COUNTY OF SALT LAKE)

  I hereby certify that on this _23_ day of December, 1997, personally appeared before me Rulon T. Jeffs, who is known to me to be the person whose name is subscribed to the foregoing instrument as President of The Fundamentalist Church of Jesus Christ of Latter-Day Saints, and duly acknowledged to me that he executed the same as such President.

NOTARY PUBLIC
Residing in _SALT LAKE COUNTY_

My Commission Expires:

  _8·8·98_

State of Utah | This form must be type written or computer generated. **EXPEDITE**

Department of Commerce
Division of Corporations & Commercial Code
Corporation Registration Information Change Form

Date: 02/15/2011
Receipt Number: 3481449
Amount Paid: $90.00

RECEIVED
FEB 15 2011
Utah Div. of Corp. & Comm. Code

Non-Refundable Processing Fee: $15.00   Entity File Number: 1107221-0145

Entity Name: The Corporation of the President of the Fundamentalist Church of Jesus Christ of Latter-Day Saints

For each Yes button that you mark the question will appear below for you to fill out.

1). Do you want to Change the Business Purpose?   ○ Yes   ● No

2). Do you want to Change the Registered Agent or the Address of the Registered Agent?   ○ Yes   ● No

3). Do you want to Change the Principal Address of the Business Entity?   ○ Yes   ● No

4). Do you want to Add individuals to the Business Entity?   ● Yes   ○ No

4). If Yes, who do you want to Add to the Business Entity and what Position will they hold?

Name: Warren Steed Jeffs   Position: President
Address: P.O. Box 840900   City Hildale   State UT   Zip 84784
Name: Warren Steed Jeffs   Position: Corporation Sole
Address: P.O. Box 840900   City Hildale   State UT   Zip 84784

5). Do you want to Remove individuals from the Business Entity?   ○ Yes   ● No

6). Do you want to Change the Address of the Business Entity's Principal(s)?   ○ Yes   ● No

Optional Inclusion of Ownership Information: This information is not required.
Is this a female owned business?   Yes   No
Is this a minority owned business?   ○ Yes   ○ No   If yes, please specify: Select/Type the race of the owner here

Under GRAMA {63-2-201}, all registration information maintained by the Division is classified as public record. For confidentiality purposes, you may use the business entity physical address rather than the residential or private address of any individual affiliated with the entity.

Under penalties of perjury and as an authorized authority, I declare that this statement of change(s), has been examined by me and is, to the best of my knowledge and belief, true, correct and complete.

Name/Title: Warren S. Jeffs/President   Signature: *Warren S. Jeffs*   Date: 2-10-2011

Mailing/Faxing Information: www.corporations.utah.gov/contactus.html Division's Website: www.corporations.utah.gov

State of Utah
Department of Commerce
Division of Corporations & Commercial Code
Heber M. Wells Building
160 East 300 South
Salt Lake City, UT 84111

CERTIFICATE

TO WHOM IT MAY CONCERN:

I, the undersigned, WARREN STEED JEFFS, have been called and sustained as the President of The Fundamentalist Church of Jesus Christ of Latter-Day Saints, and by virtue of such calling I am the corporation sole of the Corporation of the President of the Fundamentalist Church of Jesus Christ of Latter-Day Saints, organized under the laws of the State of Utah.

Entity Name: The Corporation of the President of the Fundamentalist Church of Jesus Christ of Latter-Day Saints

Entity Address: 1020 West Utah Avenue
                    P.O. Box 840900
                    Hildale, UT 84784-0900

Entity Number: 1107221-0145

IN TESTIMONY WHEREOF, I have hereunto subscribed my name this _10th_ day of February, 2011.

Warren S Jeffs
Warren Steed Jeffs

Utah Business Search - Details

CORPORATION OF THE PRESIDENT OF THE FUNDAMENTALIST CHURCH OF JESUS CHRIST OF LATTER-DAY SAINTS INC.

Entity Number: 1107221-0145
Company Type: Corporation - Sole
Address: 1020 W UTAH AVE P O BOX 840900 Hildale, UT 84784
State of Origin: UT
Registered Agent: BOYD L KNUDSON
Registered Agent Address:
1020 W UTAH AVE P O BOX 840900 Hildale UT 84784

Status: Active

Status: Active ● *as of 08/04/2011*
Renew By: N/A
Status Description: Good Standing
Employment Verification:Not Registered with Verify Utah

History

Registration Date: 02/06/1991
Last Renewed: N/A

Additional Information

Refine your search by:

- **Search by:**
- **Business Name**
- **Number**
- **Executive Name**
- **Search Hints**

Name:

Utah Business Search - Registered Principals

Registered Principals

Name	Type	City	Status
CORPORATION OF THE PRESIDENT OF THE FUNDAMENTALIST CHURCH OF JESUS CHRIST OF LATTER-DAY SAINTS INC.	Corporation	Hildale	Active

Position	Name	Address	
President	WARREN STEED JEFFS	P O BOX 840900	Hildale UT 84784
Registered Agent	BOYD L KNUDSON	1020 W UTAH AVE	Hildale UT 84784

If you believe there may be more principals, click here to

Search by:

- Search by:
- **Business Name**
- **Number**
- **Executive Name**
- **Search Hints**

Name:

AFFIDAVIT OF BOYD L. KNUDSON
THAT THE CONGREGATIONS ASSEMBLED UPHOLD BY THE LAW OF COMMON CONSENT THE CALLING AND POSITION OF WARREN STEED JEFFS AS THE PRESIDENT OF THE FUNDAMENTALIST CHURCH OF JESUS CHRIST OF LATTER-DAY SAINTS

TO WHOM IT MAY CONCERN:

STATE OF TEXAS   )

                                : ss.

COUNTY OF SCHLEICHER   )

      1.   I, the undersigned Boyd L. Knudson, am the Official Representative and Registered Agent of The Corporation of the President of the Fundamentalist Church of Jesus Christ of Latter-day Saints which is a Corporation Sole entity as allowed by Title 16, Chapter 7 of the Utah Code with an entity number 1107221-0145 assigned by the State of Utah.

      2.   I am a member in good standing of the "Church" known as the Fundamentalist Church of Jesus Christ of Latter-day Saints.

      3.   I am over 18 years of age and am otherwise competent to testify to the facts set forth herein.

      4.   I have personal knowledge of the matters set forth herein.

      5.   On February 6, 1991, Rulon T. Jeffs organized The Corporation of the President of the Fundamentalist Church of Jesus Christ of Latter-day Saints. See attached "Exhibit A" for a "Utah Business Search - Details" verifying the entity name, number, address, registration date and registered agent. On December 26, 1997, the Amended and Restated Articles of Incorporation signed by Rulon T. Jeffs, attached hereto as "Exhibit B," were filed with the State of Utah.

      6.   On April 10, 2011, I sat before a Special Conference held in Colorado City, Arizona of the Church of Jesus Christ of Latter-day Saints known as the Fundamentalist Church of Jesus Christ of Latter-day Saints and there witnessed the congregation of near 2,000 Melchizedek and Aaronic Priesthood bearers with other officers of the Church in conference assembled vote unanimously as individuals and as a congregation according to the Church law of common consent and according to the Church tenets, rites, rules

Page **1** of **2**

and laws to uphold and sustain Warren Steed Jeffs as President of Priesthood, President of said Church, and Presiding Bishop of said Church.

7.　　On April 3, 2011, I sat before a General Assembly in Colorado City, Arizona of over 4,000 Church members and witnessed them individually and together as a congregation of the Church of Jesus Christ of Latter-day Saints known as the Fundamentalist Church of Jesus Christ of Latter-day Saints, according to the tenets, rites, regulations, discipline, rules and laws of said Church and according to the Church law of common consent, unanimously stand and raise their hands and voices in favor of sustaining Warren Steed Jeffs as President of Priesthood, President of said Church, and Presiding Bishop of said Church.

8.　　Warren Steed Jeffs is the President of the Fundamentalist Church of Jesus Christ of Latter-day Saints and by virtue of this office is the Corporation Sole and President of the Corporation of the President of the Fundamentalist Church of Jesus Christ of Latter-day Saints, organized under the laws of the State of Utah.

9.　　The Certificate attached hereto as "Exhibit C" signed by Warren S. Jeffs on February 10, 2011 as filed on February 15, 2011 with the State of Utah, Department of Commerce, Division of Corporations & Commercial Code in testimony that Warren Steed Jeffs is the President of The Fundamentalist Church of Jesus Christ of Latter-day Saints and is the Corporation Sole is true, correct and valid according to the rules of the Church. See attached "Exhibit D" for a "Utah Business Search - Registered Principals" verifying the President and registered agent of the Corporation Sole.

I, Boyd L. Knudson, being first duly placed under oath by the undersigned official authorized to administer oaths under the laws of this State, do solemnly swear that the information herein is true and correct.

_____
Boyd L. Knudson

Subscribed and sworn to before me this 22nd day of July, 2011.

_____
Notary Public
Commission Expires: _12 - 3 - 2013_

EDMUND LORIN BARLOW, SR
Notary Public, State of Texas
My Commission Expires
December 03, 2013

Page **2** of **2**

AFFIDAVIT OF LYLE S. JEFFS
THAT THE CONGREGATIONS ASSEMBLED UPHOLD BY THE LAW OF COMMON CONSENT THE CALLING AND POSITION OF WARREN STEED JEFFS AS THE PRESIDENT OF THE FUNDAMENTALIST CHURCH OF JESUS CHRIST OF LATTER-DAY SAINTS

TO WHOM IT MAY CONCERN:

STATE OF TEXAS   )

                              : ss.

COUNTY OF SCHLEICHER   )

1.   I, the undersigned Lyle S. Jeffs, am Special Counselor to the President of the Fundamentalist Church of Jesus Christ of Latter-day Saints and Bishop in the Fundamentalist Church of Jesus Christ of Latter-day Saints.

2.   I am a member in good standing of the "Church" known as the Fundamentalist Church of Jesus Christ of Latter-day Saints.

3.   I am over 18 years of age and am otherwise competent to testify to the facts set forth herein.

4.   I have personal knowledge of the matters set forth herein.

5.   On February 6, 1991, Rulon T. Jeffs organized The Corporation of the President of the Fundamentalist Church of Jesus Christ of Latter-day Saints. See attached "Exhibit A" for a "Utah Business Search - Details" verifying the entity name, number, address, registration date and registered agent. On December 26, 1997, the Amended and Restated Articles of Incorporation signed by Rulon T. Jeffs, attached hereto as "Exhibit B," were filed with the State of Utah.

6.   On April 10, 2011, I sat before a Special Conference held in Colorado City, Arizona of the Church of Jesus Christ of Latter-day Saints known as the Fundamentalist Church of Jesus Christ of Latter-day Saints and there witnessed the congregation of near 2,000 Melchizedek and Aaronic Priesthood bearers with other officers of the Church in conference assembled vote unanimously as individuals and as a congregation according to the Church law of common consent and according to the Church tenets, rites, rules

            Appendix C -- Legal Documents

and laws to uphold and sustain Warren Steed Jeffs as President of Priesthood, President of said Church, and Presiding Bishop of said Church.

7. On April 3, 2011, I sat before a General Assembly in Colorado City, Arizona of over 4,000 Church members and witnessed them individually and together as a congregation of the Church of Jesus Christ of Latter-day Saints known as the Fundamentalist Church of Jesus Christ of Latter-day Saints, according to the tenets, rites, regulations, discipline, rules and laws of said Church and according to the Church law of common consent, unanimously stand and raise their hands and voices in favor of sustaining Warren Steed Jeffs as President of Priesthood, President of said Church, and Presiding Bishop of said Church.

8. Warren Steed Jeffs is the President of the Fundamentalist Church of Jesus Christ of Latter-day Saints and by virtue of this office is the Corporation Sole and President of the Corporation of the President of the Fundamentalist Church of Jesus Christ of Latter-day Saints, organized under the laws of the State of Utah.

9. The Certificate attached hereto as "Exhibit C" signed by Warren S. Jeffs on February 10, 2011 as filed on February 15, 2011 with the State of Utah, Department of Commerce, Division of Corporations & Commercial Code in testimony that Warren Steed Jeffs is the President of The Fundamentalist Church of Jesus Christ of Latter-day Saints and is the Corporation Sole is true, correct and valid according to the rules of the Church. See attached "Exhibit D" for a "Utah Business Search - Registered Principals" verifying the President and registered agent of the Corporation Sole.

I, Lyle S. Jeffs, being first duly placed under oath by the undersigned official authorized to administer oaths under the laws of this State, do solemnly swear that the information herein is true and correct.

_____
Lyle S. Jeffs

Subscribed and sworn to before me this 22nd day of July, 2011.

_____
Notary Public
Commission Expires: _12 - 3 - 2013_

EDMUND LORIN BARLOW, SR
Notary Public, State of Texas
My Commission Expires
December 03, 2013

Page **2** of **2**

Notice for Inquiries

I, Vaughan E. Taylor, have been appointed to receive any inquiries.
Please call (702) 686-1180.

Additional copies of this publication and others listed below are available for purchase at
www.flds.org or by sending your request and payment to:

Vaughan E. Taylor
PO Box 1708
Colorado City AZ 86021-1708
USA

Item#	Description	Price
101	Proclamation to the Nation 2010-07-17	$ 3.00
102	Warning to the Nations 2010-10-31	$ 4.75
103	Continued Warnings of Son Ahman to the Leaders of the Nations of the Earth	$ 6.00
104	The Coming Crisis	$ 1.00
105	Prepare for the Day of Visitation	$ 1.00

Sincerely,

Vaughan E. Taylor
Patriarch in the Fundamentalist
Church of Jesus Christ of Latter-day Saints